Understanding the Global Spa Industry: Spa Management

Marc Cohen
and
Gerard Bodeker

ELSEVIER

AMSTERDAM • BOSTON • HEIDELBERG • LONDON • NEWYORK • OXFORD •
PARIS • SAN DIEGO • SAN FRANCISCO • SINGAPORE • SYDNEY • TOKYO

Butterworth-Heinemann is an imprint of Elsevier

Butterworth-Heinemann is an imprint of Elsevier
Linacre House, Jordan Hill, Oxford OX2 8DP, UK
30 Corporate Drive, Suite 400, Burlington, MA01803, USA

First edition 2008

Copyright © 2008 Elsevier Ltd. All rights reserved

British Library Cataloguing in Publication Data
A catalogue record for this book is available from the British Library

Library of Congress Cataloging-in-Publication Data
A catalog record for this book is available from the Library of Congress

ISBN: 978-0-7506-8464-4

For information on all Butterworth-Heinemann publications
visit our web site at http://books.elsevier.com

Transferred to Digital Printing in 2010

Preface

With the spa industry fast becoming the world's largest leisure industry, an accompanying need for information arises. The industry is naturally looking to define best practice, determine successful business models, prioritise human resource issues develop standards of quality control, create effective marketing strategies and examine past and future trends. Yet, while the services, products and profits of the industry have grown exponentially, the information gap has grown wider.

At the inaugural Wellness Summit in Hua Hin, Thailand , organized by Spa Asia Wellness Associates in October 2005, we, the editors of this book, had a conversation about where we could a book with information on all of the above points. From related yet somewhat different academic backgrounds, we converged on a need to fill gaps in our own knowledge about this vast global industry.

One of us, Professor Marc Cohen, a medical doctor and academic at the Royal Melbourne Institute of Technology University in Australia, had been working for 3 years with the Mandarin Oriental Hotel Group spa division on incorporating wellness concepts into spas. He has also been working on developing curricula for university-based wellness education which required justifying that there would be vocational outcomes for gradates with wellness qualifications. At the time this was not an easy task for there was an absence of academic literature on the spa industry with no books or academic publications outlining its scope.

At the same time, Professor Gerard Bodeker, a public health specialist at Oxford University, UK, and Columbia University, New York, had focused for many years on the health traditions of developing countries and had, earlier that year, produced for the World Health Organization the WHO Global Atlas on Traditional, Complementary & Alternative Medicine.

From this global perspective the international march of the spa industry seemed a health trend worthy of documentation and study.

Over lunch we asked ourselves how could it be that despite the spa industry being a multibillion dollar global industry– growing at a rate of approximately 20% each year – spa litera- ture has remained in the domain of consumer trade magazines and coffee table books? Where, we wondered, could we find a reference that would address the professional, management, design, therapeutic, personnel, ethical, ecological and societal dimensions of the global spa industry?

And what of the industry itself – its needs for focused knowl- edge, the need to learn from those who have already traveled down the road that so many are embarking on? It seemed unlikely that no other industry of comparable size has such a gap in publicly available knowledge of relevance to the indus- try's own growth and maturation. In finding an absence of published analytic literature, the decision was made to make a start on filling the knowledge gap in one of the world's largest and fastest growing leisure industries that includes the well- ness and tourism sub-sectors.

On reviewing our ambitious proposal, Elsevier Press, the world's largest academic publisher, came back and asked us for not one but for two books – one on the business dimensions of the spa industry and another on health and therapeutic services. This volume is the first of these books. It's companion volume on spas health and the wellness experience will follow in the coming year.

When considering a structure for this book it seemed natural to refer to five elements, which are widely used in the world's traditional health systems and seem just as applicable to busi- ness. Accordingly, the book focuses on 'planning', 'profit', 'product', 'planet' and 'people'.

The "Planning" section outlines the historical and evolution- ary development of spas along with current spa trends and benchmarks. "Profit" presents an outline of the business mod- els and processes, accompanied by accounts of how spas have operationalised and been incorporated into luxury hotels. The "Product" section outlines the branding, product develop- ment, retailing, technological devices and marketing aspects of spa business. "Planet" addresses the designed and built environment along with environmental sustainability. And the "People" section focuses on leadership, recruitment and training, along with the ethical dimensions of corporate social responsibility and working with indigenous communities and traditional knowledge.

As editors, we would like to acknowledge and thank the chapter authors for their significant contribution of knowledge and time. These authors are all industry leaders in their own right who have helped to create the industry and who draw on countless years of collective experience. Prior to this, their expertise was available only to a select few – to members of their own organizations or via private industry reports and consultancy services. They have generously shared much of their proprietary knowledge and experience for the sake of advancing the industry. In this, they have worked to establish the beginnings of a platform to determine best practice, mechanisms of quality control, and systems of accountability and catalysed a large step forward towards industry-wide standards of professionalism.

What they have highlighted is that the standards they outline for best spa practice will, in turn, have ripple effects to the wider worlds of healthcare, health service delivery – including future health centres and hospitals – and for new levels of responsibility and quality in the global hospitality industry. It is also obvious that the spa industry is part of a wider global movement towards sustainability, equity, consciousness and connection and that the global spa industry can be seen as a response to humanity's desire to live well in the world. It, therefore, has the potential to contribute to a positive trend in human evolution.

We hope that this text will play a positive part in this evolution.

Marc Cohen & Gerard Bodeker

Contents

Contents

List of Contributors

Ben Bayada
EC3 Global, Australia
Ben Bayada is responsible for overseeing the day-to-day customer relationship management for new and existing clients participating in benchmarking. Ben's experience derives from fine-tuning and updating the global benchmarking database, data analysis and reporting, as it relates to Green Globe customers and other EC3 Global clients. As Relationship Manager, Ben is also responsible for offering benchmarking technical support to clients as well as enhancement of benchmarking products and maintenance of internal data systems.

Anna Bjurstam
Raison d'Etre, Sweden
Anna Bjurstam has worked in the wellness industry for 19 years. With hands on expertise in wellness and a Master Degree in Business, Anna has successfully led Raison d'Etre Spas to become one of the leaders in the spa business. Before joining Raison d'Etre, she excelled in fitness, both as a Nike sponsored athlete, as well as in management, leading 300 staff in the fitness industry in Scandinavia. As MD of Raison d'Etre, Anna has become the guiding light for an ever-growing company of globally placed professionals in world renowned spas such as Aman, One & Only, Taj, Four Seasons, Capella and many more.

Gerard Bodeker
University of Oxford, UK
Prof. Gerard Bodeker, whose doctoral studies were at Harvard, holds faculty appointments in public health at Oxford and Columbia Universities. He chaired the Commonwealth Working Group on Traditional, Complementary and Alternative Medicine and has advised UN agencies in this field. He chairs

the Global Initiative For Traditional Systems (GIFTS) of Health (www.giftsofhealth.org) and has authored several books and has published extensively in leading journals. Prof. Bodeker edited the WHO Global Atlas on Traditional, Complementary and Alternative Medicine (2005) and is on the editorial boards of several scientific journals. He is a contributor to Elsevier's Encyclopedia of Public Health (2008).

Matthew W. Brennan
Spa Strategy Inc., USA
Matthew W. Brennan is the Financial Analyst at Spa Strategy Inc. Through working with major hotel brands and hoteliers on a wide range of projects located throughout the world and tracking global consumer trends in both the spa- and wellness-related industries, Brennan has developed a keen understanding of the global spa industry. Brennan holds a Bachelor of Science in Business Administration with a concentration in Finance from the University of Denver.

Dieter Buchner
Urban Healing Company Ltd. Thailand
Dieter is the Founder and Managing Partner of Urban Healing, a Bangkok-based provider of educational wellness solutions. For over 20 years, Dieter enjoyed a successful career in learning and development in the hospitality industry with companies such as Banyan Tree, Hyatt International and Rezidor SAS. In 1994, Dieter was a key player in the pioneering team that created the first Banyan Tree Resort & Spa in Phuket. More recently he held the post of Director of Education & Research for MSpa International, a Bangkok-based Spa Management company. Dieter trained at the Maui Academy of Healing Arts, Hawaii where he gained experience in holistic massage, reflexology, Zen touch Shiatzu, Lomi Lomi and other healing modalities. He is also qualified in Thai massage.

Gemma Burford
GIFTS of Health, Oxford University, UK
Gemma Burford is a development practitioner and author based in Arusha, Tanzania. Raised in Britain, she holds Masters degrees in biological science from Oxford and environmental anthropology from the University of Kent. She is a co-director of the Global Initiative for Traditional Systems (GIFTS) of Health. Gemma co-edited the WHO Global Atlas of Traditional, Complementary and Alternative Medicine (2005) and Traditional, Complementary and Alternative Medicine: Policy and Public Health Perspectives (2007). She has published

in peer-reviewed journals on traditional medicine and midwifery and currently works with Maasai and Chagga communities in northern Tanzania establishing grassroots education promoting transfer of indigenous knowledge between generations.

Marc Cohen
RMIT University, Australia

Professor Marc Cohen is currently the Foundation Professor of Complementary Medicine at RMIT University, and immediate Past-President of the Australasian Integrative Medicine Association. He is a medical doctor with degrees in western medicine, physiology, psychological medicine as well as having PhDs in both Chinese medicine and biomedical engineering. Prof Cohen has been involved in research and education in the area of holistic health and wellness for over two decades. He has published widely in the area of holistic health and recently established the world's first online Master of Wellness program, which aims to train practitioners and managers to work in the spa and wellness industry.

David Cunliffe
South Australian Department of Health, Australia

Dr David Cunliffe is the Principal Water Quality Adviser with the South Australian Department of Health. He has over 25 years experience in dealing with public health aspects of drinking water, recreational water quality and recycled water. He has contributed to the development of a range of national and international guidelines dealing with drinking water quality, water recycling, desalination and recreational water quality as well as guidance on *Legionella* control and use of rainwater tanks. He is a member of the National health and Medical Research Council's Water Quality Advisory Committee and the Joint Steering Committee for the *Australian Guidelines for Water Recycling*.

Richard Dusseau
Spa Strategy Inc., USA

Richard Dusseau is the President and Managing Partner of Spa Strategy, Inc. a leading consulting, brand development and interior design company with projects spanning the globe with clients including Ritz Carlton, Jumeriah, and Starwood Hotels and Resorts. Dusseau is also the CEO of Spatality Inc., a global spa management and operating company featuring innovative spa brands such as *Nectar*, the first 'off the shelf' spa of its kind. Recognized as a visionary in the spa industry, Dusseau is frequently featured as a guest speaker at industry seminars and conferences.

Pete Ellis
Spa Finder Inc., USA
Pete Ellis is Chairman and CEO of Spa Finder, Inc., the world's largest spa marketing and media company. Under his leadership, Spa Finder has worked to connect the players that comprise the once-disjointed spa market ... day and stay spas, spa merchandisers, consumers, marketing partners, and travel agents in creative, opportunistic ways that result in new benefits for all parties. Mr Ellis has a background in building companies that dominate their markets and using technology to redefine entire industries. In 1995 he launched the first on-line car buying website, Autobytel.com, which introduced an efficient automotive marketing and transaction platform that revolutionized the world's largest industry.

Susie Ellis
Spa Finder Inc., USA
Susie Ellis is President of SpaFinder, Inc., the world's most prominent spa marketing and media company. Susie holds an MBA from UCLA. She began her career in spa at the Golden Door, in the 1980s. She now authors the popular 'Ask Susie' column for ClubSpa, is editor for The Spa Enthusiast, writes,' Susie's Blog ' on Spafinder.com, and the SpaFinder Insider industry e-newsletter, and is recognized as a leading authority on the spa industry and the evolving spa consumer and spa-related health, wellness, beauty, fitness and lifestyle trends. She also leads the company's charitable ventures including an initiative to address melanoma skin cancer.

Samantha Foster
The Wellness Group (TWG) China
Sam began her spa career in Australia with Jurlique, moving to Asia in 2000 as a spa consultant. She enjoyed five years as Business Development Director for Thailand's famous Chiva-Som health resorts and is now Managing Director of The Wellness Group (TWG) China and Chairman of the Asia-Pacific Spa & Wellness Council where she has helped to set up 5 national spa associations. Samantha is a proven spa manager, trainer, retailer, therapist, and one of Asia's most experienced spa consultants. She is qualified in a wide range of holistic modalities, beauty therapy and cosmetic science, with a solid background in branding and marketing.

Julie Garrow
Intelligent Spas, Singapore

Julie Garrow is the Founder and Managing Director of Intelligent Spas, an independent research company specialising in the spa industry. Julie pioneered spa benchmarking across the Asia-Pacific region and now conducts research in over 35 countries. She has also authored a series of Spa Operations Manuals to raise industry standards. Julie gained tourism, leisure and hospitality consulting experience with PricewaterhouseCoopers, Singapore and KPMG, Melbourne, conducting market research, industry surveys, marketing strategies and feasibility studies. Previously, she was Market Information Manager with a Sydney based hotel group responsible for major corporate projects and advising individual hotels on market research, business plans, product development and campaign analysis.

Andrew Gibson
Mandarin Oriental Hotel Group, Hong Kong

With a B.A in Recreation Management and Environmental Conservation and over 25 years experience Andrew has covered most aspects in the spa industry.

He has worked in construction specializing in building health clubs and spas. He established the global development of the spa brand for one of the leading luxury eco-resort brands. He conceptualized, designed and project managed his own luxury resort spa. And he was a partner in one of the world's leading spa consultancies working with the best hotel groups in the world.

Currently he is the Group Director of Spa for Mandarin Oriental Hotel Group providing global support to the design, development and operation of Mandarin Oriental Spas.

Geraldine Howard
Aromatherapy Associates, UK

Geraldine Howard is President of Aromatherapy Associates, a UK company which develops specialised aromatherapy products and treatments to a professional and therapeutic standard for spas worldwide. Besides working on all Aromatherapy Associates' formulations, Geraldine remains a practicing aromatherapist. She regularly contributes to spa articles globally, and Aromatherapy Associates has earned a number of prestigious beauty industry awards.

Geraldine trained in beauty therapy and cosmetic science at the London College of Fashion, obtaining a City & Guilds diploma in 1973. In 1974, she qualified as an aromatherapist working with Micheline Arcier and Dr. Jean Valnet. In 1985 she co-founded The International Federation of Aromatherapists.

Michael Loh
Spa Asia Magazine, Malaysia
Michael Loh is Founder and Publisher of SpaAsia Magazine. Trained in Architecture at De Montfort University, he went on to take a second degree in Town Planning at Oxford Brookes University. In 2002, a life-changing experience led him to found SpaAsia to share with and educate the world about spa and wellness. Realizing that the evolving spa realm needed benchmarking, he introduced the SpaAsia Crystal Awards in 2004. This paved the way for the inauguration of the SpaAsia Wellness Summit in 2005. Michael Loh now lives in Malaysia and spends most of his time contemplating the future of the Wellness Industry.

Jeff Matthews
Mandara Spa Group, USA
Jeff Matthews is President and Chief Operating officer of Mandara Spa – the world's largest resort spa management company. After international experience with chains such as Four Seasons and Hilton Hotels, Jeff joined Mandara Spa in 1997 and became a partner in 1998. Under his management, Mandara Spa expanded rapidly throughout Asia and, in 1998, was established in the USA. Mandara Spa is now global – throughout Asia, continental US and Hawaii, Micronesia and the Caribbean. Jeff currently leads Mandara's strategic expansion into the Middle East, India, Europe and Kazakhstan. Jeff has a strong sense of team and this has nurtured Mandara's global success and expansion.

Seán O'Connor
Mandarin Oriental Hotel Group, Hong Kong
With a Masters Degree in Recreation Management from Loughborough University (UK) Seán embarked on a career in the early 1980's – initially designing and developing and later operating hotel based recreation, fitness, wellness, spa and resort facilities. Founding partner of Hong Kong based International Leisure Consultants in the late 1980's, Seán built a portfolio of successful clubs, spas and resorts around Asia and further a field before joining Mandarin Oriental Hotel Group in 2006 as Group Spa Manager responsible for spa and resort/recreation design and development globally. He is an avid scholar of applied technology in a low tech environment.

Peter Remedios
RS Designs, USA
Peter Remedios is a Hong Kong born Macanese who graduated from the School of Design at the HK Polytechnic. He heads the design firm Remedios Siembieda Inc, one of the most innovative design firms worldwide, specializing in upscale hotels and resorts. He has been involved with many prestigious hotels including the Four Seasons NY, the Grand Hyatt Tokyo, the Raffles L'Ermitage Beverly Hills, the Mandarin Oriental Munich, the Landmark Mandarin HK, Shilla Korea, and the Crown Macau. Peter's design philosophy allows each project to have it's own personality, reflecting its architecture or locale. His work tends to be evocative rather than literal, creating uniqueness and contextual element through this 'Sense-of-Place.'

Daniella Russell
Spa Resources International LLC, Dubai
Daniella Russell is a founding member and Director of Spa Resources International LLC and the first Middle East Board Member of ISPA. With 30 years of pioneering experience in the well-being industry, her career journeyed from Therapist at Champney's Health Resort, UK, certified teacher in Holistic Therapies, practitioner of pre & post-treatments for plastic surgery, owner of a holistic center, Director of Health and Leisure at Chiva Som in Thailand, to her current position of Director of SRI LLC. Her extensive knowledge has led her to chair many international spa and wellness seminars in the UAE, UK, Asia, Russia, Hungary, Slovenia, Europe, Australia, USA, India.

Ingo Schweder
Spatality Inc., Thailand
Ingo Schweder is partner and MD of Spatality Inc and co-owner of Bodhi Dhama, a lifestyle and yoga retreat on Koh Samui. Ingo is considered one of the world foremost spa experts. From 2001-2006 he developed the MOHG's Spa Division. Under his leadership, this became the world's most awarded spa group. Previously, he was MD of the Monaco-based Rafael Hotel Groups' activities in South Asia, where he helped establish 'Ananda in the Himalayas'. Ingo's achievements have received multiple industry awards including: 'Spa Personality of the Year', 'Most Inspired Industry Motivator' and the 'Gold Key' Award at the 'Excellence in Hospitality Design' event in New York.

Sonu Shivdasani
Six Senses Resorts & Spas, Thailand
Sonu Shivdasani is Founder, Chairman & CEO of Six Senses Resorts & Spas. A descendant of Indian Parents, Sonu is an alumni of Eton College with an MA in English Literature from Oxford University. In 1990, he leased an island in the Maldives with his Eva, his Swedish-born wife, and they opened their first resort, Soneva Fushi in 1995 which boasted the Maldive's first spa. This led to the creation of the Six Senses group; a company whose *Core Purpose* is: *To create innovative and enriching experiences in a sustainable environment.* Six Senses currently has a portfolio of 26 resorts, and 41 spas.

Russell Arthur Smith
Cornell-Nanyang Institute of Hospitality Management, Singapore
Dr. Smith is a hospitality and tourism development expert who has extensive academic and professional experience in the Asia Pacific, as well as North America and the Middle East. He is Founding Vice Dean, Cornell-Nanyang Institute of Hospitality Management, at the Nanyang Technological University, Singapore. Dr. Smith has headed multi-disciplinary teams for the preparation of major hospitality and tourism development plans. In addition, he has served on many private and public boards and committees throughout the Asia Pacific. He holds a doctorate from Harvard University and degrees in architecture from the University of Queensland. He is a Certified Practising Planner.

Alison Snelling
Urban Healing Company Ltd, UK
Alison gained a Masters Degree in Business Administration from the University of Leicester, UK and has a rich mix of experience drawn from a career in leisure and hospitality management and over 20 years both in operational and training and development roles. She is also an experienced coach, an Avatar Master and NLP practitioner and is qualified in utilising psychometrics in assessment and development settings. As a Managing Partner of Urban Healing, Alison applies her expertise in the development and delivery of interactive and innovative management development programmes, trainer development workshops, recruitment and assessment tools, and bespoke guest service and sales programmes.

Daryl Stevens
Arris Pty, Australia
Dr Daryl Stevens graduated with First Class Honours from La Trobe University before completing his Doctorate of Philosophy

at the University of Adelaide, Australia. He has worked as a research scientist specialising in terrestrial toxicology for the University of Adelaide, CSIRO and Arris Pty Ltd. His research and technical advisory roles have specialised in water quality and water recycling from an environmental and irrigation perspective. He has been an advisor to the World Health Organisation and recently coordinated the Environmental Risk Component of the Australian Guidelines for Water Recycling. Currently he is the National Coordinator for Recycled Water Development in Australian Horticulture and leads a research project for the Australasian Spa Association (ASpa) into water use in Victorian Spas.

Mary Tabacchi
Cornell University, USA
Professor Mary H. Tabacchi, Ph.D., R.D., has been on faculty at Cornell University since 1972, and teaches in the School of Hotel Administration at Cornell University. She is a respected author and researcher, having published numerous papers and books on nutrition, spas, etc, as well as conducted research on the spa industry. She works globally on research, education and consulting projects in Europe, Asia and North America. Dr. Tabacchi has served on the International SPA Association Board of Directors, is past president of the ISPA Foundation and numerous spa-related boards and committees. ISPA created a scholarship in Prof Tabacchi's name in 2006.

Guy Vincent
Aromatherapy Associates, UK
Guy Vincent joined Aromatherapy Associates in 2003 and as Head of Research and Development he is involved in many aspects of formulation development from design through to manufacture. His knowledge and creativity in formulating blends using some of the world's finest essential oils and naturally active ingredients has introduced a new dimension to the company's reputed range of aromatherapeutic products Guy has acquired advanced olfactory skills, manufacturing capabilities and knowledge of natural medicine. He trained in perfumery and has specialised in creating professional spa and retail products for over 15 years.

Melinda Watt
EC3 Global, Australia
Melinda Watt is responsible for overseeing the day-to-day customer relationship management for new and existing clients and offers extra support where possible. Much of Melinda's

experience derives from developing and maintaining bench-marking services to a wide client range and in this role, Melinda continues to coordinate benchmarking projects. As Vice President, Melinda is also responsible for developing and implementing in-house training for staff as well as training of partners and clients in EC3 Global's product range. Melinda is highly experienced in the Green Globe program and currently liaises with the On-site Auditor network.

Donna Wells
Wellness Media Ltd, USA
Donna Wells began her spa career in Bali in 1999, consulting on concept development, PR, marketing and spa openings for Mandara Spa. In 2006, she returned to Australia to co-found Spa Sessions with Naomi Gregory, and later resumed freelance consulting. She now lives on Koh Samui, working as Director of Communications for Kamalaya.

Mark Wuttke
Wuttke Group, LLC, USA
Mark Wuttke heads the Wuttke Group, a business develop-ment team that focuses on sustainable luxury, spa, boutique retail, organic luxury and the emerging category of eco-chic. Active in the international luxury spa market, Mark is a founding Board Member of the Global Spa Summit, Founding Editorial Advisory Board Member of Organic Spa Magazine, Board Member of the Green Spa Network, and works closely with the International Spa Association, LOHAS, and Natural Beauty Summit (Americas and Europe). Global in outlook, Mark's experience includes 14 years as President/CEO within the wellness movement and has served over 12 years on numerous boards in green industries.

List of Figures

List of Tables

PART 1

Planning

Spas, wellness and human evolution

Marc Cohen

The emergence of a new global industry

The spa industry has recently emerged as a global phenomenon through a convergence of industries, traditions and therapeutic practices. Spa therapies have been around since ancient times in many different forms that reflect the cultural, social and political milieu in which there are embedded. These practices are now being rediscovered, integrated and branded to create a new global industry that draws from a range of aligned industries. These include beauty, massage, hospitality, tourism, architecture, property development, landscape design, fashion, food and beverage, fitness and leisure, personal development, as well as complementary, conventional and traditional medicine.

The global spa industry is a melting pot for a range of products and services that enhance health and well-being. As such, it combines features from regions around the globe, including American commercialism with its emphasis on beauty, pampering and destination experiences; Asian service ethics, holistic therapies and spiritual practices; European medical traditions and clinical acumen; and the indigenous knowledge and environmental consciousness of various tribal cultures. The convergence of these influences has seen spas being taken up by the international hospitality industry, fuelled by the merging of the travel dollar with the health dollar. Thus, spas are now springing up all over the world and have become a standard feature of luxury hotels and resorts.

The global spa industry is still in its infancy and, as yet, there are few robust figures documenting its size and scope. However, even without robust data, it is clear that the spa industry is already large and is growing. It is estimated that spas are a $40 billion global industry with at least 16,000 spas in the USA alone, and over 50,000 spas around the globe (Spafinder, 2007). It is also reported that spas are the fastest growing leisure industry with US figures showing a growth rate of around 20% per year. Furthermore, it is estimated that by 2001 revenues from spas had already overtaken revenues from amusement parks, box office receipts, vacation ownership and ski resorts (ISPA, 2002).

The rapid growth of the spa industry has created many challenges. As a high-touch, people-based business, training, recruiting and managing staff have emerged as major issues. Other major issues are the development of appropriate business models and valuation methods to enable investors to transparently asses their potential for returns. As well as being challenged by financial reporting, spas, like all other businesses, are also being challenged by issues of sustainability and the rise in consumer consciousness that is demanding greater disclosure of business practices as well as environmental and social performance.

While the global spa industry is still evolving, it is apparent that the industry is beginning to embrace wellness as part of its core business. The emergence of the global spa industry can therefore be understood as a natural response to the human desire for wellness and viewed in the context of the evolution of consciousness, globalisation and the many crises the world is now facing.

The birth of a new millennium

A growing body of opinion holds that the new millennia will mark a new phase in human evolution. It is clear that within the lifespan of the current generation, humanity will need to come to terms with the limits to growth and develop sustainable ways of 'living well in the world'.

Since the publication of 'Limits to Growth' by the 'Club of Rome' in the early 1970s, there has been an awareness that the world is limited in terms of its physical resources and that the continued existence of humanity is dependent on drastically altering many of the current structures and ways of doing business and developing a sustainable relationship with the environment (Meadows et al., 1972). Humanity has reached a 'tipping point' bringing the possibility of either a massive breakdown or a breakthrough into new ways of living.

The new phase in human evolution represents a culmination of thousands of years of human history during which many different cultures, philosophies, traditions and technologies have attempted to address the questions of life, ageing, illness and death. It seems that all people have tried to tackle with the question of: How to live well in the world?

Now, at the turn of the millennium, when humanity has finally fully colonized the planet and has come up against the limits to growth, the question has become even more pertinent with the answers being relevant to the species as a whole. It is also now that the spa industry has emerged as a melting pot for the world's traditions and knowledge. In doing the spa industry has become a global phenomenon that is poised to unite humanity in the common goal of working out how to be 'well'. The spa industry is therefore also poised to lead the way and offer solutions on how to achieving sustainable wellbeing on a finite planet.

The health spectrum

Humanity's search for well-being follows the evolution of medicine which has seen the elaboration of two distinct yet complementary approaches. These approaches parallel the rational and intuitive modes of human consciousness and the top-down and bottom-up approaches to knowledge and are represented by Eastern medicine.

Eastern and Western health traditions are based on holistic thinking that maintains a cosmological perspective outlining a philosophy of life, while Western medicine is based on a reductionist approach, emphasising controlled scientific experimentation and mathematical analysis. These two broad approaches have led to the development of two different approaches to achieving health and well-being (Cohen, 2002).

If health and disease are considered to be at opposite ends of a spectrum, then it is possible to classify health into three broad areas: ill health, average health and enhanced health (Figure 1.1). The divide between ill health and average health is generally defined in Western medical terms which classify diseases based on symptom patterns or other diagnostic parameters. Western medicine uses a bottom-up approach that aims to define and understand illness and develop interventions such

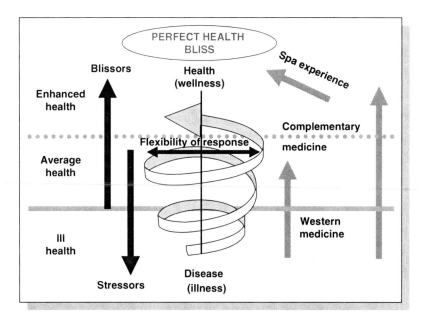

Figure 1.1
The health spectrum

as drugs and surgery to treat or prevent the disease and control factors that reduce well-being ('stressors').

Compared to the divide between ill health and average health, the divide between average health and enhanced health is less distinct. Enhanced health is more than just being disease free, it assumes high levels of physical strength, stamina, mental clarity, as well as physical beauty and maximal enjoyment and fulfilment from life. This requires the holistic integration of multiple factors that determine physical, psychological, emotional, social, economic, environmental and spiritual health (Cohen, 2003). Within many Eastern philosophies the idea of enhanced health can be extended to the concept of 'perfect health' or 'enlightenment', whereby a person is 'at one with the universe' and hence in a state of perfect bliss or 'nirvana'.

Bliss is the ultimate aim of Eastern healing and spiritual practices which adopt a top down approach by attempting to elicit bliss through meditation and other practices that enhance wellbeing ('blissors'). Bliss, or 'ananda' in Sanskrit, is considered by Vedic scholars to be innermost level of the individual self, as well as the nature of the whole universe. It is the goal of the path to enlightenment and is found in the deepest experience of meditation and the innermost level of our being (Maharishi, 1986).

The state of bliss can also be considered as the highest aim of the 'spa experience' and to be the ultimate in achieving human potential. As the late anthropologist Joseph Campbell states: 'I think that most people are looking for an experience that connects them to the ecstasy of what it could feel like to be totally alive. To know the unburdened state of total aliveness is the pinnacle of the human potential' (Campbell, 1998). This state of 'total aliveness' referred to by the Campbell is what many people may consider to be 'wellness'.

What is wellness?

While wellness has an emphasis which is quite distinct from the Western medical focus on illness and pathology, there is, as yet, no rigorously developed definition, theory or philosophy of wellness. At a basic level, wellness can be equated with 'health' which, according to the World Health Organization (WHO), is: 'a state of complete physical, mental and social well-being and not merely the absence of disease or infirmity' (WHO, 1992). The notion of wellness may be extended further to include not only physical, mental and social dimensions but also sexual, emotional, cultural, spiritual, educational, occupational, financial, environmental, ethical and existential dimensions. As a holistic concept wellness assumes that if any one of these dimensions is deficient then complete wellness cannot be achieved.

Wellness is defined by Corbin and Pangrazi (2001) as: 'a multi dimensional state of being describing the existence of positive health in an individual as exemplified by quality of life and a sense of well-being'. Another definition by Muller and Kaufmann (2000) suggests that wellness is: 'A state of health featuring the harmony of body, mind and spirit with self-responsibility, physical fitness/beautycare, healthy nutrition/diet, relaxations/meditation, mental activity/education and environmental sensitivity/social contacts as fundamental elements'.

While these definitions attempt to capture the essence of wellness by referring to 'health', 'harmony of body, mind and spirit', 'quality of life' and 'well-being', they are more descriptive than definitive. Perhaps a more comprehensive definition is that: 'Wellness is the multidimensional state of being "well", where inner and outer worlds are in harmony: a heightened state of consciousness enabling you to be fully present in the moment and respond authentically to any situation from the "deep inner well of your being". Wellness is dynamic and results in a continuous awakening and evolution of consciousness and is the state where you look, feel, perform, and stay "well" and, therefore, experience the greatest fulfilment and enjoyment from life and achieve the greatest longevity'.

This definition implies that the state of wellness allows the greatest flexibility to respond to situations and therefore provides the greatest resilience to stress and disease. Wellness is therefore the best preventive medicine. This definition also suggests that wellness is not a product you can buy or sell. Rather, it is a state of consciousness that guides the quality of our relationships with the world and therefore cannot be viewed separate from the environment in which it occurs. Thus, if 'health' is 'wholeness', then wellness is the experience of an ever-expanding realisation of what it means to be whole.

Wellness now defines a form of secular spirituality that transcends formal religion. Spas and wellness resorts may therefore be conceptualised in cultural/sociological terms as modern day temples where people can experience rituals, learn to deepen their personal wellness practices, raise their consciousness, become open to enhanced ways of being and deepen their experience of being alive.

At a personal level, striving for wellness directly involves raising consciousness and becoming more aware of both internal and external worlds. Spas have been predicted to play a major role in this process with the suggestion that 'in the future, wellness retreats and spa will become centers of education, teaching the client how to take care of themselves and enjoy optimum health' (Stapleton, 2003).

On a transpersonal level the evolution of the spa and wellness industry can be understood as a natural consequence of the evolution of human consciousness whereby humans are coming to terms with how to live well on the planet. However, while humans have always sought out ways to live well in the world, most global indicators at the turn of the millennium suggest that humanity as a whole is not doing well in this task.

The world in crisis

Disease, poison, violence, accidents, so-called 'acts of god' creating climatic or environmental upheaval: these are the major causes of individual mortality and morbidity. Similarly, humanity is facing these issues on a global level with the potential for pandemics, pollution, wars and terrorism, military or industrial accidents and climate change threatening the safety and survival of the human species.

There is currently a drastic inequality in the world, much of which is captured in data presented by numerous international agencies. According to a study on the distribution of household wealth by the World Institute for Development Economics Research of the United Nations University (WIDER-UNU), there is an ever increasing wealth inequality with the richest 2% estimated to own more than 50% of global wealth while the poorest 50% of adults own barely 1%. This inequality is likened to one person in a group of ten taking 99% of a pie and leaving the other nine people to share the remaining 1% (Davies et al., 2006).

Thus, currently 3 billion people in the world struggle to survive on US$2 per day and one-third of the world is starving with someone dying of hunger the equivalent of every 3.6 seconds; yet it is estimated that to satisfy the world's basic health and nutrition requirements would cost US$13 billion – the yearly amount spent in the USA and European Union on perfume (www.globalissues.org). Meanwhile, more than US$1 trillion is spent on the military (Stålenheim et al., 2006) and there are more than 1 billion overweight adults with the number of overweight children in the USA doubling and overweight adolescents tripling since 1980 (Puska, 2003). This inequality is also the cause of social upheaval and fuels war, terrorism and other violence.

In addition to social inequality, it is also clear that the world is becoming increasingly toxic with worldwide dissemination of industrial chemicals, pesticides, heavy metals and radioactive elements. Many of these toxins have demonstrably harmful effects including cancer, reproductive metabolic and mental diseases. Furthermore, combinations of toxins, which may combine to have greater effects than single toxins exist in wildlife and humans around the world (Cohen, 2007). Many toxins are also stored in fatty tissue enabling them to bioaccumulate up the food chain as much as 70000 times (WHO, 1993) and infants can be exposed to pesticides and other chemicals at levels greater than the Acceptable Daily Intake (ADI) from their mother's breast milk (Quinsey et al., 1995). In addition to chemical toxins, radioactive waste that will be toxic for many millions or even billions of years is accumulating at an increasing rate and being dispersed around the globe.

There is also a crisis in healthcare with an ageing population, increasing healthcare costs and an epidemic of lifestyle-related diseases such as obesity, diabetes, heart disease and cancer. Due to unhealthy lifestyles, it has been predicted that for the first time in history, the lifespan of the next generation in the USA may be less than their parents (Olshansky et al., 2005). A 2005 report by the WHO titled 'Preventing Chronic Disease: A Vital Investment' estimates that of all the 58 million deaths in the world in 2005, 35 million (60%) will be caused by chronic diseases such as heart disease, stroke, cancer, chronic respiratory diseases and diabetes. The report goes on to suggest that 80% of premature heart disease, stroke and type 2 diabetes is preventable and that 40% of cancer is preventable with the main modifiable risk factors for these diseases being lifestyle related including unhealthy diet, physical inactivity and tobacco use (WHO, 2005). In addition to the growing prevalence of lifestyle-related disease, there is a concern over the potential for a global pandemic such as bird flu or other infectious disease to decimate larges sections of the human population.

While inequality, pollution and disease are all emerging as global issues, the one issue that currently seems to be receiving the most attention is climate change.

Climate has currently become the topic for a global conversation occurring between governments, scientists, industries, investors and non-governmental agencies. Discussions on climate change are also driving a sustainability agenda in the corporate world (see Chapter 20) as it is becoming clear that drastic change is required and as former Chief World Bank Economist Nicholas Stern concluded in his report: 'business as usual is not an option' (Stern, 2006).

While the conclusions of the Stern Report refer to the economics of climate change, the multiple crises facing the global community suggest that we are on the brink of a radical shift in the ways humans live. This breakthrough will require humans to develop sustainable ways of living and it is suggested that this will in turn require a breakthrough in the evolution of human consciousness.

The evolution of consciousness

Much has been written about the evolution of consciousness and the next phase of human evolution. In his book 'The Global Brain Awakens: Our Next Evolutionary Leap', Peter Russel describes how higher levels of consciousness emerge from lower levels of complexity (Russel, 1995). Thus, 10 billion atoms can form a living cell and 10 billion cells can form a human brain giving rise to a self-reflective mind with each level having a consciousness higher than its constituents. Taking the analogy a step further, Russel suggests the possibility of 10 billion minds forming a Gaian, global, super-consciousness.

While humanity is now entering the order of magnitude of 10 billion people, just as 10 billion cells do not necessarily make a mind, 10 billion minds will not necessarily make a global consciousness. The emergence of higher conscious states requires individual elements to be highly connected, integrated and working to a common purpose. There are also stages along the way. In the human body cells first form organs and tissues that work to a common purpose before they form self-reflective minds. Similarly, before uniting on a global level, minds must first form smaller collections such as communities, companies and cultures that share a common vision and purpose.

The search for wellness provides such a common purpose and humanity's search for wellness can be understood to be a conscious extension of the basic animal instinct to avoid pain that has its origins with the dawn of humanity when consciousness first became self-reflective (Cohen, 2000).

Since the emergence of self-reflective consciousness, every culture at every point in history has maintained various practices that aim to ensure the well-being of individuals and the wider community. These practices invariably include the use of the local environment, food, water and plants along with various indigenous healing practices, such as massage along with traditional cultural practices that are performed to focus the mind and anchor the experience of being well in ritual, routine and direct sensual experience. These are the very elements that the spa industry uses to create the spa experience.

While every culture throughout history has had its own well-ness practices and philosophies, there has never before been a culture that has been global or sustainable. Even the Roman Empire, which had a dominant culture that embraced what we now term spas and wellness over 2 millennia ago, was not truly global and was inherently unsustainable, as it was based on slave labour and forced human conquest. In the current millennia, however, the global spa industry has the potential to be a globally sustainable phenomenon based on technology, commerce and the emergence of a 'global spa culture'.

The global spa culture

The global spa culture appears to be emerging from the intersection of the global, jet-set elite and the hippy counterculture both of which transcend national borders and have arisen from the baby boomer generation. Baby boomers grew up with an expanded view of individual freedom associated with feminism, civil, gay, handicapped and animal rights, and a shift away from formal religion towards an emphasis on personal spiritual experience. Furthermore, the baby boomers were the generation that witnessed first-hand the world becoming a truly global marketplace and the emergence of an experience economy where value is placed on personal transformation (Pine and Gilmore, 1999).

Virtually the entire world is now accessible to the general consumer. The advent of modern technology, travel and globalisation has enabled people to travel around the globe and reside in luxury hotels which defy their guests to know which country they are in. There are now greater similarities between airports and luxury hotels spread across the globe with the same global brands and consumer goods on offer, than there are between these hotels and many of the local communities in which they are situated.

In the past, intrepid travellers would return transformed as a result of their travels. This is no longer the case and global travel has now become a mundane reality for many. Yet, the current merging of the travel dollar with the health dollar suggests that the desire for being transformed by travel remains. The global spa industry is now emerging to fulfil on this desire by placing the wealth of the world's wellness practices on offer and turning wellness into a commodity that can be bought by the hour under the guise of a 'spa journey'.

In embracing wellness and focusing on 'experiences', the global spa industry can be seen as a vehicle for raising consciousness. In this regard the spa industry is following the lead of the 'Cultural Creatives' and the 'Lifestyles of Health and Sustainability' (LOHAS) consumers which represent a rapidly expanding marketplace for goods and services that appeal to consumers who value health, environment, social justice, personal development and sustainable living (see Chapter 12).

Conshumanism

The LOHAS movement has arisen out of a growing awareness that rampant consumerism seems to be taking over and destroying the planet. Unchecked and unconscious consumption can be seen to be at the root of many of the world problems. Thus, while consumers currently have access to a seemingly unlimited choice of goods in every size and colour, people remain disconnected from the products and services they purchase.

In response to this disconnection, there is a growth in conscious consumer trends that include LOHAS, as well as a variety of trends labelled under different names such as: 'green', 'natural', 'organic' fair-trade', 'corporate social responsibility', 'eco', 'ethical investment', 'sustainable' and 'barefoot luxury'. These have given rise to locovor restaurants (that source food within 100 miles), carbon offset programs, 'green buildings', 'carbon neutral businesses', 'eco-tourism', 'ethno-tourism', 'voluntourism', 'downsizing, 'tree change', 'social capital', and 'triple and quadruple bottom line reporting' (see Chapter 20).

It is suggested that this range of conscious consumer trends can be integrated under the banner of 'conshumanism', which is a term that defines 'conscious and humane consumption' or 'consumption with maximal awareness, efficiency and enjoyment and minimal pain, energy, waste and pollution'. Conshumanism embraces an overarching concept that can integrate multiple consumer trends towards greater transparency, equity, accountability, social responsibility environmental sustainability and ethics.

The common feature of these trends is increasing information and consciousness about consumption habits. Thus 'conshuman consumption' implies that consumers ask a range of questions about the products they are consuming such as: What is in it? Who made it? Who benefits from the purchase? Where did it come from? How did it get here? What is its lifecycle and embodied energy? What is its environmental and social impact? What are the alternatives? Is the product really necessary?

Having these questions answered will result in a much greater awareness of the impact of consumption habits on the planet and other people, thus enabling enhanced sustainability, equity and well-being. However, while most people are not yet ready for this level of disclosure and most businesses are not prepared to disclose this information, there is a clear trend towards increasing consciousness in our consumption patterns and the lure of wellness demands that this continue. Furthermore, the consequences of continued non-disclosure and rampant unconscious consumption are becoming all too obvious.

The Cultural Creatives and LOHAS consumers are currently driving the 'conshuman' agenda. These groups whose choices are aligned with their values are also deemed to be early adopters and natural opinion leaders with the ability to be evangelists for services and products they believe in.

While the spa and wellness industry has the opportunity to directly engage the LOHAS consumer, this may not necessarily be occurring as spas may be seen to embrace frivolous pampering and wasteful luxury rather than sustainable health and wellbeing. Furthermore, wellness, cannot be viewed separate from the environment in which it occurs. Thus a 'wellness spa' that depletes and degrades the environment with unsustainable practices or exploits staff and the local community will be seen an inauthentic and will degrade the image of spas to the very market segment that it is trying to engage.

There is an imperative therefore, for spas to embrace 'conshuman ideals' and actively lead the LOHAS movement by embracing sustainability and addressing climate change through the use of reusable energy and carbon offsetting. This imperative further extends to the use of organic products, fairtrade principles, engagement with local communities, and attending to the quality of life of its staff.

Towards a global health service

In offering to deliver on wellness, the spa industry is moving beyond luxury and pampering into the area of providing healthcare and raising consciousness. As such, the global spa industry is a melting pot for a whole host of products and services that encourage enhanced health and well-being drawn from a wide variety of traditions that include conventional, complementary and traditional medicine. Thus spas are adopting an integrative approach and taking holistic medical concepts out of clinics and combing them with the world of hospitality and leisure to place them in sustainable and nurturing environments.

It is clear that an integrative and holistic approach to medicine is becoming increasingly sought after. This is evidenced by the growing emphasis on disease prevention and health enhancement and the increasing utilisation of complementary therapies. These trends can be seen to reflect a growing disenchantment with the medical profession's seemingly one-sided emphasis on science and technology, as well as a growing demand for autonomy in healthcare decisions. Certainly, the general population is now better informed than ever and has greater access to health information. The public is subsequently demanding more from healthcare providers and are not only interested in treating illness. Instead they want to maximise their health, prevent or slow down the ageing process and achieve higher levels of functioning (Cohen, 2001).

In contrast to integrative medicine which emphasises wellness and a preventive approach, Western medicine is based on an illness model with most money and effort being spent on developing drugs and therapies to treat disease rather than enhance well-being. For example, it is considered normal for doctors to treat coronary heart disease with bypass surgery costing around US$20000, rather than encouraging patients to change their lifestyle and relax, exercise, eat good food and share their feelings, even though conclusive research has proven the efficacy of this latter approach (Ornish et al., 1998). As a result, over 500000 bypass operations were performed in the USA in 2000, with in-hospital costs of cardiac disease in 2003 being estimated at $94 billion (Eisenberg et al., 2005).

While high-tech medical interventions aimed at treating illness have created a massive industry that is now extending into the developing world with the advent of medical tourism, there are no global health service providers. It is also becoming clear that the current illness-based medical model is not sustainable and will never be able to meet the needs of the global population.

In a PriceWaterHouseCoopers (PWC) report on the future of healthcare called 'HealthCast 2020: Creating a Sustainable Future' (PWC, 2005), it is suggested that 'There is growing evidence that the current health systems of nations around the world will be unsustainable if unchanged over the next 15 years' (PWC, 2005, p. 2). The report found that there is a convergence of healthcare solutions in the global healthcare market and suggests that we need to apply global solutions to local healthcare problems and that consumers will play a much larger role in healthcare. The report also concluded that 'Preventive care and disease management programs have untapped potential to enhance health status and reduce costs' (PWC, 2005, p. 4).

Hotels have a much greater appeal than hospitals. Thus, by combining hospitality with an integrative medicine model that emphasises lifestyle change and personal empowerment, the spa industry has the potential to transcend conventional medicine and create a globally sustainable health system. While most spas do not as yet create formal medical records, instigate diagnostic tests or perform medical procedures, these are all taking place in some medi-spas and destination spas, and some spas are beginning to integrate both conventional medicine and complementary medicine services along with hospitality services such as accommodation and food and beverage to create hybrid hospital-spa-hotels ('hos-spa-tels'). As these are integrated into international hospitality chains, they create the potential for the delivery of a global integrated health service based on wellness principles.

Wellness principles

With the advent of wellness-based health services being delivered through the hospitality industry rather than the healthcare industry, there is an opportunity to use wellness concepts and principles to redefine healthcare based on consumer demands. Wellness does not as yet have an integrated theory yet, there are general principles that recur as themes in different healthcare paradigms, including conventional, complementary and traditional medicine.

Perhaps the most ubiquitous wellness principle in traditional medicine is the idea that life is dependent on a subtle form of energy. This energy, which has been described by many different healing traditions as 'life energy', 'vital force', 'prana, 'chi' or 'Qi', is said to flow along defined pathways and support the functioning of living systems. Traditional Chinese Medicine (TCM) has developed a sophisticated framework for conceptualising this energy which is seen encompass the concept of 'flow' and to move according to the dynamic interplay of the opposite yet complementary forces of 'yin' and 'yang' which guide the process of transformation whereby nonliving things become animate. In this view, pain and disease are said to result when the energetic flow is disrupted and healing is aimed at restoring the natural balance and flow (Figure 1.2).

As science does not recognise a form of energy specific to living systems, many concepts underlying Eastern medicine have been criticized as being unscientific. Yet many parallels exist between Eastern and Western concepts (Figure 1.3). For example, the concept of 'Tao' can be compared to the mathematical concept

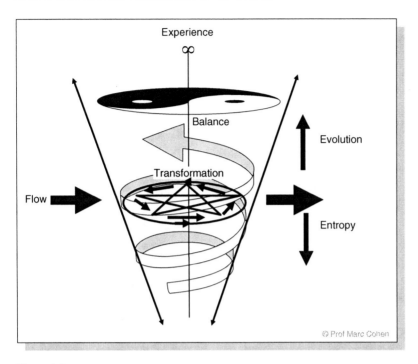

Figure 1.2
Pictorial conceptualisation of wellness concepts from traditional Chinese medicine

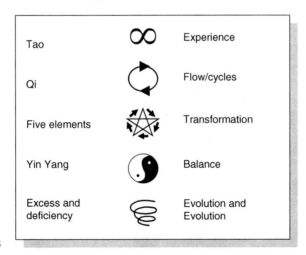

Figure 1.3
Basic philosophical
concepts of TCM and
their graphical and
conceptual counterparts

of 'absolute infinity' or the infinite nature of direct experience, which like the 'Tao' are seen as inherently incomprehensible. Similarly the concept of 'yin' and 'yang' which refers to inter-dependent yet mutually exclusive opposites can be compared with the concept of 'complementarity' in quantum physics or the concept of homeostatic balance in physiology (Cohen, 2002).

Table 1.1 Different conceptualisations of five elements

Five phases (elements) in TCM	Metal	Water	Wood	Fire	Earth
Basic TCM concepts	Tao	Chi	Yin and Yang	Five phases of transformation	Excess and deficiency
Five elements in Western science	Information	Energy	Space	Time	Matter
Western concepts	Experience	Flow	Balance	Transformation	Evolution and entropy
Five capitals	Social	Human	Natural	Manufactured	Financial
Business cycle	Planning	People	Planet	Product	Profit
Stages of computing	Program	Language	Interface	Process	Output
Communication	Source	Transmitter	Channel	Receiver	Destination

Another concept that appears throughout medical thought is that of five elements or phases of transformation. This is common to Chinese medicine, Ayurvedic medicine and Greek medicine (which considered quintessence as a fifth element in addition to air, water, fire and earth). The five element model may be extended to other diverse fields of thought such as the types of capital (Porritt, 2005) (see Chapter 20), the phases of a business, which include planning, people, planet, product and profit, as well as other areas such as five stages of computing and communication (see Table 1.1).

One of the most significant parallels between Eastern and Western thought may be the similarity between the concept of 'Qi' in Eastern medicine and the concept of 'information' in thermodynamics. Information can be measured in terms of energy as 'joules/degree kelvin' and the Eastern concept of disease arising from a blockage of 'Qi' can be seen to parallel the Second Law of Thermodynamics, which describes a tendency towards disorder or entropy in an isolated system.

Thus, pain, disease and the adverse effects of ageing, which include progressive degeneration of tissues along with loss of function, can be related to an increase in entropy as a consequence of blockages or isolation of different systems.

In contrast, the ability of living systems to grow, evolve and learn appears to defy the Second Law and can be related to an open exchange between organism and environment. Positive psychological states and well-being also require 'open systems' that are recognised in common language with the idea of an 'open heart' or 'open mind'. This can be extended to the concept of 'nirvana', or perfect bliss whereby a person is 'at one with the universe' where there is no distinction between self and non-self thus creating an open system that is no longer subject to entropy (Cohen, 2002).

Creating connections

If isolation and disconnection underpin disease processes, then it seems natural that key concepts in many healing traditions are 'connection' and 'wholeness'. Spas facilitate this via 'spa journeys', which are designed as psycho-sensory experiences that evoke the senses and induce states of relaxation where the body can find its natural balance and where connection is created between inner and outer worlds.

In addition to putting people in touch with themselves and their environment, spas are also places where physical touch occurs between therapists and guest. Touch is a basic human need and is the only one of the five basic senses that is deemed necessary for survival. Studies have demonstrated that infant monkeys will die without touch and will forgo food to receive tactile stimulation (Harlow, 1958), and that untouched human babies fail to thrive (Field, 1995). Touch has even been found in animal studies to prevent cardiovascular disease with a classic study on rabbits finding that rabbits that were petted had a 60% reduction in atherosclerosis compared to non-petted rabbits despite being fed the same high cholesterol diet (Nerem et al., 1980).

Physical human touch is more than the transfer of mechanical forces. Touch can create emotional connection and intimacy, communicate empathy, presence and awareness, and facilitate more subtle energetic exchange. Despite touch being a basic need, modern societies have become extremely 'low-touch' due to the increasing use of technology, disconnected lifestyles and the fear of inappropriate touch. 'Skin hunger' has therefore become a common, yet often undiagnosed and untreated, malady.

Spas directly treat skin hunger by creating safe environments for physical touch to occur. This is done through the use of design features that allow privacy, rituals that engender trust and professionalism of therapists who are licensed to touch and who create connection through focused intent and 'palpatory literacy' (Cohen, 2005).

As well as providing a venue for physical touch, spas provide environments that can facilitate very intimate and meaningful exchanges between people. If a therapist only cares to ask, people will often reveal things that they would not tell anyone else. This includes very personal information such as the colour, quality and timing of their bodily excretions, to highly emotionally charged information about personal relationships. Thus a spa encounter can be a very intimate exchange and it is likely that the most profound healing will occur when a practitioner can evoke the greatest trust and intimacy (Cohen, 2004).

In addition to creating intimate connections, spas are also environments where guests are more likely to be receptive to explore new information and experiences. They are therefore ideal places to introduce people to healthy lifestyle practices including healthy cuisine, the use of herbal teas and organic ingredients, relaxation and mind–body techniques, and holistic exercise programs, as well as simple daily health rituals and lifestyle practices.

Spas also make people feel good, and both commonsense and scientific evidence suggest that feeling good is life affirming and enhances health. Research from the growing field of psycho-neuro-immunology, which investigates the relationship between the emotions, the brain and the immune system, has demonstrated that we are 'hard-wired for bliss' and that feeling good can positively enhance our ability to deal with and prevent illness, as well as facilitate spiritual awakening leading to increased joy and fulfilment (Pert, 2006).

Working towards wellness

While treating illness has traditionally been the domain of the medical system, there is a realisation that a wellness model requires action from all levels of society including individuals, government and non-government agencies and the corporate sector. Therefore, in attempting to address wellness, it is likely that there will be increased convergence and collaborations between the spa industry and other sectors. Thus spas are likely to converge with and possibly transform big business.

This is suggested by a recent report prepared by PWC for the World Economic Forum, titled 'Working Towards Wellness: Accelerating the Prevention of Chronic Disease' (PWC, 2007) which found that 33% of companies surveyed were rolling out comprehensive wellness programmes in multiple countries although there were challenges in implementation, evaluation and monitoring of such programs.

While the corporate sector is being challenged to include issues of wellness and sustainability, these issues are also being addressed by the financial community and the investment sector. Recently, property developers have come to see opportunities in addressing wellness and there are now many 'spa communities' under construction, with developers realising they can receive a premium for 'wellness residences' that include spa-like facilities.

Conclusion

The new millennium has seen the global spa industry emerge as a melting pot for a whole host of products and services that enhance health and well-being. This emergence can be viewed as a response to the human desire for wellness in the context of the evolution of consciousness, globalisation and the many crises the world is now facing.

The growing emphasis on wellness and sustainability, along with the convergence of the health, travel and hospitality sectors, bears well for the continued evolution of the spa industry. However, there are still many challenges ahead. The global spa industry is still in its infancy and there is much work to do to better define measures of well-being, document the benefits of spa therapies, provide greater transparency and disclosure about the use of products and services, and develop robust systems for evaluating spas' financial, social and environmental performance.

As development on the planet pushes the natural limits to growth and inequality, and environmental toxicity and chronic disease reach crisis levels, the spa industry promises a solution to many of the current world problems. The spa industry also promises to integrate wellness knowledge and thus combine the ingenuity and enterprise of the USA; the service and holistic thinking of Asia; the formal traditions and rational thinking of Europe; and the environmental consciousness and cultural wisdom of indigenous tribes.

Thus, the global spa industry may not only help raise the consciousness and enhance the well-being of individuals, it may also contribute to shaping a new global culture that is highly conscious of its consumption habits. Spas may also provide the basis for sustainable business models that can last for millennia. In doing so, the spa industry may help to unite humanity in an enterprise that celebrates ethnic, geographical and cultural diversity, and act as a vehicle for humanity to expand and redefine its understanding of itself and its place in the world.

References

Campbell, J. (1988) *The Power of Myth*, Doubleday, New York.

Cohen, M. (2000) The evolution of holistic medicine. In: Cohen, M. (Ed.), *Pathways to Holistic Health*, Monash Institute of Public Health, pp. 11–24.

Cohen, M. (2001) From complementary, to integrative and holistic medicine. In: Cohen, M. (Ed.), *Perspectives on Holistic Health*, Monash Institute of Public Health, Clayton, pp. 33–42.

Cohen, M. (2002) Energy medicine from an ancient and modern perspective. In: Cohen, M. (Ed.), *Prescriptions for Holistic Health*, Monash Institute of Health Services Research, Clayton, pp. 97–108.

Cohen, M. (2003) Integrative medicine, principles of practice. In: Cohen, M. (Ed.), *Holistic Health in Practice*, Australian Integrative Medicine Association, Clayton.

Cohen, M. (2004) The challenges of holistic and integrative medicine in practice. In: Cohen, M. (Ed.), *Holistic Solutions for Sustainable Healthcare*, Australian Integrative Medicine Association, Clayton, pp. 49–62.

Cohen, M. (2005) *The Power of Touch*, Turning Point Spa Summit, Singapore.

Cohen, M. (2007) Environmental toxins and health: the health impact of pesticides, *Australian Family Physician*, 36(12):1002–1004.

Corbin, C., Pangrazi, R. (2001) Toward a uniform definition of wellness: a commentary, *Research Digest* 3(15):1–8. Washington, DC, President's Council on Physical Fitness and Sports, available at: http://www.presidentschallenge.org/misc/news_research/research_digests/dec2001digest.pdf (site accessed 14 February 2007).

Davies, J., Sandström, S., Shorrocks, A., Wolff, E. (2006) The World Distribution of Household Wealth, World Institute for Development Economics Research of the United Nations University (UNU-WIDER) Helsinki, available at: http://www.wider.unu.edu/events/past-events/2006-events/en_GB/05-12-2006/.

Eisenberg, M.J., Filion, K.B., Azoulay, A., Brox, A.C., Haider, S., Pilote, L. (2005) Outcomes and cost of coronary artery bypass graft surgery in the United States and Canada, *Archives of Internal Medicine*, 165:1506–1513.

Field, T. (1995) *Touch in Early Development*, Lawrence Erlbaum Associates, NJ.

Harlow, H. (1958) The nature of love, *American Psychologist*, 13:573–685.

ISPA (2002) The International Spa Association's 2002 Spa Industry Study, *PriceWaterhouseCoopers*.

Mahesh Yogi Maharishi, (1986) Thirty Years Around the World – Dawn of the Age of Enlightenment, Vol. One, Maharishi Vedic University Press, Vlodrop. 1957–1964

Meadows, D.H., Meadows, D.L., Randers, J., Behrens, W.W. (1972) *The Limits to Growth: A Report for the Club of Rome's Project on the Predicament of Mankind*. Earth Island, London.

Muller, H., Kaufmann, E.L. (2000) Wellness tourism: market analysis of a special health tourism segment and implications for the hotel industry, *Journal of Vacation Marketing*, 7(1). available at: http://jvm.sagepub.com/cgi/content/refs/7/1/5

Nerem, R.M., Levesque, M.J., Cornhill, J.F. (1980) Social environments as a factor in diet-induced atherosclerosis, *Science*, 208:1475–1476.

Ornish, D., Scherwitz, L., Billlings, J., Gould, L., Sparler, T.S., Armstrong, W.T., Ports, T.A., Kirkeeide, R.L., Hogeboom, C., Brand, R. (1998) Intensive lifestyle changes for reversal of coronary heart disease, *Journal of American Medical Association*, 280:2001–2007.

Olshansky, S.J., Passaro, D.J., Hershow, R.C., Layden, J., Carnes, B.A., Brody, J., Hayflick, L., Butler, R.N., Allison, D.B., Ludwig, D.S. (2005) A potential decline in life expectancy in the United States in the 21st century, *New England Journal of Medicine*, 352:1138–1145.

Pert, C. (2006) *Everything You Need to Know to Feel Go(o)d*, Hay House.

Pine, J., Gilmore, J. (1999) *The Experience Economy*, Harvard Business School Press, Boston, MA.

Porritt, J. (2005) *Capitalism as if the World Matters*, Earthscan, London.

PriceWaterHouseCoopers (2005) *HealthCast 2020: Creating a Sustainable Future*, available at: www.pwc.com/il/heb/about/svcs/publication/alerts/2HealthCast_2020.pdf.

PriceWaterHouseCoopers (2007) *Working Towards Wellness: Accelerating the Prevention of Chronic Disease*, World Economic Forum, available at: http://pwchealth.com/cgi-local/hregister.cgi?link=reg/wellness.pdf

Puska, P., Nishida, C., Porter, D. (2003) *World Health Organization Global Strategy on Diet*, Physical Activity and Health, WHO, available at: www.who.int/dietphysicalactivity/publications/facts/obesity/en

Quinsey, P.M., Donohue, D.C., Ahokas, J.T. (1995) Persistence of organochlorines in breast milk of women in Victoria, Australia, *Food And Chemical Toxicology: An International Journal Published for the British Industrial Biological Research Association*, 33(1):49–56.

Russel, P. (1995) *The Global Brain Awakens: Our Next Evolutionary Leap* (1995). Updated version of *The Global Brain* (1983) which was published as *The Awakening Earth* (1982) in the UK.

SpaFinder (2007) Day Spa Industry Report including data on business performance and revenue, operations, facilities, marketing, personnel management, treatment offerings, retail business, technology adoption, trends in spa clientele, etc.

Stålenheim, P., Fruchart, D., Omitoogun, W., Perdomo, C. (2006) Military expenditure. *Stockholm International Peace Research Institute Yearbook 2006 Armaments, Disarmament and International Security*, SIPRI, Stockholm, available at: http://yearbook2006.sipri.org/

Stapleton, J. (2003) *Keynote Address at the International Spa Association*, Europe Congress, Slovenia.

Stern, N. (2006) *The Economics of Climate Change*, H.M. Treasury, London.

WHO (World Health Organization) (1992) *Basic Documents*, 39th edn, WHO, Geneva.

WHO (World Health Organization) (1993) *Environmental Health Criteria 140; Polychlorinated Biphenyls and Terphenyls*, 2nd edn, WHO, Geneva.

WHO (World Health Organization) (2005) *Preventing Chronic Diseases: A Vital Investment*, WHO, Geneva. WHO Global Report, available at: www.who.int/chp/chronic_disease_report/en/index.html

Websites

www.consumersinternational.org.

www.globalissues.org.

www.ilo.org.

www.maquilasolidarity.org.

www.oneworld. org.

CHAPTER 2

American and European spa

Mary Tabbachi

Introduction

Spas or bathing have been part of every culture since aboriginal man with hot springs or thermal bathing being found worldwide with both modern and historical concepts. Most major religions require some form of cleansing before entering the house of worship, and baptismal rites require water. The culture of the spa as we know it today draws from traditions around the world, including Japan's 'onsen' (hot springs), with their fine food and Zen gardens, Finland's saunas, with their sweat room and ice plunges, and the Ottoman's hammams, with their steam rooms and private washing quarters.

While each spa has its own culture, values and beliefs, the essence of the spa – a place of restoration and health – has remained remarkably constant, even as the popularity of spas has ebbed and flowed throughout their long history. As oases of wellness, activities at spas have revolved around baths, massages, and other health treatments. Above all, spas have been places apart from the work-a-day world. This chapter briefly explains how the threads of spa history have been woven with current day trends to create the spa industry as we know it today.

European origins

The first natural springs became famed Roman baths, which foresaw European bathing culture. The typical European spa in the 1900s revolved about hydrotherapy and bathing, as spas had for centuries. European spas were originally of two types: (1) mineral springs spas (Thermals, Terme, Balneaire depending upon the language) including natural hot springs, which were thought to have healing properties and cold water springs used for drinking and (2) thalassotherapy spas based upon hydrotherapy using sea water, seaweed, seaweed cosmetics, and mineral bath sea salts.

European spas appealed to the rich and famous who escaped hot cities for the pastoral countryside. Spa 'cures', 'taking the waters', medical treatments, and relaxation for the leisure classes were combined with gambling, sporting events, orchestras, and chamber music. Spa physicians also dealt with injuries, asthma, rheumatism, gout, psoriasis, allergies and other conditions.

Birth of the destination retreat

Following Europe's spa tradition of enjoying mineral springs, when European colonists came to the Americas they sought out similar springs. Typical of these locations were White Sulphur Springs, Saratoga Springs, Arkansas Hot Springs, Calistoga, French Lick, and Desert Hot Springs. As visitors returned to 'take the waters' year after year, the proprietors of these locations began to offer activities beyond bathing and health treatments.

At White Sulphur Springs, West Virginia, residents of America's southern region, gathered each summer in what was originally a tent city (Conte, 1989). Eventually, the resort now known as the Greenbrier was developed by the railroad interests that took over the site and provided transportation for its guests. In addition to expanding the Greenbrier's health treatments with hydrotherapy, these owners added activities such as golf, horseback riding, and eventually haute cuisine.

The Greenbrier and the nearby Homestead are exemplars of the old-line, American-style destination resort. These are large, stately lodging facilities built around a hot spring, which include a spa with health treatments, but also feature a wide variety of activities – most notably their world-class golf courses. Ironically, as interest in the mineral-water aspects of spas faded in the middle of the 20th century, golf would prove to be the salvation of such old-line resorts. During the wars, the Greenbrier, for one, was converted to a hospital by the military.

The contemporary destination spa

With the development of antibiotics and modern mood-modulating drugs, the spa 'cure' was nearly abandoned in the USA. Spa resorts either decayed or relied on other pursuits to attract guests. However, the core idea of a spa as a place apart from regular existence, that is given over to personal health, was not forgotten. Even as the Second World War absorbed the energies of a generation, the spa was reborn in yet another incarnation – this time for a generation concerned about nutrition and weight control.

In 1940 Deborah and Edmond Szekely founded Rancho la Puerta just over the border in Tecate, Mexico. Rancho la Puerta is credited as being the first new-style destination spa – emphasizing fitness of body and mind, but without the hydrotherapy aspect of the old-line resort spas. Originally deemed a crypto-religious health cult' due to its emphasis on organic vegetarian food, daily meditation and exercise, and the mind–body connection (Rucker, 1949), the Ranch grew and prospered, becoming renown as a haven for the healthy. With the success of Rancho la Puerta, Deborah Szekely in 1959 established The Golden Door spa in California, again focusing on preventive principles of fitness, nutrition, meditation, and spa treatments (Mazzanti, 1977).

Together, the Golden Door and Rancho la Puerta pioneered the local organic, whole foods concept (Szekely and Stroot, 1982), as Golden Door Chef Michel Stroot developed the first US haute spa cuisine (Stroot, 1997). Different approaches to spa treatments were also explored in the 1970s in California's Ashram and at Canyon Ranch in Arizona, both of which focused on weight loss and fitness.

Boomers the engine of expansion

Once these new-style destination spas had opened, the elements were in place for the spa explosion that we have seen today. Old-line resorts with spas offered their hydrotherapy and wellness programs, newer destination spas aimed at fitness and nutrition, and day spas emerged offering services such as manicures and massages. The arrival of the baby boomers with a 'voracious appetite for products that will help them live longer, better (and better-looking)' (Crawford, 2008) provided the energy for spas to cross-pollinate, expand, and prosper.

Famously self-absorbed, the baby boomers had become well acquainted with concepts of health and nutrition in their youth. Running and aerobics, introduced by Kenneth Cooper in the 1960s (Cooper, 1968) and popularized by Jim Fixx in 1978, with The Complete Book of Running (Fixx, 1978), drew the attention of large numbers of baby boomers who had already begun their quest to remain young and vital. With so many individuals in this cohort (the usual figure is in the neighborhood of 76 million (DeFrancesco, 1999), spas would benefit even if only a small percentage of baby boomers became guests.

The baby boomers are no longer youthful at this writing, but the statistics make clear that a considerable group of baby boomers, far beyond a small percentage, and now their Generation-X children, are enjoying spas, as observed by the Hartman Groups' Consumer Trends Report for the International Spa and Fitness Association (ISPA) which found: 'an increased trend towards adult children introducing their parents to the benefits of spas. Gifts for anniversaries, birthdays, and Mother's and Father's Day appear to be the catalysts for children sending their parents on an expense-paid visit to a spa. Gen-Xers are removing the 'old taboos' of spa-going – such as it being a luxury or an unnecessary indulgence – and are teaching their parents the value of taking care of themselves from the inside out' (Locker, 2004).

Expanding the concept of the destination spa

Answering this demand, a series of spa developers expanded and refined the concept of the destination spa. For example, The Oaks at Ojai, California, opened by Sheila Cluff, featured long desert treks as part of its wellness program. This spa was also noted for innovating menus with 'spa comfort food'. At this spa and at its progeny, exhilaration replaced complacency and wellness became the responsibility of individuals. Fresh air, beautiful scenery, whole nutritious food, and physical, mental, and spiritual fitness became trademarks.

The Oaks and other pioneering destination spas created concepts where guests came home much healthier than when they left, and enjoyed vacations without weight gain, fatigue, and over-indulgence. Thus, the destination spa became synonymous with vibrant health, improved appearance, and a feeling of well-being.

By 1986, demand was strong enough to support a travel agency that specialized in spa vacations. This agency, now known as SpaFinder, has since become one of the world's largest spa information, marketing, and publishing companies (www.spafinder.com). By its own admission, the company has played a pivotal role in making 'spa' the fourth largest leisure industry in the USA, generating more revenue than ski resorts, amusement or theme parks, and even box-office receipts for feature films (Taschetta-Millane, 2006).

Day and hotel spas

Spas' fortunes rose and fell as each generation 'discovered' wellness (by whatever definition). More important, the form and features of spas changed in response to popular demand. Early in the 20th century, for instance, the needs of busy New Yorkers were satisfied by Elizabeth Arden's Red Door Salon, which is considered to be the first day spa. Rather than massages or baths, the Red Door offered manicures and facials. Despite its midtown location, it remained a place apart and by its own definition, a place of wellness.

The 1980s saw another development in the evolution of spas, with the rise of the hotel day spa. Casting about for competitive advantage in a newly crowded marketplace, hotel chains engaged in what could be characterized as a battle of amenities (see, for example, Dubé and Renaghan, 1999). Hoteliers first implemented health clubs as a popular amenity, but seeing the success of day spas, some chains opened spas of their own, thus offering their guests a much deeper experience than could be found in the high-energy health clubs.

Combined with the existing popularity and convenience of independent day spas, hotel and day spas together are the largest segment of the spa industry. Hotel operators suggest that their spas are an ideal place to commence a visit, as guests feel relaxed, energized, and motivated. In keeping with their new wellness focus, these hotel properties provide health-ful meal choices. To complement their spa services, resorts provide hiking trails, running maps, yoga, and meditation. Despite all this interest, few data are available to explain con-sumers' behavior with regard to wellness, and more research is necessary to develop this concept.

An initiative of Smith Travel Research (STR) now aims to provide an indicator of the importance of spas to the lodging industry by creating financial benchmarks for hotel spa opera-tions. Backed by the Mandarin Oriental Hotel group and the Fairmont-Raffles Company, STR is asking American spa com-panies to contribute to an industry database tallying rooms available, rooms sold, and rooms revenue. With those statistics, STR analyst Jan Freitag proposes to develop a series of finan-cial metrics for spa operators. He hopes to expand the data-base to international operators after the US pilot is completed (Spaopportunities, 2007).

From pampering to wellness

Despite spas' longstanding focus on health and well-being, the industry may still have to interpret exactly how spas relate to wellness trends. Some hotel spas and day spas focus on pampering and beauty treatments, for instance, even though beauty treatments per se are not considered to be an official part of the spa industry. Beauty treatment practitioners argue that pampering and beauty treatments are relaxing, enhance endorphin production, bring a glow to the skin, and inspire the wellness concept.

The spa concept goes far deeper than pampering. Proprietors of both day spas and destination spas suggest that wellness is a holistic process with many elements. To that end, some upscale hotel spas are developing a wellness and prevention concept more familiar at destination spas. Even within a busy hotel, the spa can be a place apart that promotes health and wellness.

Although some guests seek out the full range of spa services, particularly in destination spas, massages (including body wraps and facials) constitute the largest portion of the day and hotel spas' business – 73% in 2006 (Frietag, 2007a). In part, PKF Consulting's Bruce Baltin observed that spa customers may shy away from more exotic treatments, while they are well aware of the indulgence and relaxation in a massage. In addition to facials and massages, spas outside the USA see strong demands for saunas and steam baths (Clausing, 2008).

A 2004 study commissioned by ISPA found that in addition to massage, American spa goers were interested in yoga or pilates-type routines. Also gaining interest has been Thai massage, in part because the loose-fitting clothing typical of Thai massage eases guests' concerns about clothing (or the absence thereof) in traditional massage. Although hydrotherapy has not always been popular in the USA, ISPA found that guests who are new to spas are often more receptive to hydrotherapy than to more typical treatments such as massages (Locker, 2004).

Integrative medicine

Without doubt, wellness will be defined in part by the aging boomers and Gen-Xers who are cognizant of health issues. Many seek illness prevention and fitness of body, mind, and spirit typically found at spas. Spas will respond to guests' concerns regarding obesity, cardiovascular disease, diabetes, cancer, and stroke. The spa community has emphasized prevention by working with the National Institutes of Health and with the surgeon general. Moreover, as mentioned above, complementary and alternative medicine (CAM) coincides with spa concepts, with its noninvasive, preventive approaches to health care.

Spas are not the only health-related organizations that have recognized the value of wellness. The famed Mayo Clinic's website states 'Mayo Clinic's Complementary and Integrative Medicine program was created to address growing patient interest in wellness-promoting activities' (Mayo Clinic, 2007). WebMD newsletter is of interest in this regard, proclaiming 'Live the happiest healthiest lifestyle possible!' and offering links to sites for healthy cooking, beautiful skin, sleeping well, and weight loss (WebMD, 2007). The website explores integrative medicine and complementary therapies, biofeedback, meditation, acupuncture and hypnosis, the mind–body connection, heart disease, chronic stress, and the mind–skin–health connection are discussed. Using integrative medicine as a model, it is difficult to separate medicine from spa concepts.

In addition to their alternative wellness concepts, certain spas offer medical services. Canyon Ranch Lenox has six board-certified MDs, for instance, and Canyon Ranch Tucson has seven physicians. In addition, these spas offer acupuncturists, behavioral therapists, chiropractors, dermatologists, exercise physiologists, healing touch practitioners, movement and aquatic therapists, and podiatrists. This is in addition to more typical spa features such as huge fitness centers, outdoor sports activities, health lectures, healthful food, and the spa itself.

Michelle Higgins, writing for the *New York Times* (Higgins, 2005), reviewed 'well-being' complexes at Canyon Ranch, The Hyatt Regency in Cambridge, Maryland, The Cooper Clinic, Texas, and The Westlake Village, California. All have upscale hotel rooms, spas, and medical centers. In this era of managed care, when doctors' appointments have been reduced to impersonal blurs, spas offer patients alternative sources of information and health services.

With the wider acceptance of non-traditional treatments, the spa community has come full circle from 1949, when a journalist suggested that the Szekelys' Rancho La Puerta was a cult because it featured outdoor exercise, meditative walks, and organic food.

Spa organizations: education and credentials

With the growth of the spa industry came a realization that the industry would benefit from a trade association, both to improve spa knowledge and to establish credentials for spa practitioners. This need was answered in 1991 with the constitution of the ISPA. ISPA has now grown to be a repository of statistics and information about the spa industry, and as part of the professionalization and credentialing of the field it has put forth a code of ethics and established standards of practice including categories for safety, guest relations, and service (ISPA, 2008).

ISPA has been a driving force in the evolution of the US spa industry particularly through creating a forum for presenting ideas and seeking expertise from outside the industry at its annual national conferences. At the first meeting in 1991, 150 people from 10 countries attended. By 2000, attendance at the annual ISPA conference exceeded 2600.

At the 1993 ISPA meeting at PGA National Resort and Spa in Palm Beach, Deepak Chopra urged spa operators to examine alternative medicine. Impressed and influenced by this speech, delegates began the quest for what is now known as Complementary and Alternative Medicine or CAM. Following this, Deborah and Alex Szekely commissioned Cornell University to complete a review of complementary medical concepts to be used in spas (Tabacchi, 1996, 1997). The 1997 report on complementary medicine, which suggested that Ayurveda, traditional Chinese medicine, and energy medicine practices were legitimate and should be used by spas, seemed controversial at the time, but many of the concepts in that report are now accepted practice in spas and many hospitals.

In August 1994 at Palm Desert, California, Mary Tabacchi gave the first ISPA/Cornell research report, 'The Non-Spa Goer', which explored possibilities of increasing the spa market (Orbeta-Heytens and Tabacchi, 1995). Dr. Pamela Peeke began the first of a series of National Institutes of Health speakers, which subsequently included a presentation by C. Everett Koop, formerly surgeon general of the USA. In July 1995, President Alex Szekely and Dr. Pam Peeke presented 'The Role of Spas in Preventive Medicine' at the first ISPA media luncheon in New York City. By this time, the mainline media took note of ISPA as a growing organization that produced research and formed vital committees to professionalize spa operations.

While ISPA's activities gave impetus to spas offering preventive therapies – which has been a role for spas since ancient times, ISPA was initially focused on destination spas and resorts and did not include day spas. That changed in 1998, when the International Spa and Fitness Association became the International Spa Association in recognition of the tremendous growth of day spas. By 2002 day spas constituted three-quarters of the US spas (PriceWaterHouseCoopers, 2002).

As the industry grew and changed, the destination spas were concerned that destination spa interests would not be fully represented. Consequently, the ISPA Board of Directors searched for ways to balance needs of all members and in 1997 the Destination Spa Group was formed as an organization independent of ISPA, which itself still has destination spas as members.

Destination spas differentiate themselves from resort and hotel spas with a holistic wellness approach, emphasizing programs that strengthen fitness of body, mind, and spirit. Destination spas constitute a complete wellness experience and their mission is to encourage healthier lifestyles by educating the public about their wellness and self-improvement opportunities (Destination Spa Group, 2007).

Spa industry statistics

The following graphs depict the growth of spa industry in the USA (Figure 2.1) (Association Resource Centre, 2004, p. 14).

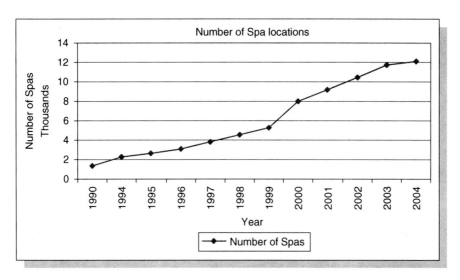

Figure 2.1
Historical USA spa growth 1990–2004

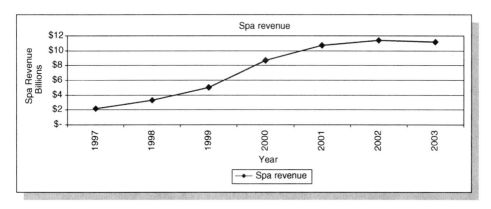

Figure 2.2
Spa revenue by year

Spa revenue growth, according to ISPA's 2004 Industry Study, is significant and is influenced by the sheer quantity of day spas (Figure 2.2) (Association Resource Centre, 2004, p. 19).

The revival of European spas and birth of the European International Spa Association

Even as spas boomed in the America, European spas underwent great change in the 1990s as government support dwindled due to financial strains. Until this point, European citizens could obtain financial assistance to visit spas. Hotel rooms, food, travel, spa activities, and spa medical treatments were reimbursed depending upon income, and European spas thrived. As governments cut back, the Continent's spas had to be reinvented.

Since reduction of governmental support, Europe's spas ventured into new markets. Just as America's spas originally mirrored the European model of situating a grand hotel near mineral baths, European spas borrowed some of the American destination spas' focus on nutrition, wellness, and meditation. In addition to mineral baths, Europe's spas have expanded to such locations as ski resorts, cities, and the seaside. Aided by cultural belief in Europe that spas are a necessary component of health, European spas attracted wealthy individuals who spent more money throughout the hotels, resorts, and immediate localities than non-spa goers.

In 1996, led by Bernie Burt and Martha Ashelman, many ISPA members traveled to Tuscany to meet with European colleagues. This was followed by a meeting in Baden-Baden in 1997. The Baden-Baden experience was novel to Americans and the American spa experience of sustained fitness was novel to Europeans. Later in 1997, those meetings led to ISPA Europe being formed at Rogner Bad-Blumau in Austria. The American newspaper, *USA Today*, covered the conference thoroughly – again indicating the extent to which the spa concept had become accepted in the American culture. Those in attendance learned that spas on both continents shared similar values. Concerns were economic growth, standards, safety, labor, training, and an emerging industry. What did new spa consumers expect? How could expectations be met?

European spas are now represented by the European Spa Association (ESPA) trade association. ESPA argues that spas, health resorts, and spa facilities in Europe represent an indispensable part of the health system of each country. Moreover, ESPA points to the spas' influence on the cultural background of the region, and their an importance as economic and social factors – not to mention their status as a source of employment (ESPA, 2007).

Increased capital investment

Perhaps the 'newest tradition' for spas is real-estate communities. Just as tent villages grew up around the American hot springs in colonial times, so certain destination spas are developing residential communities for owners of second homes or retirees that include privileges at the spa and its resort.

Upscale residential properties report strong interest among consumers for spa and spa activities (Cohen and Canyon, 2007). For example, Canyon Ranch has developed residences in Miami ranging in price from US$1 million to $5 million. Utah's Red Mountain Spa has developed adobe villas with prices beginning at just over US$500000, and Miraval plans an expansion of its concept into homes in Arizona, with prices starting at $1.7 million (Foster, 2007). While there is angst in many US housing markets, Mel Zuckerman, founder and co-owner of Canyon Ranch believes upscale consumers are recession proof (Zuckerman and Canyon, 2007). Real-estate experts report enhanced valuation of properties with spas (Chandnani, 2007).

The year 2006 saw investors and developers pour cash into hotels, resorts, and spas. Starwood Capital, led by Barry Sternlich, is developing a new series of über luxury hotels and spas, along with a spa company separate from Starwood's existing lodging brands. Blackstone, CNL, and Morgan Stanley among others are investing in spa properties. Many major Asian companies, such as Banyan Tree, Shangri La, Mandarin Oriental, Six Senses, Oberoi, Taj, seek Western Hemisphere locations. Meanwhile Fairmont, Hyatt, Starwood, and Four Seasons are finding new properties in China.

STR (Frietag, 2007a,b), PKF (Mandelbaum and Lerner, 2007), and HVS (Sahlins and Peterson, 2007) all suggest continued growth and growth opportunities for hotel and resort spas. Through studying luxury hotel–resort properties STR demonstrated increased RevPAR due to spas without sacrificing occupancy while PKF found increased spa revenues of 10 percent, comparing 2005 and 2006 data. Spa consultants are also reporting increased activity (Singer & Monteson, 2007).

Conclusion

With their current popularity, expectations are high for spas' popularity to continue growing. In that regard, spas are also expected to continue the trend of drawing together elements from various cultures to create an overall sensation of well-being and health for guests. The European hydrotherapy tradition is likely to continue to expand in the USA, as guests appreciate the benefits of water therapy. SpaFinder suggests that the global staffing shortage will also cause spas to encourage guests to work with hydrotherapy, which is often user driven and not labor intensive (SpaFinder, 2007).

The tide seems to be running strong for spas, given cultural mores, promoting the ideas of wellness, nutrition, and stress reduction – all of which are spas' strong points. As with all hospitality-industry concepts, spas face a danger of overbuilding at some point, but at this writing that eventuality remains in the future. In the meantime, the role of spas as places apart seems well accepted as a valuable and essential service.

References

Association Resource Centre (2004) *The International SPA Association 2004 Spa Industry Study*, Research and Strategy Division, International Spa Association, Lexington, KY, pp. 14, 19

Chandnani, R. (2007) *Profitability of Spas, Global Spa Summit*, The Waldorf-Astoria, New York.

Clausing, J. (2008) *Hotel Spa Profits Grow. Travel Weekly*, available at: www.spafinder.com/NewsReleases/January14/PKF.pdf

Cohen, J., Ranch, C. (2007) *Dean's Lecture Series*, School of Hotel Administration, Cornell University, Ithaca, NY.

Conte, R.S. (1989) *The History of the Greenbrier: America's Resort*, Greenbrier, White Sulphur Springs, WV.

Cooper, K.H. (1968) *Aerobics*, Bantam Books, New York.

Crawford, E. (2008) *Baby Boomers Help Drive Emerging Life Sciences Trends*, AVM Interview with Ilya Nykin, managing director, Prolog Ventures, available at: http://www.american-venturemagazine.com

DeFrancesco, A. (1999) *Baby Boomers: Drivers of Change*, Department of Economic and Community Development, CT.

Destination Spa Group (2007) Available at: www.destination-spagroup.com/ (site accessed 16 December 2007)

Dubé, L., Renaghan, L. (1999) Sustaining competitive advantage: lodging industry best practices, *Cornell Hotel and Restaurant Administration Quarterly* 40(6): 29.

ESPA (2007) *Official Internet Portal of the European Spas Association*, available at: http://www.european-spas-health-resorts.com/european-spas-association/ (site accessed 16 December 2007).

Fixx, J. (1978) The Complete Book of Running (Lehmann-Haupt), Random House.

Foster, A. (2007) Director of Strategy, Miraval, Class Project, Cornell University, School of Hotel Administration, Ithaca, NY.

Frietag, J. (2007a) *Profitability of Spas, Smith Travel Research, 3rd Annual Cornell Hotel School Spa Symposium,* The Hotel Del Coronado, Coronado, CA.

Frietag, J. (2007b) *Profitability of Spas, Smith Travel Research, Global Spa Summit,* The Waldorf-Astoria, New York.

Higgins, M. (2005) *The Spa Experience: Mud Bath, Massage, M.R.I, The New York Times* Travel Section, December 30, 2005, New York

ISPA (2008) *Code of Ethics,* available at: www.experienceispa. com/ISPA/.

Locker, D. (2004) *ISPA Consumer Trends Report,* available at: . www.experienceispa.com/ISPA/

Mandelbaum, R., Lerner, G. (2007) *Hotel Operators Massage More Profits from Their Spa Operations: Trends in the Hotel Spa Industry,* PKF Consulting, Atlanta, GA.

Mayo Clinic (2007) *Complementary and Integrative Medicine,* available at: http://www.mayoclinic.org/general-internal-medicine-rst/cimc.html (site accessed 17 December 2007).

Mazzanti, D.S. (1977) *Secrets of the Golden Door,* William Morrow and Company, New York.

Orbeta-Heytens, A., Tabacchi, M. (1995) *A Market Survey of Non Spa-Goers,* International Spa and Fitness Association, Lexington, KY.

PriceWaterHouseCoopers (2002) *The International SPA Association's Spa Industry Study,* International Spa Association, Lexington, KY.

Rucker, E. (1949) *Romanian Professor Founds Cult Across Border at Tecate,* The San Diego Union, San Diego.

Sahlins, E., Peterson, A. (2007) *The Financial Impact of Hotel Spas,* HVS International, San Francisco, CA.

Singer, J.L., Monteson, P.A. (2007) *Spas: Challenges and Opportunities: Trends in the Hotel Spa Industry,* PKF Consulting, Atlanta, GA.

SpaFinder (2007) *5th Annual Spa Trends Report, 10 Spa Trends to Watch in 2008,* available at: www.spafinder.com/about/press_release.jsp?relId = 114

Spaopportunities (2007) *Spa Benchmarking Initiative Revealed*, available at: www.spaopportunities.com/newsdetail.cfm? codeID=47233

Stroot, M. (1997) *The Golden Door Cookbook*, Broadway Books, New York.

Szekely, D., Stroot, M. (1982) *Golden Door Cookbook: The Greening of American Cuisine*, Golden Door, Escondido, CA.

Tabacchi, M.H. (1996) *The Efficacies and Cost-Effectiveness of Complementary Medical Concepts Most Commonly Used in Spa Settings.*, International Spa and Fitness Association, Lexington, KY. Part 1

Tabacchi, M.H. (1997) *The Efficacies and Cost-Effectiveness of Complementary Medical Concepts Most Commonly Used in Spa Settings.*, International Spa and Fitness Association, Lexington, KY. Part 2

Taschetta-Millane, M. (2006) *Trends in the Spa World. Skin Magazine*, available at: www.results.pointcom.com

WebMD (2007) *Integrative Medicine Resource Center*, available at: http://www.webmd.com/content/pages/25/113599.htm (site accessed 17 December 2007).

Zuckerman, M., Ranch, R. (2007) *Dean's Lecture Seriesy*, School of Hotel Administration, Cornell University, Ithaca, NY.

The spa industry in Asia

Michael Loh

Introduction

Asian spas draw upon the rich traditions of healing cultures of the East. These are in some ways intertwined with the philosophies and teachings of the major religious traditions of Hinduism, Buddhism, Confucianism and others that form the core of the Asian persona. Though the countries in Asia appear to be neatly compartmentalised in their respective nation-states and have varying ethnicities, they are somehow bound by a history of shared traditions that overlap across many levels.

Indian–Chinese influence

Long before Europeans were persecuting people for declaring the earth was round, Asian adventurers had been travelling across the great Asian landmass – from one end of China across to India and then onward across the burning sands into Arabia. Some even made their way southwards down the west coast of Africa. Others used the seas, making their way through Southeast Asia, which was like a corridor between India and China, the two great civilisations of the time. As a result both Indian and Chinese culture and norms became part of the Southeast Asian psyche and in the areas of philosophy, religion and other cultural practices, the imprints of these two civilisations are unmistakable. Indonesia, Malaysia, Thailand, Cambodia, Myanmar, Laos and to a certain extent the Philippines and Vietnam share common grounds in a variety of social components, albeit modified and adapted.

Eastern healing traditions that may have had their theoretical roots in Indian and Chinese traditions have built on local health traditions and have adapted into their own systems. They have now become distinct modalities identifiable with the various cultures and sub-cultures. The Japanese, Indo-Chinese, people of the Archipelago and those of the Middle Eastern regions have developed their own healing traditions though they have been rooted in Indian and Chinese traditions of healing. Unani, or Graeco Arabic medicine, originating with Hippocrates in Greece and coming to India with the Moghuls, is widespread throughout India, Pakistan and Bangladesh, and has become an established Middle Eastern tradition. Shiatsu and Su Jok have both sprung from the Chinese tradition of meridian points and acupressure (see Chapter 24). Modalities found in traditional Thai medicine are good representations of the confluence of traditions. Ayurveda predominates, but influences of traditional Chinese medicine, as well as traditions and practices of the hill tribes of the neighbouring regions, are significant.

However, despite their subtle differences or stark departures from one another, these healing traditions of the East share one common thread. They place great emphasis on a principle of balance of mind, body, spirit and environment as the basis for health. From this vantage point, they employ holistic routes to delivering personal care and wellness. This reverence for the individual's body is a common denominator in several Eastern cultures; the body is seen as a temple in which dwells the Divine. It is this understanding that underpins many cultural and spiritual rituals as well as Eastern holistic healing practices, and forms the basis for the Asian spa experience. Asian spas are also able to exploit the lush environments typical of Southeast Asia with its unique and ancient rainforest biodiversity, tropical weather, abundance of water, fragrant and vividly coloured blossoms, exotic foods and herbal ingredients.

Riding on traditions

The rapid growth and evolution seen in Asian spas is partly because they have been able to adopt and adapt a rich diversity of modalities that draw from the regions equally rich array of healing traditions. Long before the science and mysteries of the mind became a subject of study in the West, sages of the East recognised the connection between breathing, stillness, silence and optimum functioning of the mind and body. The ancient Taoist practice of banishing distracting thoughts and seeking the stillness within is a common prescription of traditional Chinese medicine, along with a good night's rest.

In adopting traditional Eastern healing practices, Asian spas have been able to capitalise on the disenchantment with conventional Western medicine and ride the wave of consciousness towards holistic, sustainable and preventive health. Throughout the world, ancient Eastern practices that have been tried and tested throughout generations have now become celebrated as pathways to wellness and holistic healing. Long-lost traditions and practices have been given a new lease of life. Yoga has been brought out of the confines of ashrams and temples into studios and hotels. Acupuncture, once considered an exotic and mysterious healing art, is gaining credibility as a legitimate and effective form of healthcare.

Entrepreneurs have been quick to add value by turning to the esoteric worldview of Eastern healing traditions and marketing the time-tested lure of exoticism. The Asian traditions of care and service have also been conveyed in response to consumer demands. Shrewd marketing has seen spas becoming a major product and a vehicle for the Asian tourism industry.

The advent of Asian spas

The spa made its debut in Asia in the mid-1990s and from humble and tentative beginnings, the Asian spa industry has since grown into a runaway phenomenon. This is due to a number of factors that have created fertile soil for the industry's growth, including the ability to tap into Asia's rich cultural heritage and healing traditions, the lure of unspoilt environments, the increasing ease of travel, favourable exchange rates and the merging of the travel and health dollar.

Industry surveys in Asia showed that potential holidaymakers now take into account the presence of spa facilities in hotels and resorts when choosing holiday destinations. The novelty factor, coupled with that of favourable exchange rates during its formative years, was a major catalyst for the industry. Buoyed by lower labour costs and rental rates than their European or American counterparts, yet charging close to international rates for their services, high-end Asian spas also became very profitable. Indeed, spas provided an economic lifeline to an important sector of the region's economy.

Associate Professor Rujirutana Madhachitara, PhD. of Penn State University in her paper *Opening Up a Services Market – The Thai Spa Industry*, observed 'From what we learn in the classroom and witness in real business life, markets usually do not grow as explosively as health spas have done in Thailand' (Madhachitara, 2007).

Entrepreneurs have been quick to see the potential of the Asian spa movement, and to a large extent the rise of spas has changed the face of the hospitality industry in the region. Thailand leapt from having no spa in 1995 to being the spa capital of the Asia Pacific region in just 10 years. As recently as 2004 to 2005, the growth rate was still at a healthy 26% and new areas with rich heritage and a market largely untapped are waiting to be discovered. Malaysia is one of them. Vietnam and the other countries of the region, such as Laos and Cambodia that have been culturally dormant due to man-made derailments, are also back on track to claim their stake.

In the case of Thailand, one of the worst hit by the 1998 Asian Financial Crisis, the spa industry came as a blessing. In a rather paradoxical manner, one could also say that the Asian Financial Crisis was a blessing for the spa industry which was just finding its footing. Tourists came in droves to take advantage of the bargain prices offered for dental and medical services in Thailand. Spa treatments and therapies that were seen as novelties offered at low prices were included on the 'must-do' list of the average tourist's itinerary.

By 2005, the Tourism Authority of Thailand estimated that Thai health spas were contributing a total of US$170 million into the economy (Madhachitara, 2007). By the start of the 21st century the industry has seen multi-fold growth and has continued to transform at such a fast pace that the terrain seems to change every few years.

The changing profile of spa-goers

Unlike their equivalents in Europe, home to some of the oldest spas which are more akin to health clubs patronised mainly by men, spas in Asia are relatively new having evolved from beauty salons and health centres catering to women. While frequenting spas was once the domain of women of high society (or those who wished to be so perceived), this is changing. The range of services offered has also changed from those that address vanity and pampering to holistic treatments that promise long-term benefits.

Acceptance of spas as centres for healing and nourishing the body, mind and soul has been growing steadily. In Asia, people go to spas for fitness and beauty, to manage stress, seek peace of mind, receive pleasure, achieve wellness and health, and for myriad other reasons. As a result, more first-timer and occasional spa-goers are visiting spas as a form of welcome respite. While women may have led the development of Asian spas, it is reported that the number of men taking spa treatments for the first time is increasing at an annual increase of between 25% and 30% (Durocher, 2007). However, looking back through the pages of history, it should not be a surprise to note that men want indulgence and to look and feel good. Ancient Babylonian and Chinese men indulged in manicures and pedicures as far back as three millennia.

So-called, 'metrosexuals', spa-going men who make regular visits for long-term benefits, form the most promising consumer market segment. Collectively they have helped to shape the landscape of what is fashionable and, by extension, determine the kinds of services offered. A greater number of men have no qualms about having their fingernails buffed and their toenails primed. The wave of consciousness about health and good values continually revitalises the industry, and from this springs a new culture and lifestyle among the new generation. Wellness has become the buzzword.

Benchmarking the Asian spa industry

The rapid growth characterised above has also left in its wake a host of needling questions:

- Is the industry moving too fast?
- How faithful are the adopted and adapted healing modalities to their original forms?
- Are entrepreneurs too dominant in dictating the direction of an industry that has within itself the seeds for a more equitable distribution of wealth?
- Is altruism dead?

Asian spas are fortunate in that the techniques, and underlying expectations and standards have already been set by the various cultures and traditions from which their healing modalities originate. However, the tendency to deliver traditional healing techniques in luxury settings may be interpreted as an attempt to blanket efficacy with luxury, especially if the modalities delivered are less than effective. Narrow interests motivated by the desires of a few can easily derail the original purpose and the onus rests with the spa operators to integrate ethics and luxury and authentically honour the diverse traditions of Asia.

Reflecting its tender age, the spa industry does not have a rating system, by which to measure and rank spas, unlike hotels which have the star-rating system in place. In a sense, spas are straddling a stream defined by two industries: they are neither hotels nor medical institutions. However, consumers globally need a reliable yardstick by which to gauge spa services, to ensure consistency and value for money. Similarly, the industry needs a measure to ensure that quality is delivered at all times, that professionalism is maintained at all levels and that the high ideals of the industry remain intact.

Even so, because of differing parameters and criteria from one hotel or resort to another, as well as wide-ranging customer preferences and expectations, a rating system can at best be a general measure. In this light, a consumer-based yardstick for deciding what is being passed off as excellent, good or mediocre maybe best. As the bar on standards keeps rising, those that fail to meet the consumers' expectations will be seen to lag behind the rest of the industry. Here, the media has a responsible role to play.

Setting industry benchmarks through the SpaAsia Crystal Awards

SpaAsia (www.spaasia.com), a leading spa and wellness magazine in the Asia Pacific region, has been at the forefront of educating readers and consumers of spa services for the last 5 years. With a footprint covering Japan, Southeast Asia and the Middle East, the magazine has the responsibility of educating its large readership base in terms of shaping their expectations. Since 2005, *SpaAsia* has instituted the SpaAsia Crystal Awards (SACA) which have serve as an informal awards system that has now become a part of the industry's 'software'.

The SACA were instituted with the expressed aim of educating consumers as to the level that they can expect from the industry in terms of services and quality. The Awards, which also serve to educate spa operators as to the growing discernment of consumers, may be seen as a precursor to an industry ranking system.

One of the main objectives of SACA is to honour the best, irrespective of size. The built-in advantage that bigger brands have is obvious: the playing field is uneven. However, this is not necessarily true for all categories. The maxim 'quality and not quantity counts' should be allowed to take root and this is clearly demonstrated in the preamble for some award categories. In the Best Spa Consultant/Company category, whether or not the set-up is a one-person operation or a large corporation has no bearing on their eligibility to participate. Neither does it govern the outcome. What is more important is whether the minimum criteria have been met.

Ensuring the integrity of the awards

SpaAsia worked with a panel of industry experts and consultants to develop the criteria for each award category. The development of these criteria is an important part of the awards process, as it helps to ensure that spas are entering an award category that accurately reflects their offerings and defines their business goals and achievements. The award categories encompass an array of spa experiences: from resort/hotel, destination, day spas and academies, along with targeted recognition for best practice in human resources and training and industry contribution. In 2007, product supplier categories were added to honour excellence in treatment development and delivery.

Applicants select their chosen award category through an online application process and are asked to clearly demonstrate how they meet the specified criteria. In some instances, they are asked to supply supporting documents such as photographs and service menus to illustrate their unique position. A pre-selected panel of judges shortlists the first round and then each finalist is audited. In 2007, SACA contracted an independent company, SpaAudit.com, to secret shop the top 10 finalists in each award category. SpaAudit.com took each category's award criteria and aligned this with a set of required competencies on which each finalist was evaluated. The competencies were developed to evaluate the following key areas of the spa facility: ambience, cleanliness, safety, comfort, communication, customer service and technical ability.

The judges are selected for their diversity in background – an inbuilt mechanism to create discussion and debate. Each individual in the awards secret shopping team – which is made up of individuals with experience in the hospitality, spa and wellness industries – must also have closely aligned attitudes and opinions on what is good and what is not to ensure the scoring is as consistent as possible. These opinions and attitudes are refined via a group discussion before the secret shopping process begins, in which opinions and perceptions are discussed and debated so that the team set out with a like-minded approach.

The secret shopper begins their evaluation from the time the reservation is made through to the arrival and pre-treatment stages, as well as the treatment experience, and finally the time to depart. The secret shopping process for the awards is quite intense, and shoppers are required to do a number of audits, sometimes within different categories. It is therefore important to ensure that each audit experience remains fresh in the mind so that differentiating details can be recalled. This is achieved by the explanations of 6 or lower and 'perfect' 10 scores and the additional requirement for each secret shopper to keep a detailed log of key points for each experience.

Benchmarking via 14 award categories

SpaAsia has generated 14 award categories that it considers provides a quality-driven approach to honouring the best. Key features of the awards are that they:

- honour excellence regardless of the size of the spa operation;
- perpetuate ongoing improvement in standards within the industry;
- set benchmarking standards that guide the consumer in making an informed choice amongst the best Asian spas;

- define indicators of excellence to drive the industry forward in its expansion and development and guide future investors in the industry.

To qualify for some categories, a particular establishment must embrace *SpaAsia's* definition of a 'spa'; which is a place where:

- a person goes to improve their wellness in body, mind and spirit;
- the spa operator and all their staff make a connection with the guest in body, mind and spirit;
- the spa experience is delivered to guests through the vehicles of their five senses;
- the guest's expectations of wellness are met;
- the business is driven with integrity and a commitment to quality.

The 14 *SpaAsia* award categories are summarised below. A full description with award criteria can be accessed at: www. spaasia.biz/events/saca/default.asp.

Best Spa Education Programme. This is awarded to a spa, spa academy or educational institution that sets leading standards in the industry for spa training through structured, measurable and committed training programmes and their implementation.

Best Spa Academy. The Spa Academy Award is presented to a spa academy that is committed to making an enduring and sustainable contribution to the betterment of the individual learner, company, community and country. It will have a comprehensive curriculum which aims to develop values, skills, knowledge and attitudes of the individual learner while reflecting actual and evolving needs of the spa and wellness industry (by keeping 'its ear to the ground' and initiating a training needs analysis, as appropriate). It will have the relevant accreditations with complete local and national operating license/permits and should also be accredited by at least one credible international therapy examination body (CIBTAC, ITEC, CIDESCO).

Best Human Resource Programme. This award is presented to the spa operation that sets the standards for Human Resource (HR) practice within the industry through structured, measurable, committed and ethical HR policies and their implementation. It will also have a forward-thinking approach in its HR practice that ensures the long-term development and retention of its staff.

Best Spa Consultant/Company. This award is for a one-person firm or a large operator that implements innovative, trend-setting spa concepts that assist in driving standards up and the industry forward and is recognised by the industry as being a leader in the field.

Best Wellness and Spa Group is awarded to the company that is the most innovative, benchmarking operator in the business and that has a forward-thinking approach to business development coupled with quality and integrity that not only grows and sustains their business, but drives standards up and the industry forwards. It will be accepted as an industry leader.

Best Hotel Spa is awarded to the Hotel Spa that has treatments on its menu that delivers wellness of body, mind and spirit and has a brand identity and spa concept that is clearly evident in architecture, fixtures, fittings, equipment, treatments and products. As well as having distinct signature treatments, it offers, within the hotel, a health-conscious menu that embraces elements of the host country's local food.

Best Resort Spa. This award recognises the Resort Spa that provides a relaxed and informal haven of rest and rejuvenation amidst the beauty and tranquillity of nature, and incorporates elements of nature within the spa.

Best Day Spa is awarded to the Day Spa that offers rest and rejuvenation for mind, body and spirit amidst the hustle and bustle of everyday life.

Best Destination Spa. This is an award that honours sustained excellence and a spa that is chosen by guests because the spa experience is more important than the hotel/resort experience in choosing the destination.

Best Wellness Retreat is awarded to the Wellness Retreat that has a menu of holistic treatments that delivers wellness of body, mind and spirit, and that allows the therapist to cater to individual needs.

Best Signature Experience. An award for the highest standard of signature experience or treatment which is published and available to guests at time of publications.

Best Complementary and Alternative Medicine Wellness Centre. An award that incorporates those companies who provide complementary and alternative medicine (CAM) treatment, Ayurvedic treatment or traditional Chinese medicine (TCM), where the entire focus within the operation is on therapeutically improving health and wellness.

Best Product: Signature Body Treatment. This award honours the best product house signature body treatment which has proven sustained excellence in more than three spa locations in the Asia Pacific Region and which use only products branded by this single-product line. It is awarded for the signature body treatment which is published and available to guests at time of publications.

Best Product: Signature Facial Experience. This award honours the best product house signature facial treatment which has proven sustained excellence in more than three spa locations in the Asia Pacific Region and use only products branded by the single product line. It is awarded for the signature facial treatment which is published and available to guests at time of publications.

Publisher's Choice. This award goes to the business identified by the publisher as having contributed the most in the preceding year to driving the industry forwards and setting standards of excellence for existing and future operators to aspire to. They are awarded directly by the publisher.

Asian spas in the future

Throughout history almost all phenomena fizzle out after shining brilliantly for some brief moments. In this light, will the spa industry suffer the same fate? Some believe that spas have seen their best days. If this is true, what is next for the industry?

Compared to that of Asia, the growth of the spa industry in Europe and the USA is noticeably slower. Spas in the West focus on delivering wellness through three distinct methodologies – aesthetics, medical approaches and holistic modalities. These are often delivered in hi-tech surroundings with commensurate equipment and techniques. It may be said that such focus on technology, as contrasted with spas in the East that are high-touch and low-tech, may be attributed to the strong culture of research and development in the West. In addition to higher labour costs in the West, another reason could be the lack of creativity in harnessing the traditional modalities of Western cultures.

To some significant extent, the USA and Europe look to Asia for benchmarking, as Asia enjoys a very varied selection of modalities and cultural traditions of healing. A current phenomenon that is causing some concerns among the spa fraternity in the East is the migration of trained and highly skilled Asian therapists to the West and the Middle East. With the growing popularity of Eastern healing traditions within Western and Middle Eastern spas, skilled therapists are being lured away from the East with the promise of greater financial incentives. This migration has left a vacuum, causing a dearth of skilled therapists in spas in the East.

The merging of Eastern and Western traditions raises a number of pertinent questions:

- Can the low-tech high-touch delivery of the Eastern therapist, at home in the lush natural environments of Southeast Asia, be comfortably supplanted into the Western setting that is more familiar with a high-tech clinical environment?
- What if the white-coat phenomenon takes over and modifies thousand-year-old traditions and passes them off as new, or worse, calls them their own.
- Will the Asian cultural imprint be diluted or even wiped out once the forces of commercialization take over, or will spas be able to serve as cultural conservators and adopt 'endangered' healing practices thus saving cultural features of the region from being washed away forever by modernity?

An ongoing court case in the USA illustrates how corporate manoeuvring could leave 'uncopyrighted' traditions such as yoga exposed to the vagaries of the commercial world (see Chapter 25). Such tactics have a way of limiting availability of the world's heritage to all. However, the converse may also be the case where the rich and highly personalised traditions of the East, through globalisation, may offer new healing and personal evolutionary journeys to the wider world.

References

Durocher, B. (2007) Global Medispa Trends, *SpaAsia*, 5(6):142–145.

Madhachitara, R. (2007) Opening Up a Services Market – The Thai Spa Industry, *The Management Case Study Journal*, 7(1):13–32.

CHAPTER 4

Spa industry benchmarking

Julie Garrow

Introduction

The word benchmarking was originally a term used by land surveyors and referred to a mark made on a rock or wall as a reference to determine the position or altitude in topographical surveys or tidal observations. Today a benchmark is a sighting point to enable a measurement or a standard which something may be measured against (Patterson, 1996, p. 4).

Benchmarks are key inputs for reliable business planning. They enable businesses to monitor performance and industry trends with the aim of improving competitiveness and profitability. The activity of benchmarking incorporates measuring the performance of a business using predefined measurements and may be performed in two main ways:

1. Internal benchmarking tracks and monitors the performance of a business to identify growth or decline in specific areas over time.
2. External benchmarking compares the internal benchmarks of a business against industry benchmarks, where industry benchmarks are the collation of the internal benchmarks of multiple businesses within a marketplace. Industry benchmarks are commonly the average performance of those in the marketplace.

Once benchmarks are available, other key performance ratios may be calculated for detailed business analysis including analysis of the business's strengths, weaknesses, opportunities and threats (SWOT). The outcome of such analysis empowers business owners and managers to make information business decisions and initiate changes to reduce risk and maximise return.

The purpose of benchmarking

There are many business benefits to benchmarking. Benchmarks provide a clear understanding of market conditions and enable assessment of how the business is performing within a marketplace. The activity of benchmarking enables a business to make tactical and strategic business decisions based on facts rather than guesswork. By using industry intelligence, a business is less likely to make potentially damaging decisions and instead, control its performance and direction.

Benchmarking is also a pre-requisite to justifying expansion and attaining external funding to develop a business. While benchmarking can be used to identify new opportunities in a market, just as importantly, it may highlight market opportunities in decline, allowing a business to minimise over-investment of time, funds and other critical resources.

Benchmarking has been conducted in the hospitality industry for years, with hotels and resorts participating in benchmarking programs in order to track key performance indicators, namely average occupancy, average revenue per available room and average daily rate. These surveys are conducted by many hotel accounting and consulting firms and over time are used to track the performance of the industry, typically by country and city. For example, the HotelBenchmark™ Survey by STR Global tracks data on occupancy, average room rate and Revenue Per Available Room (RevPAR) on a monthly basis. Hotels use this data to benchmark their performance against the industry averages which enables them to identify changes in the marketplace and act to maintain and increase their performance. These benchmarks are also used to set performance goals of employees and determine remuneration bonuses.

Benchmarking and the spa industry

Benchmarking is a relatively new concept in the spa industry as professional spa industry survey reports have only been published since 2000. Before reviewing the current practices in more detail, it is important to define 'spa' and identify and describe common spa industry benchmarks.

The importance of defining 'spa'

The definition of spa is fundamental to the calculation and analysis of spa industry benchmarks in order to compile a set of comparable and relevant benchmarks for spa businesses to use. The definition is required to differentiate real spa businesses from non-spa businesses such as beauty salons, hotel massage services, clinics and other types of businesses that do not offer spa treatments. For example, it is not accurate or useful to compare average revenue of a full service day spa with that of a hotel offering two types of massage or a beauty salon that only offers facials, nail services and waxing. Also, if spa is not defined correctly, the number of spas in a market cannot be counted, and it is therefore impossible to accurately calculate the benchmarks based on the total spa population.

For the purposes of benchmarking, spas have been defined as 'a business offering spa treatments based on authentic water-based therapies which are practiced by qualified personnel in a professional and relaxing environment' (Intelligent Spas, 2007). This definition incorporates a water element based on the original definition of spa interpreted as 'healing through water', as well as includes a relaxation element to address contemporary spa consumers' definition of spa as 'a place to relax' (Garrow 2005, p. 5). These two key elements are necessary to exclude the thousands of beauty salons, massage centres and medical clinics, and ensure that data collected is relevant to spa businesses.

Spa industry benchmarks defined

Spa industry benchmarks are calculated from information collected from spa operators. Self-administered surveys are typically completed by spa owners, directors or managers of individual spa businesses or in the case of spa management companies, surveys are often completed at corporate headquarters level. The survey results are collated to establish industry averages by country and where response rates are high enough, more specific benchmarks may be calculated, for example, by spa type and specific location.

Spa industry benchmarks can be broken down into the three main categories – spa profile benchmarks, spa performance benchmarks and spa benchmark ratios (Garrow, 2008, p. 7).

Spa profile benchmarks

Spa profile benchmarks enable the qualities and characteristics of the spa to be measured. Some key spa profile benchmarks include:

- Number of spas – count of total number of spas in the market.
- Type of spa by main type – day spa (no accommodation on site) or destination spa (accommodation on site).
- Type of spa by sub-type – club spa, medical spa, hotel spa, resort spa, salon spa, etc.
- Location – urban, regional, island, other relevant to the specific market such as state, province or city.
- Size – total indoor area, breakdown of indoor area and total outdoor area.
- Treatment rooms and stations – total number and breakdown of treatment rooms and stations, occupancy capacity (single or double occupancy) and purpose of use (wet, dry or combination of treatments).
- Business structure – ownership, management and marketing structures.
- Infrastructure and facilities available – availability of relaxation rooms, change rooms and water-based support facilities such as plunge pools and steam rooms.

- Treatments and services available – therapies, treatments, services, consultations, programs, activities and classes available.
- Pricing – starting prices of standard spa treatments by treatment time.
- Trends – current industry trends and observations as noted by spa owners and managers.

Profile benchmarks establish a sound foundation for key cross-tabulation of data which is required for detailed analysis, for example comparing the results by type of spa and location. These benchmarks are typically not considered confidential information and high survey response rates enable this analysis to be reliable.

Spa performance benchmarks

Spa performance benchmarks or key performance indicators enable a spa to measure and monitor its business performance, and are typically considered confidential or competitively sensitive. Spa performance benchmarks include:

- Revenue – total industry revenue, average revenue per spa, breakdown of revenue by type of treatment/service, department, other revenue such as memberships and retail.
- Expenses – total industry expenses, average expenses per spa, breakdown of expenses by type of treatment/service, department, other expenses such as salaries, benefits, training, rent, maintenance, marketing, insurance and cost of sales.
- Visitors – total industry visitors, average visitors per spa, breakdown visitors by demographics (gender, residence, age), repeat visitation and treatment choices.
- Human resources – total industry employees, average number of employees per spa, breakdown by job type, qualification levels, salaries and benefits by job type.

Spa benchmark ratios

The collection of spa profile and performance benchmarks enables the calculation of important analysis ratios which are used to determine the state of a spa business as well as the state of the industry. Key spa benchmark ratios include:

- Revenue ratios – average revenue per visitor, treatment, occupied treatment room, available treatment room, treatment table/area/station, square metre, therapist, return on investment and payback period.
- Expense ratios – average cost of sale, treatment, goods sold and expenses as a percentage of revenue.

- Visitor ratios – average visitors by number of rooms, operating hours and employees.
- Treatment ratios – average treatments per visitor, treatment room/area/station, therapist and average treatment prices.

Who uses spa industry benchmarks?

Spa industry benchmarks are critical to the sound development of the industry and provide a clear understanding of market conditions. Spa facilities use benchmarks to:

- monitor and improve operational performance;
- identify potential business risks;
- highlight areas requiring improvement;
- discover opportunities to expand;
- control costs and increase profits;
- develop business plans;
- communicate goals and standards to employees.

By reviewing internal benchmarks and comparing them against industry benchmarks, spas are able to control their direction and maximise their business performance.

Spa benchmarks are also used by a wide variety of business types that support the spa industry. For example:

- Journalists require spa industry statistics to support articles.
- Suppliers use benchmarks to develop and modify their products and services to meet the changing needs of spa businesses.
- Consultants require independent spa benchmarks to keep up-to-date with industry trends and to support the advice they give to their clients. Benchmarks are key inputs for feasibility studies and business plans.
- Financial institutions and investors require facts to calculate the risk of funding applications before approving loan applications and investment opportunities.
- Spa associations require reliable spa benchmarks such as the size and value of the market to effectively promote the industry and develop incentives and benefits for their members.
- Government and tourism departments require spa benchmarks to develop financial incentives to support the industry including, for example, promotion, training and taxation initiatives.
- Trainers and educational institutions require spa benchmarks to understand the industry and assess the requirement of new training programs and courses and identify relevant content for course materials.

Ideal spa benchmarking practices

To date, spa industry research has been conducted by research companies, consulting firms, suppliers and associations with varying degrees of success and rigour. The accuracy of the research, however, is highly dependent on the methodology implemented. Industry research is a complex science and high-quality spa industry research requires the following:

1. **Estimating the total spa population**: A reliable estimation of the total spa population is required in order to accurately calculate many benchmarks and ratios which are based on a proportion of the total spa population. To obtain an accurate estimation of the total spa population the research methodology should incorporate extensive desk research, verification calls and telephone interviews to actually confirm the total number of spas in a market.

2. **Consistent definitions:** It is critical to define 'spa' and the various spa types in order to calculate accurate benchmarks for the spa market and conduct detailed breakdown analysis by specific spa type. If spa and other industry terms are not defined correctly, survey design and analysis problems are possible. For example, the International Spa Association (ISPA) stated their 2006 US spa industry survey report included revisions of the industry size estimates previously published in three earlier reports as spa businesses had not been accurately categorised and counted (International Spa Association, 2007, p. 1). This problem affected their estimate of the number and type of spas in the market and changed all the benchmarks and conclusions of the study which were based on the total spa population.

3. **Industry knowledge and expertise**: If the research is not conducted by spa industry research experts, the quality of the research may suffer due to poor design and implementation. For example, in 2007 ISPA was forced to recall study results after publishing preliminary information citing numerous statistical and analytical errors associated with the research (International Spa Association, 2007). Although a global market research consulting company was commissioned to conduct the study, a lack of industry knowledge compromised the design of the survey and the findings were deemed unreliable.

   Similarly, other industry surveys developed by associations without market research qualifications have included faulty survey design such as incorrect or incomplete ranges and response options, which produces invalid information.

Another problem is where anonymous surveys are used as this allows non-spa businesses to complete the survey and submit irrelevant data. This also does not allow the data submitted to be checked for errors so accuracy cannot be determined.

4. **Independence and reliable response rates**: High response rates are necessary to calculate accurate spa benchmarks and thus provide an assessment of the true state of the industry. High response rates are likely to be achieved only when the confidentiality of sensitive data can be assured, and the research is seen to be unbiased and totally independent. This requires the research company to fund its own research and to have no industry ties through consulting contracts or collaborations with any third parties. Response rates can also be increased when potential respondents are offered the incentive of receiving at least some of the survey results.

   This model can achieve very high survey response rates, for example using this model a 2006 survey conducted in Australia achieved a 64% response rate (Garrow, 2006, p. 14). In contrast, a number of spa industry reports have been published by associations with a response rate of less than 5%, which in industry research terms is questionable and potentially unreliable (Association Resource Centre Inc, 2007, pp. 2–4). Poor response rates are typical with research conducted or commissioned by organisations that cannot assure confidentiality of the data. This can occur with research conducted by spa associations where the boards and committees include spa operators, making it difficult for competitors to feel comfortable in sharing their data. Similarly, key information may not be gathered and/or the true state of the industry may not be disclosed if the research is conducted or commissioned by an organisation which is not independent or has a real or perceived conflict of interest. Such conflicts may occur between associations and their sponsors and/or members; suppliers and their clients or where responses could be used for other purposes, including private studies commissioned by individual spa businesses. Bias may also occur where third parties have the opportunity to influence the research design, methodology or the manner in which survey findings are published, or where the publisher of the research has a vested interest in the results.

5. **Disclosure of sample and sub-sample population**: Where only a segment of the spa population is surveyed, for example an association's members or a supplier's clients, the

research is unlikely to be based on a representative sample and the resulting survey findings may not be reliable. Fully disclosing the sample and sub-sample sizes for a report (and for each question) provides transparency so that readers can accurately interpret the results.

Challenges of spa surveys

The two main challenges faced when conducting spa industry surveys include:

1. **Lack of understanding about benchmarking**: Benchmarking has been conducted in various industries for many years, however as it is a relatively new concept in the spa industry, some spas continue to decline the invitation to participate in industry surveys due to fear their data may not be kept confidential. Intelligent Spas has addressed this issue by developing a 'Spa Industry Profile Survey' which does not request confidential information. This concept aims to educate spa owners and managers about the benefits of benchmarking and encourage their support. To date, it has proved very successful with the achievement of extremely high response rates including 64% of all spas in Australia, 61% of Indonesian spas and 54% of spas in the Philippines during the first survey conducted. Such high response rates provide extremely reliable benchmarks for those spa markets.

2. **Some spas do not record data**: Some spas do not record and analyse key information which does not allow them to complete all the survey questions. Many spa owners are from beauty therapy or massage service backgrounds and have not been trained on the business side of spa management. Therefore, systems to collect data are often not in place.

Summary of published spa industry benchmarks

A summary of findings from Intelligent Spas', Spa Benchmark Program in key markets across the Asia Pacific region based on survey data collected in 2006–2007 is presented in Table 4.1 (Garrow, 2007, pp. 16–17):

Australia

The Australian spa market was the second largest in the region and has experienced strong growth since 2002. Dominated by day spas and individually branded spas, it continues to grow at a steady pace. The following industry trends were recorded:

- The increase in male spa visitors was the most common industry trend, with 29% of Australian respondents making this observation.
- 22% of spas surveyed stated there was more focus on wellness and related modalities.
- An increase in couples and group bookings was noticed by 12% of respondents.

Indonesia

Indonesia hosted the largest spas in terms of indoor space, and over half the spas were destination spas. The prices of standard spa treatments were the second most affordable in the region after the Philippines. The key industry trends observed by spa owners and managers included:

- Increased demand by clients for holistic spa treatments (22%).
- 20% of respondents observed the variety of treatment packages offered by spas.
- 11% stated clients were preferring products with natural ingredients in their treatments.

Table 4.1 Asia Pacific spa industry overview

	Total Spas	Survey response rate (%)	Historical growth rate (%)	Growth period	Day Spas (%)	Destination spas (%)	Indoor Spa size (SqM)	Treatment rooms	1 hour body wrap (USD)
Australia	503	64	129	2002–2006	65	28	237	6.0	94
Indonesia	390	61	160	2003–2007	42	52	713	9.0	27
Malaysia	151	35	202	2002–2006	54	40	393	7.7	48
Philippines	87	54	74	2003–2006	76	20	609	10.9	31
Singapore	173	35	63	2003–2006	58	14	603	8.7	71
Taiwan	317	14	–	–	81	6	457	7.8	78

Source: Intelligent Spas, Spa Industry Profile Benchmarks Asia Pacific report.

Malaysia

The Malaysian spa industry has experienced over 200% growth since 2002 and is forecast to continue strong growth. Just over half the spas were day spas and on average, spas were relatively small compared to other markets across the region. Survey respondents noted:

- Increased interest in traditional massage (30%).
- 26% stated there was increased customer awareness about spas.
- 22% received more requests for relaxation-related treatments.

Philippines

The Philippines is the smallest market featured in this report, however, its spas had the highest number of treatment rooms on average. Over three quarters of the spas were day spas. Strong growth is predicted over the next couple of years. Key industry trends included:

- 35% of spas noticed there were more spas opening in hotels, resorts and malls.
- An increase in the number of medical spas was observed by 30% of respondents.
- 20% stated spas were promoting more to tourists.
- An increase in natural products used during treatments was noticed by 20% of respondents.

Singapore

Singapore's spa market is relatively mature, yet it is predicted to continue growing at 11% over the next couple of years. Half of the spas were day spas and a relatively high proportion of spas were salon spas. Spa owners and managers observed the following industry trends:

- 31% said competitive and affordable prices were currently being offered.
- 28% noticed an increase in the number of medical-related treatments being introduced.
- 24% stated more clients were emphasising, they wanted a total spa experience.

Taiwan

Taiwan hosts over 300 spa facilities and 81% were day spas. Spa franchises are very common and the majority of spas use group brand names. Relatively slow growth is forecast over the next couple of years. Key industry trends include:

- 59% of respondents observed clients were increasingly demanding high-quality services from spas.
- 53% stated spas were setting varied prices for the same type of treatments.
- 35% said some existing spas were opening more spa branches.

Preliminary research of other spa markets based on survey data collected in 2007 is summarised in Table 4.2:

Table 4.2 Preliminary research of various spa markets

	Total spas	Day spas (%)	Destination spas (%)
New Zealand	160	75	25
Thailand	590	43	57
Vietnam	110	47	53
Cambodia	40	35	65
Hong Kong	130	70	30
Mainland China	90	23	77
Korea	40	42	58
India	130	20	80
Sri Lanka	20	17	83
Maldives	60	0	100
Mauritius	40	0	100
United Arab Emirates	60	50	50
South Africa	180	45	55

Source: Intelligent Spas, spa benchmark program.

- Thailand hosts the largest spa market in the Asia Pacific region with approximately 590 spas, 57% of these are located in hotels, resorts and retreats.
- Day spas dominate the markets in New Zealand and Hong Kong.
- The majority of the spas in the Maldives and Mauritius are located in hotels and resorts.
- Hotels and resorts are developing spas in the emerging markets of Cambodia and Sri Lanka.

The future of spa benchmarking

As competitiveness in an industry increases, so does the requirement for benchmarks. Businesses operating in the spa industry need reliable benchmarks to accurately assess and monitor their performance in order to control their direction and sustainability. Benchmarking programs are expanding to cover new spa markets and with continued education about ideal research practices and the benefits of benchmarking, the availability and range of reliable spa industry benchmarks is likely to expand.

References

Association Resource Centre Inc (2007) *2006 Spa Industry Statistics Summary Report*, International Spa Association, USA.

Garrow, (2005) *Female versus Male Spa Consumers: Survey of Behaviours, Expectations, Preferences and Predictions*, Intelligent Spas, Singapore.

Garrow, (2006) *Spa Industry Profile Australia 2002–2007*, Intelligent Spas, Singapore.

Garrow, (2007) *Spa Industry Profile Benchmarks Asia Pacific Report*, Intelligent Spas, Singapore.

Garrow, (2008) *Using Spa Industry Benchmarks for Success*, Intelligent Spas, Singapore.

Intelligent Spas (2007) *Spa Definitions*, available at: http://www.IntelligentSpas.com (site accessed 15 November 2007).

International Spa Association (2007) *Press Release*, available at: http://www.experienceispa.com (site accessed 15 November 2007).

Patterson, (1996) *Benchmarking Basics: Looking for a Better Way*, Crisp Publications, Inc, USA.

Trends in the global spa industry

Susie Ellis

Introduction

Understanding current trends and anticipating those of the future can be an invaluable tool in business. It is foundational for strategic planning and can help spa entities find a clear direction to better allocate resources, ensure a competitive edge, and raise the level of benefits and satisfaction for consumers.

Tracking trends can also be inspirational, as it is one of the best ways to motivate, stimulate and encourage people. Possibly most exciting of all, analyzing trends may result in the rewarding opportunity to help shape future trends.

This chapter begins with defining the term 'trend', explaining each word in the phrase 'Global Spa Industry', and establishing once and for all just when the Global Spa Industry began. The chapter continues with examining historical spa trends by continent and by decade, the current macrotrend landscape, potential troubling trends which may be brewing, and concludes with a look at some probable spa trends of the future.

Definition of trends

The word 'trend' can be defined as 'the general direction in which something tends to move' (American Heritage, 2004). Understanding trends in the spa industry gives us foresight regarding where things are headed, and also provides insight into the current state of the industry itself. Trends are not fads. They are not here today and gone tomorrow. Trends evolve rather than magically appear; as is often said, 'A trend is my friend' since this kind of knowledge is as close as one can get to seeing the future.

Defining the global spa industry

Looking at the words 'spa', 'global' and 'industry' will help give us a starting point from which we can study spa trends. The term 'spa' is generally considered to have had its origins in Europe. Some believe the term evolved from the Latin *spargere*, meaning 'to scatter, sprinkle or moisten', while others embrace the word as an acronym for the Latin phrase *sanitas per aquaam*, meaning 'health through water'. Others trace its origin back to the 14th century, when mineral springs were discovered near Liège, Belgium, in the town now known as Spa (Croutier, 1992, p. 136).

'Spa' was adopted in the USA after Native Americans introduced early settlers to mineral springs. By the mid-1800s, people routinely took curative vacations to an area in upstate New York with a variety of naturally carbonated mineral waters called Saratoga Springs. In the 1930s a great new health center was built and named Saratoga Spa.

From there the term 'spa' spread, first associated with other international natural mineral or hot springs and later adapted to describe enterprises offering similar ways to relax and rejuvenate. Around 1950, the Jacuzzi brothers (who had immigrated to the USA from Italy and were making hydraulic aircraft pumps) developed a hydrotherapy pump to ease the leg pain of a family member. Later marketed as a Jacuzzi and referred to as a hot tub or spa, the product introduced many people to the term 'spa'. In the late 1990s, the International Spa Association (ISPA) crafted a definition for the term which is still used by many today: 'Spas are places devoted to enhancing overall well-being through a variety of professional services that encourage the renewal of mind, body and spirit' (Types of Spas, 2007). While some people still feel that any definition of spa must include the use of water-based therapies, this is unlikely to be a winning argument in the future. The term 'spa' has been rapidly adopted by associated businesses and studies show that consumers in many parts of the world no longer consider water therapies a component of their definition of spa.

For a concept, product or industry to be considered 'global' it needs to appear, or be used, in various parts of the world. While the term 'global spa industry' may not have been used worldwide until recently, the concept of spa has been part of every civilization since the beginning of time. All cultures have unique ways of renewing body, mind and spirit; a glance at Table 5.1

Table 5.1 International language of spa

Alpine Wellness	Egyptian Oils	Japanese Shiatsu
American Aerobics	French Thalassotherapy	Javanese Lulur
Australian Indigenous	Finnish Sauna	Mexican Temescal
Balinese Boreh	German Kur	Philippine Hilot
Brazilian Wax	Hawaiian Lomi Lomi	Russian Steam
British Health Farm	Hungarian Mud	Swedish Massage
Chinese Acupuncture	Indian Ayurveda	Swiss Shower
Chinese Medicine	Indian Head Massage	Thai Massage
Dead Sea Salts	Italian Fango & Terme	Turkish Hamam
	Japanese Onsen	

lists terms from various countries and regions which have become part of today's universal spa vocabulary.

The term 'industry' is described as 'the aggregate of productive enterprises in a particular field, often named after its principal product' (Industry, 2007). Sources show that the first worldwide spa listings were compiled in the USA by Jeffrey Joseph, a travel and tour specialist who became the first person to specialize in selling spa vacations around the world. He printed a comprehensive catalog of health and fitness resorts which included 'spa' businesses from every continent except Africa. Joseph's publication, called *SpaFinder*, was printed in 1987 (Joseph, 1987, p. 2). One can therefore conclude that the official beginning of the global spa industry, where the terms 'global', 'spa', and 'industry' came together for the first time was in 1987.

Other international guide books and magazines would follow. In 1991, a group of health and fitness resort owners formed an association which was later called ISPA, and held their first conference in Neversink, New York, attended by people from 10 different countries. Other developmental milestones for the industry included the first worldwide spa awards given out by Condé Nast in 2003, and the spa crystal awards by SpaFinder in 2004, the first Global Spa Summit (GSS) held in New York in 2007, the first Global Spa Economy Report Commissioned by the GSS in 2008 as well as the publication of this book, the first text on the global spa industry.

Historical look at spa trends

Pre-1987 spa industry trends by continent

Prior to the late 1980s when spas became an international industry, each continent had unique places devoted to the overall well-being of the mind, body and spirit. Although it would be fascinating to delve into each country or region's spa industry trends, for the purposes of this chapter we will look in general at each continent's spa history and the hallmarks of its contribution to today's industry.

Europe

The popular notion of 'taking the waters' can be traced back to many countries in Europe where it gained immense popularity, as the affluent flocked to natural springs and nearby towns in pursuit of health, beauty, inspiration and even sexual pleasures. Later many of these establishments took a more medicinal approach before falling out of favor after both world wars and the evolution of scientific cures. Nevertheless, the significance of water and the alignment with medicine remained as modern spas emerged and are considered important characteristics of today's international spa community.

Asia

Although there was emphasis on water, in the traditions of onsen bathing in Japan or steam baths in Russia, Asia's contribution to the spa industry is the preservation of holistic therapies. From Ayurveda in India, TCM in China, Shiatsu in Japan or Thai Massage in Thailand, their systems and treatments for health and rejuvenation naturally recognized the body, mind and spirit as an inter-related, whole entity.

Australia

With its history closely aligned with Britain and its proximity to Asia, it is no wonder that the combination of eastern and western medicine found a natural home here. However, Australia distinguished itself through a focus on nature, the healing environment of the outdoors and the value of organic and eco-conscious philosophies. Many current trends in spa product brands and sustainable practices trace their roots to this continent.

South America

This land of warm, fun-loving and beautiful people adopted the term spa later than North America, Europe, Asia and Australia, although indigenous healing traditions and beauty practices have existed in the region for centuries. In particular, South America is known for ancient herbal techniques: shamans, healers and medical lore. Hispanic cultures have combined physical and spiritual elements quite naturally. In addition, this continent's focus on physical beauty would contribute to a worldwide phenomenon, vaulting them into a trend-setting role in aesthetic alteration and the growth of medical tourism.

Africa

This continent, with its mystique, allure, vast diversity and political challenges, has also had a worldwide impact on the spa industry. Though it is clearly still evolving, the importance and value of indigenous practices and products has become a foundational component of the spa industry today. South Africa's reputation for medical excellence, its attractive climate and wine-producing regions have caught the imagination of many adventurous spa-goers. The continent's native practices, flora and wildlife have also spurred health and tourism combinations such as spa and safari.

North America

Though several natural springs grew into spa facilities, the North American spa industry did not capitalize on bathing and water therapy. Rather, it developed around fitness, weight loss, health and beauty. Spa industry pioneers introduced a for-profit model of spa, emphasizing the physical body in original programming developed around 1- or 2-week stays. Popularized by media, celebrities and marketing know-how, the interest in spas spread quickly and birthed a myriad of offshoots including day spas, medical spas, spas-at-sea, club spas, mobile spas and residential living spas.

Spa industry trends in the 1980s

This decade saw a smattering of trends on various continents, with North America emerging as the venue for the newly aggregated for-profit spa industry. One major factor contributing to the consumer-funded model in North America was the lack of government healthcare systems which funded 'relaxation' vacations for Europeans. In addition, America was experiencing a decade of abundance. An excess of food, drink and other pleasures would necessitate the need to pursue health and weight reduction while simultaneously fueling the desire for pampering aspects of the spa tradition. This focus on fitness, weight loss and beauty resulted in high level aerobic exercise, very low calorie diets and celebrity-defined beauty. Spa-goers woke early, climbed mountains, attended exercise classes, ate healthy food and were rewarded with a massage, facial or occasional herbal wrap.

Meanwhile, in Europe, many spa-type places were still water-focused, government subsidized and supervised by doctors. The kur in Germany, thermae in Italy and thalassotherapy in France were visited regularly by citizens at their governments' expense. For preventative reasons, many would visit for weeks at a time. In Great Britain, estates like Champney's, Grayshott Hall, Radgale Hall and other so-called 'health farms' identified with the term spa which was becoming a popular topic for journalists. Eventually these dedicated facilities would later be called 'destination spas'.

Apart from these total immersion spa experiences, resorts and hotels began adding 'and Spa' to their names, capitalizing on luxuries like massage, beauty treatments and sophisticated dining in order to tap into the popular glamour of the spa getaway. Adding a spa as a hotel or resort amenity offered a solution to differentiate a hotel from its competition; places such as La Costa in California and Brenner's Park Hotel in Baden Baden, Germany added 'and Spa', garnering significant visibility and guests.

Eventually, it became obvious that governments would no longer fund spa visits. Nevertheless, wealthy patrons began spending their own money at spas, even if they were not reimbursed. For example, Clinique La Prairie in Switzerland founded half a century earlier, was becoming famous for its Revitalization Therapy – fetal sheep liver cell injections which attracted clientele from all over the world. Although the clinic did not use the term spa, its international patrons did. The notion of anti-aging became linked with the idea of spa visits from that time forward.

Though the term 'spa' in the 1980s was relatively unknown outside of the USA and Europe, there were exceptions. On Japan's East Coast the Beppu Spa, located near several hot boiling ponds, was known for shooting mud and water high into the air. In Australia, mineral springs in the Daylesford/Heburn reserve were named the Spa Hydro Therapy Center, offering massage, baths, Pela mud and valerian. Rotorua, the site of spectacular thermal activity in New Zealand, was described as a place for 'abundant spa-like services and natural outdoor activities'.

Also in the 1980s, the Cunard Cruise Line asked Deborah Szekely to establish a branch operation of her then famous Golden Door spa (in California) aboard the QE2 which, when opened in 1982, became the first spa-at-sea. A few years later, Steiner Salons (UK), began to open spas onboard ships as well and quickly became the dominant player in the cruise ship spa arena.

By the end of the decade, 'day spas' emerged. With no overnight accommodations, they offered a wide variety of treatments, some with added fitness options. Due to the sheer number of people who would ultimately patronize these facilities, the day spa became a powerful tool for the growth of the industry on an international scale.

Spa industry trends in the 1990s

This decade witnessed explosive growth in the number and types of spas, as well as in the number of people who sampled them or became regular spa-goers. Spa industry professionals became more organized and concerted efforts were made to promote the industry. Due to public relations and increased marketing expertise, a broader base of consumers was introduced to the alluring world of spas. This resulted in a welcomed trend of the democratization of spas; these luxuries, formerly reserved mostly for the affluent, were now available to new consumer groups.

At the beginning of the decade, ISPA joined industry owners, managers and suppliers in an effort to define and standardize industry terms. In 1995, the European Spa Association (ESPA) was founded by several existing organizations, including the German Spa Association, the Spa Business Association (formerly the British Spas Federation) and Le Federation Internationale du Thermalisme et du Climatisme (FITEC).

Terms such as destination spa, resort/hotel spa, day spa, mineral springs spa, club spa and cruise ship spa became more universal. In the following decade categories such as medical and med spas, residential living spas and mobile spas would be added to the spa vocabulary. Other categories, trumpeted by various countries and organizations, represented unique points of view. These included: Thalassotherapy Spas, Wellness Centers, Bathhouse Spas, Nordic Spas, Airport Spas, Dental Spas, Holistic Spas, Spa Retreats, Thermal Spas and Urban Spas, to name a few. While there is still no universal agreement on the definitions of the various spa types which have evolved, the differences are becoming smaller. A greater spirit of cooperation has emerged as industry professionals realize that consistency for the benefit of media, investors and above all consumers is a benefit for all.

This decade also produced some of the first spa industry research. Cornell University's School of Hotel Administration added a class on spa and students began research studies to help identify actual figures of the US spa industry. ISPA funded research beyond the Cornell studies, identifying revenues, expenses and profits in addition to examining consumer behavior for this growing industry.

The emergence of spa trade magazines and consumer spa publications helped promote the industry and encourage spa-going.

More hotels and resorts began adding spas to existing properties or developed luxurious designs for new properties. This trend was especially noticeable in Asia which had many of the ingredients required for successful spa operations: an abundant labor supply, undeveloped land in beautiful locations and spa as part of the culture. Famous brands like Mandarin Oriental,

Banyan Tree, Mandara and Six Senses began placing more emphasis on spas, primarily expanding in Asia where large profits (due to low labor costs) were assured. Others such as Shangri-La, Taj and Peninsula soon followed. The seeds of spa brands were planted; larger companies began to see the advantages of a branded product.

Due to the dramatic rise in the number of hotel and resort spas, stand-alone spas offering a full-immersion 'pure' experience needed to differentiate themselves. In the 1990s, the owners of Canyon Ranch, the Golden Door, the Oaks at Ojai and approximately 15 other establishments formed a group and called themselves 'destination spas'.

Meanwhile, the day spa market was growing like wildfire, particularly in the USA. By the end of the decade, there were more day spas than all other types of spas combined. Marcia Kilgore founded two Bliss day spas in New York City with a younger, quirky and hip personality. She established a retail product line to match, and captured the industry's attention regarding the value of retail spa products after selling Bliss to LVMH for a reported $30 million (Maneker, 1999).

Spa cuisine became industry vocabulary as flavorful and tempting healthful dishes became popular. In the 1990s, spas also began to embrace philosophical and spiritual aspects of wellness; spas added yoga programs, built labyrinths, introduced meditation and incorporated other types of spiritually oriented experiences.

Spa industry trends in the new millennium

At the turn of the century, the spa industry as a whole was robust. One major shift which took place in the first decade of the 21st century was the idea of spa expanding from merely a place to visit to a well-rounded way of life. The term 'spa lifestyle' emerged, affecting fashion, travel, home design, business and every other aspect of a person's life. The only spa category which remained stagnant was the destination spa because people began spending more time at work. Going away for a week or two at a time became less popular and shorter spa vacations grew in popularity.

The events of September 11, 2001 cut deeply into travel and tourism industries, affecting the spa industry as well, albeit more lightly. With the cover story 'Spas for Challenging Times' on newsstands shortly after the New York attack, *SpaFinder* magazine had a big seller. The desire to improve one's health and appearance was not the only reason that drove visitors to spas; the opportunity to heal and revive was also a powerful motivator.

In this new Millennium, spas began to reach out to medical professionals to provide services that customers had started to demand but for which they were not licensed. In turn, medical professionals took note of the vibrant spa industry which was beginning to lure away clients. Consumers liked the synergistic combination of a medical professionals' expertise and a caring, nurturing atmosphere.

The trend of mixing medicine and spa had a variety of interpretations. To some, medical spas were about prevention and wellness. To others, it was a facility offering complementary, alternative or integral modalities. Still others considered the medical spa a place focused on cosmetic dermatology and aesthetics, where a growing number of substances and techniques (i.e. Botox and fillers) appealed to consumers. New categories of products called nutraceuticals, cosmeceuticals and other hybrids from the medical and spa worlds became popular. Later in the decade the term 'wellness' would gain significant popularity and become an umbrella term under which many of these medical and spa concepts would fall.

Although men frequented spas regularly in some countries – especially Japan – male specific treatments added another wave of consumer interest in this decade. Men became more aware of health issues and the desire to maintain a youthful appearance and began visiting spas in greater numbers, usually to 'work' on an issue such as improving a golf game, helping a back ache or lowering blood pressure.

Spa suites became a trend. Many were built to accommodate two massage tables; some even offered private amenities such as steam rooms, saunas and whirlpools that couples could enjoy together. The 'couple's treatment' expanded to involve friends, groups of three or more and eventually parties for bridal showers and birthday parties of all ages. The first generation to watch their parents visit spas regularly, teens began to incorporate spa-going into their own routines. Later pre-teens joined in, kid spas opened and eventually moms and babies would be welcomed together at spas.

The spa industry began seeing consolidation and increased competition in this new Millennium. At first, the competition came from industry-related companies (Dove, Kohler, Evian, etc.). Later other corporations would join the spa bandwagon (Bulgari, Prada, Coldwater Creek, etc.). Differentiation became a trend that helped spas stand out. Some facilities offered vegetarian menus or alcoholic beverages; accommodated pets or babies; provided help with detoxification, sexual or fertility issues; offered adventure opportunities; catered to business groups or offered executive physicals; provided packages called baby-moon vacations (a final vacation before giving birth); targeted an ethnic population's unique needs and customs or focused on weight loss. An increased interest at both ends of the pricing spectrum resulted in affordable experiences counterbalanced by over-the-top customized spa opportunities. Express, no frills or no fuss spa services were offered for the time deficient. Spas at airports and mobile spas, which came to people's homes, attracted an additional demographic of spa-goer. Consumers reacted positively to the use of indigenous ingredients, like mud, cocoa, cornmeal, water from the rainforest and even maple syrup. Spas began adding services inspired by local traditions, such as Korean scrubs, Thai massage or the Philippine Hilot, regardless of where they were located.

The presence of a spa continued to drive sales at hotels and resorts. The Mandarin Oriental Hotel Group discovered that guests who used the spa spent more money at the hotel, stayed longer and were more likely to book suites (Gibson, 2007). Spas had made the complete transformation from amenities to profit centers to room night drivers.

Meanwhile the spa industry became more professional. New consumer and trade publications appeared like *SpaAsia, Asia Spa, Spa India, European Spa* and *Spa Business*, joined by online resources such as *Spa Trade* and *Spa Opportunities*.

Spa directories and gift card programs were seen in virtually every country. Gift certificates or vouchers became lucrative business strategies, bringing even more consumers to spa experiences. Studies showed a large percentage of new spa-goers had been introduced to their first spa experience through a gift certificate or voucher.

The rise of the Internet helped spread the spa gospel internationally. Spas developed websites, online booking became the norm and the smallest day spa was able to attract distant customers for nominal marketing fees. However, this connectivity also resulted in the invasion of 'high tech' into the high touch spa environment, challenging spas and consumers to choose between 'plugging in' or 'unplugging' at the spa.

As business tactics advanced, the spa consumer became more knowledgeable and discerning. Spa-goers liked what they saw in spas and wanted it for their homes. Thus, the trend of home spa design emerged, incorporating the spa look in bathrooms, meditation rooms, living rooms and even bedrooms. The idea of 'living' at a spa was the logical next step. When Canyon Ranch Living announced the first spa lifestyle real estate project (which they opened in Miami, Florida in 2008), the idea of living the spa lifestyle took on its ultimate meaning. The anticipated success of that venture spawned the trend of mixed-use developments and integrated resorts around the world with spas adding residential components, developers adding spas and hotels and resorts with spas adding condos.

Other trends of the 21st century included a rising concern about organic, green or sustainable issues, resulting in the development of the eco-spa. Sleep health became an important wellness pillar, fully integrating into existing spa programming. Emotional health and the value of relationships emphasized a social spa-ing trend that made many spa experiences just plain fun!

Economic realities spurred change as high costs of labor, general expenses and increased competition made it more difficult for spas to be profitable. New business models emerged emphasizing hydro or thermal experiences for large groups (de-staffed spa treatments) and a high volume, no frills, no fuss angle to services. Revenue management techniques and benchmarking became part of spa business vocabulary.

Current macro trends influencing the global spa industry today

It is useful to examine current dominant macro trends, using the STEEP approach to highlight Social, Technological, Economic, Environmental and Political macro trends and their likely affect on the global spa industry of the future (PEST Analysis, 2007).

Social trends

Demographic trends

In many parts of the developed world, including North America, Australia, Europe and Japan, the population is aging and the birth rate is decreasing. This population will require more medical care, while the middle-aged group (often called 'Boomers') will have a strong desire to stay youthful and vibrant for as long as possible. Other demographic trends include a shift in ethnic makeup, an increase in population and urbanization of the developing world, a shortage of highly skilled talent and a rise of income inequality.

What this means for the spa industry is a continued and increased interest in spa-going with shifts in participant make-up and challenge in terms of staffing. Health and beauty treatments will remain appealing to the aging, urban population, whose medical needs support the fusion of practical medicine and spa philosophies. At the same time, the Gen X and Gen Y generations of spa goers will flood the industry with their new open attitude toward all things spa; since they had grown up watching their parents take part.

However, fundamental human needs and desires are so strong that they will continue to overshadow potential shifts in other arenas. The spa industry addresses many of the concepts included in Abraham Maslow's Hierarchy of Needs: the physiological needs for food, water, air and sleep; the need for safety, security, love, belonging, esteem and self-actualization; and the desire to gain and understand knowledge, create and experience beauty, and reach a place of transcendence where one becomes aware not only of his or her own potential but the fullest potential of human beings at large (Sorensen, 2006).

Technological trends

Technological advancements are continuing at an accelerating pace, causing ubiquitous connectivity, improving our ability to access and share information, as well as communicate and interact with others. Geography and location are losing importance. Competitiveness is accelerating.

What this means for the spa industry is access to an increased number of spa services, including health management and cosmetic procedures like genetic screening, advanced executive physicals, scans, DNA analysis, biomarker measurements, toxicology assessment, laser procedures and safe injectables. With advancements via the Internet making information on medical wellness and cosmetic med spas more viable, continued interest is assured. The arena of medical tourism will become more robust as people from one country travel to another for less expensive services which may also be limited at home. Spa settings surrounding medical procedures will make these options even more attractive.

Economic trends

The aging baby boomers have a great deal of money but are also inheriting the accumulated savings of their parents' frugal generation. In addition, large populations in various parts of the world, specifically India, China and Russia, are just now becoming global consumers. By 2015, the spending power in emerging economies could nearly match the spending power of Western Europe. It is anticipated that 100 million Chinese households will achieve European income levels by 2020. Furthermore, the Hispanic population in the USA will have a spending power equal to 60% of all Chinese consumers (Wagner, 2007).

For spas, this means a further increase in consumer demand. Aristocrats originally took to the waters in Europe, enjoying other aspects of the wellness experience: nature, beauty, conversation, good food, wine, art, music, etc. As affluence increases, more people will be attracted to spas and able to afford them. Increased prosperity has also been known to stimulate health issues (stress, weight, substance abuse) to which spas can also respond.

The appeal of luxury consumption is influencing an entirely new middle-class market, thus the continual race to design the latest luxury experience. In addition we see a trend of wealthy consumers choosing to use their own resources to open spas for their health, or that of family and friends.

With costs of healthcare skyrocketing worldwide (a great concern for businesses, governments and citizens), prevention and self-care will become all the more important, to which spas can make a significant contribution.

Environmental issues

Growth in population and emerging economies utilizing resources will place further strain on the environment at unprecedented rates. Consequently, spas will see an increase in demand for healthy and eco-friendly spa experiences and facilities. Because spas renew the body, mind and spirit of consumers, they understand that a healthy planet is necessary for optimum results. As natural resources are jeopardized, more emphasis will be placed on detoxifying at a spa. Spas in natural settings will become even more appealing.

The very affluent are often criticized for using a disproportionate number of resources, raising yet another reason for environmentally friendly practices. Using large amounts of water, in Vichy Showers or personal bath experiences for example, will no longer be tolerated in areas plagued with water shortages.

Political trends

The potential for world conflicts, natural disasters and threats of terrorism cause feelings of powerlessness and anxiety.

As seen with past disasters such as September 11, 2001, an increased interest in spa participation and spiritual renewal are common responses to these events. Stress reduction is, of course, the number one reason people go to spas and that seems poised to continue. A state of anxiety of this magnitude may cause people to travel less, conserve resources or turn to more personal spiritual refuge as comfort. The trend to spa at home may become more popular.

Troubling trends

Though a positive future for the spa industry is likely, it is prudent to take a look at troubling trends which could, unless kept at bay, yield negative effects for the industry. Some thoughtful foresight and planning could help reduce the likelihood of these coming to fruition and lower their negative impact should one or more of these trends come about.

Excessive building of spas may result in oversupply and lack of differentiation causing saturation. Costs may become excessive due to a global labor shortage, high energy costs and increasing liability expenses, ultimately making spas unviable. A backlash against the entire spa industry may arise from a perceived overuse of resources or frivolous indulgence in light of serious global problems resulting in a widespread (and negative) public attitude toward spas.

Spas may create problems by implementing undesirable practices such as unsubstantiated claims, high pressure sales techniques, occult practices conflicting with people's beliefs or a reversion back to an association with sexual activity. Spas could cause physical or emotional harm due to inappropriate use of equipment or lack of adequate self-regulation. Regulation could be forced upon the industry to combat medical liabilities and improve practicing standards. Businesses (and consumers) could be harmed by disagreements about intellectual property rights, patents, fair trade or negative public relations.

Spas might lose the caring touch they are known for as they are influenced by the medical arena in which high tech trumps high touch resulting in significant depersonalization. If indigenous practices are not honored, the spa experience could become less meaningful, another negative result of globalization. Large brands focused primarily on generating profits may suppress the 'soul' of the spa experience which was birthed by entrepreneurs who nurtured and grew their businesses slowly.

Worldwide catastrophes such as war, terrorism, environmental disaster or a nuclear holocaust could change civilization so radically that spas would no longer be relevant. Should a more successful way for people to reduce stress emerge, or if the spa experience would be taken over by a new business model, the industry may find itself overshadowed completely.

Benchmarketing efforts, educational programs and widespread support for sustainable practices are just a few ways that the spa industry has already adapted to face the possible onset of some of the troubling trends list above. As long as demand continues to grow and quality supply does not exceed demand, the global spa industry's future looks promising.

Future trends in the global spa industry

New trends will arise in the very foundations of the spa experience: water, exercise, cuisine, therapies and beauty treatments, rest, education, as well as intangibles such as connection, community, inner growth and spiritual renewal. Each of the five senses will be taken to new levels (in unique ways) and a true exploration of the sixth sense will find a comfortable home in the spa arena. And watch for an often unstated shift from the consumer, 'In our health vacations we no longer want to relax, we want to change'.

Expect fresh discoveries in the healthcare field (some as a result of stem cell and DNA research, for example) which produce new ways of managing chronic diseases such as diabetes, heart disease and mental problems like Alzheimer and memory loss. New arenas such as the field of psychoneuroimmunology (PNI), which looks at such issues as how emotions and health are related and the link between stress and disease, might find the spa setting an ideal laboratory as well as a place of great hope. Salutogenic theories, complementary and alternative or natural medicine, and points of view not yet expressed will be part of the tapestry created by the coming together of spa and medicine.

Hospitals of the future may feel more like spas just as spas may be more akin to hospitals. The possibility of health coverage, government or employer reimbursement for spa treatments may become reality, an outcome of economic studies which show a definitive financial value in preventative medicine.

New markets will open. For example, as we stand on the horizon of civilian space travel, the need for a space travel conditioning and training program is right around the corner. Getting people physically, mentally and spiritually ready for their space flight would be an exciting endeavor. And what about the elite athlete or the person interested in extreme health, wellness or longevity?

Other trends to watch include the exciting field of energy medicine and the incorporation of indigenous practices and modalities previously considered unproven or experimental. In addition, new ways of thinking about aging populations frequenting spas are sure to arise.

Welcomed changes would be the use of higher quality resources: water which would no longer need to be chlorinated, air clear of radicals and purer, cleaner and more nutrient-rich food, and better and more effective products. With advances in understanding the makeup of water, its vibration and resonance and even how our thoughts might influence it, we may yet realize the ultimate irony – that water, which ushered in the notion of spa to begin with, may hold some of the most exciting breakthroughs to improved health and well-being. And would not a global spa industry committed to the health of our planet's water supply be a most appropriate contribution to a healthier world?

With an improvement in so many aspects of spa-going, it is likely that an entirely new level of spa experiences would emerge. This may, for example, come in the form of the arts and spa coming together. Distinctive architecture, superior interior design elements, performing arts, literature and music, for example, all touch our spirits profoundly; watch for these elements to mix into the process of renewing body, mind and spirit in the spa setting.

That being said, it may finally become transparent that the real magic of the spa experience is multidimensional, enough so that we become comfortable with its existence even though we are unable to fully explain it. These are places for renewal and relaxation, for change and transformation, where we are touched on many levels, where we connect with our true selves and purpose and where we love and are loved. This may finally define not only the truly memorable and healing spa experience of the future, but the state in which we all want to live.

References and selected reading

Croutier, A.L.L. (1992) *Taking the Waters*, Abbeville Publishing Group, New York. p. 136

Dosh. C. *Hotels Meeting Spa Demand with New Facilities*, Business Travel News Online 06 November 2006, 03 January 2008, available at: <http://www.btnmag.com/businesstravelnews/headlines/frontpage_display.jsp?vnu_content_id = 1003352725/>.

Gibson, A. (2007) *Spas in Hotels: How to Decide the Right Ownership*. Global Spa Summit, 2007, Waldorf-Astoria Hotel, New York.

Industry. *InfoPlease*. Random House, Inc., 4 October 2007, available at: <http://www.infoplease.com/ipd/A0490028.html>.

Introduction. *European Spas Association*, 3 January 2008, available at: <http://www.espa-ehv.com/>.

Joseph, J. (1987) Spa-Finders; Jeffrey Joseph's Spa-Finders Travel Arrangements Ltd, *The Spa Finder*, 2.

Kurinformationen. *Deutscher Heilbäderverband*, 3 January 2008, available at: <http://www.deutscher-heilbaederverband.de/>.

Maneker, M. Marital Bliss, *New York Magazine*, 6 December 1999, 3 January 2008, available at: <http://nymag.com/nymetro/news/bizfinance/columns/bottomline/1660/>.

News: About Us. *Spa Business Association*, 3 January 2008, available at: <http://www.britishspas.co.uk/news/about_us.php>.

PEST Analysis. *Mind Tools*, 4 October 2007, available at: <http://www.mindtools.com/pages/article/newTMC_09.htm>.

Sims, A.C. *Say Ahhh! At the Dental Spa*, FoxNews.com, 27 February 2003, 3 January 2008, available at: <http://www.foxnews.com/story/0,2933,79719,00.html>.

Sorensen, K. Maslow's hierarchy of needs and subpersonality work, *Psychosynthesis*, 31 May 2006, 3 January 2008, available at: <http://two.not2.org/psychosynthesis/articles/maslow.htm>.

SpaFinder Offers Sneak Preview of Spa Trends to Watch in 2005, 2006, 2007, 2008. *SpaFinder Press room – Press Release*, 3 January 2008, available at: <http://www.spafinder.com/about/press_release.jsp?relId = 54>.

The International Spa Association, and the Hartman Group (2006a) *ISPA 2006 Consumer Report: Spa-Goer and Non-Spa Goer Perspectives*, The International Spa Association, Lexington, KY.

The International Spa Association, and the Hartman Group (2006b) *ISPA 2006 Spa-Goer Study*, The International Spa Association, Lexington, KY.

Trend (2004). *The American Heritage Dictionary of the English Language*, 4th edn, Houghton Mifflin Company, 05 October 2007, available at: <Dictionary.com http://dictionary.reference.com/browse/trend>.

Types of Spas. *International Spa Association*, International Spa Association, 4 October 2007, available at: <http://www.experienceispa.com/ISPA/Visit/Spa + 101/Types + of + Spas.htm>.

Wagner, H. Taking global macro trends to the bank, *Investopedia*, 22 February 2007, 4 October 2007, available at: <http://www.investopedia.com/articles/07/global_trends.asp#>.

PART 2

Profit

CHAPTER 6

Business plans for 'state of the art' spas

Andrew Gibson

Introduction

Dictionary.com defines state of the art as: 'the latest and most sophisticated or advanced stage of a technology, art, or science'.

Entrepreneur.com defines a business plan as – A written document describing the nature of the business, the sales and marketing strategy, and the financial background, and containing a projected profit and loss statement.

This chapter will help to explain the current concept of a 'state of the art' spa business plan by focussing on the financial strategies that are currently used to achieve a profitable business. The chapters on marketing and feasibility should complement this chapter for anyone wishing to build their own business plan. Examples will be drawn from the hotel spa industry, spa management companies, mega spa complexes, destination spas and day spas. Any limitations on the business plan for each category will also be exposed.

The current concept of spa is quite simple regardless of location. Most spas provide treatments for guests based on therapist skills, products and experiences. The treatments are categorised into massage and its derivatives, skin care (e.g. healthy ageing, damaged skin, Botox, whitening), beauty treatments (e.g. waxing, facials, manicure/pedicure) and optional bathing/water experience. Other spas may include fitness activities (gym, Pilates, yoga, etc.), retail, food and beverage (F & B) and wellness consultations. Today the word 'spa' is global and spas are starting to appear in the most unlikely of places such as the Blue Lagoon in Iceland, on the ski slopes in Val d'Isere, France or in Baku, Azerbaijan. In 2007 over 14 000 spas are registered in the USA as reported by International Spa Association (ISPA).[1]

Nearly all spas have the following common features:

1. reception and ability to take bookings and welcome guests;
2. treatment rooms;
3. retail;
4. somewhere to change – either in the treatment room or changing rooms.

The more luxurious spas may have:

1. changing facilities;
2. fitness/gym;

[1] International Spa Professional Association–2007 Spa Industry Study.

3. activity room;
4. sauna, steam, hot tub;
5. relaxation.

And if the spa is expected to succeed in a competitive market it requires 'attractions' that create the 'wow' factor. Any state of the art spa will have a combination of the above and may add the following:

1. thermal experience (a dedicated designed facility that includes different heat and wet experiences such as sauna, steam, vitality pool, experience showers, ice fountains, heated floors and benches, massage fountains);
2. meditation rooms;
3. purpose built activity rooms (e.g. Pilates, yoga, kinesis, hydro baths, floatation chambers);
4. retail shops;
5. F & B;
6. waiting lounges;
7. gardens.

The difference between a 'state of the art' spa and an ordinary spa is not necessarily in the composition of the facilities but more in the thought, concept and design of the spa. A spa that has been conceived with a clear vision of the end purpose and has identified the anticipated guest profile is more likely to become a 'state of the art spa'. A good place to observe such spas is within hotels because hotels have established brand standards for the hotel group and have used much of the same procedures to apply to spas. Mandarin Oriental Spas, Willow Stream Spas at Fairmont, Chi spas at Shangri La, Bliss at Starwood are just a few examples. To compete in the marketplace and secure a state of the art spa or spa brand, almost every luxury hotel brand in the world now has a Global Spa Director or senior executive responsible for the group's spa strategy. However, the first Global Spa Directors did not appear until the beginning of 2002 and so these brands are relatively new (see Chapter 10).

The only other type of spa activity that has a global reach within spa management is with the specialist spa management companies such as E'spa, Mandara/Steiner, MSpa in Asia, Angsana (Banyan Tree). Often these companies do more than manage the spa; they design spas that are state of the art. It is no coincidence that three of those companies have a strong Asian influence as will be explained later.

Independent self-managed spa operators on a global scale are unknown when compared to the fitness industry (which is about 30 years older than the spa industry). In the fitness industry chains such as Golds, Fitness First, Virgin Active, Holmes Place (Europe), California Fitness (Asia) are relatively well known. Why is this? – perhaps there are limitations to the success of a state of the art spa business plan? This chapter helps to explain how different types of spa establish an effective business plan and report on profits.

The state of the art spa has three main handicaps to overcome in order to have a profitable business unit:

Higher capital costs: State of the art spas require the latest innovations. Dry floatation beds, customised water features with computerised thermal suites, multi-tasking spa software, fully integrated music and lighting that have centralised mood settings for each area in the spa, are just some examples. In addition to the higher build costs there are likely to be higher design fees to engage specialist design and spa consultants.

Operating costs: The business of spa treatments is inherently a one-on-one relationship. Add the administrative and support staff and the ratio increases to more than one member of staff to each guest. Consequently the ability to make a spa a successful business generally rests on the ability to diversify beyond providing treatments.

Economies of scale: Since the spa industry is a labour-intensive industry it is difficult to sell the services in more than one location without adding more human resources. Unlike fitness chains that can provide a room full of equipment to satisfy guests, spas that only provide treatments require suitably qualified therapists or need to find acceptable ways of offering treatments that do not require therapists.

The first stage before any comparisons can take place is to get acceptance and adoption of a uniform system of accounting. The hotel industry has a uniform system of accounts for the lodging industry that originated in the early 1920s. Today it is in its 10th edition.[2] This system has evolved over many years and became necessary in order to establish a commonly accepted system of accounting for auditing purposes, transparency of records and ability to be able to benchmark performance.

---

[2] Educational Institute of the Amer Hotel; 10 edn (November 2006) ISBN-10: 0866122826, ISBN-13: 978-0866122825.

One of the drawbacks to the spa industry is that until recently there has not been a consistent system of financial recording making it virtually impossible to compare the profitability of any two spas. This was addressed in 2004, with the first Uniform System of Financial Reporting for Spas being introduced by ISPA after 2 years of research.[3] This system was modelled on the system adopted by the hospitality industry and does an excellent job of explaining, detailing and categorising the financial analysis and reporting lines for a spa.

In this chapter we can observe how different spa categories define their business model by examining the different types of approach to recording expenses.

In a typical spa in the USA a profit and loss (P & L) format may look like Table 6.1. To make a spa profitable, the challenges of a potentially high capital outlay, high manpower requirements and low economies of scale need to be overcome. How each spa type tackles these obstacles is described below with each section examining the most common practices and approach to capital expenses and formatting of P & L statements.

The hotel spa

Some of the spas in hotels such as the Spa at Mandarin Oriental Hotel, New York, or the Spa at Sonoma Mission (operated by Fairmont) have become as famous as the hotel. By now most readers will have heard of at least one of the following hotel spas – Willow Stream (Fairmont), Bliss (Starwood) or Chi (Shangri La). And if the branded spa has not been heard of, then the spas in Ritz Carlton, Four Seasons and Mandarin Oriental are equally well known. These global hotels have become as well known for the quality of their spas as their guestrooms.

Hotel spas can be operated by the hotel operator (as above for example) or by a third party such as E'spa within the Peninsula group or Mandara in a number of branded hotels. This distinction is important because the return on investment (ROI) varies depending upon the management structure. This section will examine a typical spa that is operated by the hotel operator. The third party management agreement will be examined in the next section.

[3] Educational Inst of the Amer Hotel and ISPA; 1st edition (2005) **ISBN** 0-86612-264-8.

Table 6.1 Example of a Profit and Loss Statement

<table>
<tr><td colspan="3" align="center">Statement of Income</td></tr>
<tr><td></td><td colspan="2">Period</td></tr>
<tr><td></td><td>Current year</td><td>Prior year</td></tr>
<tr><td>Net revenue</td><td></td><td></td></tr>
<tr><td>Massage</td><td>$</td><td>$</td></tr>
<tr><td>Skin care</td><td></td><td></td></tr>
<tr><td>Hair</td><td></td><td></td></tr>
<tr><td>Nail</td><td></td><td></td></tr>
<tr><td>Fitness</td><td></td><td></td></tr>
<tr><td>F & B</td><td></td><td></td></tr>
<tr><td>Health and wellness</td><td></td><td></td></tr>
<tr><td>Memberships</td><td></td><td></td></tr>
<tr><td>Retail</td><td></td><td></td></tr>
<tr><td>Rentals and other</td><td></td><td></td></tr>
<tr><td>Other operating activities</td><td></td><td></td></tr>
<tr><td>Total net revenue</td><td></td><td></td></tr>
<tr><td>Cost of goods and direct expenses</td><td></td><td></td></tr>
<tr><td>Massage</td><td></td><td></td></tr>
<tr><td>Skin care</td><td></td><td></td></tr>
<tr><td>Hair</td><td></td><td></td></tr>
<tr><td>Nail</td><td></td><td></td></tr>
<tr><td>Fitness</td><td></td><td></td></tr>
<tr><td>F & B</td><td></td><td></td></tr>
<tr><td>Health and wellness</td><td></td><td></td></tr>
<tr><td>Retail</td><td></td><td></td></tr>
<tr><td>Other operating activities</td><td></td><td></td></tr>
<tr><td>Total direct expenses</td><td></td><td></td></tr>
<tr><td>Gross margin</td><td></td><td></td></tr>
<tr><td>Indirect expenses</td><td></td><td></td></tr>
<tr><td>Indirect operating expenses</td><td></td><td></td></tr>
<tr><td>Indirect support labour</td><td></td><td></td></tr>
<tr><td>Total indirect expenses</td><td></td><td></td></tr>
</table>

Table 6.1 (Continued)

Statement of Income		
	Period	
	Current year	**Prior year**
Undistributed operating expenses		
General and administrative		
Marketing		
Facility maintenance and utilities		
Total undistributed operating expenses		
Income before fixed charges		
Fixed charges		
Insurance		
Management fees		
Rent		
Real estate/personal property taxes		
Total fixed charges		
Income before depreciation and amortisation, interest expense and income taxes (EBITDA)		
Depreciation		
Amortisation		
Interest expense		
Gain and loss on disposal of property		
Income before income taxes		
Income taxes		
Net income	$	$

Source: Reproduced by the kind permission of ISPA and the Educational Institute of America: Uniform System of Financial Reporting for Spas, p. 20.

Tackling the capital costs in a hotel spa

The true ROI for the hotel spa is difficult to calculate for while it is generally acknowledged that the spa is likely to produce room bookings and extra spend in the hotel, there are no accurate methods of calculating this. In addition the relative importance to this question is minor in relation to the ROI on the overall spend for the project. For example if the hotel is costing US$150 million and the spa US$7.5 million then the spa investment represents 5% of the total. With revenues contributing about 2–4% of total hotel revenue it is understandable that not all investors require such a detailed breakdown of returns.

However, in recent years, there has been a noticeable change. Many global chains are either public companies or owned by asset management companies. Both types of owner require records of financial performance and the ability to be transparent with costs and returns. This has resulted in the need to look at every square metre of the hotel as an opportunity cost. Some hotel groups have attempted to determine the ROI on the spa whilst others have opted to look at the ROI on the business unit of the real estate rather than breaking it into individual components.

In recent years hotel groups with Global Spa Directors such as Fairmont, Starwood, Shangri La, Hyatt[4] and Mandarin Oriental have conducted research and established models to determine incremental revenue to the Rooms and F & B based on the presence of the spa. They vary in approach to methodology and how they use the information. In some cases a contribution is added outside of the spa P & L account to show incremental revenue to the hotel based on the spa presence in the hotel.

One approach is to calculate an overall ROI for the entire business entity with the spa being considered to be as much a part of the entire business model as the F & B operation, banquets or the hotel lobby all of which have standards used to create the hotel brand. Conference organisers will often choose a hotel based as much on the size of the pool and spa as the size of the meeting room space. Yet the same conference organisers will fill up the itinerary that gives delegates no time to use the pool or spa. Does this mean that the spa has not contributed towards the revenues for the hotel operation?

At Mandarin Oriental the ROI is calculated on the overall business need and is supported by an independent market survey to research the spending patterns between hotel guests using the spa against non-spa users. These surveys clearly show that the spa attracts more leisure guests and extends their length of stay.

In 2005, the typical spa guest in the USA spent around an extra $200 in room contribution (excluding their spending in

[4] Discussion with the Global Directors of Spas for these hotel groups from October to December, 2007.

the spa).[5] In just one hotel this could equate to an additional US$4 million in revenues to the hotel (and virtually all bottom line profit since it is predominantly extra room revenue). It is almost impossible to say if the spa attracted those guests and therefore was the cause to the additional revenue or if the big spenders in the hotel just happen to use the spa services. It does, however, provide some attempt at putting a monetary value on the ROI of a spa. It also provides the basis of a rudimentary ability to establish a suitable budget for the capital costs of a spa.

Smith Travel Research made an independent survey of the US luxury hotel market and confirmed that spas in luxury hotels contribute to the bottom line for the hotel. According to Smith Travel Research a premium of about $76 is added on to the average room night for a luxury hotel in the USA.[6] Although it is unlikely that this revenue would ever be recognised within the spa P & L statement it does help to explain why hotel spas can be 'state of the art' and offer outstanding designs. The justification for bigger budgets and the best designers on the spa can be based on the need to maintain an image to support the entire brand.

Tackling the operating costs in a hotel spa

Where the hotel and spa are operated under the same management there are a number of costs that may be termed central costs and therefore may not be allocated to the spa. In other words the hotel may be able to show the spa operating costs in a favourable position by non-allocation of the undistributed costs.

The normal set up for a hotel spa P & L is shown in Table 6.2. It includes various revenue line treatments, retail, membership, F & B, activities and others.

Notice how the expenses differ to those in Table 6.1. Although cost of sales and payroll are the same, the other operating costs differ. This table can look very different within each hotel since the allocation of costs will match the existing hotel system for other operating departments. Furthermore, the attitude to accounting may vary and the central costs may be treated differently. Cost associated for central services such as accounting, marketing, legal costs, public relations and sales costs may not always be allocated to the spa. In some properties the allocation

[5] ICLP survey 2005 for MOHG.

[6] Smith Travel Research – Finding for luxury hotels with and without spa 2007, presented by Jan Freitag at Global Spa Summit, NYC.

Table 6.2 Any spa, any town, anywhere

	Year 1
Revenue	US$
Massage	
Body treatments	
Facial treatments	
Beauty	
Manicure/pedicure	
Package	
Membership	
Retail (percentage of treatment revenue)	10%
Total revenue	
Total costs of goods sold	
Massage	7%
Body treatments	10%
Facial treatments	10%
Beauty	10%
Manicure/pedicure	10%
Retail	50%
Total costs of good sold	
Percentage of revenue	
Labour	
Total salaries	
Commission	10%
Training	2%
Employee benefits spa	
Total labour	
Percentage of revenue	
Operating expenses	
Linen	10%
Laundry	2%
Cleaning supplies	0.2%
Decoration	1%

Table 6.2 (Continued)

	Year 1
Guest supplies	1%
Electricity	7%
Printing and stationary	1%
Telephone	0.25%
Uniforms	
Travel + entertainment	1%
Dues/subscriptions	0.2%
Sales and marketing	2.5%
Maintenance	0.2%
Miscellaneous	3%
Total operating expenses	
Percentage of revenue	
Spa profit/loss	
Percentage of revenue	*8%*

of utilities such as water and electricity may also be omitted if they are not separately metered. Similarly, if the hotel operator man ages the spa it is unlikely that rent would be shown in the spa's P & L statement. Non-allocation of these expenses has the favourable effect on the net operating profit for a hotel spa when compared to any other type of spa operation.

Making a profit may only be one of a number of priorities for the hotel spa. The spa may be part a strategy to fill rooms and attract guests to the hotel. Whilst it does contribute a healthy profit, the award winning spa at the Mandarin Oriental in New York has found that spa promotions account for 40% of the publicity used to promote the hotel. The spa has also attracted favourable reports for the entire hotel and resulted in free advertising that cannot be valued on a P & L statement. Furthermore, the spa at New York is often full. The 2006 spa guest at the Mandarin Oriental, New York was likely to spend an additional $234 per day on their stay per night and contribute a massive $514 extra spend per night in the hotel (on room, F & B, etc.).[7]

[7] ICLP survey for MOHG 2007.

The spa has assisted the leisure mix of guests, extended the average length of stay, increased the sale of suites and altered the weekly occupancy patterns of the hotel. Where staff costs can be as high as 60% of revenues the marketing edge and ability to promote other parts of the business become crucial.

Some spas have attempted to reduce labour costs by charging guests to use unmanned areas such as thermal bathing facilities, fitness/gyms and pools or by introducing mechanically operated equipment such as massage chairs and floatation chambers. Whilst these may reduce staffing needs it is important to determine if this is acceptable for the quality your guests are seeking. Although labour costs are transparent and difficult to hide, a hotel spa can still appear profitable because many other indirect costs may not be applied. Other operating costs may be reduced to 10% of the overall revenue where costs can be centralised in the business operation.

Tackling economies of scale in a hotel spa

The start up costs of a branded hotel spa may be reduced because it can achieve an economy of scale based on replicating the group standards and best practices. The spa may benefit on division of labour, established capital costs and reduction of 'central' costs not attributed to the spa P & L. Then as the hotel chain develops, a database of human resources is built up and it may be possible to reduce the payroll in the area of recruitment costs based on internal transfer and career development programmes.

Third party management of the spa

A third party management agreement simply means that the owner of the hotel has opted for one party to manage the hotel operation and a third party to manage the spa operation. An example of this would be where the hotel owners of the Arts in Barcelona appoint Ritz Carlton group to manage the hotel and the Six Senses Spas group to manage the spa. Some examples of spa management companies that have international experience are E'spa, Mandara, Steiner, Angsana, Mspa, Six Senses, Raison d'Etre, Spatality and Spa Resources International LLC (based in Dubai).

There are many different types of arrangement between the three parties that can determine the ROI and business strategy.

Tackling the capital costs in third spas

In most cases (but not all) the owner of the hotel normally pays for the building and Fixtures, Fittings and Equipment Listing

(FF & E) of the spa. It would be very rare for the hotel operator to pay for any capital investment in the spa unless they have contracted a third party to manage the spa on their behalf.

If the owner wants to manage the return on their investment they can easily calculate the 'rent' on the space. The rent can be a fixed fee on the square footage provided or a split of the revenues and profits. In the USA or with American companies the fixed rent tends to be favoured whereas the European and Asian operations tend to favour the split of revenue and profit. The option taken can be looked at as an attitude to risk. The reason for hiring a third party is to reduce the risk and add value to the property. A current trend by the property market is to use a spa brand to leverage the retail prices on the properties by adding perceived value. The perceived value is that the property owner has access to the spa and possible health benefits the spa business offers.

In order to determine business viability and a suitable business model it is necessary to look at third party management contracts from three perspectives:

1. The owner of the property
2. The operator of the hotel
3. The operator of the spa.

In the event that the attitude to risk is the most likely determinant of the type of contract that is agreed then the business model may make the following generalisations:

1. The owner needs a third party to make his entire business enterprise successful. Profit in the spa may or may not be the primary objective.
2. The hotel operator wants no risk and no costs associated with the spa whilst trying to maximise on the positive aspect of promoting a spa and increasing room occupancies. The hotel group will be concerned that the spa operator meets the hotel operator's standards.
3. The spa operator recognises that they are in demand and want to minimise risks associated with their investment and effort. They also want to maximise their revenues as quickly as they can since they are vulnerable to an early exit strategy by the owner.

Unless the spa operator can remove their assets easily from the spa they are unlikely to want to invest in the operation. The spa operator can argue that the construction and FF & E are bespoke items that cannot be removed or reused elsewhere and therefore are a benefit and cost to the owner. The owner may argue that they do not have the skill to design and build a spa and therefore offer a shell and an opportunity to the spa operator.

The US model of a rent option provides the ability for both parties to factor in capital costs of the spa but it may be a more difficult agreement to assess fairly. There is little data available to calculate the kind of rental prices spas pay compared to the wealth of data available to determine shop floor rents. Consequently a shop floor rent is often the starting point for space negotiations. This may or may not be fair depending on the location of the spa. Shops are normally located in places of high passing traffic such as lobby and hotel public areas. Almost 100% of the hotel guests pass by the shops. Until recently spas seemed to be confined to the basement or back of house areas. Even well-performing spas may only attract 20–25% of the hotel guests and are expected to provide amenities free of charge such as fitness/gym, sauna, steam, etc. It is therefore irrelevant and illogical to apply the same kind of floor rent as a shop when looking at only the opportunity cost of the floor space.

The advantage of the US model rests with the owner by reducing the owner's risk entirely. The disadvantage of this system is that if the rent has been poorly set then the spa operator may suffer in times of difficulty and potentially fail with the business. There is little incentive for both parties to ensure success if one party is guaranteed to receive their income irrespective of performance. One option often taken to alleviate the higher start-up risk is to provide a rent holiday for an agreed period – possibly the first 6 months or first year. This allows the spa operator to establish and stabilise a business and still allows the owner to budget an ROI.

The advantage of the European/Asian model is that both parties have an incentive for the spa to succeed. It encourages dialogue between the parties and joint initiatives for the success of the spa. The disadvantage is that it is more difficult to forecast the ROI and the repayments of capital may differ to the income received.

Tackling the operating costs in third party spas

In the rent model all operating expenses are likely to fall on the spa operator. If the rent is a fixed item then the rental expenses will vary as a percentage of overall costs each month. The owner has passed all risk on to the spa operator and looks forward to a guaranteed rental payment. The parties have to make an agreement on central costs that are either absorbed or split so that the spa operator does not meet all the costs. These types of costs will be discussed in the next section.

In the revenue split agreement the spa operator may be able to pass on many and sometimes all the costs to the owner or the hotel operator. If the spa operator follows a similar contract to the hotel operator then they may be successful to negotiate either a paid royalty fee for managing the spa or a percentage of the revenue and a performance incentive based on the net operating profit. In this case the risk falls entirely on the owner. The spa operator has no assets invested in the spa and only their reputation at risk if they fail.

In Asia, the revenue split has a slightly different approach whereby the spa operator takes a higher proportion of the revenue but then meets nearly all the operating costs. There will still be negotiation over central costs but the labour, cost of sales and direct costs are debited from the spa operator revenues. The reason that this is still acceptable in Asia is mainly due to low labour costs that enable the business plan to succeed. This maybe why the Asian spa management companies are successful since they operate spas in low labour cost countries such as Thailand, Indonesia (Bali) and China whilst taking a more cautious approach in countries such as Hong Kong and Japan where labour costs are higher.

The spa management agreement may be directly between hotel owner and spa operator or it may be between hotel operator and spa operator. If the deal is done with the hotel operator, the spa operator may expect higher operating expenses because the hotel operator will charge for everything they can since they are not deriving any tangible[8] revenues out of the spa. There may be meters allocated to monitor utilities and costs loaded for marketing, administrative charges and storage space.

The operating costs are likely to be discussed with negotiations on items such as laundry, marketing, non-metered utilities, security, landscaping, administrative and financial support and storage. If the spa management company also produces products such as E'spa, Givenchy, La Prairie, then it will nearly always include the obligation to buy the branded products. There may be minimum quantity orders stipulated. These strategies help maximise the profitability for the spa management company and reduce their risk.

Spa management companies have various risks associated with any agreement to manage a spa on behalf of an owner. Although the preceding sections may indicate that the spa

---

[8] Note that the intangible revenues such as extra room revenue, F & B spend, extended stay, etc. are rarely considered since they are rarely accurately measured.

operator may have a low risk operation there are numerous other risks that can affect their business.

1. The spa operator may be required to sign an exclusivity agreement that restricts their business opportunities with a defined geographical region for a defined period.
2. The owner may plan to learn from the spa operator and then seek an early exit to the agreement. The spa operator will want to minimise this risk by recovering their costs as fast as possible.
3. The spa operator may be entirely dependent on the hotel business and have little opportunity to influence their business levels. This may be particularly relevant in a rent agreement where there is little association between hotel and spa operators.
4. The spa operator is often working in a country where all laws, customs and culture favour the local owner in the case of legal disputes and payment issues.

The spa operator may therefore request design fees, pre-opening technical fees, exit penalties, restrictions on hiring employees by the owner and using any other methods to protect their business (Table 6.3).

In conclusion, management companies can either take on, or try to pass on, the risk to another party. The risk is more likely to be accepted if the spa operator is very confident they can make a return on their investment quickly (within 2–3 years). With increasing competition amongst management companies and a developing bank of resource information, the typical contract of 5–10 years (with options to extend) has been under pressure and companies are accepting 3 years with extensions based on performance.

The revenue split scenario can take place where one of the obstacles of high capital costs, high labour costs or economies of scale can easily be overcome. It is therefore more likely to be prevalent in countries with low capital and low labour costs (hence the prevalence of management groups in Asia such Mspa, Six Senses, Angsana, Mandara Spas) or in places where there are large spa operations (see below).

Tackling economies of scale in third party spas

In the management fee agreement or royalty example, the spa business model is very different and economies of scale are reached by providing services to many owners at the same time. The centralised administration can provide the support

Table 6.3 Illustration of some different types of management agreements and allocation of revenue and expenses

Example Statement of Income

| | | Revenues and expenses allocation to spa operator | | |
		Revenue split	Management fee	Royalty
Net revenue	$			
	Total net revenue	65%	3–5%	None
Cost of goods and direct expenses		All	None	None
Gross margin				
Indirect expenses				
	Total indirect expenses	All	None	None
Undistributed operating expenses				
	General and administrative	Negotiated		
	Marketing	Negotiated		
	Facility maintenance and utilities	Negotiated		
	Total undistributed operating expenses	Negotiated	None	None
Income before fixed charges		100%	10–25% based on targets	None
Fixed charges				
	Management fees	None	None – as above	An agreed annual amount
	Rent	None/ negotiated	None/negotiated	None
	Real estate/personal property taxes	None	None	None
	Total fixed charges			

to many spas that benefit from centralised marketing, human resource support, training, media support, standards and product guidelines. The management fee allows spa management companies to capitalise on their expertise. However, spa management companies have to continually provide value for money since the temptation to cancel a contract is high once the owner feels he has learnt everything from the spa management company.

Mandara spas that operate from an Asian base are a very good example of how a management company can deploy these strategies to their advantage. One of the biggest success strategies was to work in countries with low labour costs combined with the ability to charge tourist prices for treatments to a captive market (see Chapter 9).

The large spa

In this section the definition of a large spa is any spa with more than 20 treatment rooms. There are relatively few such spas and the most likely place to find them is where there is a large captive audience such as at mega resorts, casinos, cruise ships or city shopping malls. The really big spas can be found at entertainment destinations such as Las Vegas and Macau. The Venetian hotel in Las Vegas has 3000 guestrooms and a Canyon Ranch spa. The Medinat Jumeirah resort in Dubai has 3 hotel properties on one site and a 33 treatment room spa. Similarly Elounda in Crete has approximately 900 rooms and a thalassa spa with 22 treatment rooms.

Tackling the capital costs of large spas

Often the operator of the spa is not the owner of the premises, as is the case with Canyon Ranch in the Venetian, Las Vegas or International Leisure Consultants (ILC) in the Venetian, Macau. The first step is to therefore agree on the size of space and who will pay for the fit out of the spa. In simple terms the arrangements and line items are similar to those of the rental agreement in the previous section. The common scenario is that the spa operator will be required to make an investment into the spa.

Although the capital costs may be high they are justified by an expectation of a high volume of guests. The ratio of treatment rooms to other facilities must therefore be balanced out. There are likely to be more revenue streams. Membership fees may form a significant part of the revenue line whereas in smaller spas there may not be the facilities to offer a membership. Large spas are able to add facilities based on economies of scale where volume makes the activity viable, such as retail, F & B, gyms, memberships and teacher led group activities such as yoga, Pilates, aerobics. The Canyon Ranch club at the Venetian boasts 69 000 square feet (6400 square metre) with 62 treatment rooms and over 120 activities.[9] The spa at the Venetian Macau will grow to 85 000 square feet under the management of ILC.

Casino spas have another unique advantage. In the casino there is a 24-hour operation which actively works to encourage guests to disregard the normal patterns of daytime activity. The spa is therefore able to extend operating hours and revenue potential.

Due to the volume of business in a large spa, the incremental revenues from retail sales, F & B and activities can contribute more to the profit line without higher staffing. Classroom activities such as yoga may attract a higher number of participants simply because the spa has a greater volume of customers. The net result will be that the fixed costs of the spa will reduce as a percentage of the revenue and the capability for income before fixed charges will increase as a percentage of total revenue.

Tackling economies of scale of large spas

A large spa is able to achieve economies of scale by better distribution of the fixed costs. Whilst the division of labour on the treatment side of the business is untouched the division of labour in class activities and administration becomes viable and consequently the payroll and benefits become a lower percentage of the overall revenue. Although actual figures are difficult to obtain one report from Macau has estimated payroll of a casino spa to be 25% of total revenues compared to 36% for a nearby hotel spa.[10]

Destination spa

Destination spas are built with the primary purpose of providing spa/wellness activities for guests. Think of locations such as Champneys, UK; Chiva Som, Thailand; Peurta La Rancha, Mexico and Canyon Ranch, Tucson USA. For a hotel the

[9] See www.canyonranch.com/spaclubs/las-vegas.
[10] Anecdotal evidence in conversations with two spa directors in Macau October/November 2007.

105

primary purpose of business is selling rooms and the spa is a support service. In a destination spa the primary purpose of business is the activities and the rooms are built to support this. Consequently, the business plan for destination spas is likely to be a part of the business plan for the entire entity. The Uniform System of Financial Reporting for Spas does not cover destination spas as a business entity.

Almost every destination spa is able to hide the true cost of the spa within the overall cost of the business. The destination spa wraps up meals, resort activities and some form of treatment in a package with the room. Chiva Som, Thailand (www.chivasom.com is a good example where bookings are made by selecting your retreat and then choosing a room. All retreats are priced the same and include:

- Three Chiva-Som Spa Cuisine meals per night of stay.
- Choice of daily massage per night of stay.
- Health and Wellness Consultation on arrival.
- Participation in the daily fitness and leisure activity programme.
- Complimentary use of the Water Therapy Suite which includes Steam, Sauna and Jacuzzi.

This type of programme exists in many other destination spas such as Champneys, in the UK (www.champneys.com) and Miraval in the US (www.miravalresort.com).

Destination spas benefit through achievement of efficient distribution of labour by providing multi-revenue options in rooms, F & B, retail, guaranteed treatments and activities. Additionally they have economies of scale by attracting guests with the objective of engaging in activities they offer, whereas a hotel attracts guests that may or may not use the spa. Whilst they may have higher capital costs for spa equipment in relation to other types of spa, they are more likely to get better utilisation of the equipment since it is programmed into activities for guests rather than provided as an option.

Day spas

Perhaps the most transparent form of spa business is a operator-owned day spa. The entire business plan can be observed without hidden costs. The day spa operation may be considered as one of the most difficult operations to succeed in the spa business.

Perhaps two of the most globally well-known day spa operations are the sanctuary in Covent Garden, London (www.the-sanctuary.co.uk/) and Cleopatra's Day spa in the Wafi Centre, Dubai (http://wafi-health-leisure.com/wafiH&L/PH&L.asp).

The Sanctuary has its famous pool in the centre of London while Cleopatra's has an Egyptian theme located in a pyramid and many innovative attractions such as a vitality pool with countercurrent for swimming. These spas may be considered state of the art and has been in existence for over 10 years.

Tackling the capital costs of day spas

Even these successful day spas have a business plan that involves more than just spa treatments to survive. Although their business accounts are not open for public viewing it should be noted that the Sanctuary took several years to become profitable. It now derives the most significant income from Sanctuary products.

The Sanctuary in Covent Garden is a ladies only spa formed in 1987. Despite excellent publicity it took more than 5 years for a profit to be shown. Today it has a turnover in excess of GBP £6 million and is a thriving business. A strategic choice was taken more than a decade ago to protect against down swings in the day spa business by moving away from management contracts of which it had originally started.

Cleopatra's Spa at the Wafi Centre is also a successful day spa that has been operating since 1998.[11] The construction was part of a larger commercial development that included shops, apartments and entertainment.

Tackling the operating costs of day spas

Without a doubt the most genuine P & L account likely to be seen in the spa business will be from a day spa. There are normally no other places to distribute costs and therefore the true cost of operations will be shown.

Even the most successful day spa operators required perseverance to succeed and have needed to diversify in order to continue. Product companies such as La Prairie and Givenchy operate 'day spas' in many locations around the world. They would probably not be considered state of the art spas using the definition in this introduction. Visit any one of the spas and observe that the typical layout is one with a large retail, fairly small treatment rooms and virtually no other facilities. In the case of these spas (or salons) the primary purpose is to sell the products. Treatments in these spas enable the client to 'test' the product and receive expert advice.

[11] Information supplied by the current owners – Leisure Resources Middle East.

State of the art innovations may have a place in a day spa if the business is able to charge guests for their use – such as use of thermal suites or swimming pools. A day spa operation rests critically with the management of payroll costs.

The income before fixed charges is not the final determinant for a successful business for a day spa. Even in countries with low labour costs the capital costs and the rent need to be carefully considered. Tax, capital and interest repayments need to be factored in to the cash flow to succeed. Cash flow management becomes one of the biggest differentiators between this type of spa operation and any other.

Tackling economies of scale of day spas

Successful day spa operators have realised that economies of scale are difficult to achieve if the company relies on treatments. Even in countries with low labour costs it is difficult to find a day spa operation that has state of the art facilities comparable with a luxury hotel spa.

The Sanctuary at Covent Garden is able to support the upkeep of state of the art facilities in central London because it created a unique and interesting concept that was considered ahead of its time and had the competitive advantage for many years. Today it has the financial support of a company that has switched its prime business to retailing spa products based on the spa at Covent Garden.

Cleopatra's Spa prospered by adding a membership, good F & B services created with nutritional guidance. In 1999 an International Beauty Commercial training centre was added and in 2000, Spa Resources International LLC was created by diversifying their business to a consultancy group that covers project and design consultancy, product distribution, recruitment and operational management contracts.[11]

In late 2007, Champneys from the UK announced plans to roll out a day spa operation loosely based on their destination spa experience with a target of 50 spas over the next 5 years. In an interview in *Spa Business Magazine*[12] they state that retail will play an important role in the success of these spas. It is also worth observing that their model does not include 'state of the art' facilities such as thermal suites or relaxation.

[12] *Spa Business Magazine* (2008) Vol. 1, p. 19.

Conclusions

The main conclusions to be drawn from this chapter are:

1. Successful 'state of the art' spas are most likely to be found in a business where the spa is a support service. Most state of the art spas start as a support service that provides an attraction to the core business.
2. The success of a state of the art spa business plan should be determined from the success of the entire business enterprise of which the spa is supporting.
3. The spa industry has categories of spa that have a different way of reporting the financial performance of the spa.
4. A system for establishing standardised formats for accounting and auditing purposes has only been launched since 2005. It is therefore difficult to accurately compare spa profitability.
5. The spa industry is a service industry that has a large human resource component in relation to the services that are offered. Reliance purely on treatment revenue is rarely sufficient to sustain a business for a long term.
6. With the exception of day spas, the ROI is not normally taken into account since the spa is part of a bigger business entity.
7. Where spa services are the core business, successful spa companies diversify and offer more than just treatments.
8. Standards, legislation and scrutiny from the financial industry will improve the state of the spa industry and eventually create a recognised system to determine the ROI for a spa.

CHAPTER 7

Spa feasibility: Steps and processes

Richard Dusseau and Mathew W. Brennan

Understanding the competitive marketplace

The spa industry in the USA and internationally is one of the fastest growing and most constantly innovating in history. In the last year, 15% of the US population visited a spa, and that number is only increasing each year (International Spa Association, 2006). Because of the significant industry diversity and fast-moving market trends, competitive spa research and feasibility have become an important piece in the development of a competitive spa business.

Identifying competitors for a spa requires the spa to predetermine its exact positioning and segmentation within the industry. Segmentation within the spa industry allows consumers to identify the types of services they would like to experience. As the spa industry matures and expands spas are targeting specific consumers through targeted services and marketing. Examples of Industry Segmentations include (International Spa Association, 2004):

- *Day Spa (Definition)*: A spa offering a variety of professionally administered spa services to clients on a day use basis.
  - Days Spas represent about three-quarters of the industry.
  - They are the smallest spas in terms of square feet (typically only 3500 square feet on average).
  - They are among the lower revenue generating types of spas.
- *Medical Spa (Definition)*: Individuals, solo practices, groups, and institutions comprising medical and spa professionals whose primary purpose is to provide comprehensive medical and wellness care in an environment with integrated spa services, as well as conventional and complementary therapies and treatments.
  - Medical Spas are the fastest growing spa segment.
  - They generate the least amount of revenue.

- *Resort/Hotel Spa (Definition)*: A spa owned by and located within a resort or hotel providing professionally administered spa services, fitness and wellness components, and spa cuisine menu choices.
  - Resort Spas are typically larger (on average 21 100 square feet) and offer more services.
  - They also have the highest priced spa treatments, compared to other spa categories.

The remaining chapter will focus on spas located within hotel and resorts that also provide guestroom accommodations.

However, many of the principles discussed also apply to Day Spas and Medical Spas.

The financial impact of spas

Building a spa is one way hotels and resorts can increase revenue from reaching hotel guests, whether on business or leisure, as well as the local population. If built and managed correctly, a spa will add revenue to a hotel's bottom line by allowing an increase in room rates, which in turn increase revenue per available room, or RevPAR. Figures 7.1 and 7.2 were compiled by Smith Travel Research and presented at the 4th Annual Cornell Spa Symposium which display the dramatic effect a spa has on both average daily rate (ADR) and average property occupancy.

Figure 7.1 displays the positive impact that a spa has on average occupancy. Average property occupancy dramatically increases after a spa has opened.

Figure 7.2 displays the positive impact that a spa has on ADR. ADR increases by nearly $50 just due to a full service spa facility. Even though cost of construction continues to rise, making spas more expensive to develop, a developer or hotelier will still realize a positive return on investment due to increases in ADR and average property occupancy.

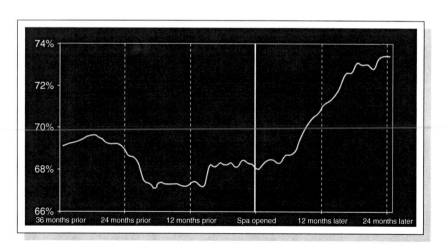

Figure 7.1
Luxury hotels with spa (in occupancy percent compared to open date)

Surveying the competitive marketplace

Before a spa is built it is advisable to perform a detailed feasibility study. Areas to be considered when developing a quality spa facility are the facility design and its size, the treatment spaces and treatments offered, the pricing strategy and amenities, and the level of quality which is to be maintained throughout the facility in order to create a loyal client base.

Spa facility

A spa facility is defined by a space that is designed and created to serve the particular function and service of spa-related activities. The entire spa facility is typically measured in square units, feet or meters, depending on the region in which it operates. When measuring a spa facility it typically includes both revenue generating and non-revenue generating spaces. A revenue generating space is an area which is programmed and used to deliver revenue generating services, or in the case of a spa, treatments. Most often these spaces include spa treatment-rooms, retail space, and a food and beverage outlet. A non-revenue generating space is an area which serves as an added amenity to the spa. These spaces do not provide any direct revenue, but they create added value to the spa and can, therefore, drive higher treatment pricing. Non-revenue generating spaces include saunas, stream

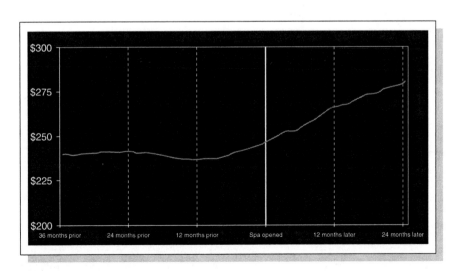

Figure 7.2
Luxury hotels with spa (in ADR $) compared to open date

rooms, changing rooms, relaxation areas, whirlpools, and any other areas which are open to spa guests as part of a service, but are not sellable areas within the spa. These two types of spaces combine to encompass the entire spa facility.

Some spaces within a spa are not included within the measurement of the spa facility because they are not considered within the definition of a 'spa'. Examples of these types of areas include: fitness centers, pools, and gardens. These are areas which are not directly related to the spa or its services and should not be included when measuring the size of a spa facility. Many times these areas are located in close proximity or even within the spa, making them difficult to separate.

Treatment-rooms/treatment spaces

A treatment space or treatment-room is generally designed to serve a specific purpose or treatment. Treatment-rooms can be rented out numerous times throughout the day, making revenue per treatment-room (RevPAT) higher than revenue per available hotel guestroom (RevPAR) (Wohlberg and Foster, 2006). Typically, a moderate to large size spa will have different treatment-rooms for massage treatments, facial treatments, manicures and pedicures, hydrotherapy services, and sometimes will even have separate rooms for couples and beauty services.

Number of treatments offered

A treatment is a service or application intended to relieve illness or injury, tension and stress, remove toxins from the body, improve physical functions and appearance, and provide general wellness through internal balance and external relaxation. Treatments typically offered at a spa include massages, facials, body treatments, and nail care. These treatments vary greatly and are many times combined in multi-treatment packages. Treatment menus are an area for spas to stand out from their competitors, provide innovation, and develop a competitive advantage though a particular story, menu concept, and positioning.

Treatment pricing

The price of a service or treatment is similar to the pricing strategy in any other industry. It is affected by demand, supply, economic stability, inflation, and the location of the market in which it is sold, making the price variable.

The price of a spa treatment is determined by:

- therapist compensation;
- the price of the professional used during the service;
- demand for treatment;
- controllable operating expenses of the spa.

The price of spa treatments will also vary based on the primary and secondary competitive markets in which the spa operates. The cost of living within the market in which the spa is located, known as the primary competitive environment, will determine the disposable income of the market population. Treatment pricing will vary to accommodate this disposable income. Additionally, the pricing strategy will change to compete with other spas that demonstrate a similar competitive advantage or serve a similar niche market.

Facility amenities

Within a hotel or resort, the amenity platform, which includes all non-room-related services such as food and beverage outlets, recreation, and spa and wellness departments, can support a higher average daily room rate. Similarly, the hotel rate can become a driver for the amenities that need to be provided. For instance, guests who pay a higher rate on a room are more inclined to spend additional discretionary dollars on the property's outlets and recreation services. This remains true within a spa. Spa pricing is partially contingent on the number of value-added amenities provided, which will change significantly depending on the size of the spa. However, spa amenities also include other value-added services like fitness centers, healthy cafes, yoga studies, and lifestyle programs.

Quality of facility

The quality of a spa should mirror the quality of the resort or hotel in which it is located. If it is a five star hotel, the spa must reflect that quality. Therefore, the space allocated to public areas and the finishes used throughout the facility must be parallel to that of the resort or hotel. Additionally, the brand of the hotel will provide perceived quality to the spa through its own brand equity.

Elements of a quality spa facility include:

- attention to interior design, increasing guest relaxation;
- transition areas and generous public spaces;

- multiple relaxation areas:
  - outdoor/indoor;
- environmental controls for guest comfort;
- a spa concept which is parallel to the design of the spa facility.

Quality of service

The quality of a spa's service is the most important component of operating a profitable spa. It is an intangible quality that has the ability to generate guest satisfaction and greatly increase the sense of a quality, valued experience. Because spas operate within the leisure industry, they are held to the highest expectation of quality. Spas not only need to train employees on spa services, protocols, and techniques like spa treatments and wellness trends, employees should also be educated on product lines, so that staff are knowledgeable about what to use on specific guest's skin types and how to offer the product for home use once the treatment is finished.

An important part of customer service in a spa is turning a visitor into a returning client. Implementing a system for customer recognition aids in developing this customer base. Supporting technology, like CRM (Customer Relationship Management) systems, help spas keep track of vital customer information. (The CRM Association (crmassociation.org) is a helpful resource for understanding the implementation, development, and use of CRM.) These preferences can include anything from a gender preference for their therapist, to skin type, product choice, favorite scents and music, or special dates like anniversaries and birthdays. This helps the spa take a much more personalized approach to pleasing each specific guest and maintaining a long-term relationship.

How to determine a competitive advantage

The information that is collected in relation to spa size and hotel size can be analyzed in a few ways to generate statistics that can be used to compare facilities across the industry. The following example is not representative of any particular market, it is a fictional example used only for the purpose of demonstrating the following principles.

Spa One

Spa One is located in a large hotel with 226 guestrooms. The spa is 40 000 square feet, with 30 treatment-rooms. Its treatment menu has 69 total treatments including 16 massages, 9 facials, 15 body treatments, and 4 nail care services.

Spa Two

Spa Two is located in a smaller boutique hotel with 29 guestrooms. The spa is 2000 square feet, with 8 treatment-rooms. Its menu has 20 total treatments including 3 massages, 7 facials, 4 body treatments, and 2 nail care services.

Some spa services are not included within the totals in the Spa One and Two examples above. This is because they are not directly spa related to the spa's services (i.e. waxing, hair services, and makeup). However, they are included in the total treatment count within these examples because they are a part of the spa's menu.

Tables 7.1–7.3 represent the breakdown of the competitive information related to the two example spas and their competitors. The data set titled: 'Competitive Set Averages,' represents the respective averages within the competitive market in which these two spas operate; they are a snapshot of the market to illustrate what is offered. It is calculated by surveying the properties within the area for vital statistics, like total number of treatment-rooms within the spa, spa square feet, and total number of guestrooms within the property, then calculating the industry average for that particular competitive market.

When analyzing the size of a facility, averages help to compare one spa to all the others within a particular competitive

Table 7.1 Competitive set averages and facility size

Name	Treatment-room/guestroom ratio	Square feet per treatment	Guest rooms	Spa square footage	Treatment-rooms
Spa One	0.13	1333	226	40 000	30
Spa Two	0.28	250	29	2000	8
Competitive set averages	0.10	1136	111	12 500	11

Table 7.2 Competitive set averages and number of treatments

Name	Massages	Body treatments	Facials	Nail services	Total treatments
Spa One	16	15	9	4	69
Spa Two	3	4	7	2	20
Competitive set averages	8	8	7	3	36

market. In Table 7.1, it is easy to tell that Spa One is larger than the average in this particular competitive environment when comparing size of the hotel, size of the spa, and the number of treatment-rooms. Spa Two is smaller than average in all of these areas.

Additionally, using this facility size information, two very important size comparison figures can be calculated: square footage per treatment-room and the treatment-room to guestroom ratio. Square footage per treatment-room is a ratio that displays the total square footage of the spa facility to the number of treatment-rooms. The luxury standard for this calculation is 1000 square feet per treatment-room. It should be noted that this calculation takes into account the total spa facility's size. Treatment-room to guestroom ratio is used in hotels to determine the number of treatment-rooms required. If the spa facility has too many treatment-rooms, the rooms will sit idle and will negatively impact the spa's profitability. On the other hand, if the spa facility offers too few treatment-rooms, the spa will not be able to accommodate high demand which will also negatively impact the bottom line.

Many times the size of the facility dictates the number of treatments the spa can offer. The following chart is a break-down of the number of treatments offered by each spa compared to the competitive average.

In Table 7.2, it can be seen that Spa One offers significantly more treatments than Spa Two, this is because it not only has more treatment-rooms to provide more services, but also because it has a lower treatment-room to guestroom ratio, putting each room at a higher demand. Table 7.3 shows the pricing structure within the competitive market and how each example compares.

Table 7.3 Competitive set averages and pricing

Name	50 minute massage	80 minute massage	50 minute facial	80 minute facial	Basic body scrub	Basic mani cure	Basic pedicure
Spa One	$155	$295	$155	$255	$135	$65	$85
Spa Two	$125	$195	$135	$175	$115	$40	$55
Competitive set averages	$141	$213	$141	$190	$132	$58	$70

Note: Spa menus are typically very similar when broken down. Most will offer massages in 25, 50, and 80 minute intervals; facials in 50 and 80 minute intervals; and at least one basic manicure and one basic pedicure. These times can fluctuate depending on the spa, but will be based on a similar structure. This makes comparisons on a price point basis much simpler.

When developing a competitive pricing strategy, the spa must consider the market positioning it wants to support and base treatment pricing on the competitive marketplace. It can be seen in Table 7.3 that Spa One is positioned at a higher price than the average spa in the competitive market in which it operates, while Spa Two is positioned at a lower price point. This can greatly affect the quality expectations for the spa.

Developing an accurate business model

Developing an accurate business model based on specific assumptions and industry data is the foundation of the feasibility process. An accurate business model will allow the potential business owner or investors to determine a return on investment as well as provide the operator of the facility annual forecasts and targets to achieve and measure against. Because spa facilities have increased in demand and popularity, they are becoming sustainable business models within hotel/resort developments generating revenue and profit that can increase overall property performance. Business models should include either 5, 10, 20 year projections depending on the type and scope of the project.

Because facilities vary in size, cost, forecasted revenue and strategy, business models will differ in calculating a reasonable return on investment.

Business models must be based on data gathered through due diligence, and must be project and location specific. The following sections will specifically describe all the data needed and the process in how to develop a business model from the ground up.

Accurately estimating spa demand

Accurately estimating the demand for spa services and treatments is the most important aspect when developing a business plan. If the estimated number of guests using a spa is too aggressive or too conservative, the business model will be inaccurate, resulting in an unprofitable operation. To estimate spa demand, one must be familiar with property specific demand indicators. Important demand indicators include:

- *Property size*: The number of available guestrooms within the hotel/resort. Guestrooms, also known as 'Keys', include standard rooms, guest suites, and any additional condo and residential units available for rental.
- *Property type*: The property classification, brand affiliation, urban, resort, destination, luxury, or others.
- *Average annual occupancy*: The percent of time all keys are being occupied by property guests.
- *Number of guests per occupied room*: The number of guests staying in each occupied room. Please note that this number may be above 2.0 if the property offers a large supply of condominium/residential units available for rental.

Once all of this data is collected, the following formula should be used to determine the total number of available guests the spa facility could capture for spa treatments and services.

Number of available guests = Number of keys available annually × Annual occupancy percentage × Number of guests per occupied room*

Once the total number of guests available is determined, the next piece of information needed to accurately estimate guest demand is the type of guests staying on the property; group, transient, or others. This information is important to collect from the property and will be a determining factor of the average number of daily guests the spa facility can expect to capture. The percentage of guest types will differ based on property location and type. For example, an urban property based around a convention center will have a higher percentage of group guests than a luxury urban property which will capture a high amount of transient or leisure travelers.

When the total number of guests by type is determined, the next step is to estimate spa demand by guest type. Table 7.4 displays historical observed capture rate ranges by guest type from full service spa facilities. Full service spa facilities include value-added amenities located within a dedicated spa facility. If the property can only offer a small spa facility with no value-added amenities or only in-room spa services, capture rates will be reduced. These percentages should only offer a starting point in the process and will need to be tailored based on project specific parameters.

Historical spa capture rates

Transient travelers offer the best opportunity for a spa facility to capture guests as they are less time sensitive and are looking to experience property amenities (Dusseau). Group guests are more time sensitive and are primarily business travelers who are less likely to purchase spa treatments and services (Dusseau, 2008). Luxury spa facilities have the best opportunity to capture transient and group spa guests. Because groups of guests staying at luxury properties are generally smaller in size than business groups and they are more familiar with spa services. In addition, luxury properties capture more transient guests for spa services because they are more familiar with spas and generally evaluate a spa facility when determining where to stay (Table 7.4).

The following formula can be used to determine the number of estimated guests who will use the spa while staying at the property:

Number of spa guests = (Number of available group guests × Group spa capture rate) + (Number of available transient guests × Transient spa capture rate)*

Depending on the property, spa facilities also have the opportunity to capture spa guests from additional guest segments. These segments include local, residential, and facility membership. All three of these segments as well as any additional project specific guest segments must be analyzed to determine adequate and reasonable capture rates. Some important data that must be considered is: the number of competitive spa facilities in the area, residential living patterns (i.e. are residential guests only there for a quarter to a half of a season), and the number of members belonging to the fitness, golf, or the social component of the property.

Table 7.4 Property classification against business groups and transient guests

Property classification	Group (%)	Transient (%)
Urban property (100–500 guestrooms)	2–8	8.0–18
Urban (group house) (1000 + guestrooms	1–3	5.0–7
Resort (spa as primary or secondary amenity)	6–14	8.0–20
Highly rated (ADR $350+)	8–20	15.0–30

These different guest segments, although they are not the primary guest segment of a hotel or resort spa, offer the spa the ability to drive traffic into the spa facility during low demand periods, minimizing operational inefficiencies. Strong marketing campaigns and other sales techniques should be utilized to increase awareness of the spa facility within the local marketplace. These segments can make up anywhere between 5% and 50% of the total spa guest capture depending on the location of the property (Dusseau, 2008).

Accurately estimating potential revenue

Although a spa primarily functions as a space where spa guests purchase spa treatments and services, there are other potential revenue centers located within a spa facility. This section will discuss the typical revenue centers, as well as additional revenue centers, that when placed in a spa facility can increase the profitability of the facility.

Spa treatments

Upon determining the estimated annual number of spa guests by guest segment, the next step in the business plan creation process is to determine the services these guests will be purchasing. Figure 7.3 displays typical spa treatment capture rates.

Spa treatment capture rates will be highly dependent on geographic location and may need to be adjusted. The following

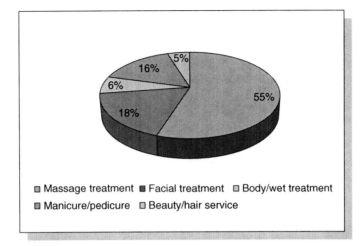

Figure 7.3
Typical treatment capture percentages

□ Massage treatment ■ Facial treatment □ Body/wet treatment
□ Manicure/pedicure □ Beauty/hair service

formula can be used in determining the estimated number of spa treatments purchased by treatment type.

Number of massage treatments = Number of spa guests
purchased   × Number of treatments
                            purchased per spa guest
                            × Massage treatment
                            capture percentage*

When the estimated number of treatments is determined, take the decision upon pricing strategy for the proposed spa program, and complete the formula to determine the amount of revenue to be generated by each treatment type. The average treatment pricing may be lower or greater than that of the competitive set depending upon the strategy chosen. In addition, if the property is anticipating offering a high number of express spa treatments to cater to the group segment, treatment pricing may fall below average to reflect that scenario.

Additional spa revenue centers

In addition to generating spa revenue through the sale of spa treatments and services, spa facilities have the ability to generate spa revenue through additional services. Additional spa revenue centers may include retail sales, spa food and beverage sales, general health and wellness services, facility day access, fitness services, and spa membership programs.

Due to an increase in demand for general health and wellness services and the desire of many spa guests to bring the spa experience home, spa facilities have the opportunity to offer these additional services and products to guests. Each one of these aspects needs to be examined based on property specific parameters.

Retail revenue should always be included when estimating gross spa revenue. Retail sales offer spa facilities the opportunity to add incremental revenue provided that the retail program is correctly designed and the staff receives appropriate training. According to industry averages, retail revenue can vary between 10% and 50% of total treatment revenue.

Accurately estimating payroll and operating expenses

The most variable aspect of a business plan for a spa facility is operational costs and payroll. It is important that operational costs and payroll be calculated independently, including all necessary costs and staff requirements to operate the spa facility. If all associated costs are not considered, the net profit margin and the cash flow projections will be inaccurate, leading to an inaccurate estimate of return on investment. This section will outline how to create a operational budget and staffing guideline for a spa facility.

Cost of sales

Cost of sales is defined as the cost to the facility for purchasing retail product, treatment product, and treatment supplies used when administering spa treatments. In addition, cost of sales should include any cost of purchasing food and beverage items for sale. The cost to the facility for purchasing retail product must also account for shipping and handling, although this figure may differ depending on facility location and the amount of tax charged for importing/exporting. Figure 7.4 displays the average cost of each treatment by type.

These percentages include the cost of treatment product and supplies used when administering spa treatments and are calculated from the revenue produced by each treatment type. Massage treatments generally have the lowest cost of sales. Facial and body or wet treatments cost the most to perform because they are the most product intensive. Total cost of treatment should range anywhere from 3% to 12% of total treatment sales and is also dependent upon property location and the ability to use indigenous ingredients.

Operating expenses

There are numerous costs associated with operating a full service spa facility that must be considered. Such costs are laundry, facility cleaning, advertising, and general guest supplies

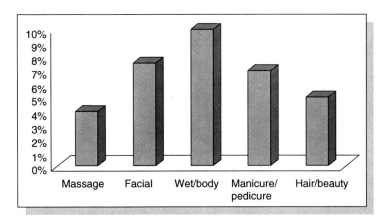

Figure 7.4
Cost of Percent of
treatment sales

for the locker rooms. In addition, other expenses that will be incurred are linen replacement, cleaning supplies, equipment maintenance or replacement, facility decorations, printing and stationary, staff education and continuous training, office supplies, complimentary services, spa software licensing fee, uniform replacement, membership and associations, insurance, telephone and Internet and postage and magazine subscriptions for relaxation and waiting room areas. It is important to look at the monthly costs of each line item when analyzing the forecast amount and determine if that amount is enough to run the type of spa facility being built. When creating an operational budget for a spa facility, it is extremely important to include all costs so that a correct business plan can be created. Depending upon facility size, total operational expenses typically fall somewhere between 12% and 25% of gross revenue, if the facility is properly managed.

Staffing

There are many different positions needed to run a spa facility. They include Facility Director, Facility Supervisors, Front Desk Agents, Reservations Agents, and Facility Attendants. In addition, staffing may be required for other areas such as Fitness Attendants, Juice Bar/Café Attendants, Retail Associates, and Spa Concierge. Staffing must be considered during the development process because it plays an important role in the profitability of a spa facility. If staffing is not adequately managed once the spa is operational and staffing issues are not resolved immediately, the spa will more than likely perform poorly. Total payroll and related expenses in profitably operating facilities can be anywhere between 20% and 70% depending

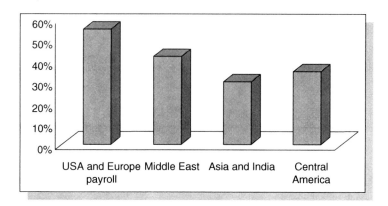

Figure 7.5
Total salaries and wages by region

on the region which highly influences pay rates. Figure 7.5 displays observed industry payroll averages based on geographic location.

Please note that percentages are of gross spa revenue. Gross spa payroll will differ depending on the country and geographic location, for example, payroll in developing countries is much less than in the developed world and payroll in major cities is much higher than payroll in the secondary cities and towns. Staffing wages and salaries should reflect regional staffing wages, both for salary and hourly employees. It is important to analyze the competitive marketplace to determine the correct salaries and wages.

Therapist and service provider pay rates will also vary based on property location. When forecasting therapist payroll it is important to understand the different ways therapists can be compensated (see Chapter 22). Therapists can be compensated on a commission structure only, where they receive a percentage of all treatments performed by them that week or that day. Therapists under this type of compensation package are generally hired on a contract basis during high demand periods and do not receive benefits. Other therapists are paid an hourly wage, and then also receive a certain percentage of revenue from treatments performed in the form of a commission structure. Commission structures for therapists under this compensation package will vary based on the therapists' qualifications. Top performing therapists who are qualified will generally be salaried employees receiving an agreed upon wage. In addition to all of the above compensation options, therapists may also receive gratuities from clients satisfied with the treatment administered. When creating a staffing guideline for a business plan, it is important to determine what compensation package is chosen and forecast accordingly. In addition to salaries and wages, spa staff can also be offered incentives to sell specific treatments or retail products to spa guests.

The bottom line

If all the above steps are followed and revenues, operational costs and staffing requirements are considered, the business plan should determine the net operating profit for the spa facility. Estimated cash flows generated from general business operations can be used to determine a return on investment. It is important that all of these levels be built and analyzed, not from a financial perspective but from an operations perspective, in order that revenues, costs, and staffing are closely analyzed to make certain they are realistic and attainable.

Facility design, construction, and appropriate space planning based on demand indicators

There are many factors that influence the architectural program for a spa and how the space is used within the facility (see Chapter 8. It is critical that the architectural program be dictated by the demand study and includes the proper space allocation for amenities and revenue generating spaces such as treatment-rooms, studios, and retail store.

Maximizing the amount of direct or indirect revenue generating space should be the objective of the architectural program. There are a multitude of factors which influence these allocations such as the cost of construction in a specific location, pedestrian access for retail or potential day-spa business, construction restrictions due to pre-existing building conditions, and schematic adjacencies. All of these factors influence the development of the architectural program and allocation of space within the spa.

The number of treatment-rooms has a direct impact on the ability of the spa to generate revenue. Designating the number of treatment-rooms as well as the type of treatment-room, such as couples, suites, wet, facial and dry or massage, should be influenced by the proposed treatment and service menu that supports the positioning and specific market segment the spa is designed to attract. The exact number of treatment-rooms, by type, should support a targeted annualized occupancy between 50% and 65% once the business has stabilized. This target occupancy will allow for maximum usage or 100% occupancy comparatively, during peak periods of high demand when the spa experiences peak compression and treatment-room utilization is maximized.

In addition to the direct revenue generating spaces such as treatment-rooms and the retail store, it is important not to overlook the value-added spaces such as changing rooms, transitional spaces, relaxation lounges, and possibly wet areas or thermal circuits. These spaces enhance the spa's ability to generate a higher yield by providing amenities that guests have grown to expect in luxury spas and desire in mid-market spas. A spa's ability to maximize its yield and create a competitive advantage is often predicated by the extent to which these amenities have been included within the spa. The architectural program should include all aspects of the facility as noted in the sample program below. Noting a percentage of space allocated to each area from the total square footage or meters allows for an assessment of the ratio of spaces dedicated to specific areas such as transition lounges, treatment-rooms, and circulation.

Conclusion

Due to an increase in global demand for spa and health and wellness treatments and services, Spa and Wellness Facilities are receiving more attention from property managers, property owners, and individual investors. Spa and wellness facilities either located within a hospitality development or a stand-alone business are developing into business outlets that are generating substantial margins and return on investment. According to Figures 7.1 and 7.2, luxury properties with spa facilities are generating both higher ADR's and occupancy percentages than luxury properties without a spa facility. Due to this, and an increase in demand for spa and wellness treatment and services property managers, property developers, and individual investors are willing to invest additional capital into spa projects. Higher investment into these projects will gain consumer recognition and ultimately positively impact the value of the asset, this either being a hotel property, resort development, or a stand-alone business. As additional capital begins to be earmarked for spa and wellness projects, more importance will be placed on accurate feasibilities studies. Therefore, following the steps previously discussed is necessary when conducting a feasibility study for a spa or wellness project.

References and selected reading

ISPA (2004) Industry Study. International Spa Association. Association Resource Centre Inc., 2004.

Consumer Report: Spa-Goer and Non-Spa-Goer Perspectives. International Spa Association (2006), pp. 1–132.

Consumer Trends Report Variations & Trends on the Consumer Spa Experience. International Spa Association (2004), pp. 1–62.

Cornelia, 11 November 2007, available at: <www.cornelia.com >.

Dusseau, R. (2008) *Spa Strategy Proprietary Information*, Spa Strategy Inc., Denver.

Freitag, J.D. (2007) Performance of US hotels with & without spas, *Smith Travel Research*, .

Renaissance Aruba Resort & Casino, Marriott (2007) *Marriott International*, 11 November 2007, available at: <www.marriott.com/hotels/travel/auabr-renaissance-aruba-resort-and-casino/>.

Silverstein, ,M.J., Fiske, N. (2003) *Trading Up: The New American Luxury*, The Penguin Group, New York.

Spa Consumer Survey Asia 2003. Intelligent Spas, 2004.

Spa Industry Profile Australia 2002–2007, Intelligent Spas, 2006, pp. 1–70.

The Ritz-Carlton, Bachelor Gulch, The Ritz-Carlton (2007), The Ritz-Carlton Company, L.L.C., 11 November 2007, available at:<www.ritzcarlton.com/en/Properties/BachelorGulch/Default.htm>.

Wohlberg, A., Foster, A. (2006) Hotel spas as independent profit centers, *PKF Consulting and PKF Hospitality Research*, 1–6.

Websites

Spa search engines

Spa Finder: www.spafinder.com

Way Spa: www.wayspa.com

Spas of America: www.spasofamerica.com

Spa Index: www.spaindex.com

Industry publications

American Spa Magazine: www.americanspamag.com

Spa Magazine: www.spamagazine.com

Spa Business: www.spabusiness.com

Spa Trade: www.spatrade.com

Hospitality.Net: www.hospitalitynet.org

Condé Nast Traveller: www.cntraveller.com

Affiliation

International Spa Association: www.experienceispa.com/ISPA

CHAPTER 8

Spa design, development and construction

Seán O' Connor

Introduction

This chapter explores the commonsense, methodical steps required in the design and delivery of a successful, world-class spa and wellness facility.

The design process is a mixture of art science and serendipity that is also a journey of discovery and documentation that commences with a vision, proceeds through testing that vision and forming a model, putting together an appropriate team of specialists and then guiding them through the delivery process up until the realisation of the project.

Along the design and development journey there are many, many common and easily avoidable pitfalls. The largest section of this chapter is devoted to this topic – since simply following the above modus operandi, and avoiding common pitfalls should at least ensure that the business is robust – even if the serendipity is rationed in short measure – or completely absent!

It is useful to divide the process into coherent phases, identify the critical milestones in each phase and list them in rational and logical steps. The critical phases are:

(a) Concept development
(b) Finding a location
(c) Market research
(d) Area programming
(e) Assembling the professional team
(f) Critical path planning
(g) The design process
(h) Pre-opening preparations
(i) Handover and commissioning
(j) Post-handover tasks

It may be noted that the above step-by-step protocol applies not only to spa development, but also to any hospitality or related business – be it a restaurant, health club, bookshop, barbershop, salon, cinema or wine bar.

Concept development

Every spa should begin with a vision – a concept with a 'story'. Each and every concept should have something unique and extraordinary.

World-class spas may have many unique aspects and these may relate to its unique location, the proportions and dimensions of the spaces allocated, the arrival sequence and sense-of-place, the colours and textures and how they are combined, the facilities themselves and/or unique treatments, ceremonies and rituals that have not been seen in that catchment area before. In developing the concept, the key proficiency is in teasing out the vision and committing this to paper in the form of a Concept Statement.

Very often an owner or developer may have a wonderful dream and vision, and an exceptional location where that concept may materialise and make its mark on the spa industry – yet that owner may quite possibly lack the capability to adequately express the concept in understandable terms and vocabulary, nor summarise it and expand it out for the development team to comprehend.

Even experienced architecture or engineering professionals may struggle to communicate a new concept to those expert in their own field of operations. Yet by their nature, spas require specialised areas of proficient and the more novel and unique a concept, the more difficult it is to express to professionals involved in developing and delivering the final result.

It is important to recognise that the Concept Statement has a number of audiences that must all be able to read and comprehend the overall picture, but at the same time, must know how their specialist contribution can be consolidated in the overall scheme.

The first audience is the owner of the vision and the financier of the project. They have to understand and agree with the principles and approve it for the next stage of the development process. Others that need to be 'on the same page' include the professional team (architect, interior designers, engineers, contractors and of course the eventual operator). There is more detail on these key players under the heading 'Assembling the professional team'.

Location identification and qualification

As with many businesses that rely on customer interaction, location is the most important aspect in any venture. No matter how appealing and attractive a spa concept is conceived and delivered, if the location is wrong then the business will fail. Ease of access is key here and where the spa is not a part of a hotel or resort – that has a relatively captive audience – this is all the more important.

In a community where customers are likely to walk to the venue, then the way-finding signage must be intelligible and the name and logo of the spa must identify the entrance prominently at all times of the day and night. This 'shop front' signage may also act as advertising and 'imprinting' of the spa for passing traffic.

Other means of transport may feature in the location qualifying process. In a city where underground and overground public transport is extremely efficient, and therefore possibly a preferred method of getting around, links from transport stops and interchange nodes become very important.

Equally important for all modes of transport is the link from the transport stop/node to the front entrance of the spa. In places where the extremes of torrential rain and blistering sunshine may affect the level of business, the safe and comfortable passage of potential and actual visitors is crucial. Otherwise business levels will fluctuate according to local climate and weather systems, and this may have severe consequences on cash flow and profitability.

If the clientele is likely to arrive by self-driven private car, then adequate car parking, especially during predicted peak periods, is essential. If they are likely to be dropped off by a driver, then a convenient lay-by at the front entrance or the entrance of a transfer link to the spa reception is required.

Market research

Market research can be an expensive exercise, and it can still be unhelpful if not properly conducted. If this is out-sourced to a third-party specialist, it is important to verify that they will be asking the right questions and gathering the right data, and that they are equipped to convert this data into useable information.

A typical approach to market research is to divide the scope as follows:

(a) Desk research
(b) Site research
(c) Feasibility study
(d) Business planning

Desk research

Desk research refers to home-town-based research such as internet surfing and search engine enquiries, library resource investigations and phone calls to gather relevant background information on the location and characteristics of the site and the marketplace. This is superficial research, but it does help to identify the universe, horizons and boundaries for the next level of more detailed research.

Site research

On-site research entails a trip to the locality of the project and deeper investigation of the targets identified as 'important' in the desk research conducted earlier. Such deeper query decorates the tapestry of the desk research and would be broken down as follows:

(a) Competition analysis – existing peers
(b) Competition analysis – 'stretch' peers
(c) Competition analysis – future competition

Competition analysis – existing peers

Having postured the backdrop of the project with desk research, a review of existing 'market players' is a valuable insight into what the local market currently enjoys and potentially expects from a spa. Gaps in operation and facility provision may surface and may underline the potential of the concept under consideration.

Competition analysis – 'stretch' peers

It may be that there exist a number of operators with regional, national or international recognition that currently enjoy superior or dominating status. These would be considered 'stretch peers' and it may well be useful to investigate what they are doing to ensure that the project concept stands up to scrutiny compared to these operators.

Competition analysis – future competition

Since it takes a while to plan and develop, launch and stabilise a spa facility, it is a useful exercise to be inquisitive about other spa and related projects that may not be operating currently, but are also currently under planning – and their concept and projected opening dates.

All of these inputs assist tremendously in reinforcing the project concept – or re-directing it as appropriate.

Feasibility study

A feasibility study is a very academic 'modelling' exercise in that the whole premise works off a series of declared assumptions, and these assumptions are not entirely set in stone. Different variations on the model can be entertained (see Chapter 7).

Some parameters indeed may be fixed (investment capital available, size of space available, market resistance to pricing, etc.). Assumptions should be reasonably made and then altered later to test the sensitivity of outcomes to find the best fit or most comfortable level.

Three models are recommended: an anticipated 'best guess' model, a more conservative variant and a more aggressive model. All should be possible based on the research gathered, with conservative guesswork being better than reckless optimism.

There is a fine divide between being 'precise' and 'accurate'. Many feasibility studies adopt very precise, yet hardly accurate assumptions and end up precisely inaccurate!

Business planning

The business plan is a document that could potentially be submitted to a finance institution to persuade, convince or prove that the business result is worth loaning the capital to invest in or complete the project. The business plan is built up from key factors reflected in the assumptions of the feasibility study, but presented as a day-to-day operating synopsis with monthly and annual results.

The business plan must consider factors such as rental (or revenue share, if applicable) opening hours, prices of treatments, number of treatment rooms/beds, minor revenue centres, manpower plan and shift planning, payroll costs and payroll-related costs, anticipated therapist utilisation, utility expenses, cost of sales in retail, etc.

Area programming

Spas must have a logical flow that constitutes what may be referred to as the 'spa journey' or 'spa experience', from pre-arrival, through meeting and greeting, preparation for therapeutic treatment(s), post-treatment experience and farewell. These 'journey sojourns' may be punctuated with various complementary 'stops' that contribute to the experience and journey. These should include the three R's:

(a) *Retail imprinting:* The display of products that, when reinforced by therapists' recommendations, result in a commitment to purchase. This is not 'hard-sell' rather, it is a transaction based on trust, built up from a confidence in a professional specialist resulting in a satisfying concluding transaction.

Some spas introduce clients to retail imprinting at check-in, again in the locker room and relaxation lounge areas, yet again in the treatment rooms or suites, as well as at check-out and in the retail boutiques. This is an effective method of educating and inspiring confidence in clients about the benefits of products – and in achieving sales.

(b) *Relaxation:* It is important that users can relax in single gender lounges, but equally important that couples can relax together in a co-ed lounge.

There has been recent recognition that co-ed relaxation lounges should be provided in both dry (waiting areas) and wet areas (wet area lounges). It is important that couples can be reunited socially to compare notes on their experiences as they happen, and also to plan adjustments in their schedules as they alter during their independent or combined spa journey.

(c) *Refreshment:* Spa cuisine is not universally attractive or enticing. However, it is essential that clients are well hydrated, especially during and after thermal bathing.

Other experiences that require rehydration may include fitness and wellness activities such as lifestyle counselling and exercise workouts, Pilates, yoga, stretching, etc.

Area programming falls into three main areas in a spa and wellness facility:

(a) Front-of-house facilities
(b) Back-of-house facilities (heart-of-house in deluxe spas)
(c) Unique 'signature' features

Front-of-house facilities

Front-of-house facilities can be logically grouped according to the arrival sequence – this may begin in a basement car park or an elevator – so it important to set the mood right from the start. Retail can be grouped with reception and waiting so that users can browse and try out products.

Locker rooms should not allow cross circulation of wet and dry foot traffic, but should flow from dry to semi-wet to wet areas, and bathing or pool access. High energy areas such as salons and fitness should be acoustically separated from the tranquil lounge and treatment areas.

Back-of-house facilities (heart-of-house in deluxe spas)

It is important that the back-of-house facilities fully support the front-of-house facilities, otherwise a compromise will seriously impact operations. Many (if not most) operators get this wrong and this is one magical ingredient that can make or break an operation. Secure storage areas, therapists lounge areas, spa pantry, mop sinks in thermal bathing areas, circulation and stacking of facilities, etc., all contribute to sense of peace and harmony that spas engender.

There are logical groupings of these facilities. Such groupings can be divided between front-of-house and back/heart-of-house areas (see Spa area programme sample in Appendix III). It is important that the umbilical cord between these distinct areas resonates with clients – when a spa pantry door is opened, there should not be a flood of white fluorescent light and therapists chatter into the corridor. Conversely, these all contribute to the powerful enchantment of a world-class spa, an invisible and intangible characteristic. An undefinable trait that makes a spa special and superlative.

Unique 'signature' features

Every spa must have a unique signature: this may be in the look and feel of the interiors, the architecture of the facility, and the richness of the finishes, the views presented by the public areas or treatment rooms or the lighting (a crucial element for the success of any spa), or some special operational element such as a foot cleansing ritual, a tea ceremony or some such other reach-back to a cultural or ancient 'signature' (Chinese, Indian, Aztec, Mayan, Greco-Roman or some other established indigenous culture).

Assembling the professional team

The following team members are essential to the design and development of a successful spa:

(a) Owner's representative – usually one person
(b) Architectural team – usually a senior person with support persons
(c) Interior design team – usually a senior designer plus a junior and a Computer Assisted Design (CAD) design operator
(d) Engineering team:
    (i) Structural
    (ii) Mechanical
    (iii) Electrical
    (iv) Spa and wellness
    (v) Plumbing and drainage
    (vi) Acoustic
    (vii) Audio Visual (AV)

(viii) Information Technology (IT)

(ix) Telephone

(e) Graphics and signage

(f) Specialist advisors

These team members are essential to achieving the end result, and any cost-cutting in this regard has shown time and time again to be both fruitless and detrimental. Quality workmanship, waterproofing, conduit and cable management, plumbing and signage may end up being key differentiators.

Critical path planning

Critical path planning is an essential element of producing an on-time, within budget project. A 'critical' element in the design process is one upon which other item(s) depend on to commence or complete. Any delay in this component will inevitably stall the process overall. It is important where possible to accomplish tasks and procedures in parallel, and note those which must be completed in a timely fashion so as not to disrupt the overall progress of the project. It is important also to be aware of those elements that have a 'long lead time' to complete.

Easy examples occur in the ordering of equipment and supplies. When standard items are ordered there is usually a lead time for delivery. However, if items are made-to-order, manufacture, testing, packaging, shipping, delivery, and installation phases may take longer which must be considered in the ordering process.

There is more on this topic under the heading 'The design process' of this chapter, critical milestones (please see below).

The design process

There is a logical starting point from the progression from vision and concept development, market reality-check, area allocation and facilities brief, assembling the team and planning the courses of action and progress. While there is a flow in this process and areas may overlap, the first few steps are clearly the lead-in to the matters that occur at a later stage.

The design process may be listed in order as follows:

(i) Block planning

(ii) Detailed design development

(iii) Bidding and award of contracts

(iv) Contract management and project management

(v) Critical milestones

(vi) Payment schedules and cash flow management

Block planning

Always, the first stage of the actual design process is block planning. This may take the form of a hand-drawn 'bubble diagram' that simply shows the relationship between blocks of space such as reception, waiting area and retail area or dry locker room area, semi-wet locker room area and wet locker room area. This block plan should indicate the relationship between spaces (spatial planning), whether there are views over other areas or connections between areas (e.g. lounge area, overlooking activity areas or juice bar with a view over outdoor landscaping, or fitness area with views over outside areas).

If the facility is spread over multiple floors then the relationships and connectivity of relevant spaces are all the more important. This is called a 'Stacking Plan', a 3D version of the bubble diagram – and positioning of various elements involves the efficient stacking of facilities that require mechanical, electrical and especially plumbing and drainage components. Electrical, IT and telephone services are relatively simple to move around, but water supplies and drainage are more problematic.

It is prudent to be mindful that there are both client and staff requirements in many areas and the flow between spaces may require certain front-of-house connections, but also parallel back-of-house connectivity. This is especially important in areas where personal privacy or solitude and seclusion is ideal for clients' benefit.

Detailed design development

Design development proceeds from the Bubble Diagram to a scaled drawing layout plan that takes into consideration fixed building constraints such as the footprint of the building, columns and shear walls, fire egress and stairways, elevators and ducts that run vertically through the building, etc.

Once the 'playing field' has been established (the parts of a given floor that are usable) then the Block Plan is reconsidered intelligently to find the best fit for the various components shown in Appendix I, as appropriate. It is quite usual to conduct many rounds of refinements and revisions to the floor plan until it is accepted by all parties in the professional team, and site issues are resolved to achieve the targeted end-result.

Bidding and award of contracts

Normal procedure calls for a broadcast of a tender document to at least three, but probably not more than five, qualified bidders for a project. Three allows a 'good, bad and ugly' comparison of quotations, and five begins to get unmanageable from a review and decision-making basis.

It is important that the tender document is clear and concise and that deadlines for submission allow reasonable and adequate time for a contender to prepare a proposal. Very often a bidder may have excellent input that can enhance the project, but this sort of input requires time to reflect and consider all aspects of the concept. Bidding deadlines should be no less than 30 days from issue of requests for proposals.

In a similar vein, bids must be analysed in great depth. Often the bidders will stray from the brief and this may be a positive direction worth exploring. Simply choosing the lowest bid may be considered a lazy, cheap or short-cut approach. So additional time should be planned and set aside for tender review and discussion, and maybe re-tendering, based on issues brought up in the first tender exercise.

Contract management and project management

Contracts have two principle aspects: scope of work delivered and payments out. Managing a contract simply requires the scope of services and relevant, agreed payment milestones to match up.

Project management is much more complex. Issues often arise that could never have been predicted and a pragmatic 'what if I was in your shoes' approach is useful. Making a contractor or supplier perform under unfair circumstances is neither conducive to completing the project, nor establishing a reputation for excellence in the wider community.

Critical milestones

The critical milestones in a project are as follows:

(a) Kick-off briefing when the team assembles to unite on the project.
(b) 50% completion of design (50% CD) where changes and input are welcomed, this is the real design development phase where creativity can come to the fore.
(c) 90% design completion (90% CD) where changes and inputs are NOT welcomed as so many hours have been devoted in CAD, and usually the structure is fixed or changes can no longer be accommodated.
(d) Completion and handover.

There is more on the heading 'handover and commissioning' of a project of this chapter (Please refer to page 143).

Payment schedules and cash flow management

During contract management and project management stages of the project, it will have been agreed when payments will be issued based on satisfactory delivery of services and the installation of equipment. Cash flow planning is therefore essential as adequate funds must be made available to meet financial commitments to ensure that contractors, manufacturers and suppliers do not walk away from the job.

Pre-opening preparations

Pre-opening activities usually commence 12 months prior to opening a facility. Pre-opening activities are divided into major categories of involvement such as:

- Budgets and startup
- Licenses and inspections
- Insurances and contracts
- Human resources and recruitment:
  - Preparation of job descriptions and scopes of work for each and every position
  - Planning local and regional/international advertising of positions available
  - Interview appointments
  - Standard operating procedures (SOPs)
- Key performance indicators (KPIs)
- Training schedules
- Uniform design
- Operating equipment and supplies listing (OS&E)
- Fixtures fittings and equipment listing (FF&E)
- Purchasing
- Printing materials and collateral
- Signage and graphics design
- In-house control forms
- Operations manual
- Pricing structure(s)

Having developed the pre-opening checklist, it is essential to 'guesstimate' the time required to complete each task, with some contingency, just in case. At the same time, it may be useful to highlight the tasks that may become critical in the overall process of preparing for an opening and accelerating these tasks or prioritising them. Finally, it may be prudent to delegate portions of the listing to capable subordinates and taking a background supporting and co-ordinating role in this process.

Handover and commissioning

Handover and commissioning is an important milestone in the development process. This is where suppliers will attempt to get their clients to accept the work that they have completed.

A handover and commissioning procedure would normally be a session where the relevant parties assemble with a contractor (appointed supervising consultants, engineers, operations teams, housekeepers, etc.) and review methodically the contractors work in order to accept that work and release any outstanding payments. It is useful to adopt a cynical standpoint from the outset, and assume that the contractor/manufacturer/supplier is trying to trick the project into accepting the contractor's workmanship and handiwork. Perfection is not difficult to assess, either the products or finishes are perfect or they are not!

When conducting a handover session, it is necessary to ensure that the commissioning agent provides on-the-spot training to engineers or operational staff that will be expected to operate the facility being commissioned. Manuals (in the relevant languages for both operational and management staff) also need to be handed over and signed for.

Defect rectification and improvement works

In any project, it is fundamental to appreciate that there is a difference between a 'defect' and an 'improvement'.

During the design and development process, various tenders and bidding documents are drawn up and issued. Bids are tendered by interested parties and an appointment is made to carry out agreed works. Any variation from this agreed scope is called a 'variation order', and these can be very costly. Some larger projects are bid by contractors at a low price in the hope that the profit on the job may emerge from costly variation orders.

When accepting a project through the handover and commissioning procedure, there may be certain aspects that deviate from the original specification. Some variations may be perceived 'improvements', while others may be considered defects. If there is a defects list that is not disputed and an improvements list that is desired, then a deal is in the making!

While 'perfect' is an admirable target, there may be some compromises that could be considered acceptable. Offering to swap 'acceptable' defects (expensive for the contractor to fix), for desired improvements, may be a successful strategy to materially improve a spa project, at little or no cost.

Common avoidable mistakes

Table 8.1 presents a list of common avoidable mistakes in the planning and development of contemporary spa projects. Paying particular attention to these issues should contribute significantly to the successful planning and development of a facility that can have the best opportunity to succeed in any marketplace.

Conclusion

The design and delivery of a successful, world-class spa requires the transformation of a concept into a plan that can then be understood and worked through to deliver the final product. This process requires meticulous planning and staging including finding an appropriate location, market research, competition analysis, feasibility studies, business planning and area programming.

Once this preliminary work has been done, a professional team needs to be assembled and critical path and block planning along with detailed design and development can be performed so that work can be contracted out and effectively project managed. Once work has commenced, then critical milestones need to be met and cash flow managed to deliver a final facility.

Along this journey, there are many things that can alter from the original plan; however, the more robust the planning, the greater the ability to cope with the unexpected and the greater the likelihood of avoiding common mistakes.

Appendices

(I) Spa design development checklist
(II) Market research – key questions
(III) Sample facilities brief – urban spa sample

Table 8.1 Common avoidable mistakes

- Underestimating budgets – particularly the cash flow required for operating equipment and supplies, pre-opening costs such as training and marketing
- Copying mistakes made by others
- Insufficient storage space – retail, linen/laundry, professional products, etc.
- Allocation of space dedicated to ongoing training
- Assumption that your designer is an expert in spas
- Frequently changing the design – particularly at late stages where significant costs may be incurred
- Matching equipment into bespoke furniture and millwork
- Cross circulation – wet and dry
- Sizing of facilities – maximum capacity for key compaction areas:
  - Lounges
  - Waiting
  - Lockers
  - Pantry
  - Fitness equipment – ratio of space allocated to cardio and strength
- Provision for janitorial services
- Floor finishes – selection of appropriate materials, especially in wet bare foot areas
- Retail display and storage design
- Consideration for privacy where needed
- Provisions for refreshments
- Safety signage
- Future provision for expanded information technologies
- Use of domestic appliances in a commercial environment
- Waterproofing in thermal bathing areas
- Noise pollution
- Location and design of relaxation spaces
- Showers – side facing and details
- Back of house provisions – particularly for preparation areas, storage and administration
- Clean and soiled laundry and linen management
- Lighting design
- Air conditioning
- Millwork – burying reception and retail hardware into the furniture tastefully
- Consideration for disabled access and comfortable use by seniors

Appendix I

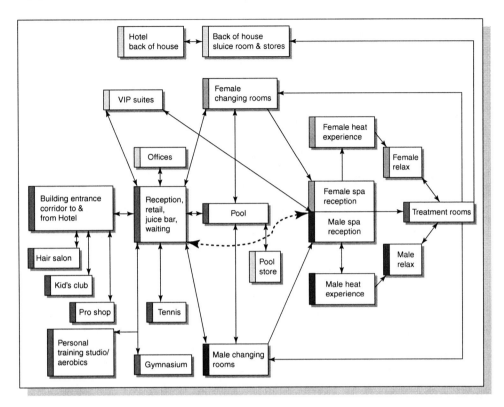

Combined spa and fitness centre

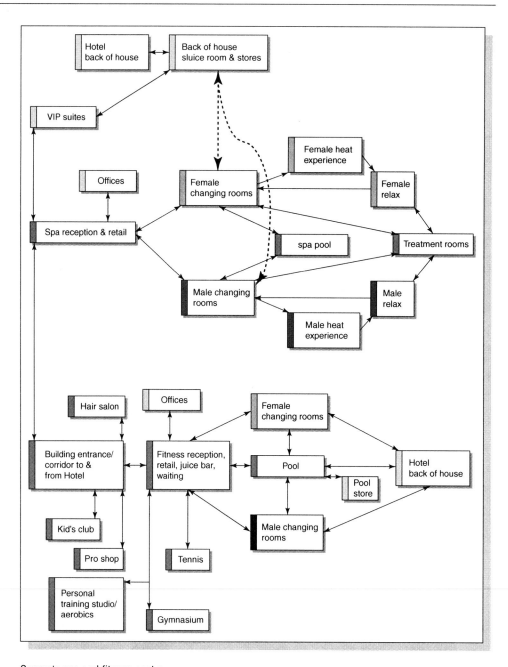

Separate spa and fitness centre

Appendix II

Market Research Questionnaire – Key questions asked

1 **Spa Catageory** (check one)
Day Spa
City Resort
Hideaway
Other

2 **Indicate size of facilities in relation to size of property (for hotels) and state the mix of facilities for each spa.**

Fitness & Wellness
Overall size
Number of cardio units (treadmills, bikes etc)
Full or partial manning of Fitness/Wellness areas
Fitness Assessment Office
Multipurpose Studio(s) size(s)
Yoga Studio
Pilates Studio
Fitness/Pool Locker Rooms – number of showers
Fitness/Pool Locker Rooms – number of lockers
Fitness Opening hours

Spa
Spa Retail area size
Dedicated Spa Training Room – size
Spa Locker Rooms – number of lockers
Spa Locker Rooms – number of showers
The number of single treatment rooms
The number of couples + VIP
Thermal bathing facilities
    Sauna – size or seating for how many
    Steam – size or seating for how many
    Whirlpool/Vitality Pool – size or seating for how many
    Relaxation lounge – size or seating for how many
Spa Opening hours

3 **To obtain the following key performance indicators from at least two of the major competitive spas:**
gross revenues
net operating profit
average cost per treatment per hour
ratio of retail sales to treatment sales
therapist utilization = (number of treatment hours per day/ number of working hours per day)
room utilization = (number of hours of treatments per day/number of hours available per day)
Indication of the most popular treatments

147

4 Obtain any information relating to payroll and benefits packages for the spa

5 Obtain any information relating to market mix of local guests.

6 Details of any future spa developments in the competitive region

7 If time permits and cooperation is granted or if the competition is considered a 'peer' – gather the following also;

The professional products/brands currently used.

The retail items sold in the Spa.

The nationalities of the Manger and the operational staff

The number of full time/part-time staff

Type of membership offered

Types of treatment rooms – standard beauty, with shower, wet treatmen areas?

Spa Concept/theme and ambience

Website – provide address if possible

Treatment packages offered and discount structure

8 **Prices:**

Basic:

Massage (time)

Facial

Manicure

Pedicure

Wrap

Appendix III

Spa area programme – urban location

Front-of-house facilities
These include logical groupings of facilities such as:

Front of house
(a) Spa reception area
(b) Spa reception desk
(c) Spa retail boutique reception desk
(d) Spa retail boutique displays
(e) Spa herbal tea lounge
(f) Ladies hair and beauty salon
(g) Barber: Gentleman's grooming and skin care salon

Back of house
(a) Spa reception admin office
(b) Spa retail boutique product stockroom
(c) Spa herbal tea lounge pantry

Locker rooms dry areas
(a) Locker dry areas
(b) Janitorial room – dry

Wet areas
(a) Locker room wet areas
(b) Janitorial room

Heat and wet experiences
(a) Steam room
(b) Dry Sauna
(c) Vitality pool
(d) Ice fountain
(e) Hamam
(f) Rhassoul
(g) Laconium
(h) Tepidarium
(i) Caldarium
(j) Aroma bath
(k) General bathing and lounging areas
(l) Janitorial room – bathing

Spa treatment areas
(a) Standard couples treatment suite
(b) Standard couples treatment room
(c) Couples oriental treatment suite
(d) VIP couples deluxe treatment suite

(e) Standard single treatment room
(f) Single treatment suite
(g) Single oriental treatment suite
  - H–ydrotherapy treatment zone
  - Scrub room and vichy shower
  - Experience shower
  - Manicure and pedicure areas
  - Water therapy pool

General spa areas front of house
(a) Spa relaxation

Back of house
(a) Spa pantry and preparation room
(b) Professional spa products store
(c) Therapist lounge and staff wardrobe
(d) Training room
(e) Clean laundry and linen store
(f) Soiled laundry and linen store

Fitness and wellness areas
Front of house:
(a) Fitness and wellness centre
(b) Fitness and wellness assessment lounge
(c) Group exercise studio
(d) Pilates studio

Back of house:
(a) Fitness and wellness office
(b) Equipment store room

Lifestyle guest rooms
(a) Lifestyle guest room

Administration
(a) Lifestyle counselling office
(b) Spa manager's office
(c) Scheduling centre
(d) Technical store (AV room)
(e) Spa operations manager's office

Swimming pool
(a) First aid room
(b) Pool deck
(c) Interior and technical design

SPA chain operations: the experience of the Mandara Group, a division of Steiner Leisure Limited

Jeff Matthews and Donna Wells

Managing a chain of spas is not very dissimilar to managing a chain of stores or restaurants. The key to optimum success in each case is having the right systems and human resources in place to facilitate remote management while still ensuring accountability in individual outlets. Regardless of whether each outlet is an exact replica of the next or if each one is unique, systems are the foundation and they belong in each aspect of the business. That means systems and reporting mechanisms are required in finance, operations, training, purchasing, sales and marketing, human resources and whatever other departments may exist.

Of course, every type of chain operation faces its own peculiar issues, so while the need for systems and structure may be common, the systems and structure each one uses will be very different. In this chapter, we will discuss some of the issues of spa chain operations and the systems and strategies that are the foundation of success.

Defining spa chain operations

Before focussing on the issues, challenges, opportunities and strategies for dealing with spa chain operations, it will be helpful to first determine what constitutes a spa chain and look at some of the major operators. There are two main types of spa chain operators:

1. A spa chain operated by a spa management company. This is where a third party organisation operates multiple spas for one or more host hotels, resorts or properties. The spas may operate under the management company brand, the host business brand or even a neutral brand. Angsana, Mandara Spa and Six Senses are examples of this type of spa chain.
2. A spa chain operated by a hotel group. This is where a hotel group creates and operates spas under its own brand. Usually, the hotel group will form a separate spa division to oversee the operations. Some examples are Banyan Tree, Chi the Spa (Shangri-la Hotels) and Mandarin Oriental Hotel Group.

While the above scenarios are the most common, crossover does exist. For example, Angsana Spa, the sister brand to Banyan Tree, manages some spas on behalf of third party hotels and others within Angsana branded resorts. Similarly, Six Senses operates spas within its own resorts and also under third party arrangements for other hotels and resorts. Regardless of the scenario, the common denominator is the operation of spas in multiple locations (Table 9.1).

Table 9.1 Breakdown of major spa chain operators

Spa chain operator	Number of spas	Number of countries	Within own hotels/resorts	For third party hotels/ resorts
Angsana	36	18	•	•
Banyan Tree	14	8	•	
Chi the Spa (Shangri-la Hotels)	10	6	•	
Hyatt Pure	65	25	•	
*Mandara Spa	70	20		•
Mandarin Oriental Hotels	17	12	•	
Six Senses	24	15	•	•
Starwood Spa Collection	53	25	•	

Sources: www.angsanaspa.com [site accessed 14 November 2007]; www.banyantreespa.com [site accessed 14 November 2007); www.shangri-la.com [site accessed 14 November 2007]; www.hyatt.com/hyatt/pure/locator/ [site accessed 16 December 2007]; www.mandaraspa.com [site accessed 14 November 2007]; www.mspa-international.com [site accessed 18 November 2007]; www.mandarinoriental.com [site accessed 14 November 2007]; www.sixsensesspas.com [site accessed 14 November 2007]; www.starwoodspacollection.com/common/Home.asp [site accessed 16 December 2007]

*Mandara Spa figures include spas operated by MSpa International under the Mandara Spa name.

Spa chain is not synonymous with 'cookie-cutter'. While consistency is both necessary and desirable when managing multiple spas, there are still opportunities to make each spa unique and relevant to its particular location or concept. In fact, spa chain operators have some great advantages:

- More people means more expertise to draw on.
- Better cost efficiency through economy of scale.
- More structured and systematic training.
- Opportunities for higher consumer awareness and trust.
- Marketing leverage.
- Better career path opportunities for employees.
- Less exposure to economic crises that are isolated to one country or region.

The evolution of Mandara Spa: Mandara Spa's four pillars of success

This chapter will focus on the strategies and systems required to successfully manage a spa chain operation, drawing on the experience of Mandara Spa and what we call the Four Pillars of Success:

- Pillar 1 – Training is the foundation
- Pillar 2 – Brand strategy and marketing
- Pillar 3 – Create your own path
- Pillar 4 – Systems and structure are essential

Before exploring the Four Pillars, it will be helpful to understand Mandara Spa's history to discover how and why the Four Pillars were developed.

Mandara Spa is part of a family of companies that operates spas in various parts of the world, including over 130 cruise ships and over 70 land based spas. It is known for its success in taking the spa concept global and introducing the tropical spa experience to locations as diverse as Bahamas, Caribbean, China, Hawaii, Indonesia, Japan, Malaysia, Maldives, Mexico, Micronesia, the South Pacific, Thailand, United Arab Emirates and the United States. Mandara Spa's reach also extends to the "Spas at Sea" division which takes the spa experience to the oceans through business relationships with lines like Norwegian Cruise Line, Orient Lines and several others.

A Case Study

When Mandara founders, Tom Gottlieb and Mark Edleson opened the first Mandara Spa in Bali, in 1996, they never guessed that the company would become the global success that it is today. Nor did they imagine that within less than ten years, the company would be valued at US$70 million. By the time that Jeff Matthews joined them in 1997, the success potential was evident. There was just one problem; the company lacked the structure and systems to support rapid growth. Things were slipping through the cracks, including profits.

It began with the wrong idea

In 1995, Tom Gottlieb found a piece of land in the heart of Kuta, Bali surrounded by hotels with no spas. He had an idea to build a stand-alone spa

---

on this site, expecting to draw guests from the surrounding hotels. In hindsight, this was a bad idea! Why? If Tom had gone ahead and built that spa it would have seen 2 years of good business before the spa boom started and the hotels began to setup their own spas. In those 2 years, it is unlikely he would have recouped the costs of build and setup.

Serendipity steps in and a great idea unfolds

While Tom was planning his Kuta spa, Mark Edleson was wondering what to do about low occupancies at his new hotel in Ubud. Mark approached Tom with a suggestion – take over two guest suites and offer his hotel guests simple massage services.

That's how the first Mandara Spa debuted in May 1996 at The Chedi, Ubud, in two modified guest rooms. It began with four massage oil blends and four traditional body scrubs, developed by Tom's wife, Carol Gottlieb. Carol, who had a passion for the spa industry, worked closely with some Balinese contacts to create the signature blends, which are still in use today.

Word soon spread and within 6 months other hotel General Managers were asking for the same. This new 'accidental' business model had more merit and less capital expense than Tom's original idea, so the Kuta spa idea was dropped and Tom and Mark joined forces to establish Mandara as a spa management company.

The big picture requires structure, standards and systems

By May 1997 – after 1 year of operation-Mandara had four hotel spas under contract. The management focus was on growth – getting more contracts – but with two visionaries running the business and nobody to focus on existing contracts, Mandara Spa was finding it difficult to keep up with demand and profits were yet to be realised. Jeff Matthews, with his 20-year background in hotels and experience in managing multiple outlets, then took on the role of General Manager.

By the end of 1997, Mandara had six spas, and Tom and Mark set their sights on a new goal – to build the company to become an attractive buyout proposition for a more established company. Over the next few years, Mandara Spa expanded into other countries. The rate of growth continued to increase, and in 1998 Mandara Spa established a US division and the following year another 13 spas were opened in Asia. The challenges of going international were many, and without a strong foundation of standards and systems, Mandara often had to resort to reactive management. But the group had to grow fast, in order to keep up with overheads. It was during these exciting and often trying times that Mandara Spa's Four Pillars of Success were developed.

Pillar 1: Training is the foundation

While it may be fine for a single outlet spa to flourish with an 'organic' training approach, spa chain operators will find that success comes much more easily with a standardised, centralised and systematic training strategy in place. Anything less means increased operating costs, staff retention problems, lack of integrity and consistency and the inability to react appropriately to training shortfalls. That translates to reduced profit, operational challenges and deficiencies, and probably disappointed guests and bad press.

In-house versus out-sourced training

A spa's reputation and brand identity is built on the ability of its staff to deliver services in the way that management expect them to be delivered. Relying on out-sourced training in a multiple outlet spa operation does not work because trainers need to live and breathe the spa's philosophy and inject its values into every aspect of training. Even the best out-sourced trainer will find it difficult to succeed on this level.

Additionally, when managing a spa chain, training and retraining the required number of therapists becomes a full-time job for a team of trainers. Mandara Spa started out with one out-sourced trainer, but quickly discovered how labour intensive the business was and how few trainers were available. When rolling out multiple spas and adding new treatments to existing spas, management cannot afford to wait until a suitable trainer is available. The need for regular 'refresher' training, further highlights the futility of relying on out-sourced training.

When Mandara Spa went international, management decided to employ two trainers based in Bali and one travelling overseas. That quickly turned into 12 Bali-based trainers, with three of them travelling overseas to conduct 'refresher' training. Soon after, Mandara recognised the challenges of getting visas for the Bali trainers to enter certain countries. This in turn led the group to set up other regional training centres in Guam, Thailand and Malaysia.

To keep up with industry trends and develop the spa's services menu, it is necessary to invest in on-going training for trainers. This is where out-sourced trainers do have a place in spa chain operations. Mandara Spa uses 'guest' trainers to conduct 'Train the Trainer' programmes.

Training administration and support

With one spa, it's relatively easy to ensure consistency in training and be able to react quickly to any training issues in the spa. However, a spa chain operator requires a strong administrative function to support standards, procedures and control systems.

To take experienced or raw recruits into a spa or spa school and train them in the spa's curriculum is one thing; and in many ways it is the easy part. With training manuals in place and a good team of trainers, it is simply a matter of following the programme. However, if the same plan is applied in 20 different countries, the group is faced with a logistical nightmare.

It takes a long time to train a therapist just on the basics, and this is compounded by the addition of complicated or specialised treatments. If staff leave part way through a contract, they must be replaced and thus there is a need to have a 'stock' of staff ready to go.

Spa management should record the training history of every therapist – the treatments they have been trained in, when they last received 'refresher' training, when their next 'refresher' training is due, trade test results, etc. Then there are visas, flights and treatment trials to organise, all of which require careful coordination.

The training department operates best in a stand-alone capacity, taking responsibility for its own budgeting, placing orders with the purchasing department, coordinating laundering of linen, managing the training calendar and ensuring that therapists are tested frequently during the training programme so that the spa group's standards are always met.

These logistics are best handled by an effective administrator working alongside the spa trainers. This person does not need hands-on training experience but they must understand the various functions and be able to coordinate the list of needs for the operation to ensure a ready supply of suitably trained therapists is available (Figure 9.1).

The issue of consistency

Consistency is a topic that generates a lot of debate when raised at industry conferences. Some industry people say that it is detrimental to the spa experience, but the opposite can be the case, particularly in the case of spa chains that operate multiple outlets under the one brand.

Staying with the case study of Mandara Spa, the group takes pride in the fact that it has trained hundreds of therapists to deliver its treatments consistently. This is held to be a key factor in Mandara's success, attracting a loyal following of guests and their referred friends who visit different Mandara Spas

SPA THERAPIST TRAINING MATRIX
Spa A
September 2006

Last Training : 28 Mar - 27 May 2006
Trainer : Rajimah (MSM) & Nirmala (MSI)

NAME	BODY / MASSAGES									FACE		SCRUBS				SPA PACKAGES								
	Balinese Massage	Mandara Massage	Warm Stone Massage	Fancy Foot Work	Express Massage - (25 minutes)	Foot Massage - (25 minutes)	Smooth Down - (15 minutes)	Silk Slipper - (15 minutes)	Mini Massage - (5 minutes)	Pure Nature Facial	Refresher Facial - (25 minutes)	Soothing Coconut	Bali Coffee	Javanese Lulur	Balinese Boreh	Spa Sampler - (80 minutes)	Nirvana - (80 minutes)	Harmony - (110 minutes)	Dream Weaver - (110 minutes)	Ocean Detox - (110 minutes)	Yin Yang - (110 minutes)	Ultimate Indulgence - (140 minutes)	Aromatherapy Floral Footbath	Aromatherapy Floral Bath
Therapist	C2	C2	A2	C2	A2	C2	A	C	C	C3	C3	C3	C3	C2	C2	C2	C2	C1	C	C	C	C2	C3	C3
Therapist	C2	C2	A1	C2	A	C3	A	C	C	C3	C3	C3	C3	C3	C2	C	C	C	C	C3	C	C	C3	C
Therapist	A3	A3	A3	A3	A	A3	A	A	A	A3	A3	A3	A3	A3	A3	A3	A3	A3	A	A	A	A	A3	A3
Therapist	A3	A3	A3	A3	A2	A3	A	A	A	A3	A3	A3	A3	A3	A3	A3	A3	A	A	A	A	A	A3	A3
Therapist	A3	A2	A2	A2	A	A2	A	A	A	A2	A2	A	A	A	A	A	A	A	A			A	A	A
Therapist	A2		A3	A3		A2	A	A	A	A2	A2	A2	A2	A2	A3	A3	A	A	A	A			A3	A3
Therapist	C3	C3	A1	C3	A	C3	A	C	C	C3	C3	C3	C3	C3	C	C3	C3	C	C3	C	C3	C	C3	C3
Therapist	A2	A2	A2	A3	A	A2	A	A	A	A2	A2	A	A	A	A	A	A	A	A			A	A	A
Therapist	C2	C3	A2	C3	A	C3	A	C	C	C2	C2	C3	C3	C2	C2	C	C	C	C	C3	C	C	C3	C
Therapist	A3	A3	A3	A3	A	A3	A	A	A	A3	A3	A3	A3	A3	A2	A3	A3	A	A	A	A	A	A3	A3
Therapist	C3	C3	C3	C3		C3		C	C	C2	C2	C3	C3	C3	C3	C3	C3	C3	C	C3	C	C3	C3	C3
Therapist	A2	A2	A3	A3	A	A2	A	A	A	A2	A2	A2	A3	A2	A2	A3	A3	A	A	A	A		A3	A3

A : Less than 6 months ago   1 – Does not meet expectation
B : More than 6 months ago   2 – Met expectation
C : More than 12 months ago   3 – Exceed expectation

Figure 9.1
Example of therapist training record

around the world, confident that the Four Hand Mandara Massage they had in Bali will be equally enjoyable in Hawaii. The Mandara group considers that consistency is what makes it familiar, and that familiarity has helped to create a strong brand identity in an increasingly crowded market.

Irrespective of whether the group is Mandara Spa, Six Senses, Mandarin Oriental or any other spa chain, if a treatment is offered in more than one outlet, guests will expect the treatment to be the same irrespective of which country they have it in. Spa groups owe it to their guests to deliver on that expectation.

Pillar 2: Brand strategy and marketing

In the early days, Mandara Spa didn't consider brand strategy. Spa names or the common threads that distinguished them as being distinctly Mandara Spas was not of concern. There were three different brands – Mandara Spa, Chavana Spa and Indo Spa – and absolutely no strategy! The Mandara team just liked opening spas and wanted to keep opening more.

Mandara didn't consider it necessary to spend money on marketing, believing that it was up to the host property to market the spa. This was a mistake – for two reasons. First, the primary business target was, and still is, hotel operators. In order to win more contracts in an increasingly competitive market, Mandara needed to back up performance figures with a strong brand. Second, the pool of potential hotel partners wanted a brand that spa consumers knew and found appealing.

By 1998, the Mandara group realised that it had a problem. Its hotel partners were pressuring it to spend money on marketing but having three different brands made this an expensive proposition. Worse, everyone was asking: 'so what is Mandara Spa?', and Mandara management stumbled trying to find the answer.

Fortunately, the spa boom was still in its early stage, competition wasn't as strong as it has become and there was time to take a step back and develop a brand strategy. In the current climate, an operator cannot afford to start up without a brand strategy as it is too easy to get lost in the marketplace and lose sight of the brand values that will guide growth.

It's important to note that a brand is far more than a logo and a certain look or style (see Chapter 11). Ultimately, a brand's identity is formed in the mind of a business's consumers, and this impression is shaped by every interaction and every communication that takes place. Customers are not so interested in what a brand says about itself; their brand perception is much more influenced by how a business operates, how it talks to them, how it treats them and how well the staff deliver on what the brand promises.

Mandara Spa is now back to three brands – Mandara Spa, Chavana Spa and The Spa by Mandara – but this time there is a strategy and the necessary resources to develop that strategy through every part of the company.

The costs of marketing

Marketing is one of several areas where spa chain operators can benefit from the economies of scale. The cost for a single spa operation to take out a full page colour advertisement can be prohibitively expensive. The price of advertising space varies, but a glossy spa magazine is likely to cost at least US$5000 for one insert, even prior to design and production costs. The impact will be minimal, since for advertising to be effective, it needs to be repeated continually. Advertising becomes a much more affordable proposition in the case of a spa chain, with one advertisement featuring the full portfolio of spas, thereby significantly reducing the cost per spa of advertising and offering excellent brand exposure.

The situation is even better for a spa chain operating in hotels and resorts, as marketing in these environments is more targeted and less expensive than marketing a stand-alone spa. A stand-alone spa is targeting a diffused market, and marketing costs can range from 4% to 9% of gross spa revenue, depending on the location. When business is successful, spas need to continue their marketing; when business is not doing well they need to market even more. Conversely, a hotel or resort spa is primarily targeting a captured market of in-house guests with holiday money to spend. The spa needs to show them why that money is best spent in the spa versus, for example, a jet ski ride or other tour. This is relatively easy to do, particularly in a remote resort environment where spa capture rates can average over 20%, compared to an average of 7% in city hotels.

The other cost advantage for hotel and resort spas is that the host property's Sales and Marketing department will include the spa in all of their marketing activities.

Creative brand marketing

Marketing a brand doesn't have to be just about advertising and PR. The goal of getting a brand into the minds of potential customers can be reached by less obvious means. It was with this in mind that Mandara Spa opened in Tokyo in 2003.

Mandara Spa has a high number of spas in locations that are popular with Japanese tourists, such as Bali, Guam, Hawaii and Saipan. In these locations, Japanese guests far outnumber any other nationality at Mandara spas and the brand is well regarded by Japanese travellers. Mandara wanted to leverage that advantage by ensuring that their brand remained strong and awareness expanded within the affluent Japanese market. They could have spent significantly on a targeted advertising and PR campaign, but decided instead on a more strategic route that would not only create excitement and brand loyalty, but would also add to the group's revenue. So, Mandara partnered with Royal Park Shiodome Tower and opened the first Mandara Spa in Japan. Spa profit margins in Japan are much smaller than in other parts of Asia, however the marketing value gained from having a spa in Japan makes it worthwhile.

Pillar 3: Create your own path

There is a diverse range of different spa experiences available today, catering to an equally diverse range of spa consumers. In addition to the mainstream segments, such as Resort Spa, Destination Spa, Day Spa, Medi Spa, etc., there are spas that have a holistic focus, spas for men, spas for women, those with spiritual leanings and others that draw on ancient traditional practices. Clearly then, just as different hotels attract different guest profiles, different spas attract different types of guests with different expectations. Accordingly, it is important to understand one's own spa identity and also to know who the guests are and what they want. Then, the spa can create its own path and follow this with exceptional skill and execution, confident that present and future customers will find it appealing.

Mandara Spa found this Pillar to be particularly challenging. Pressure from hotel partners, competitors and from emerging trends within the rapidly diversifying spa industry can be seductive, and Mandara sometimes found that it was trying to be all things to all people.

There were times when the Mandara group tried to introduce services that either didn't fit with its philosophy or that were beyond its areas of expertise. In every case, this was done on the insistence of Mandara's hotel partners, who wanted it either because their competitors had it or they had read about it and thought it sounded good. In most cases, it was a disaster. One example was the introduction of an Ayurvedic treatment, which a hotel partner had insisted they wanted on the menu. Mandara explained that Ayurveda was much more than a single treatment and that authenticity required highly trained specialists who had studied and understood the Ayurvedic philosophy. The hotel partner still insisted, so Mandara organised a guest trainer to teach its therapists one Ayurvedic treatment. Once it was on the menu, Mandara was criticised for offering something that didn't follow the true protocols of Ayurveda.

The lesson learnt – several times over – was stay true to the core philosophy, know what the customers want and deliver it seamlessly every time.

It is critical that spa operators take note of what is happening in the industry and evaluate new trends. The key word there is 'evaluate'. Every spa operator needs to continually look at new ways to differentiate from competitors and broaden their market appeal. They should be strategic about it though, being guided by their philosophy and values, working with and developing their strengths and giving customers what they want with exceptional skill.

The figures will always indicate what works best in the market. This underscores the importance of having a reporting mechanism that not only tells the spa how much money guests spend, but what they spend it on. For a chain operator, this is likely to be different in each location so services menus and new treatment offerings will need to be tailored accordingly.

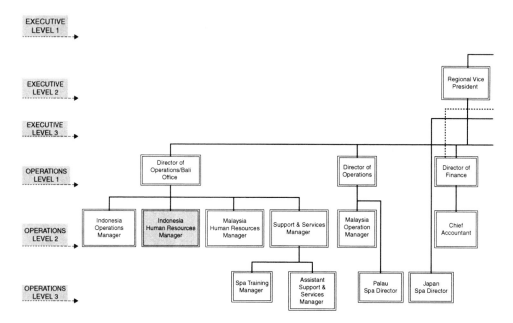

Figure 9.2
Mandara group organizational chart

Pillar 4: Systems and structure are essential

None of the Pillars mentioned thus far would be effective without the proper reporting and administration systems in place. Without systems and structure, much of what is done will be guess work or trial and error. This is exactly the way it was in Mandara Spa's early days, when management was reactive rather than proactive, scattered rather than focussed.

Having the right systems and structure enables a spa to motivate and reward staff, track results, understand guests better, attain financial objectives, find problems before they get out of control and run a profitable business with satisfied partners, team members and customers.

Organisational structure

Obviously, if a company is going to run successfully and drive revenues of millions of dollars it will need a very well-planned structure. If it is a spa business, it will also need a careful balance

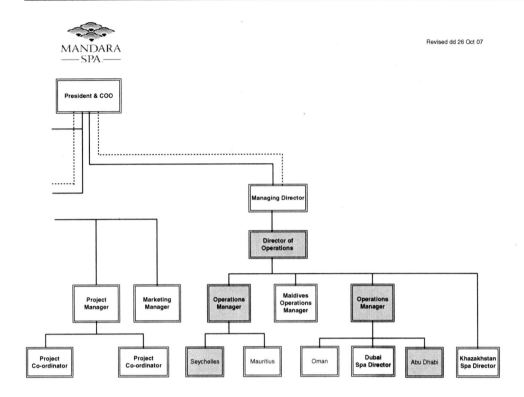

of managers – some with business backgrounds and some with spa and wellness backgrounds.

The minimum department head level needed to manage multiple spas is General Manager; Finance, Sales and Marketing; Training, Operations and Human Resources. To manage multiple spas in multiple countries, more layers are needed. For example, country Directors overseeing five or more spas, reporting to Managing Directors overseeing two to three countries, reporting to regional Vice Presidents (refer to Figure 9.2 for an example from Mandara Spa).

Daily operations reporting

When managing multiple spas, it's essential to know on a daily basis how every spa is performing, regardless of where the group manager might be in the world. If any of the spas are having problems, management will need to respond immediately in order to lessen the impact. There are two key components that are vital in this reporting: Key Performance Indicators (KPI) and progressive financials.

Table 9.3 Example of daily sales report from Mandara Spa

Revenue							Date:	
	Treatment							
Spa's	**TODAY**			**MTD**			**TODAY**	
	Actual Treatment	F'Cast Treatment	Variance Treatment	Actual Treatment	F'Cast Treatment	Variance Treatment	Actual Retail	F'Cast Retail
	USD	USD	USD	USD	USD	USD	USD	USD
Spa 1								
Spa 2								
Spa 3								
Total								

Statistical

			Treatment			
Spas	Total Occ. Rate	# of Rooms	Total Guests	In-house Guests	Capture Rate	Total Revenue
Spa 1						
Spa 2						
Spa 3						

Key performance indicators

KPI are the gauge by which success – or the lack of success – is measured and tracked. They are vitally important because they help to drive revenues, whether 1 spa or 20 spas are being operated. The basic KPIs are spa guest capture rate, outside guest capture rate, average treatment check, average retail check, spa bed occupancy and repeat guest numbers.

There are substantial differences in KPIs for spas in the East (i.e. Asia-Pacific) and those in the West (Europe, North America). In the East, the average check for spa revenue runs between US$65 and US$85 while in the West it averages from US$90 to US$140. Significant differences also show up in capture rates between resort spas and hotels spas, with resort spas generally being higher.

Financials

Financial reporting is about more than the money. It is a diagnostic tool, a planning tool and vital indicator of opportunities

Retail				Total Revenue					
MTD				TODAY				MTD	
Variance Retail	Actual Retail	F'Cast Retail	Variance Retail	Actual	F'Cast	Variance	Actual	F'Cast	Variance
USD	USD	USD	USD	USD	USD	USD	USD	USD	USD

Retail			M-T-D					M-T-D	
Total Guests	Capture Rate	Total Average Revenue Check	Total Guests	Capture Rate	Average Check	F'Cast Revenue	Budget Revenue		

and threats. If a daily report shows a spa under-performing, the first thing to do is find out why. It may simply be because it was the first sunny day in weeks and guests are out enjoying the weather. Or, it may be a problem with the operation that needs attention. Similarly, if a spa is significantly over-performing, management will want to know immediately so it can capitalise on a potential opportunity.

Financial reports will ideally show daily figures alongside month to date and indicate budgeted forecasts against actuals and what the variance is (Table 9.3).

Third party contracts

For a spa chain operator working with third parties, one of the most basic structures is the contract that governs distribution of revenue and expenses. There are three scenarios for creating a third party spa contract.

Revenue sharing model with no investment

The spa collects 100% of the revenue but shares a percentage of the gross revenue with the host hotel. The operating expenses are shared, proportionate to the revenue split. Depending on the country, the share to the hotel is between 20% and 40% off the top. Contract term is between 7 and 12 years with a renewal option.

Revenue sharing with full investment

This depends somewhat on the amount invested. For example, if investment is US$5 million for the build and fit out of a spa in a 500–800 room hotel, the contract term is likely to be 12–16 years with a renewal option in favour of the spa operator. The revenue sharing in year 1 would be zero, year 2–5 the hotel would get 8%, years 6–8 12%, and years 9 onwards 15%. This allows the operator to recover the investment in the first 7 years. This may vary, depending on the country, the selling prices at the spa, the guest demographic and the hotel occupancy. These and other various KPIs are carefully calculated into a spreadsheet that will give internal rate of return (IRR) and determines commercial terms of the contract.

A percentage of Gross Operating Revenue (GOR) and Gross Operating Profit (GOP)

This structure is very similar to a typical hotel management contract. There is no investment and no on-going costs for the spa operator. The spa operator receives a percentage of the top line, usually between 5% and 12%, and a percentage of GOP, usually between 9% and 14%. Naturally, these all depend on the type of hotel guests and other various KPIs used to calculate the potential revenue.

Other systems and structure

Beyond what is discussed above, structure and reporting mechanisms are required in every department. Here is an overview of the most basic structures:

● *Standard operating procedures (SOP)*: A key component for managing multiple locations. It is management's responsibility to ensure that staff live and breathe these standards, or else run the risk of delivering an inconsistent and substandard product.

- *Human resource (HR) systems*: As well as the obvious structure for such areas as the administration of employment contracts and leave entitlements, the HR department will need some form of performance management system that clarifies individual KPI and allows for appraisals, recognition and career development. For example, bonuses could be linked to guest satisfaction index, return guest ratio, yield management of beds, average revenue and occupancy per bed as well as success in retail upselling. On a staffing level, the performance management system could reflect the success of the management in reduction of turnover, positive employee opinion surveys and career growth within the team. Guidelines could then be set for the manager against these criteria and would thus become the generic KPI for each individual as well-enabling benchmarking for each spa. The individual's performance would be reviewed and appraised twice a year, during which time individual goals could be identified or redirected as appropriate based on success in the current role.
- *Production systems*: Having an in-house production department allows management to do more than control the quality of spa products and Furniture, Fixtures and Equipment (FF&E). It also saves money and can even make money if the structure allows for supplying to other spas. Supplier contracts, confidentiality agreements and stock control are some of the key systems that need to be in place.
- *Retail systems*: The fastest way to increase profit is through retail sales (see Chapter 12). If systems can be put in place through various staff incentives or the use of retail closers, profits can jump by as much as 60%. Ideally, a spa should aim for a treatment services to retail sales ratio of at least 70:30. However, this is not always achievable in a resort spa environment where repeat business and facial services are minimal. Mandara Spa's association with Elemis – another Steiner Leisure brand – has given the group some significant retail advantage. The Elemis 4 Steps to Retail Success System has helped Mandara to increase retail performance. As an example, one resort spa in Bali that had been achieving only 5% retail revenue jumped to 14% after the Elemis system was introduced. The same system used in an Elemis Day Spa saw retail increase from 15% to over 35% of revenue in just under a year. The Elemis 4 Steps to Retail Success System focuses on the following areas to increase retail revenue:
  - *Retail Training*: An on-going programme that keeps the team fresh on product knowledge and at their best technically. The focus is on product knowledge, unique

selling points for each product, link selling, upselling and client profiling that helps to adapt sales techniques.
- *Staff Incentives*: Varying incentive packages that are adapted to suit the individual spa business. These can be both individual and team based.
- *Treatment Menu Mix*: Evaluating the percentage of body treatments to facials. Although massages generally have a much lower cost in product, these treatments tend to have limited retail sales link. Encouraging more clients to try a facial and continue with retail homecare is critical to increasing retail revenue.
- *Visual Merchandising*: Clients love to shop, browse and experience. Sales increase dramatically when the products are not locked away behind glass cupboards. Testers that allow the client to try, feel and smell the product are critical to retail success. Elemis has developed tester units and glorifiers that highlight key products and keep the client stimulated and interested.

When structuring staff incentives for retail, it is important to ensure that financial targets are balanced with other customer service goals. Ideally, the retail approach should result in both increased revenue and an improved guest experience. If incentives targets are purely financial based, it can mean that sales are pursued at the expense of the guest experience.

The lessons of hindsight

During Mandara Spa's first 2 years, Tom and Mark did not take a salary and for the first 18 months actually contributed from their personal finances. Mandara Spa was under fiscal pressure to grow quickly and that pressure meant that mistakes were made.

Evaluate potential contracts

Mandara Spa used to sign up contracts based purely on their earning potential. This strategy hurt Mandara Spa's brand image for a while. Eventually the mistake was recognised and management became very defined and focussed on targeting the right kind of hotel partners for Mandara's business.

When evaluating a spa's financial and brand viability, Mandara now looks at areas such as the number of hotel rooms, actual and projected hotel occupancy, estimated spa capture rate, guest demographics and estimated average spa spend. Spa treatment prices can be estimated by looking at food and beverage, hotel room and transport costs, as these will indicate guest spending patterns.

Determine the right level of investment

One of the biggest financial mistakes a spa chain operator can make is to over invest on build and fit-out. Ideally, spa investment should be returned in 5–6 years. If an IRR above 25% can be obtained and overheads controlled, operating multiple spas can be a profitable business. However, many spas over-invest, making it difficult to achieve sustainable returns.

Make sure that systems fit the philosophy

Mandara Spa was founded on the ideal of having no replica spas. The goal was to create a collection of unique spas operating under a unified system. Those two goals were often at odds with each other. As a result, Mandara had beds that were too short for guests or too big for the room. It cost in terms of money and resources, but eventually Mandara got it right and now when a spa is opened, all that management needs to know is the size of the rooms, number of hotel guest rooms, hotel guest profile and number of spa rooms and the spa can be up and running in 4–6 months.

Going global requires research

Some of Mandara Spa's most avoidable mistakes have had to do with operating overseas. The golden rule is; if a spa group wants to go global then it must act local. And it helps to know what acting local involves before actually getting there. It is essential to know upfront if a particular country will not allow couple treatments or work visas for staff who are better equipped to perform spa therapies than local employees. During Mandara's venture into Japan, some costly errors were made that could have been avoided. More than 3000 pieces of black tea sets were sent, along with 10 000 menus with a particular white flower on the cover. When they arrived, it was found that black tea cups were not acceptable in Japan and the flower on the menu represented death! So, menu reprints had to be rushed through and new tea sets were bought in Tokyo at very high cost.

Summary

At the start of this chapter, it was noted that managing a chain of spas is not so dissimilar to managing a chain of stores or restaurants. In all cases, systems and structure are necessary for success.

The difficulty with spa chain operations is that in spas, interaction with customers is on a much more personalised and intimate level. Guests expect consistency, but they also expect the spa to have the flexibility to individualise experiences. Some people assume that to achieve this flexibility, systems should be minimised or even avoided. However, without a systematic structure and efficient reporting mechanisms, a spa chain operation is likely to experience poor financial performance, frustrated employees and disappointed guests. The real key to success is to ensure that the systems themselves are flexible and that they are developed with the guest experience in mind.

In summary, success comes easier to spa chain operators that:

- Set up excellent quality in-house training resources and systems to control that training.
- Set up and maintain standard qualities for services.
- Implement the right systems and reporting mechanisms for controlling revenues.
- Ensure that their brand values and identity are in sync with their core strengths, and that the brand strategy is filtered throughout the business.
- Implement a system to measure, reward and develop team performance.
- Focus on the quality of the experiences they deliver rather than how many different treatments they can offer.

Jeff Matthews likes to define success as: the ability to accept failure without any loss of enthusiasm, seeing it as a valuable learning experience and a catalyst for positive change. Keep your head down, your mind open and never give up!

The emergence of a new global luxury business model: a case study of the spa at the Mandarin Oriental

Ingo Schweder

The growing wellness industry

The new millennium is welcoming a series of industry and lifestyle trends arising out of a growing awareness of what it means to be well and how this can be achieved. The demand for wellness-related services is intensifying and constantly evolving and it has been observed that the public is becoming aware of the potential for optimizing health, improving performance, preventing disease and aging, and enhancing beauty from the inside out, through investment in wellness (Cohen, 2004).

In his book *The Wellness Revolution* (Pilzer, 2002), economist Paul Zane Pilzer suggests that in 2002 existing items in the US wellness industry such as spas, fitness centers and vitamins had reached approximately $200 billion. This includes $70 billion for vitamins and $25 billion for spas and fitness centers – about half the amount spent to purchase US automobiles. Pilzer further suggests that the $200 billion is only the tip of the iceberg, and wellness products and services represent the beginning of a new $1 trillion sector of the US economy. In an updated edition of his book, Pilzer estimates that in 2007 the wellness industry had expanded to over $500 billion and that the untapped market for wellness had increased in size due to millions of new wellness consumers (Pilzer, 2007).

The rise of the wellness consumer is aligned with a move towards Lifestyles of Health and Sustainability (LOHAS). In 2000 LOHAS described a $228 billion US marketplace for goods and services focused on health, the environment, personal development and sustainable living that include diverse market segments including personal health, natural lifestyles, green building, alternative energy and transportation and eco-tourism (www.lohas.com). A strong component of the LOHAS movement is trend for consumers to choose more holistic, prevention-based models of healthcare and this is evidenced by the increasing utilization of complementary and alternative medicine (Tindle et al., 2005). Spas have been predicted to play a major role in this with the suggestion that 'in the future, wellness retreats and spa will become centers of education, teaching the client how to take care of themselves and enjoy optimum health' (Stapleton, 2003).

Wellness, luxury and travel

Wellness is becoming a mainstream aspiration that is associated with luxury and prestige. Feature cover stories on wellness-related topics now frequently appear in most key global publications and multinational companies like CNN, Lloyds Insurance, HSBC and Cathay Pacific are strategically using 'wellness messages' to sell financial and other prestige products which are not necessarily wellness related. Wellness includes both physical and emotional satisfaction which may allow wellness services to demand premium prices. In 2002, the Boston Consulting Group published a research document titled 'The Trading Up Phenomenon' (Silverstein Neil Fiske, 2003). This report describes the concept of 'New Luxury' which refers to 'the phenomenon of middle-market consumers escaping the extraordinary stresses of modern life by carefully choosing high-quality, high-performance, emotionally satisfying goods and services' (Boston Consulting, 2002).

The trend towards health consciousness, emotional satisfaction and important consumer sentiments that drive spending has also been observed in the travel industry. In 2006 Kuoni – one of the world's biggest travel conglomerates – commissioned the Gottlieb Duttweiler Institute (GDI) in Switzerland to produce an in-depth report into the future of leisure travel in order to define how best to cater to new customer needs (Bosshart and Frick, 2006). This report which was based on the systematic analysis of specialist literature, trend studies and websites, along with interviews conducted with experts and online polls included the following findings:

- Our society is aging and it has been forecast that by 2020, the elderly will be the main travelers and children and young people will be in shorter supply.
- The growth of health consciousness will increase; destinations with contaminated water and beaches, polluted air, ugly buildings, risk of infections, etc. will be avoided. Unspoilt nature will become increasingly scarce and therefore more valuable.
- Instead of an ecstatic high, people want meditative tranquility and spiritual experiences. People are exhausted by life in the experience society. Opportunities for relaxation will become more important than entertainment.
- Polarization of demand will be apparent for cheap and luxury products and there will be growing pressure on the middle. There will be growing demand for individual travel and falling demand for package tours.
- Growing incomes mean that the great mass of people can travel solely for the sake of the experience, recuperation and pleasure, and there will be a search for concentrated recuperation, relaxation and regeneration with holidays

Table 10.1 The change in global hotel chain wellness center offerings

Previous millennium: Hotel fitness center model	New millennium: A holistic wellness sanctuary with therapeutic values
Gym	High-energy fitness
Pool	Holistic exercises & specialty programs
Dry sauna	Water & wet area experiences
Aerobics	Spa treatment services
Tennis	Wet area experiences
Squash	Nutrition expertise
	Spa merchandise
	Lifestyle event series
	Unique trend-setting designs
Standard offerings not linked to the brand	Brand defining core competency
No revenue/profit, but substantial investment/hotel amenity	Substantial business driver for hotel on several fronts and increased spending

viewed as emotional medicine against exhaustion, stress and depression.

- For tomorrow's health holidays, the emphasis will be less on the hardware, bathing facilities, saunas, fitness rooms, etc., and much more on the software, in other words, emotional and spiritual care.

The luxury hotel industry responds to consumer trends

With the merging of the wellness dollar with the travel dollar, there has been a corresponding shift in the health and leisure offerings of global hotel chains (Table 10.1). Previously these offerings were seen simply as an amenity that required substantial investment without bringing in revenue. This has now changed. In the current millennium there are no hotels or resorts in the first class or luxury segment conceptualized without a dedicated spa and wellness component. Spas are also considered to be much more than an amenity. Spa operations are becoming a core competency and a substantial business driver for luxury hotels and an element that can help define the hotel's philosophy and underpin its brand recognition. This represents a dramatic shift that has taken place in a relatively short period of time. The remaining chapter illustrates how this development occurred using the spa at the Mandarin Oriental, the first hotel group to develop this competency, as a case study.

The birth of spas as core competency for a global hotel group

Around the turn of the millennium after reflecting on the emerging wellness trend and the scientific and lifestyle research, the CEO of Mandarin Oriental Hotel Group (MOHG), Edouard Ettedgui, made a decision to create a new core competency for the Group and globalize the company's spa operations. His aim was to grow the company's spa, wellness and leisure offerings and thus enhance its overall positioning and image while simultaneously growing profitability and internal management know-how. This was forward thinking as at the time no luxury hotel chain had a global spa operation or had made spa and wellness management a core competency alongside Rooms and Food & Beverage (F&B) management.

To implement this strategy Mr. Ettedgui began looking for a Global Spa Director who was a global hotelier and former hotel General Manager who had worked on a minimum of three continents, had in-depth expertise in design and development, an astute hotel-related financial acumen, and was an effective team leader with a passion for wellness. In 2001 by accepting this position, the author became the first Head of the 'MOHG Spa Division'.

The position of Group Spa Director was initially a lonely, one-man enterprise with significant challenges including:

- The 'General System of Accounts' used by all hotel management companies to account for their revenue streams had no section for the spa segment. There was therefore a general lack of measures and financial systems in place to account for the ever-growing revenues and expenses this new business segment was generating within the hotel industry. This is no longer the situation (see Chapter 6).
- There were no guidelines or industry-wide understanding of how to effectively market spa as part of a global hotel business.
- Most spa consultant companies were offering hands-on training and menu planning support but not comprehensive, in-depth marketing, business and strategic advice.
- While selected product houses offered design and technical service solutions, their competency was, and still is, limited to the development of products and their associated treatments.

- There was little data available to help the industry at large to relate to the overall market dynamics and help understand the guest's preferences.
- While spa management companies like Mandara and Banyan Tree had developed an Asian tropical spa business model for hoteliers to buy into, this was limited to Asia and was impractical for global hotel companies and high end urban projects elsewhere in the world.
- There were no peers within the industry with which to bounce ideas off or compare notes with (within the next 3 years, Fairmont Hotels, Starwood Hotels, Ritz-Carlton Hotels, Hyatt Hotels and others had all appointed a dedicated senior executive to manage their respective spa and wellness operations).

The beginning of a new core competency for a luxury hotel company

In early 1993, when the spa at the Oriental in Bangok opened, it was the world's only hotel with Spa Suites. In the later part of the same year, however, the Shangri La Taipei opened with designers Peter Remedios, and George Wong along with then Hotel Manager Ingo Schweder, creating eight dedicated spa suites on the 42nd floor with views over the entire city. Nearly a decade later, in early 2001, Mandarin Oriental only had two in-house managed spas located in Macau and Bangkok, yet additional openings in London, Miami and Turn-berry Isle were planned and from 2003 onwards and further new openings were planned for prestigious Mandarin Oriental Hotels in New York, Washington, Bermuda, Chiang Mai, Hong Kong, Prague, Tokyo, Singapore, Boston, Riviera Maya and other vibrant locations and key brand defining travel destinations. All these properties required the creation of a uniquely designed, profitable and well managed spa. There was therefore an urgent need to create a structure in order to formulate the group's efforts in the spa and wellness realm.

While today there are professional spa management companies like Spatality (www.spatality.com) MSpa (www.mspa-international.com) and Raison D'Tre (www.raisondetrespas.com) offering business support structures to create and extend spa brands for hotels, at the time there was no professional spa management company deemed adequate to effectively manage MOHG's mostly urban spas in a transparent manner. Furthermore, while Mandarin Oriental had made an earlier decision to engage the consultancy services of a product company for technical services, spa product and spa menu training, it was agreed that the image and positioning created by outsourcing spa services to a product house would not support MOHG in the long run and would undermine the hotel group's valuable brand. The team therefore knew that it had to build up MOHG's very own spa identity and it became the job of the Global Spa Director to create the required company-wide structure to strengthen the Group's new business segment and establish a global awareness of the Group's expertise and leadership.

Creating the structure, image and positioning

The initial efforts of MOHG's newly created Spa Division involved assessing the needs of the group and creating the structure for a spa business model that could support MOHG's global operations. In February, 2001, a strategy document was discussed between the key company stakeholders, outlining the group's immediate and future goals necessary to identify the MOHG brand for excellence in spa and wellness services.

The outcome of the meeting was that the team was determined to fund, structure and conceptualize the Group's in-house spa concept and make it a vibrant, brand defining core competency. In practical terms, this meant that there was a need to define and develop a myriad of nuances required to create industry-wide systems and processes for MOHG's design and development, marketing and operational capabilities as well as future needs. The team determined that it would apply tailor-made, yet commonly applicable, business systems and processes to create hotel industry benchmarks. These were to have the depth to serve as worldwide guidelines that other hotel companies could benefit from.

While reflecting on a wide amount of customer and industry data and research material, the MOHG spa concept was created. The vision of this initiative was to bring alive a sincere understanding of wellness within the company involving the genuine delivery of holistic services, intrinsically linked to the Asian roots of the company and woven sensitively into the conceptualization and design of future facilities. The team then developed an overall guiding philosophy to be innovative and responsive to change within the triangle of tradition, innovation and quality. The team also developed a worldwide MOHG spa brand identifying logo in order to identify spa as a stand-alone business model that could be seen as a well conceptualized core competency that was an extension of the Mandarin Oriental brand.

Expanding the knowledge base

True to the meaning of 'spa' as 'Salus per Aquam' or 'health through water', the team aimed to ensure that bathing and the historical context of water was a dominant and clearly defined concept element of MOHG's spas. The team wanted to build contemporary spas but not miss learning from forebears who had already very advanced technologies and bathing forms integrated into historical monuments of wellness. Visits to Turkey and Lebanon were undertaken to investigate the roots of the original hammam. Time was spent in Moscow in order to research the workings, cultural associations and systems in which historical Banyas, an almost extinct bathing and entertainment form, had flourished centuries ago. Rome offered the study of the architecture and flow of the Caracalla Thermae, an ancient (212–216 AD) spa and wellness complex that could accommodate 1600 people, build on 33 acres in downtown Rome (one can still visit its ruins). Various wellness centers and onsen locales were visited in Hokkaido, Japan, to study the Japanese bathing culture.

In addition to developing an in-depth understanding of spa within the Spa Division, it was evident that in order to bring spa and wellness into the fabric of the company, it was necessary to instill in-depth professional spa and wellness knowledge amongst all senior executives and key stakeholders in the company. To achieve this a range of experts were brought in. An alliance was formed with Prof. Marc Cohen at RMIT University who conducted a series of seminars on wellness for the Group's General Managers and senior executives as well as running a series of in-depth retreats with the Group's Spa Managers/Directors. William Pfeiffer, Managing Director, Columbia Pictures in Asia/Pacific was commissioned to run a workshop on cultural sensitivities and maintaining cultural integrity while Prof. Mary Tabbachi from Cornell University gave lectures to Spa Directors on the importance of spas in new hotel developments. The groups annual general meetings and marketing meetings also included dedicated spa workshops and all Spa Managers/Directors were made to serve as executive members of their respective hotel.

While these initiatives led to a steady increase in the depth of knowledge and extent of spa and wellness know-how throughout the company, there was little data available to understand the overall market dynamics or specific guest's preferences. This was addressed from 2003 onwards by compiling in-depth research on the consumer spending of every hotel guest who simultaneously enjoyed spa services. In this way the team learned about spa-goers likes and dislikes, their preferences and choices. Detailed databases and statistics were then compiled in order to learn more about clients, allowing MOHG's spa program to react instantly in its day-to-day operations

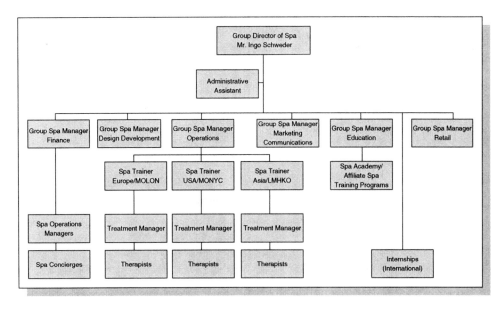

Figure 10.1
Organization chart for Group Spa Division in 2006

and incorporate this learning into all of the new projects being planned. An awareness had been generated of a new market segment – the MOHG spa savvy traveler.

Creating structure and processes

It was evident that a Division of one was not enough to sustain the progression. Little by little more individuals were incorporated to fill key roles that would bring the MOHG spa concept to fruition. By the fall of 2006, the Division of one had matured into a corporate Division of 13 staff with a defined organizational structure (Figure 10.1). Furthermore, many key initiatives were identified to take a new business segment in the hotel industry and make it a valuable contributor to the overall organization (Table 10.2).

'What does not get measured, does not get done' is a statement applicable to all business segments. In order to measure and manage performance, generate awareness of the new business and make the organization aware of the industry dynamics, monthly charts containing detailed financial information were created and distributed to all corporate stakeholders and all hotels, as well as to all regional offices. Information collected includes:

- Revenue
- Profit

Table 10.2 Changes in operations and key initiatives undertaken to create spa operations as a core competency within the MOHG, 2001–2006

2001	2006
Financial reporting and statistics	
• No synchronized reporting structure.	• New group-wide budget format with standardized panel review system. – Workshops with all financial controllers in order to ensure familiarization with new business segment, terms and business dynamics.
• Limited statistics available on guest preferences, guest purchasing patterns and the relationship between leisure and rooms.	• Comprehensive monthly P & L and guest statistic comparisons sent to corporate stakeholders, General Managers and Spa Directors. – Group Spa Director reviews and comments on all hotel budgets and makes recommendations. – Yearly survey of 19,000+ MOHG spa consumers from 2003 onwards in order to learn about their spending patterns, booking source and general likes and dislikes, see separate graph.
Revenue and profit	
• Negligible amount of revenue from spas.	• 366% increase in revenue with a corresponding increase in profit from MOHG spas between 2001 and 2005.
• 3% of total rooms revenue from spa.	• Over 10% of total company rooms revenue from spa.
Marketing	
• Little data on Key clients, distribution channels, and specifics on wellness market segment.	• Spa Software interfacing with hotel PMS for better data collection. – detailed data mining in order to feed information back into marketing plans, development strategies and ongoing operations
• No separate marketing efforts for the spa included in the hotel's overall marketing plan.	• In-depth marketing plan format for spas. – Group spa team actively participating in all group marketing and sales meetings/workshops, etc.

Table 10.2 (Continued)

2001	2006
● No website dedicated to the spa.	● Spa is a key feature of MOHG website.
● Limited marketing, communication and sales activities and programs in relation to the spa.	● Group Spa Marketing Best Practices Manual developed to include CRM, marketing communication ideas, programs, partners, sales activities, events, specialized packages, public relations, merchandising and revenue management. – Monthly meetings between Group Spa Division and Group Communications Division to structure combined efforts.
● 6 different logos and brand identities.	● Group Spa Manager – marketing hired at head office. ● Integrated worldwide applicable spa identity established. ● Authentic ethnic-inspired MO signature treatment and experiences implemented. ● MO spa merchandise on sale group-wide (CDs, signature products, lounge wear, tea and more).

People

2001	2006
● Shortage of qualified therapists, supervisors and MOHG Spa Managers.	● Spa Academy under development.
● Need identified to grow spa know-how throughout all layers of MOHG management and supervisory team members.	● Formed alliance with Prof. Cohen from RMIT University and Prof. Tabacci from Cornell University. – Annual general meetings and marketing meetings included dedicated spa workshops.
● Not sufficient in-house resources of spa treatment and spa business educated professionals.	– All Spa Managers/Directors to serve as executive members of their respective hotel. ● Cornell University graduates and Regional Group Spa Trainer in Asia and USA.

(Continued)

Table 10.2 (Continued)

2001	2006
• No collaboration with renowned hotel business university faculties like Cornell, NYU, Johnson and Wells, Michigan State University and others.	• Comprehensive training and cross exposure to Cornell Hotel School graduates at MO New York, MO Washington, Landmark Mandarin Oriental Hong Kong and elsewhere.
	• The spa is integral subject during every group-wide operations, marketing, finance review as well as all group-wide workshops.

Operations

2001	2006
• No synergy between properties.	• Group-wide comprehensive training plan initiated.
• No LQE measurements.	• Updated spa LQEs implemented in all locations.
• No accountability for spa results in openings. GMs are not held accountable for spa results.	• Developed critical path format for maximum effectiveness and efficiency in new spa openings.
	• Key performance indicators for hotels executives included measurement for overall spa operations results.
• Guest satisfaction not measured.	• Spa Guest Satisfaction Surveys refined in all hotels.
• No accountability for spa service standards.	• Spa became part of overall Richey Report hotel evaluation.
• Not sufficient hotel operations and spa management exchange in hotels leading to functional silos.	• Monthly phone calls between Spa Division and all operating units.
• No communication between properties	• Yearly group-wide Spa Seminar and cross exposure tour for all Spa Directors and MOHG Spa Division.
• Complete dependence on outside consultants to assess standards.	• Internal Mystery Shopper program.
• Outsourced operations in Singapore, Manila, Kuala Lumpur, Surabaya.	• No outsourced operation/contract will be extended.
• No spa retail know-how.	• Comprehensive range of MO branded lifestyle products, music and lounge wear created embedding the MOHG heritage and quality hallmarks.
• No comprehensive approach to maximize business understanding in team members installed.	• Group Spa Manager – Operations.
	• Group Spa Trainer for each continent – Group Spa Manager – Finance.

- Payroll
- Therapist utilization
- Treatment room utilization
- Daily revenue per treatment room
- Daily profit per treatment room
- Top guest satisfaction score – spa
- Top guest satisfaction score – fitness center
- Top guest satisfaction score – beauty

All results and achievements were ranked in order to develop a healthy competition amongst all stakeholders in the group.

Consistently striving for improvements

In order to continue to remain at the forefront, the spa team constantly initiated new group internal benchmarks:

- The menu of MO spa experiences were re-engineered twice a year and Mandarin Oriental Signature Treatments were added.
- While applying the results of the guest research, the team further defined and upgraded the LQEs (Leading Quality Standards) in order to energize customer service standards;
- The spa SOPs (Standard Operating Procedures) were further defined as a group-wide system in order to standardize minimum service levels in all global operations;
- The group's marketing efforts were strengthened by creating a detailed Marketing Best Practice Manual.
- Group Spa Director's conferences and workshops were organized. These often took place in the Asia-Pacific region in order to expose US- and Europe-based Spa Directors to the company's Asian roots.
- The spa team actively participated in supporting group-wide sales efforts with large-scale events in Moscow, New York City and London.
- A structure for activities and documentation was established to support the successful induction of new employees and managers and to support the efficient set-up of new spas.

Design and development

By 2002 it was recognized that the level of growth would require a detailed technical services guideline in order to ensure that all the design teams could simultaneously manage their design processes to the required standard. Initially the Group Spa Director created a detailed concept, area program and critical path for each new spa development and initiated extensive design and development meetings to enable their implementation. A collaboration with Sean O'Connor, who had a wide variety of experience in the fitness, golf and related leisure industry was also established and together with the Group Spa Director a detailed manual outlining the design parameters, fixture, finishes and measurements of every inch of a spa was compiled.

The MOHG spa design benchmarks became firmly established with the openings of the spa at Mandarin Oriental New York in 2003 and the Landmark Mandarin Oriental Spa in 2005 and in early 2006, Sean joined the MOHG team and became the first global head of spa design and development services working full time for a luxury hotel company (see Chapter 8).

In 2003/2004 there was a challenge to create a design brief for what was planned to be, at that time, the world's best urban spas, both located in Hong Kong and operated by MOHG, both very different and both only 100 meters apart from each other.

One became the Oriental Spa at the Landmark Mandarin Oriental. Developed by a team led by the Group Spa Director and designer Peter Remedios, this was created as a contemporary urban oasis with linear architectural lines and extensive use of warm Indian sandstone and Italian mosaic. Knowledge obtained from the previous investigative tours had substantial influence on what was done with the bathing component at this spa. This was very much a modern, lifestyle driven hotel, with shopping, pampering and contemporary interiors designed to appeal to the taste of the globe trotting, bohemian urban elite the MO wanted to attract. The spa included yoga, Pilates, a swimming pool, café and an aquatic circuit with uniquely designed vitality pools, hammams, herbal saunas and tropical rain showers at a time when most other spas in the region still bought off-the-shelf sauna units.

The other spa was situated on the top floors of the historical Mandarin Oriental hotel overlooking the Victoria Harbor and as such, a contemporary expression of the vibrancy of 1930s Shanghai. This was recreated with modern amenities, from a Kinesis studio, Kneipp walks, dedicated Thai, Shiatsu and Ayurveda treatment rooms with Neem tree tables, a modern day male barber and an Italian beauty and hair salon. All facilities and services were rooted in the eclectic, yet refined historical context of Shanghai in the 1930s.

The outcome was two urban destination spas and wellness centers which were fiercely competing with each other. However, as their design integrity, atmosphere and services were quite different, the center of down town Hong Kong had gained two new oasis of modern luxury with a wide selection of spa services available for a wide variety of consumers. The spas were extending each other, harmonizing their respective offerings, complementing their services. The only thing they really had in common was the same high level of service and quality of workmanship.

Recognition

Soon after further innovative spas were opened with features never seen before in the industry, such as in the MO Tokyo where two pools – one vitality pool and one relax whirl pool with reclining water lounge chairs – were wedged into the curtain wall of the 38th floor wet areas for both genders. By 2005, the momentum the Group had established proved that initiatives taken in the spa sector were propelling Mandarin Oriental Hotel Spas forward. Four MOHG's spas were rated in the World's Top 10 Best Urban Spas by Conde Naste Traveler, UK, in their 2005 Reader's Spa Awards:

- # 1 Miami
- # 3 New York
- # 7 Bangkok
- # 9 London

In 2005, Conde Naste Traveler, USA also gave MOHG's New York spa with the highest score for two categories – Urban Hotel Spa and Treatments. *Luxury Spafinder Magazine* honored MOHG in 2005 by including five MO spas within the top 10 urban spas in the world. In 2006 *Spa Asia* and 2005 *Asia Spa* magazine voted MOHG 'Best Spa company' and again at the European Spa Summit in Monte Carlo in early 2006. Mandarin Oriental was again voted as 'Best Global Spa Company'. In less than 5 years Mandarin Oriental had established its leadership in the spa industry by creating a myriad of brand defining holistic wellness concepts and became recognized as the world's most awarded spa company (Table 10.3).

After only 5 years Mr. Ettedgui's decision to enter the spa and wellness industry had paid off. The company had succeeded in creating substantial brand value, had maximized profits and share holder values and had identified what is today recognized as one of MOHG's key contribution to this nascent industry. That is, the acknowledgement that spa services within a luxury hotel adds more than just spa revenue/profit and a leisure offering. Rather, spas drive demand for higher paying leisure guests and spa consumers in general pay higher room rate; tend to stay longer and as such, offer a substantially higher financial value to the overall hotel.

Table 10.3 Industry awards from MOHG spa operations 2005–2006

European Spa Forum Monte Carlo 2006
    Best Spa Company or Wellness Group
    ● Mandarin Oriental Hotel Group
Spa Asia magazine Hua Hin 2006
    Best Day Spa
    ● Mandarin Oriental Tokyo
    Best Destination Spa
    ● Mandarin Oriental Dhara Devi
    Best Wellness and Spa Company
    ● Mandarin Oriental Hotel Group
    Most Inspired Industry Motivator
    ● Ingo Schweder
Conde Nast Traveller Spa Awards (UK) (2006)
    Best Overseas Day Spa – Worldwide
    ● #2 The Spa, Mandarin Oriental Miami
    ● #5 The Oriental Spa, The Oriental, Bangkok
Conde Nast Traveller Spa Awards (UK) 2005
    Best Overseas Day Spa – Worldwide
    ● #1 The Spa, Mandarin Oriental Miami
    ● #3 The Spa at the Mandarin Oriental New York
    ● #7 The Oriental Spa, The Oriental, Bangkok
    Best Urban Day Spa in the UK
    ● #1 The Spa Mandarin Oriental Hyde Park, London
Gallivanter's Guide (UK) 2006
    Best Spa in a Hotel/Resort Worldwide
    ● #1 The Oriental Spa, The Oriental, Bangkok
Mobile Travel Guide – USA (2006)
    Best Spas in America – Five Star Award
    ● The Spa at the Mandarin Oriental New York
Celebrated Living –The Platinum List 2006
    Top 10 US Spas 2006
    ● # 6 The Spa, Mandarin Oriental Miami
    Top 10 International Spas
    ● #5 The Oriental Spa, The Oriental, Bangkok
    ● #9 The Spa Mandarin Oriental Hyde Park, London
Luxury Spafinder –Readers Choice Awards (2005)
    Country Awards (China And Japan)
    ● The Landmark Mandarin Oriental, Hong Kong
    ● Mandarin Oriental, Tokyo
Baccarat Asia Spa Award – Hong Kong (2005)
    Spa Marketing
    ● Mandarin Oriental Hotel Group
    Spa Exterior of the Year
    ● Mandarin Oriental Dhara Dhevi, Chiang Mai
    Spa Personality of the Year
    ● Ingo R. Schweder, Group Director of Spa

Conclusion

The increasing public awareness about wellness along with increasing affluence, the shift towards lifestyle change and holistic models of healthcare and the merging of the health and travel dollar, has provided the foundation for the spa industry. The spending habits of the typical spa consumer have also continued to increase as consumers learn more about the benefits of leading a wellness-centric lifestyle. While luxury hotel chains have in some regards played catch-up with these trends, it is now clear that spa and wellness will be an entrenched component of the luxury hotel market for the foreseeable future.

Acknowledgement

The above was literally written days before departing from Mandarin Oriental and returning to my entrepreneurial roots. The meteoric rise and the in-depth implementation of spa as a new core competency for luxury hotels was an exceptional team effort and I want to thank all MOHG Spa Division team members for their dedication, hard work and commitment to excellence.

References

Bosshart, D., Frick, K. (2006) *The Future of Leisure Travel*, An independent study created by the Gottlieb Duttweiler Institute on behalf of Kuoni, Kuoni 2006, available at: http://www.gdi.ch/fileadmin/user_uploads/pdf_media/studien/Kuoni_Studie_2006_E.pdf).

Boston Consulting (2002) *Despite the Economy, Pursuit of 'New Luxury' Redefines How, Why and What We Buy*, According to New Report from the Boston Consulting Group, available at: http://www.hospitalitynet.org/news/4013926.search? query = the + trading + up + phenomenon + 2002 + boston + consulting

Cohen, M. (2004) *Academia Responds to Healing and Wellness Trends*, Presentation at the Turning Point Seminar, Singapore.

Pilzer, P.Z. (2002) *The Wellness Revolution: How to Make a Fortune in the Next Trillion Dollar Industry*, John Wiley and Sons, NJ.

Pilzer, P.Z. (2007) *The New Wellness Revolution: How to Make a Fortune in the Next Trillion Dollar Industry*, John Wiley and Sons, NJ.

Silverstein, M., Neil Fiske, N. (2003) *Trading Up: The New American Luxury*, Penguin, New York.

Stapleton, J. (2003) Keynote address at the International Spa Association Europe Congress, Slovenia.

Tindle, H.A., Davis, R.B., Phillips, R.S., Eisenberg, D.M. (2005) Trends in use of complementary and alternative medicine by US adults: 1997–2002, *Alternative Therapies in Health and Medicine*, 11(1):42–49.

PART 3

Product

Branding and spas

Samantha Foster

What is branding?

It has been suggested by Walter Landor that: 'Products are created in the factory; brands are created in the mind.' (Casey, 2004).

Most dictionaries tend to define 'brand' as a distinguishing name and/or symbol intended to identify the goods or services of a seller, and to differentiate those goods or services from a competitor. This simplistic definition omits the aspect of branding that is perhaps the most important in modern marketing: that is, the creation of an emotional link, or relationship, with the consumer.

Branding originated with consumer goods companies, however, in today's competitive environment, it is equally applic able to service industries such as spa. Commonly regarded as the domain of marketers, branding is in fact inseparable from overall business strategy. In applying branding to a spa, it must underpin every aspect of the operation – permeating spa design, the selection of inventory products and treatment menu, the creation of signature treatments and operating procedures, as well as the production of marketing materials.

The foundation of effective branding is a strong concept, which is translated and applied so that guests enjoy a consistent experience. It is through this consistent experience that guests build up knowledge and form perceptions about the spa. These perceptions may be created from a guest's own encounter, but also transmitted to non-guests by word-of-mouth, the media, or even gleaned from marketing collaterals and the internet. The aim of branding is partly to create these perceptions, but more importantly to facilitate their development into an enduring relationship between the guest and the spa.

Branding is about relationships

When developing a relationship with another person, first impressions are created by their appearance: Are they appealing? Are they someone that one would like to know better? When engaged in conversation, does their personality shine through in a way that is attractive? Gestures (or actions) and tone of voice add greater dimension, and help to bond people, or drive them apart. Similarities create 'chemistry', drawing people together, whilst a lack of common ground can leave people feeling that they are 'just not right for each other'. As relationships deepen, people get to know each other's values: the key drivers that shape their behaviour. At this point, they feel that they 'know' the person, and can decide to what extent they want him or her in their life.

Branding applies this same process to business. In the spa industry, guests are first drawn by the appearance or description of the spa; either its physical facilities, and/or through marketing collaterals. Upon contact, it is the staff and service protocols that start to imbue the spa with personality, making the guest feel welcome and comfortable. The 'tone of voice', reflected through décor, verbal and written communications, helps guide guests as to how they should interact with the spa. For example, a formal and elegantly restrained environment creates an atmosphere of reverent silence, whereas a colourful, lively spa encourages more casual interaction. The values of a spa are generally reflected in its policies and procedures, and become most evident when there is a problem that needs solving. An example of a value may be a spa that is committed to 'results', and manifests this value by offering a service guarantee.

Implicit in the process of branding is the concept of differentiation. Just as people differ in their choice of friends, they also differ in their choice of brands. One spa can't be all things to all people, and so spa owners and managers need to take great care in choosing a target audience who will be most responsive to their concept and the total product offering.

In the marketing classic, *The 22 Immutable Laws of Branding*, Ries and Ries assert that 'customers want brands that are narrow in scope and are distinguishable by a single word, the shorter the better' (Ries and Ries, 1998 p. 6) and also note that a brand becomes stronger as you narrow it's focus. Their Law of Singularity states that the most important aspect of a brand is its single-mindedness. The first step in branding is to develop a strong concept which encapsulates this single-minded point of difference.

Why is branding important for a spa?

Spa is a relatively young industry, and in countries where spa is still in its infancy, it remains a 'seller's market'. Excess demand generally ensures early entrants a steady stream of business, and so they need to give little heed to what the customer really wants. As Henry Ford said, when he introduced the first car affordable to the mass market: 'any customer can have a car painted any colour that he wants so long as it is black'.

When there is little competition, spa owners can do as they wish. If a customer is dissatisfied, there is always another customer ready to take their place. However, as the industry becomes more competitive, spa owners need to find some means by which to make their spa more attractive to consumers. Branding achieves this in two ways:

1. It creates a unique identity – one that will resonate with and attract the desired clientele.
2. It saves clients' time by allowing them to buy on 'trust' – the ultimate shortcut to a buying decision.

Why do clients buy on trust?

It is not that spa clients are ignorant: on the contrary, spa-goers are highly interested consumers, and are becoming increasingly savvy. They read spa and health-related articles, and actively research treatments, products and potential spas on the internet. However, they are simply bombarded with choice, and don't have the time to investigate the features and benefits of every option. Therefore they tend to buy what they trust, as this eliminates the risk of disappointment.

This is where brand becomes so valuable: a strong brand creates a relationship; a relationship creates trust, and trust encourages purchase behaviour: 'I can buy with confidence now, and think about the details later'.

To the successful brand owner, the benefits of branding are significant. In their book, *Marketing Aesthetics*, Schmitt and Simonson (1997) identify five important benefits of a reputable brand:

1. it creates consumer loyalty;
2. it enables premium pricing;
3. brand aesthetics cut through information clutter, increasing memorability of the brand's visual marks, which in turn increases chance of selection at the point of purchase;
4. it provides protection from competitive attacks;
5. it facilitates cost savings and increased productivity, as employees and suppliers need to spend less time in creating new layouts and messages.

In addition, a good brand can attract top quality employees; an important advantage given the current labour shortage within the spa industry. A Brand can also provide leverage for securing financial resources. In an article for The Economist book, *Brands and Branding*, branding consultancy Interbrand cites research showing that brand equity accounts for 51% of Coca-Cola's company value. McDonalds is even higher, with 70% of company value (The Economist, 2003). Companies can borrow against the value of their brand equity, leveraging this intangible asset for growth and development.

Concept development

Concept development requires more than a point of difference. As a fundamental part of the business strategy, the brand must also be seamlessly aligned with the business objectives. Other key considerations are the type of spa and location, as this will determine the target market and their motivations for spa use. Once a possible concept has been identified, it should then be reviewed in the context of the market, to ensure that the brand can indeed claim a unique niche relative to its competitors.

Ries and Ries maintain that authenticity is a crucial ingredient in the success of any brand and that the best claim to authenticity is being the leading product or service in your category, because consumers assume that if it is a leading seller, it must be good. (Ries and Ries, 1998)

Authenticity goes beyond mere 'claims' of leadership: any claims must be able to be supported, thereby giving consumers a solid reason to believe. Without proof, the brand is vulnerable to attack: either by competitors, or by consumers who have had an experience that does not live up to the brand promise.

Neumeier (2003) argues that if a brand can't be number one or two in the market, then it is better off redefining its category. The reason for this is that the market leader garners all of the benefits of branding as previously described. The further down a field the brand is located, the more it must compete on price. Its product becomes commoditised, and it is difficult to sustain healthy profit margins.

Planning for longevity is important, as it maximises the value of the brand over time. Ries and Ries claim that 'once you get on top, it's hard to lose your spot' (Ries and Ries, 1998, p. 32). They cite a widely publicized study of 25 leading brands in 25 different product categories from the year 1923. Seventy five years later, twenty brands are still the leaders in their categories: to this day, only five brands lost their leadership.

Concept application

Once developed, the concept needs to be applied to a defined target market. In doing this, it is helpful to segment the market not only on demographics (such as age, sex, geography, income), but also on psychographic profile: defining the customer in terms of his or her lifestyle, personality and values. Knowing that branding relies upon the formation of a relationship, the more specific the target market definition, the more likely the branding team will be able to craft the brand experience in a manner that is relevant and attractive to that market.

Schmitt (1999) concludes that an effective brand must deliver a consumer experience via one or more of five strategies:

1. Sense: the tangible aspects of the brand experience that appeal to the five senses, attracts attention and motivates.
2. Feel: eliciting moods and emotions that create an effective bond and makes the experience personally relevant and rewarding.
3. Think: encouraging customers to engage in thinking that may result in their re-evaluation of the company and products and adding a permanent cognitive interest to the experience.
4. Act: aims to create experiences through behaviour on the part of the customer. The goal is to change long-term behaviour and habits in favour of the spa's product or service. Examples of this marketing strategy may be educational workshops.
5. Relate: this strategy plays upon the identification of self with the context and associations bound up in the spa product or service. Relate-marketing often links the brand to lifestyles and aspirations and goes beyond the individual experience and makes it meaningful in a broader social context.

The mechanisms, or 'experience providers', by which these strategies are delivered, span every aspect of the business, from signage to choice of aroma.

Aspects of spa branding: tools for differentiation

When creating or analysing a brand, it is helpful to view it in five aspects (Figure 11.1):

1. the attributes (features or assets) of the spa;
2. the benefits that these attributes deliver to the guest;
3. the underlying values that shape the spa's activity;
4. the personality with which the spa communicates;
5. Brand essence: in summary, the key differentiator.

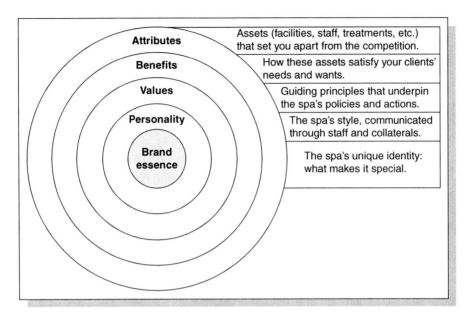

Figure 11.1
Aspects of branding

Attributes

Attributes are those assets that can differentiate the spa from its competition, and may include one or more of: concept, location, facilities, design elements, staffing, products, treatments and rituals or procedures. Each of these shall be addressed here:

Concept

Concept is critical, because it forms the foundation of the spa's identity, from which all facets of the brand are created. Concept development requires consideration of business context and strategy, as discussed earlier, but of paramount importance is selection or creation of the spa theme. The theme often draws heavily on features of the location, the indigenous heritage, the nature of the owner and the nature of the guest.

For example, the Spa at Hotel Hershey (www.hersheypa.com) centres its spa experience around Hershey's fame for chocolate, whereas destination spa Ananda in the Himalayas (www.anandaspa.com) draws on India's rich healing traditions and the grand heritage of its hotel property as inspiration for the spa's Ayurvedic concept. In contrast, Clinique La Prairie (www.clinique.au) is renowned for its cosmetic and medical procedures; its concept clearly formed around the needs of the medi-spa client.

It is important that the spa concept is carried through in the choice of spa name, tag line (if any) and logo. All should combine to tell a story, communicating a clear idea as to the type of spa, and the experience that it promises.

Location

Every spa must consider it's location during concept development, as it governs the type of guest who will use the spa. Location is particularly important in establishing the branding for hotel and resort spas, as a priority for most leisure travellers is to experience the local culture. Spa provides an ideal way to showcase the culture and deliver an authentic experience that embraces all of the five senses.

Facilities

Facilities can be used to support brand identity, although it is a risky proposition to differentiate one's spa brand solely on this basis. The industry is changing so rapidly, and facilities (such as a 'crystal steam room') can be copied or bettered in a relatively short period of time. This is especially true as the industry matures and attracts big business investment.

To stand out from the crowd, facilities need to be either unique, or sufficiently different to attract attention. It is often the design of a facility, rather than its mere existence, that makes it newsworthy. For example, when Thailand's Chiva-Som opened in 1994 it was not the first spa to offer floatation, however the spacious design of its floatation chamber, compared to the traditional claustrophobia-inducing tanks, supported the brand's luxury positioning, and garnered the health resort a lot of media exposure.

Spa design

In designing a spa, there is often a tussle between the designer and the operator over the relative importance of form versus function. Designers strive to give the spa a unique identity (which is ideal for branding), however there are many operational constraints that affect the layout, and selection of materials, finishes, and furnishings. The designer of an Asian spa may wish to line the walls with silk, for example, to introduce the rich, exotic colours and textures of Asia, however an experienced operator would resist this because of the high likelihood of oil stains and the expense of continual replacement.

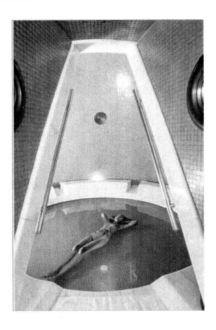

One of the most effective ways to incorporate branding into spa design is through the use of a signature motif, which can be used not only in the physical structure, but also in every element of the spa that involves design. The accompanying photos of Devarana Spa (www.devaranaspa.com), owned by Thailand's Dusit Thani hotels, demonstrate how its signature motif (of a contemporary Thai roofline) has been effectively used to brand the spa through interior design, furnishings, retail products, website and marketing collaterals.

Staffing

The type of staff that a spa employs, and the service protocols in which they are trained, can also contribute significantly to a spa's branding. As with facilities, it is risky to pin the brand entirely on staffing claims or on a particular personality (unless it's the owner) because of the high industry turnover, however the spa may have some general policies that sets it apart.

For example, a Thai spa franchise may employ only Thai therapists to perform Thai massage, regardless of where in the world the spa is located. Similarly, a wellness centre may have all health consultations conducted by qualified naturopaths or doctors. Such policies send a strong message about the authenticity of treatments, adding credibility and integrity to the brand.

Service quality can be also a differentiator, although this is hard to prove. To avoid being dismissed as marketing puffery, a company must be able to demonstrate tangible ways in which it sets itself apart. Ritz Carlton (www.ritzcarlton.com) is an excellent example of this. In his article, *Branding – a job well done*, Dale Buss reviews the 20 *sine qua nons* known as 'The Ritz Carlton Basics' that all staff are not only expected to read and memorise, but also to internalise. These basics include the company credo and motto ('we are ladies and gentlemen serving ladies and gentlemen'), and Ritz Carlton's *Three Steps of Service, Twelve Service Values*, and the *Employee Promise*, amongst other things. According to Ritz Carlton's vice president of marketing, Bruce Himelstein, 'we teach (employees) to think of themselves not only as attendants to our guests but also as actors in spreading our brand; the feeling they get after they go through our orientation and are involved in our ongoing training is that they *are* the brand (Buss, 2005)'.

Rituals and procedures

Service rituals often provide a value-added component that greatly enhances the spa experience. Rituals communicate care and an attention to detail, and can contribute to the brand with minimal impact on the time or cost of a treatment. Much of the appeal of South-East Asian spas is due to the extensive use of ritual, derived from traditional cultures. Greeting gestures, aromatic teas, and footbaths filled with flower petals are just a few of the ways that Asian spas set the scene and win the guest's heart before the treatment even begins. Rituals continue throughout the spa experience, with the end of treatment often indicated with resonant bells or cymbals, to welcome the guest gently back to wakefulness.

Product selection

Product names are usually only prominent in the branding of retail-oriented spas, which tend to be owned or operated by product companies, such as Clarins (www.clarins.com), Elemis (www.elemis.com.au), Aveda (www.aveda.com) or Jurlique (www.jurlique.com.au). In all other spas, product selection most appropriately plays a support role, reinforcing the brand identity rather than creating it.

Surprisingly, many spas overlook the impact that the choice of brands has on guest perception. For example, an Asian spa may choose a European skincare line because of its quality or relationship with the distributor, not realising the disconnect that this creates (consciously or subconsciously) in the mind of the client.

Many spas opt to carry more than one product line, thereby maximising retail opportunities whilst creating a comprehensive offering for facial care, body care and amenities. If carrying multiple lines, the brands selected should ideally be complementary – filling gaps or weaknesses in the other lines – not directly competing with them. This allows spa staff to provide a consistent 'prescription' for any given condition, rather than varying according to personal preference or incentives.

Maintaining consistency between product and brand identity is particularly important if offering a private label range – an increasing trend as spas seek to make their services more distinctive. Private label can effectively differentiate, while at the same time acting as a souvenir of the spa and improving profit (see Chapter 13). However if the product quality is inferior to the spa's brand identity in any way, it can do more harm than good. This is particularly evident in packaging (a major cost component), where details such as poor quality pumps or imperfectly applied labels undermine the spa's professional image.

Signature treatments

Signature treatments have the opportunity to encapsulate a spa's brand more than any other single element, as creation of a signature necessarily involves packaging the spa concept, treatment, product and service rituals into one seamless experience.

Imagination is the limit for signature treatments, there is no accepted guide as to what they should include. Most commonly, signatures are packages of several services (such as bath, scrub, wrap and massage) designed to encourage the guest to experience a variety of the spa's facilities over a longer period of time. European spas often favour thermal treatments, true to spa's European origin of promoting 'health through water'. However, with the rise of holistic therapies, and yoga and meditation as mind–body treatments par excellence, Ayurveda and other Asian-inspired therapies are becoming increasingly popular in western markets.

On rare occasion, signature products and treatments can take on a life of their own, as in the case of Les Sources de Caudalie (www.sources-caudalie.com). This boutique French spa resort, located in Bordeaux, pioneered 'vinotherapie' as its signature – the use of wine (and all things grape) in spa treatments. Caudalie products are now a thriving stand-alone retail business, and vinotherapy is a recognised spa treatment that is rapidly growing in popularity worldwide.

Signature treatments may be lavish, such as the 'Sultan's Royal Six-Hand Massage' at the Laveda Spa at the Ritz Carlton Instanbul (www.ritzcarlton.com), but often a little creativity can result in treatments with a sharper edge than simply overloading signatures with resources. For example, spa operator Auriga (www.auriga-spa.com) bases its signature therapies on the phases of the moon: a simple, but powerful homage to spa's philosophy of helping mankind reconnect with the cycles of nature.

While creativity is to be encouraged, treatments must be developed according to sound therapeutic principles if they are to have integrity. In an effort to stand out, many spas are developing signature treatments that are increasingly bizarre. One day spa in Thailand offers 'Meridian Fire Therapy', in which guests are covered with materials which are then set alight. Such extreme treatments may capture the attention of the media, but they may also create risks for both guest and spa. It only takes one accident to destroy a brand that took years to create.

Benefits

Having discussed the many potential attributes a spa can use for branding, it is essential that these assets are translated into a message that is meaningful for the guest. Too often spas simply promote the attribute, without making this asset relevant to the guest. A popular example is 'detox' therapies. While many people know that detox is somehow desirable, it will not be motivating unless the guest understands specifically what it can do for him or her.

This may mean presenting the same treatment in different ways to different target markets. Young women may find detox appealing because it helps to keep their skin clear and glowing, whereas many older women are motivated by trying to reduce oedema and cellulite. Sedentary businessmen may need detox to help relieve chronic disease, while anyone living in heavily industrialised cities would benefit from detox as part of their preventative health regime.

Values

Values are the guiding principles that lie deep within the spa's philosophy. They are a more subtle aspect of branding, and often are not specifically articulated. Values can be implied from a spa's mission statement and policies, however the real challenge comes when the spa operation encounters a problem. Are employees really treasured as the spa's greatest asset? Do guests' needs always come first?

In the face of adversity, values are put to the test. The decisions taken quickly communicate to staff and guests whether the values are genuine or just lip service. Over time, incongruous actions can erode employee morale, which translates into high staff turnover, creating the risk of loss of service quality and consistency. Spa clients tend to act more immediately. If they detect insincerity, it undermines their trust and they simply vote with their feet. To make matters worse, it is well-established that consumers are more inclined to spread negative publicity than good publicity. A common axiom is that 'a happy customer tells 3 people; an unhappy customer tells 10 people'. Now, via the internet and blogging, an unhappy customer can tell thousands, and so compromising on its values can have a serious impact on a spa's brand equity.

Personality

Personality, the fourth aspect of branding, is simply the character of the spa, described and experienced as human personality traits, for example: 'warm, friendly, outgoing and fun'.

A clearly defined personality provides guidance for many elements such as recruitment, interior design and all sensory details such as choice of aroma and music. It also sets the brief for marketing communications. The selection of language, style of photography, tone of voice, and use of graphics and colour all contribute to animating the spa in the guest's mind.

A world apart from the usual photos of an elegant, relaxed-looking woman with her back coated in a mud wrap, Maruba Jungle Spa in Berlize (www.maruba-spa.com) brazenly captures the fun and adventurous personality of it's spa with a few simple photos: young adults in groups and couples playing in the jungle, adorned with colourful muds applied in tribal-like patterns.

Another example is Bliss (www.blissworld.com), a well-known day spa brand that caught the spa-goer's attention with its quirky personality. The playful nature of the brand is clearly demonstrated through its cartoon graphics and fun treatment names such as 'Quadruple Thighpass' and 'Homme Improvement'. Personality is a highly impactful tool in conveying the brand, however few spas approach and implement it strategically.

Brand essence

With so many inter-related components forming the total brand identity, the chance of being mired in confusion is very real. It is often helpful to distil the spa's core differentiator down to a few words, to help focus the team in decision-making. The brand 'essence' is simply that: the essence of all the elements previously discussed, or the one key thing the spa can 'hang its hat on'? The simpler and more concise the brand essence, the more powerful it can be.

The brand essence is not necessarily a marketing tagline; it is an internal compass and decision-making tool. However, it can be translated and used to good effect in marketing communications if desired.

Consistency

'The successful company is not the one with the most brains, but the most brains acting in concert.' (management guru, Peter Drucker, as quoted in *The Brand Gap*) (Neumeier, 2003, p. 52).

Effective branding requires delivery of a consistent experience, so that guest perceptions are harmonious and not contradictory. However, consistency is not an easy thing to deliver – especially in the spa industry where the product relies on people and even more so in a multi-spa operation.

Consistency is beyond the control of the owner, manager or marketing department: all employees must play a role. Branding should therefore be considered a process which involves the collaboration of the entire spa team. Every member of the spa team impacts on the guest experience in some way, and therefore every member of the spa team must have a clear understanding of the spa's brand story, and must also be able to perform his or her role in a manner that reinforces the desired guest experience.

Training is the cornerstone to consistency; both pre-opening and on an ongoing basis. In the rush to get new staff on board, orientation is often overlooked, however orientation is a key opportunity to instil new staff with the brand culture and passion that they must to deliver to guests. Ongoing training is also essential to maintain excitement and ensure that the whole team is continuing to stay on track, delivering consistency time after time.

As spa operations grow, particularly for multi-site businesses, a dedicated brand manager should be considered to provide strong co-ordination across all business units. Beyond the marketing of the brand, systems need to be in place so that the brand can thrive independently of any specific person. This includes continuing education programmes and culture-building activities for staff, but may also include seminars and workshops for external representatives, such as suppliers. Brand strategist Martin Roll estimates that at least 50% of the success of any brand is attributable to these internal efforts (Roll, 2006).

Ultimately, the power of a brand is in how it is perceived by the guest. A spa cannot dictate what its brand is: the best that it can do is engineer the spa environment, services and communications so that the guests form the desired perceptions of their own accord. When enough consumers share the same perceptions, and these perceptions are cultivated in the marketplace through word-of-mouth and media, then the 'brand' can be said to exist.

Summary

Branding is fundamentally about creating a relationship with the consumer. This relationship is formed by building layers of interaction that add up to a unique and seamless experience, giving the guest a clear perception of what the spa is and what it promises. When delivered consistently, this perception is shared and propagated by all, and becomes 'the brand'.

The layers of interaction begin with the attributes (or assets) of the spa, such as concept, location, facilities, design, staffing, products, treatments and service. In order to inspire a relationship, it is important that these attributes are created with guests' needs and desires in mind, and then translated into benefits that are relevant and motivating. Brand personality, expressed through design, verbal and written communications, adds depth to the spa's character, while the spa's values form a solid base for behaviour, so that the guest knows that they can rely on the spa to be consistent over time.

From all these layers, a brand essence – or core differentiator – can be distilled. However, that is just the beginning of the branding process. Consistency is essential if the brand is to achieve widespread acceptance, and so all staff must collaborate to deliver an effective brand experience. Innovation is required to maintain the brand's appeal and relevance over time, and marketing must continually support the brand by maintaining awareness. Systems must be in place to ensure that the brand continues to be cultivated long after the original branding team is gone.

References and selected reading

Aacker, D. (1991) *Managing Brand Equity*, The Free Press, New York.

Aacker, D. (2003) *Building Strong Brands*, The Free Press, New York.

Adamson, A. (2006) *Brand Simple*, Palgrave Macmillan, New York.

Buss, D. (2005) *Branding – A Job Well Done*, available at: www.brandchannel.com/features_effect.asp?pf_id=286 (site accessed 3 January 2008).

Clayton, R.C. (2004) Designing brand identity: A complete guide to creating, building, and maintaining strong brands, *Journal of the Academy of Marketing Science*, 32: 100–101.

Doctoroff, T. (2005) *Billions*, Palgrave Macmillan, New York.

Grimaldi, V. *What Makes a Brand Great*, available at: www.brandchannel.com (site accessed 6 November 2003).

Grimaldi, V. (2003) *The Fundamentals of Branding*, available at: www.brandchannel.com (site accessed 3 December 2007).

Neumeier, M. (2003) *The Brand Gap*, New Riders Publishing, USA.

Payne, A. (1993) *The Essence of Services Marketing*, Prentice Hall, UK.

Ries, A., Ries, L. (1998) *The 22 Immutable Laws of Branding*, Harper Collins, New York, p. 6.

Roll, M. (2006) *Asian Brand Strategy: How Asia Builds Strong Brands*, Palgrave Macmillan, New York.

Schmitt, B. (1999) *Experiential Marketing How to Get Customers to Sense, Feel, Think, Act and Relate to Your Company and Brands*, The Free Press, New York.

Schmitt, B., Simonson, A. (1997) *Marketing Aesthetics – The Strategic Management of Brands, Identity and Image*, Free Press, New York.

Steel, J. (1998) *Truth, Lies and Advertising*, John Wiley & Sons, USA.

Trout, J. (2000) *Differentiate or Die*, John Wiley & Sons, USA.

The Economist (2003) *Brands and Branding*, Profile Books, UK. (available at www.economistshop.com/asp/bookdetail. asp?book=1691).

Wheeler, A. (2006) *Designing Brand Identity*, John Wiley & Sons, USA.

Websites

Ananda in the Himalayas: http://www.anandaspa.com
Auriga Spa: http://www.auriga-spa.com
Aveda: http://www.aveda.com
Banyan Tree: http://www.banyantreespa.com
Bliss: http://www.blissworld.com/category/spa/spa+ treatments/locations.do
Brand Channel: www.brandchannel.com
Building Brands: www.buildingbrands.com
Chiva-Som: http://www.chivasom.com
Clinique La Prairie: http://www.laprairie.ch
Devarana Spa: http://www.devaranaspa.com
Four Seasons (employment): http://www.fourseasons.com/employment/a_four_seasons_career/#division_5
Interbrand: http://www.interbrand.com
Jurlique: http://www.jurlique.com.au
Laveda Spa at the Ritz Carlton, Instanbul: http://www.ritz-carlton.com/en/Properties/Istanbul/Spa/Default.htm
Les Sources de Caudalie: http://www.sources-caudalie.com
Lime Spa at Huvafen Fushi: http://www.huvafenfushi.com
Maruba Jungle Spa: http://www.maruba-spa.com
Raison d'Etre: http://www.raisondetrespas.com
Red Mountain Spa: http://www.redmountainspa.com
Ritz Carlton (gold standards): http://corporate.ritzcarlton.com/en/About/GoldStandards.htm#Promise
The Spa at Hotel Hershey: http://www.hersheypa.com/accommodations/the_spa_at_hotel_hershey

Spa retail

Mark Wuttke and Marc Cohen

Spas primarily sell 'experiences' or 'guest journeys' rather than products, yet retail product sales is a vital and growing element of the spa industry. Shopping itself is an experience and in the growing 'experience economy', lifestyle brands have emerged from many different market segments with brands such as Abercrombie and Fitch, Quiksilver, Nike, Gaiam, Harley Davidson, Caterpillar, Apple and BMW demonstrating that retail products can enhance their customers' experience and create new business opportunities. The spa industry has also witnessed a number of retail companies such as L'Occitane, Whole Foods, Hersheys, Boots, La Prairie and Guerlain opening their own spa operations which offer experiences that complement their retail sales.

Spa retail has traditionally focused on beauty and skin care products with therapists using products in treatments and then offering them for sale. This has met resistance from some therapists who consider themselves to be caring practitioners rather than salespeople. There is a growing acknowledgement, however, that spa retail sales offer the guests an added service and do not have to be a 'hard sell'. There is also a trend towards spas employing dedicated retail staff and having online stores, as well as extending their product range beyond skin care to include food, home ware, furnishings, apparel, music, beverages, handicrafts and giftware.

Know the product and the customer

It is said that every person has a story. Similarly, every product has a story and it is the aim of retailing to have the guest's story and the product's story merge. Retail sales therefore emerge out of a conversation between the customer and the salesperson and it is the role of the salesperson to know about their products and find out as much as possible about the customer so that they can provide the most relevant product information.

In order to provide the best service to the customer and to achieve the greatest retail revenue, it is vital that salespeople thoroughly know the story behind the product regardless of the type of product. The product story may be based on the product's specialized use as determined by modern science or specific historical or cultural traditions, or on its unique natural ingredients, geographical origins or symbolic significance. Product stories may also center on the particular artisans involved in the products production or the ecological, social and/or ethical values behind the product. Whatever the product, the greater the product knowledge, the greater the ability for salesperson to engage the customer and to offer the customer products that are aligned with, or exceed, their expectations. Without this engagement, it is likely that the salesperson will merely be told what the customer came in for and this (if anything) is all they will be sold.

In order for a deep conversation to occur between the customers and salesperson it is necessary for the salesperson to get into the customer's world. The more the salesperson knows about their client the more they are empowered to sell their products and leave the customer satisfied by the experience. This requires the salesperson to understand that people process information in different ways and to learn how to present information in a way that is understandable and aligned with the customer's values, needs and wants.

Consumer values

In the current global market, people are becoming more interested in spirituality, environmental sustainability, ethics and lifestyle, and purchasing decisions and brand loyalties are becoming more aligned with personal values. This consumer movement has been termed LOHAS which is an acronym for *Lifestyles of Health and Sustainability* and is described on the LOHAS website www.lohas.com as: 'a market segment focused on health and fitness, the environment, personal development, sustainable living, and social justice. ... LOHAS consumers, sometimes referred to as Lohasians, are interested in products covering a range of market sectors and sub-sectors, including: Green building supplies, socially responsible investing and "green stocks", alternative healthcare, organic clothing and food, personal development media, yoga and other fitness products, eco-tourism and more'.

The LOHAS consumer market appears to be expanding rapidly in response to the growing awareness of global issues such as climate change, social inequality, third world sweat shops, the increasing use of toxic chemicals and the potential for lifestyle change to improve health and prevent illness.

In response to this, many companies have begun to label themselves and/or their products as 'green', 'natural', 'organic' and 'fair trade' and have begun programs involving 'corporate social responsibility', 'ecological foot-printing', 'food miles', 'carbon offsetting', 'indigenous intellectual property rights', etc. Such programs may inform consumers of the companies activities and allow them to assess the food miles associated with food purchases or offset the carbon emissions when purchasing travel. Other initiatives add a small amount onto a sale which is then given to a philanthropic fund, research or aid program or enable the calculation of the 'embodied energy' of a product.

Examples of these activities abound in the non-spa world and include initiatives by companies such as Bon Appetit's 'Circle of Responsibility Program' which informs consumers about the environmental, social and health impacts of their food choices initiatives such as 'Petsmart Charities' and 'Footprints' which allows an extra dollar to be added to online transactions and donated to aide programs and initiatives by companies such as TS Designs and Timberland which list important facts about how their product was produced including sweatshop labor, pesticides used, certified organic cotton, water based inks, energy to produce, renewable energy used, hours served in local communities, percent of factories assessed against code of conduct and child labor.

It has been suggested that the range of social, environmental, ethical and personal health issues related to consumption of con-sumer goods can all be integrated under the banner of 'conshu-manism' (see Chapter 1), which refers to 'conscious and humane consumption' or consumption with maximal awareness, effi-ciency and enjoyment and minimal pain, energy, waste and pollution. Ultimately conscious consumption comes down to disclosure of all aspects of a products life cycle including: where and when products are produced; who produced them; how they are produced; what is in them; how they are processed, stored, transported; and where they end up after being used. This can apply to all consumer goods including food, cosmetics, apparel, home ware, electronics, etc.

Label information

While the above information may be provided for certain items such as specific wines and gourmet foods, current labeling laws fall extremely short of the ideal. As consumers become more empowered and information becomes easier to access it is likely that the trend towards increasing transparency into the product life cycle will continue although full disclosure still seems a long way off for most product categories. In fact there are as yet no international standards upon which to base label claims for product quality, purity and efficacy and many prod-ucts are labeled 'natural' or 'organic' for marketing purposes only without substantiation. The spa and other industries that bandy these terms around are therefore open to valid criticism concerning the authenticity of their products.

One product category that is at least attempting to tackle the issue is natural skin care and some standards have been put forward by private and government bodies such as Ecocert in France, the Soil Association in the UK, AIAB in Italy, BDHI in Germany and EcoControl. Despite these moves, there is no worldwide recognition of what constitutes a natural or an organic cosmetic and many standards are derived from the food and agriculture industries (see Chapter 13).

In the absence of industry-wide standards, and in an attempt to adopt a more holistic approach to product standardisation, a Brussels-based group, led by European industry leaders Laverana/Lavera, Logocos/Logona, Primavera, Santaverde, Wala/Dr. Hauschka and Weleda have formed the European Natural and Organic Cosmetics Interest Group, NaTrue www.natrue.de/index.php?id=35&L=1. NaTrue, advocates for information on corporate social responsibility (CSR) issues, fair production of raw materials, gentle processing and the abolition of animal testing during development and manufacture, clear, regulatory definition of natural cosmetics, and correspondingly precise criteria for product labeling and use of the terms 'bio' or 'organic'. NaTrue also aims to protect the integrity and availability of high quality materials that may be inadvertently jeopardized by regulatory changes sponsored through European institutions and the EU member states.

Merging the product and the customers stories through direct sensual experience

Spas seem almost perfectly set to maximize the retail exposure as they have an almost unprecedented opportunity to engage in rich conversations with their guests and establish long, intimate and highly profitable relationships. Many spas begin this dialogue by issuing questionnaires to their guests in order to determine how they are feeling and how their needs can best be met. When done well this can provide the basis for adding a very personalized approach to retailing.

It is estimated that in traditional retail environments sales staff have 30 seconds to connect with the customer, yet in the spa environment it is possible to maintain contact with the guest for an extended period of time. Furthermore, spas provide an immersion experience where it is possible to create an emotional connection with the customer by engaging all five senses. The feel of a skin product or apparel, the smell of essential oils, the taste of herbal teas and spa cuisine, the sound of running water or ambient music and the sight of beautiful spaces and décor that include the use of natural materials and environments, all contribute to creating an experience which is then connected to any products on offer.

In addition to providing an immersion experience, retailing in spas can extend the spa experience so that guests can relive the experience at home. Thus classical conditioning can be used to create a link between the spa experience and the retail product. Just as Pavlov's dogs were conditioned to salivate at the sound of a bell which had been linked to the prospect of a meal, it is possible for a product used in the spa to re-establish the physiological benefits of a spa treatment. This is illustrated by the finding that people with intractable epilepsy can obtain relief though the relaxation obtained from smelling aromatherapy oils which had their scent linked to a state of deep relaxation during a series of aromatherapy massages (Betts, 2003).

If the spa journey starts and finishes in the retail boutique it is possible to build the expectation of reliving the spa experience at home from the very beginning making any product purchase a therapeutic act. It is even possible now for guests to never leave the spa as spa retail has extended to property with homes or 'spa residences' such as Miraval Living, Cliffs Communities and Canyon Ranch Living become increasingly available on the retail property market.

Retailing in Spas

In stand-alone spas, treatments are considered the bread and butter of the business and retail is seen as the cream, while in hotel and resort spas, there are increasingly high expectations from property asset managers, hotel management companies, and private equity investors, for spas to function as stand-alone profit centers rather than just an amenity. This means that spas are under increasing pressure to explore untapped revenue sources and maximize retail revenue for once a spa reaches maximum treatment room utilization, the sole way to increase revenue each month (without raising prices) is through retail.

Spa retail can give a spa a major – and immediate – financial boost without compromising the guest experience. However, while it is possible for spas to increase their revenue considerably from seamlessly integrating retail into the guest's spa journey, the old cliché of 'if you cannot measure – you cannot manage' applies. As with most business practices, it is not possible to effect change and get results in areas that are not monitored and reported on. This involves close monitoring and attention to specific key performance indicators (KPIs).

What is a KPI?

In simple terms KPIs are deemed by management to be the critical success factors, or drivers for the business. Monitoring KPIs thus provides an 'early warning update' or 'insurance policy' to ensure the critical and most important business activities are closely monitored and that any trends, either positive or negative, can be viewed at a glance and appropriate action taken. KPIs are also a great way to allow salespeople to know exactly what the performance measures are and thus monitor and measure their own performance without constant supervision.

While KPIs are an effective tool for monitoring the performance of a business, they merely report on what is happening and do not create results. If KPIs are used to punish team members they will react in an aggressive manner which will often destroy the guest experience, not improve it. However, an intelligent and intuitive leader will use KPIs to coach and mentor team members and empower them to take the guest experience to a higher level of consciousness and sensibility.

In a spa retail business, KPIs should be monitored on an hourly, daily, weekly, monthly, quarterly and yearly basis so non-performing activities can be quickly corrected and the ones that are working are continued or duplicated. The following KPIs are appropriate in a spa boutique retail environment:

1. Revenue dollars per paid hour.
2. Average dollar per sale.
3. Retail dollars to treatment dollars ratio percentage.
4. Lead generation numbers.
5. Lead conversion rate percentage.
6. Inventory turnover number.
7. Inventory shrinkage percentage.
8. Revenue dollars per linear foot/meter.

Revenue dollars per paid hour

This is the amount of dollars generated by a salesperson for every hour they are paid to work. A good rule of thumb is a 10-fold return on whatever the hourly rate is. For example, a good expectation and KPI for a team member earning $10 per hour would be $100 per paid hour. The hourly rate should include the costs of superannuation, annual leave, sick leave and any other add on costs of employment which can be substantial.

Average dollar per sale

This is the average dollar amount of each transaction. This is calculated simply by dividing the total sales for any given period (or individual salesperson) by the number of transactions. This KPI is very helpful to determine the efficiency of a salesperson once a guest has decided to purchase. A salesperson may be very good at inspiring a guest to purchase an item or the retail environment may be so seductive and conducive to selling that just about everyone will buy something. This KPI provides a benchmark for salespeople to measure their ability to achieve retail revenue and may be compared to the number of units per guest or transaction which provides a related measure without focusing directly on the dollar amount.

Once the average dollar sale is calculated there are a number of steps that can be taken to improve it, including add-on-sales or link-selling, up-selling, demonstrations, providing a gift with a purchase and simple annual price increases. The aim of add-on-sales or link-selling is to add an additional purchase to any purchase decision. For example, if a guest is interested in, or buys a bath robe, they can be invited to purchase slippers or an additional robe as a gift for their partner, family member or friend. Similarly, if a guest buys a skin cleanser, they can be introduced to a moisturizer or toner, or if they buy a tea pot they can be invited to purchase some tea.

Up-selling involves increasing the value of a purchase decision. For example, if a guest is interested in or buys an $80 bath robe, they can be invited to purchase a $160 bath robe. Similarly, if a guest buys a skin care product they can be introduced to a larger size container, or if they decide to purchase a $20 tea pot they can be introduced to a $40 tea pot.

Demonstrations can be used to add value to the guest's purchase by allowing the guest to experience a product directly thereby increasing their connection with the product and their likelihood of making a purchase. For example, guests can be invited to try on a bath robe, or a mini facial or hand massage can be performed so they can see and feel the results from the cleanser or moisturizer. Similarly, a trial size sample of a product as a gift along with a gift check or certificate to buy the full size of the product with their next visit or within a pre-determined timeframe, provides the opportunity for guests to experience a product and increase their spending. It is important however, not to heavily sample products which would normally be purchased, without a limited call to action as this will only erode further sales.

It is also important not to attempt to save a customers money unless they specifically request it. It is not uncommon for guest to want to buy more expensive products yet be talked out of it by a salesperson. A sale needs to be viewed as an opportunity to contribute to the guest. The more money the guest spends, the more value the purchase adds to their life and the greater connection with the brand.

Retail dollar to treatment dollar ratio

The retail dollar to treatment dollar ratio is a measure of the retail dollars generated compared to every treatment dollar. It is also common for spas to measure retail dollars as a percentage of total sales by dividing retail sales by total revenue and multiplying by 100. This ratio can be measured daily, weekly, monthly, quarterly or yearly, however, as with all retail ratios daily measurements provide the greatest opportunity to detect and respond immediately to any positive or negative trends.

Lead generation

Anyone who comes in contact with a spa is a prospective client and represents a 'lead'.

Leads are generated in many different ways. They may have read an editorial, an advertisement, heard about the spa through word of mouth or have simply walked by and entered the spa. It does not matter how someone heard about the spa, once they have contacted the spa, whether by phone, in person or in writing, they are a potential client. As such, lead generation measures the spas actual traffic and therefore potential revenue.

Lead generation is calculated by determining how many leads are generated through all means and therefore represents a total of how many people come in contact with the spa either physically as customers or walk ins, or through phone calls, emails and letters.

Lead conversion rate percentage

A lead conversion is the conversion of a prospect or lead into a client. A lead conversion therefore represents a sale and 'lead conversion rate percentage' is the percentage of leads converted into sales. While spas may believe that they do not have enough traffic, it is the ability to convert existing leads into clients that actually creates revenue. Lead generation and lead conversion are directly influenced by a spas operation and thus represent a measure of a spa's ability to attract revenue that can be directly influenced by management.

Inventory turnover number

Inventory Turnover measures the number of times the inventory investment is turned over and is calculated by subtracting the cost of goods sold (COGS) from retail revenue over a given time period by the average inventory value over the same period. For example if annual retail sales were $560 000, annual COGS was $280 000 and average inventory value was $50 000 then Inventory Turnover = ($560 000 − $280 000)/$50 000 = 5.6.

The Inventory Turnover rate is an important statistic because it can directly impact on a spa's profitability. Inventory essentially represents cash; thus an inventory that contains overstocked or slow moving items ties up valuable cash that could be invested in other areas for a better return. Inventory control therefore represents a vital management function that needs to be based on:

1. *Forecasting* – This can be done by combining historical data and current trends to determine future stock requirements.
2. *Seasonal Variation* – This will determine the mix of inventory required at different times of the year which may be impacted upon by season, peak periods, special events, etc.
3. *Order regularity* – This will be influenced by a range of factors including freight charges, the time required for the product vendor to deliver goods to the spa and the time it will take to sell those goods. A general rule of thumb is to have no more than 4–6 weeks of inventory on hand at any one time unless vendors are not reliable or are frequently out of stock. If vendors demand that spas order product in amounts greater than are practically required, or are unable to supply product when needed, then this can be compensated for by extended trading terms, discounts, free product or building financial penalties into supply agreements.

Managers need to be aware of a potential conflict between the spa and product vendors as vendors may like spas to purchase more product than they really need or can ever sell, while spas may like to have vendors respond immediately to requests for small amounts of goods. Ultimately, however, spas and vendors share the common interest in having the greatest amount of product sold for the greatest client satisfaction.

Inventory shrinkage percentage

Inventory shrinkage percentage is the difference between whole-sale dollar value of product purchased and received verses the dollar amount of product available for sale. Although as yet, there is no specific shrinkage data for the spa industry, there seems to be similarities across most retail industries. According to a 2004 US National Supermarket Shrink Survey (Vargas, 2004) the five key inventory shrinkage causes are:

- Employee theft – 56%
- Shop lifting – 21%
- Back door receiving – 10%
- Pricing and accounting – 9%
- Damaged goods – 4%

The finding that greatest contribution to shrinkage is staff suggests that keeping products for sale locked behind glass is not only a poor strategy for selling as it prevents customers from touching, feeling and smelling the product, but that it is also an ineffective way of reducing shrinkage. Strategies for reducing shrinkage include:

1. *Monitoring* – If staff know shrinkage is being measured it is likely to reduce.
2. *Connecting with guests* – Thieves generally do not like to be recognized or interacted with, therefore shrinkage is likely to reduce if every guest is greeted with direct eye contact and verbal interaction. This is also good sales practice and is likely to increase the number of sales as well as the average dollar per sale.
3. *Not throwing stock away* – Being mindful of what is being thrown away can significantly reduce wastage. Many times what seem to be either empty boxes or trash bags may contain something far more valuable. In one case a medium size retail location saved over $200 000 in shrinkage by ensuring only senior management had keys to the dumpster.
4. *Controlling opening and closing* – Having two or preferably three people present for opening and closing is likely to reduce shrinkage.
5. *Incentives and accountability* – If commission, bonuses, promotion and pay rises are linked to shrinkage it becomes everyone's responsibility.

Revenue dollars per linear foot/meter

'Revenue dollars per linear foot/meter' is measured by dividing the total dollars sold by the linear measurement of space occupied during a specified period, usually week or month. This measure provides information about the products and/or categories that are producing the best dollar returns for the space occupied and therefore allows the products with the greatest return to be given the greatest prominence.

If products are divided into discrete categories then the contribution of each category can be also tracked and calculating the revenue dollars per linear foot/meter for specific time periods provides valuable information about seasonal variations in product demand. This measure also allows calculations to distinguish between turnover (how often a product is sold) and efficiency (how much a product contributes to overall revenue).

Summary

It is the experience at the point of interaction with the brand that is the key element of successful retailing. Thus, the environment in which people shop has become almost as important as the product being sold with experiential retailing focusing on creating a lifestyle/social environment that engages the guest in a compelling, authentic and relevant way. This is done through direct sensual experience as well as through creation of a brand image and a story behind the product. It is also necessary to get into the customer's world so that they can be fully engaged through an individualized, personalized, approach. In this way retailing can enhance the guest experience and enable guests to increase the money they spend and hence the value they obtain from their purchases.

As with other areas of a business, when assessing the productivity or efficiency of a retail offering it is important to measure performance using defined key performance indicators. These can be used to inform management decisions and provide motivation and incentives to staff and thus maximize retail revenue.

References

Betts, T. (2003) Use of aromatherapy (with or without hypnosis) in the treatment of intractable epilepsy – A two-year follow-up study, *Seizure*, 12(8):534–538.

Vargas, M. (2004) *National Supermarket Research Group Shrink Survey*, available at: http://retailindustry.about.com/cs/lp_retailstore/a/aa030519a.htm

Websites

www.hotelportopalacio.com/en/hotel/index.html?area=spa
www.wholefoodsmarket.com/stores/preston/thespa/index.
  html
www.hersheypa.com/accommodations/the_spa_at_hotel_
  hershey/
http://bootsus.bri-global.com/main.asp?bid=59&cid=0
www.granhotelguadalpin.com/en/byblos/salud/lapraire.cfm
www.spachakra.com/guerlainspa.htm
www.circleofresponsibility.com
www.footprints.org.au
www.tsdesigns.com
www.timberland.com/shop/ad4.js
www.lohas.com
http://int.ecocert.com
www.soilassociation.org/web/sacert/sacertweb.nsf/B3/
  health_and_beautycare.html
www.aiab.it/home
www.kontrollierte-naturkosmetik.de/en/index.htm
www.eco-control.com/index_en.htm
www.miravalresort.com/Living.aspx
www.cliffscommunities.com/wellness
www.canyonranch.com/living/living-home.aspx

Product development

Geraldine Howard and Guy Vincent

Introduction

The main revenue streams in spas are from a combination of services and products with the ratio between the two varying dramatically. The industry average for product sales is considered to be around 15% of the total spa revenue, with some spas reporting only single figure numbers and others quoting figures as high as 65% (although the latter is rare). In recent years the focus on product sales has increased and it is now considered an important part of spa revenue.

The majority of the sales come from skincare/cosmetic and topical products rather than apparel, homeware or foods and this chapter will focus on cosmetic products.

Recent trends in the cosmetic industry show an increased demand for products based on natural, organic and fairly traded ingredients and those which take into account global environmental issues. The demand for totally natural products has raised some industry concerns about the safety of such products and how product production and marketing is regulated.

In spas the trend for producing signature products is regularly debated, with there being many different industry views on the subject; and this topic will also be reviewed in this chapter.

Product design

Most products used and sold in spas come under the trade marking classification of cosmetics (Trade Mark Classification ref. no. 3, 2008). Many similarities exist between cosmetic products categorised as either 'spa' or 'retail'. The latter are usually sold through department stores and pharmacies, whereas spa products are mostly distributed through spas with not all of them being sold to the end user but simply used by therapists in treatments.

The overlap between the two categories, with both types of products now being sold in either market place, is increasing. However, the defining difference lies in the compatibility and effectiveness of a product when used in a treatment to deliver a benefit to a client. A spa requires a range of products to facilitate the execution of all treatments listed on the menu. As the industry has grown, so has the spectrum of facial and body treatments on offer, which means the products needed can range from a highly scientific acid-based facial peel, to botox, right through to a very simple salt and vegetable oil body scrub.

Private label products

Spa operators constantly assess which products they should be using, and many like to consider producing a line under their own private label. The main advantage is that signature products give a spa the ability to offer something unique and many spa operators are keen to offer treatments and products that are not available anywhere else. From a marketing perspective this can be an asset, but the disadvantage can be that a savvy spa goer may well not trust in the spa's ability and expertise to create good, effective products and prefer to purchase a recognised global brand.

Before making the decision to produce private label products, the most important issue to address is the number of units and volume of product that is going to be used. Manufacturing production runs for both packaging components and filling containers will dictate whether or not a project is feasible.

It is necessary to clarify the number of treatments being carried out and therefore the total volume of professional product required, along with the projected number of retail items to be sold per annum. It can then be assessed whether or not it is possible to create the product in both professional and retail packaging, taking into consideration the shelf life of a product. If volumes and budgets allow for only one type of packaging then a decision needs to be made based on whether this will make the cost of treatment too high, since smart quality packaging can be expensive when produced in small numbers.

Once feasibility has been established, there are still many other points to consider before deciding to create either private label products or use an established brand. These are illustrated in Table 13.1.

General criteria to assess before selecting or designing all spa products

Understanding the market place

Identifying whom a spa is targeting, and fully understanding this, is vital before selecting or creating any product. For established brands it is equally important to understand which type of spas they are targeting.

A strong brand marketing story should be reinforced throughout the spa and the choice of products will go a long way towards indicating to a potential client both the quality and type of treatment they can expect. For example, if a spa philosophy emphasises environmental issues then product ingredients and packaging should reflect this.

Cultural differences

These can play a part in product selection so, again, it is important to understand who the end users are. For example,

Table 13.1 Comparison of branded and private label products

Branded products	Private label products
Brand recognition and public perception	
Already established	Need to build from scratch
Product companies have built their reputation on creating products, it is their expertise	A spa's reputation is built on execution of services. Will people acknowledge a spa as an expert in creating product?
Marketing	
Collateral such as point of sale and training literature will automatically be available – often supplied free of charge.	Collateral needs to be designed and then produced
Costs can be spread over many spas	Cost can be high if only supplying a few spas
Producing the right product mix	
Established brands will have already done the analysis in linking treatments to products and understanding which products sell well.	Important to understand the menu and ensure the product range produced covers all treatment and retail requirements.
Stock holding	
Small stock holding – Inventory can be ordered in small numbers per product as required	Usually large stock holding – the minimum number of products that can be produced per manufacturing run can lead to high inventory levels.
Stock maintenance	
Stock maintenance is done by product company and inaccurate forecasting risks are spread across more spas	Accurate forecasting and management of product sales and treatments is needed to maintain correct stock levels, since manufacturing lead times can be as high as 16 weeks
Obsolete stock/write offs	
Excess stock should be minimal since order volumes are small and controllable	Excess stock will become a write off expense. Obsolete stock can be due to new legislation requirements on packaging, discontinuation of products and treatments or products exceeding expiry date
Development	
All aspects and expenses will be covered by the product company	Time and hard costs will be incurred for research, design and management.

Asian cultures often favour skin whitening products in their skincare, whereas these are rarely seen in the West.

Indigenous treatments are currently very popular on menus so these will require special ingredients to be used in products. Since these are unlikely to be used worldwide it is important to consider how relevant retail products are to the budget or whether 'professional use only' will suffice.

When designing indigenous products it is also important to ensure that fair-trading standards are adhered to so that financial benefits can be given back to the customary owners of the formulae and the producers of the product.

The treatment menu

The selection of treatments offered in a spa are chosen according to the type of spa (hotel, day or destination), its location (city or holiday) and its clientele and their lifestyle (Spa Source The Essential Guide to Spa Development, 2007).

Understanding the needs of the spa goer will dictate the types of treatments listed on the tariff and this in turn will define exactly what products are needed in a brand line up of Stock Keeping Units (SKUs).

Traditionally there will always need to be body massage oils, body creams/lotions, muds and scrubs plus an extensive range of facial skincare products ranging from cleansers and masks to moisturisers.

Each product needs to be created to work in conjunction with others in any one specific treatment. Product combinations must all work well together in terms of texture, aroma and effect.

An example in a body treatment would be when a body scrub is followed by a relaxing massage. The aromas used in the scrub and the massage oil should both have a calming effect and blend well together.

In a rejuvenating facial for any skin type it is important that the aromas of the cleansers, toners, masks and moisturisers harmonise with each other and that the combination of using all the products through the treatment delivers the desired skin texture by the end of the treatment.

Professional and retail

Twenty years ago spas were not particularly interested in generating revenue through selling products, as the focus was more on professional products used in the treatments, or creating an ambience or enhancing wet area experiences.

In recent years this has dramatically changed, with financial personnel realising that a spa's bottom line can be greatly improved through product sales. Retail products are usually sold with a 100% mark up (50% margin) on the wholesale price and with the price of 2–3 products equalling the price of a treatment (which uses greater space and a trained therapist for at least 1 hour) it is easy to see how retail sales can deliver a positive revenue stream.

Product companies supplying spas will expect to generate more than half their revenue from supplying retail products rather than professional products. To maximise revenue for both parties all treatments should have retail products linked to them. However, the purpose of homecare products is not just to drive revenue, it is also to maximise the benefits of the treatment and extend the client's spa experience. The use of product will undoubtedly have played a part in their spa experience, either through an aromatic or a physiological benefit, so to introduce these products into their daily life will add to their complete wellness experience.

Price

The end price of a product will help a spa determine which product brand is suitable for their clientele. When developing new products for either private label or an existing brand, it is often best to decide on an acceptable market place price for the finished product and then work backwards; taking into account global price variations, margins required on retail products and treatment costs for professional products. This calculation dictates the expenditure available for both packaging components and raw materials. The look of the finished product needs to reflect the quality and philosophy of the spa or product brand, but the budget has to work to allow the appropriate ingredients to be used.

Aromatherapy provides a good example of where the cost of the same volume of different essential oils can vary from 10 to 10,000 times, as with essential oils of eucalyptus and organically certified Rose Otto.

Contraindications

Allergic reactions and sensitivity to products is increasing, so it is important to take this into consideration when designing products and to ensure that appropriate tests are done and relevant information is listed on the product label. Alternatively, ensure there are sufficient products in the complete spa offering to be able to provide services for clients with sensitive skins.

Different people will react to different ingredients but there are many common potential allergens which (in the European

Market) now have to be listed on product packaging (European Cosmetic Toiletry and Perfumery Association (Colipa) directive, 2003). This has to be considered when selecting the combination of ingredients to go into a product and also raises the question as to whether all treatment needs can be covered through creating just one type of each product. For example, one body or facial wash, one body or facial moisturiser for both dry and sensitive skin types.

Aroma

Understanding the effect of aroma on humans is an ever-advancing field. Aromas inhaled from cosmetics have been demonstrated to have a significant role in enhancing relaxation (Field et al., 2005). In the spa environment aromas can come from products, aroma vaporisers and burners. Many companies recognise that aromas now have a significant role to play in brand recognition and are taking steps to create 'signature scents' and ensure all their sales environments smell the same as well as look the same. Researchers have found that our ability to recall a specific scent surpasses even our ability to recall what we have seen (Living with Your Sense of Smell, 1992).

Smell has a fundamental relationship with memory with many smells transporting us back to a time and place without us consciously trying to remember it. Emotions are also recalled through aromas with some triggering good recollections and some unpleasant. This is due to the sense of smell being directly linked to the limbic system in our brain. The limbic system is the memory bank of smells and also controls or modifies our emotions and sexual response, hunger and thirst responses, artistic abilities, perceptions of space, body temperature regulators and cognition (Living with Your Sense of Smell, 1992). However, there is not always a direct relationship between a specific smell and a response for example the smell of lemongrass makes some people feel happy but if an individual has a memory of food with lemongrass that made them ill, this may well not be the case for them. Nevertheless, if a new smell and a pleasurable experience are married together, then classical 'Pavlovian' conditioning can occur, enabling the reliving of the pleasurable experience after smelling that aroma. Spa homecare products reproducing these aromas are definitely a formula for successful retail products.

Individual product development

The act of application of product in spa treatments plays an important role in defining what form products take and which

227

active ingredients are added for specific actions. How the product is applied, how long it will stay on the client and what the intended function is, all affect the overall form of the product and the ingredients selected. When designing products, it is advisable for product developers to review the product target action and also the customer need. For example, for a client to receive a relaxing treatment and leave the spa with their skin looking smooth radiant and well hydrated, the product mix could be as follows:

Firstly, a body scrub, to buff away dead skin cells for physical appearance but to also prepare the skin to facilitate effective passage of lipophilic (oil soluble) and hydrophilic (water soluble) components into the skin.

Secondly, a body wrap with a water based gel product that allows for hydration of the epidermis (especially the stratus corneum), plumping the skin to make it appear well hydrated.

Thirdly, a body massage with vegetable oils that not only help moisturisation and skin health but also contain aromatherapy essential oils which penetrate into the blood stream working both systemically and aromatically to relax the client.

All three of the above products act in different ways due to their chemical relationship with human anatomy and physiology, as well as having a clear link through the method of application. Retail versions of the products also need to be considered for the client to continue their treatment at home.

Throughout product development, product goals need to be kept in focus, so making sure they are clearly defined and written down is important. All marketable parameters should be defined right down to the ingredients, making the development brief as black and white as possible. More information is better, no matter how rudimentary and 'unchemistry like' it seems. Items to be considered are:-

- Required effect of product
- Texture and thickness
- How product will be applied
- Preferred product container
- Preferred ingredients – organic, natural, fairly traded
- Essential ingredients, for example, Essential oil of Geranium
- Feel of skin following product application
- Aroma

An example of a product brief for a body scrub may look something like this:

- Thick base that can be easily applied to dry skin. It is comfortable for the therapist and the client alike

- smooth sided (non scratchy) micro particles, for example, Jojoba beads but must effectively exfoliate body skin so may need reinforcement with wood derived materials
- relatively water soluble so it can washed off in the shower without excessive surfactants, making sure there is little to no waxy or oily residue
- polishes the skin leaving it smooth and soft to touch, buffs away dead cells
- must include fairly traded geranium
- fragrance to be fresh and floral

Target 'drift', where the product evolves into something that differs from the initial goal, often occurs during the development process as ingredient selection takes over. For example the fair trade geranium and exfoliating particles are sourced and formulated into a base but create an odour which is NOT fresh and floral and smells like cooked cabbage. Once the product plan is mapped out, each product can then be designed to meet its specific objectives.

Bases and actives

Cosmetic bases, known as cosmetic vehicles, deliver the primary function of a product with active ingredients, often being the more powerful part of a product, delivering more specific actions. Examples of bases commonly used in cosmetics are: vegetable oils, mineral oil, butters (cocoa and shea) and waxes (beeswax), petroleum-based gel, and water. Examples of active ingredients are: herbal extracts, essential oils, fatty acids, polymers, lipids, ceramides, proteins, peptides, antioxidants and natural moisturising factors. Choosing actives and evaluating their actions requires research into their chemistry, method of action and claim substantiation.

The marriage of the actives and bases is very important for high quality product development. Essential oils mix in with base oils or vegetable oils because they are lipophilic; aqueous herbal infusions naturally mix with water. However, oil extracted herbs (e.g. arnica) do not mix with water bases. To have the best of water and oil bases, emulsions need to be made. An emulsion is a fine dispersion of one insoluble liquid in another – oil dispersed in water for example (Schueller and Romanowski, 2008). Emulsions use emulsifiers which are a type of surfactant that allows oil-soluble and water-soluble components to remain mixed (Living with Your Sense of Smell, 1992).

The actives need to be in the correct vehicle as well as present in sufficient volumes within the formulation to be able to both reach their target and give a positive response.

All too often, active ingredients are added into products in such low doses that they do not have a chance to perform to their capacity. Moreover, actives can be trapped in unsuitable mediums limiting their function. For example anti-ageing actives that need to penetrate the first skin layer to achieve their effect are pointless in a wash-off product such as a facial cleanser.

Simple research can be done by reviewing manufacturer literature, text books and web based research and talking to cosmetic chemists. Complex formulas will often be formulated by experienced cosmetic chemists who often choose the active materials, but it is far better for developers to question and influence active ingredient selection to ensure the final product is fit for purpose within spa treatments.

Natural products

The development of natural and organic products is the fastest growing sector of the cosmetics industry in both spas and retail stores. It is generally accepted that it is growing by 15–20% a year worldwide (www.organicmonitor.com). Many products are perceived to be natural; however the classification of 'natural' is very difficult. According to the requirements set down in 1993 by the German Federal Ministry of Health, natural cosmetics in Germany may be manufactured only from natural ingredients, with the exception of nature identical preservatives and emulsifiers based on natural substances (Webber, 2007).

However, at the time of writing (2008), there is no worldwide recognition of what constitutes a natural or an organic cosmetic. Many classifications are coming from the food and agriculture industries, which are more advanced in their definitions of organic and natural.

Standards, which are becoming widely recognised in Europe, have been put in place by private certifying companies such as Ecocert in France (www.ecocert.com) the Soil Association in the UK (www.soilassociation.org) AIAB in Italy (www.aiab.it) and BDHI in Germany (www.kontrollierte-naturkosmetik.de/en). These four European bodies are currently working together to create a uniform criteria to give certification for both natural and organic products. In the USA certification comes from the USDA (www.usda.gov) and in Australia the ACO (Australian Certified Organic) (www.australianorganic.com.au). Each certifying body has differences in what constitute natural ingredients, what processes are allowed for ingredients to be termed 'based on natural substances' and when a product can be labelled as 'organic'.

The public and consumer groups are demanding more standardisation and transparency in the labelling of natural products.

However, more often than not, cosmetic companies that claim to be natural, or organic, have made the claim based on their own criteria. Brands need to understand their marketing standpoints, and their own personal philosophy as well as being aware of regulatory guidelines.

At present the use of natural ingredients versus synthetics in certain products will produce a different feel (texture) to finished products. Surfactants (foaming agents) are a good example where sodium lauryl sulphate will produce more bubbles than a natural equivalent such as Yucca Glauca. Many cosmetic scientists argue that without using synthetics it is difficult to produce skincare creams and washes that feel 'luxurious' and of 'high quality', but since this is subjective it will ultimately be up to the consumer to decide which they prefer as the use of natural ingredients becomes more widespread.

Preservation

Preserving products is necessary to stop products degrading, which can lead to obsolete stock, brand damage or, more seriously, harming the consumer. Microorganisms are all around us, in the air, on our skin and on the things we touch and eat. Many do not cause any problems but if they get into spa products and develop in significant numbers they can cause real concern. The main types of microorganisms to be considered are yeast, moulds and bacteria. For example *Pseudanomas* (a type of bacteria) in significant quantities can cause skin and eye infections, food poisoning, toxic shock, strep throat and even dental plaque. Bacillus (bacteria) can cause unsightly product contamination. The yeast, *Candida albicans*, can cause infections like thrush (Schueller and Romanowski, 2008). Microorganisms can grow and flourish very easily and all that is needed is water, some nutrients and a moderate temperature. Cosmetics and toiletries can provide the perfect growing conditions, particularly when containing plant extracts which often provide necessary nutrients for microbe proliferation. Microbes cannot live in a base of 100% oil but will grow in a base containing water, which means that any product containing water will need to have some type of preservative system.

Products can be contaminated from ingredients, manufacturing equipment, packaging and human contact (Schueller and Romanowski, 2008). This means contamination can come from any person during manufacture, spa staff or the final consumer. In spas, large size professional products sitting in warm environments and that are handled by many people are particularly vulnerable and require adequate preservation.

Preservatives are, by nature, used to kill harmful micro organisms, so it is important to keep them to a minimum to limit skin irritation whilst maintaining product integrity.

To test the robustness of the preservation system, the product needs to go through a Preservative Challenge Test or Preservative Efficacy Test (PET) or Antimicrobial Effective Test (AET). PET and AET protocols can be found in various pharmacopeias such as the United States Pharmacopeia (USP) or the British Pharmacopeia (BP). The primary objective of a PET is to accurately and reproducibly measure the ability of a product or formulation to resist both normal and abnormal microbial insult (Yablonski and Mancuso, 2007). This is where a product is inoculated with a set number of microbes; surviving microbes are counted over a period of time, usually 28 days. Adequate preservation requires that the preservative kills the microbes over that period at a steady, if not rapid, rate.

Stability testing

Stability testing evaluates a product's ability to maintain its original aesthetic, physical and chemical characteristics under controlled conditions designed to accelerate aging. Such testing can provide an early indication of problems that may occur in formulations (Schueller and Romanowski, 2008). Stability tests are important to ensure the product does not separate, change colour or change odour over its intended lifespan. Stability test results also qualify the intended lifespan or shelf life of the product defining how long stock will last unused. The most common storage conditions used in (this) industry include the following: 54°C or 50°C, 45°C, 37°C or 35°C, room temperature (25°C), 4°C, freeze/thaw, and exposure to fluorescent and sunlight (www.aseansec.org/cosmetic/6.doc). Samples are evaluated by odour, colour, appearance and viscosity at checkpoints on 1, 3, 6, 9, 12 and sometimes 24 months.

Claim substantiation

Claims are the statements made about the performance or benefits of a personal care product (Schueller and Romanowski, 2008). Any claim that is made must be supported, usually with experimental data, from the ingredient manufacturer or the product developer. Throughout the world there are consumer protection bodies (mainly governmental) that need to be satisfied that any claim made is supported with adequate evidence. Products must not mislead consumers about their benefits. Strong consumer claims should be tested by evaluating the consumer perception. Some sort of quantitative tests need to be performed to ensure the product claims can be backed up with facts. For example, if it is claimed 'Product x gives your skin 25% moisture' then a skin moisture test needs to be performed with analytical data to support the claim. Since laws differ in various countries it is important to be aware of each country's trading standards including consumer protection laws as well as trade laws that cover the sale of cosmetics and toiletries for example weights and measures and cosmetic safety regulations (SCCNFP, 1999) (www.cfsan.fda.gov/~dms/cos-toc.html) (www.accc.gov.au/content/index.phml/itemld/614012/fromltemld/268595).

Packaging

Primary packaging is any receptacle that holds the product Secondary packaging is the outer wrapping or cartons. The aesthetics of packaging plays a major role in the success of retail products but the functionality of packaging can play a major role in the ease of use for therapists during treatments. There is far too much competition in the personal care market place for consumers to suffer poor packaging, so choosing the right packaging is an important step of the product development process. The product needs to dispense easily from the container without leaving a substantial inaccessible amount in the base.

For professional use, being able to accurately calculate how much product is used per treatment is important. Pumps that give metered doses are a good way of regulating product use. Spatulas and spoons can also be used, however sterilization must follow.

Again, as with ingredients, it is becoming increasingly important to take into consideration environmental issues when selecting packaging. Packaging can be recyclable (glass or HDPE plastic – this is indicated by the recyclable symbol (www.biffa.co.uk/getrecycling/symbols.php) reusable or biodegradable. It is also preferable to select packaging materials which are from a sustainable source, such as the board used for cartons which can be obtained from sustainable managed forests approved by the Forestry Stewardship Commission (FSC) (www.fsc-uk/org/). Sourcing materials locally limits transportation and in general purchasing through ethical companies who endorse environmental practices in the work place will make the process of finding eco-friendly packaging easier.

Packaging compatibility

Packaging must be compatible with the product it contains. Plastics can be incompatible with some ingredients as they can break or allow some chemicals to pass through their walls. Polyethylene (PET) plastic can crack after exposure to certain products and some fragrances can seep through plastic walls. These incompatibilities are often not apparent until months after the package has been filled and can cause disastrous effects further down the line. Glass is a tough material but not always practical especially in wet areas where breakages can be dangerous. If plastic is needed then a packaging compatibility test is advised. The basic compatibility test involves placing filled product in an oven set at around 35°C for 28 days with regular visual and physical checks during that time. Pumps can be used, bottles squeezed and caps taken on and off. Any signs of physical stress, discoloration, bending or perfume on the outside of the packaging indicates a package incompatibility and unsuitability (Schueller and Romanowski, 2008).

Good manufacturing practice

Good manufacturing practices (GMP) for cosmetics are based on quality management systems from personnel through to quality control procedures, premises, storage, equipment, training, etc. and are essential to producing safe and effective products.(www.aseansec.org/cosmetic/6.doc) When developing products it is also important to take into account that the general increased awareness of environmental changes is leading customers to look more closely at the industrial processes used to both extract natural ingredients and to manufacture and transport products.

Safety assessments

Natural ingredients are not necessarily harmless so as with synthetics the ingredients and finished products need to follow the correct assessment procedures that are applied to all cosmetic ingredients, and safety assessments for finished products (http://ec.europa.eu/health/ph_risk/committees/sccp/documents/out12_en.pdf). Safety assessments are documents designed to give reassurance that the product is safe for use in its intended cosmetic use. It usually takes the form of a signed statement of opinion from an appropriately qualified and suitably experienced person (DTI, 2005). These statements are necessary for product sale in certain countries plus they also reassure product developers that the product is fit for use.

Summary

To summarise, when selecting products for spas it is very important to identify each spa's requirements and to calculate the advantages of private label products versus established brands.

The line up of products created should fully reflect the brands philosophy and be suited to the end users.

All product producers are obliged to ensure that safe products are created by following worldwide industry and country-specific guidelines. Lastly, it is important to note that products which stand the test of time in any market place, be it department stores, pharmacies or spas, are those that give benefit to the user. Trends, in packaging in particular, come and go but good effective products are always in demand.

References

Australia   www.accc.gov.au/content/index.phml/itemld/614012/fromltemld/268595;

DTI. 2005. *Cosmetic Safety, Guidance on the Implementation of the Cosmetic Products (Safety) Regulations* (2004). (Online) Available: http://www.berr.gov.uk/

European Cosmetic Toiletry and Perfumery Association (Colipa) Directive 2003/15/EC (7th amendment to Directive 76/768/EEC, Annex III, part I) (Online) Available: http://www.colipa.com/site/index.cfm?SID=15588&Obj=15756

Field, T., Diego, M., Hernandez-Reif, M., Cisneros, W., Feijo, L., Vera, Y., Gil, K., Grina, D., Claire He, Q. (2005) Feb *Lavender Fragrance Cleansing Gel Effects On Relaxation, International Journal of Neuroscience*, 115(2):207–222.

Living with Your Sense of Smell (1992). The Sense of Smell Institute, New York.

SCCNFP. The Scientific Committee on Cosmetic Products and Non-Food Products Intended for Consumers (1999). (Online) Available: www.dti.gov.uk/consumers/safety/products/cosmetics/index.html

Schueller, R., Romanowski, P. (2008) *Beginning Cosmetic Chemistry. An Overview for Chemists, Formulators, Suppliers and other Interested in the Cosmetic Industry*, 2nd Edition, Allured Publishing, Carol Stream.

Spa Source the Essential Guide to Spa Development (2007). Stevenson Publication Ltd, Sarah Ward.

Trade Mark Classification ref. no. 3 (2008). (Online) Available: www.patent.gov.uk.

Webber, W. (2007) Is It Natural Or What?, *COSSMA*, 10:18.

www.organicmonitor.com.

www.ecocert.com.

www.soilassociation.org.

www.aiab.it.

www.kontrollierte-naturkosmetik.de/en.

www.usda.gov.

www.australianorganic.com.au.

www.cfsan.fda.gov/~dms/cos-toc.html.

www.canadabusiness.ca/servlet/ContentServer?cid= 10819442 04554&1ang=en&pagename=CBSC ON%2Fdisplay&c=Regs.

http://www.biffa.co.uk/getrecycling/symbols.php.

http://www.fsc-uk.org/.

www.aseansec.org/cosmetic/6.doc.

http://ec.europa.eu/health/ph_risk/committees/sccp/documents/out12_en.pdf.

Yablonski, J.I., Mancuso, S.E. (2007) Preservative efficacy testing accelerating the process, *Cosmetics and Toiletries Magazine*, 122(10):51–62.

CHAPTER 14

Wellness technologies and related products

Marc Cohen

As spas move from pampering towards wellness, there is a trend to balance the high-touch aspect of spas with the use of high-tech equipment based on technologies applied to the monitoring, enhancing and maintenance of well-being. These technologies have arisen out of both conventional and eso-teric science as well as traditional knowledge and while many of these technologies are not yet widely used in spas, as they become more accessible, and as spas become more specialized, it is likely their use will increase.

While it is impossible here to give a full account of all the cur-rent health and wellness related technologies, the rest of this chapter, aims to give a broad overview of the range of tech-nologies available and provide examples of those technologies that may be relevant for use in the spa industry. These technol-ogies, which can be broadly divided into wellness assessment and therapeutic technologies, include a range of diagnostic devices, information and communication technologies as well as equipment related to electromagnetic energy and water.

Wellness assessment technologies

Wellness assessment technologies include a range of method-ologies designed to obtain information and then analyse and interpret it in order to form an understanding of a person's state of health and to then use this information, along with existing knowledge, to inform the design and implementation of the most effective therapies. There is a very wide range of wellness assessment technologies, that can be summarized under the following headings: data recording; direct questioning; tissue sampling; functional testing; and data analysis and knowledge management.

Assessing wellness versus illness

Wellness assessment, which aims to document and moni-tor a person's state of health is distinct from medical diagno-sis which generally aims to get to the cause of a symptom or detect an established disease. Wellness assessments aim to document a person's current health status and form the basis for risk management strategies, create motivation for positive lifestyle change and document any improvement or decline. Wellness assessments may also be used for insurance purposes and many companies now send their executives for 'executive health checks' as a risk management strategy to ensure their continued good health. In spas, wellness assessments can also help to establish a very personal and intimate relationship with the guest and enable the guest's experience to be highly personalized and individualized.

While wellness assessments aim to document health and wellbeing rather than diagnose specific illnesses, it is possible that such assessments inadvertently pick up diagnoses that require urgent attention. To ensure adequate continuity of care is provided, interaction with the mainstream healthcare system and the guest's usual medical providers is advisable whenever tests are performed that may reveal important diagnostic information. That there is a duty of care to act on the results of any diagnosis and or refer people for further testing and consultation with medical specialists. This duty of care has legal, ethical and moral implications and needs to be assessed from the individual therapist and company perspective.

Data recording

This includes taking direct measurements of the body (anthropometry) as well as recording images via clinical photography and medical imaging. Recordings can also be made of the electrical properties of the body to monitor organ function or assess body composition, muscle activity or sleep.

Anthropometry (body measurement)

Anthropometric measures are used to assess a person's body parameters and their change over time as well as compare to population norms and perform risk assessments. While measures such as height, weight and skin fold thickness do not require sophisticated technology, there are also highly sophisticated technologies such as dual energy X-ray absorptiometry (DEXA) and ultrasound densitometers used to record body composition including lean muscle mass and percentage body fat (Erselcan et al., 2000). There are also a number of technologies suitable for use in a spa or resort environment that can be used to provide relatively quick, simple and reliable measures of body composition such as bioimpedance devices that uses the body's electrical conductivity (Mattsson and Thomas, 2006) and devices such as the Bodpod (www.bodpod.com) which use air displacement plethysmography (Noreen and Lemon, 2006).

Clinical photography and medical imaging

Clinical photography and medical imaging are used to create images of the body for diagnostic purposes and include a range of sophisticated technologies including disciplines such as radiology, endoscopy, thermography and microscopy. While these areas are generally considered specialised fields best left to medical professionals, there are a range of imaging technologies that are more accessible and may be relevant to spas. These include the use of complementary and alternative medicine assessment tools such as iriscopes that can be used to perform iridology assessments, as well as dermoscopes to document skin lesions and provide mole surveillance.

Dermoscopy may be particularly relevant to spas as spa therapists are well placed to monitor the state of their guests' skin. Modern digital dermoscopes can very simply capture high quality images that can be used to monitor existing moles for changes in shape, size or colour as well as record the occurrence of new moles. Digital dermoscopy also provides the basis for tele-dermatology services which have recently become available to spas whereby images are recorded by the spa therapist and sent electronically to dermatologists who report on them and respond with their assessments (www.wellnessdiagnostics.com).

Other imaging technologies relevant to spas use specialized light such as the Wood's lamp, which uses ultraviolet light to help visualize and detect photodamage, topical skin infections and other skin lesions, as well as devices such as the 'biophotonic scanner' which uses specific laser light to record the skin's carotenoid anti-oxidant levels and make an assessment of nutritional status (www.pharmanex.com).

Electrophysiological measures

The diagnostic applications of different types of electromagnetic radiation (EMR) began around the start of last century with the discovery of X-rays and the use of the galvanometer to detect the electrical activity of the heart. It has subsequently progressed to where many electrodiagnostic techniques such as the electrocardiogram (ECG), electroencephalogram (EEG) and electromyogram (EMG) have become standard medical procedures.

The advent of personal computing and modern consumer electronics has seen these technologies become more and more accessible with many technologies moving away from the domain of the technical specialist within hospitals and medical clinics and becoming available to the general population via home-based and mobile platforms. Thus, new devices such as the v-patch (www.vpatchmedical.com) with the capacity for ambulatory monitoring and wireless uploading of data to the internet have the capacity to effectively monitor various aspects of well-being are may be applicable for use in the spa industry.

Sleep studies

The assessment of sleep is likely to become an increasingly common as sleep is a good indicator of well-being and quality of life and the technologies available for assessing sleep are becoming simpler and easier to use. Full sleep studies generally involve the use of polysomnography (PSN) which includes the recording of many body functions including brain, eye and muscle activity, heart rhythm, breathing function and blood oxygen levels within the confines of a specialised sleep laboratory. Sleep can also be assessed using much simpler technology such as actigraphy which measures body movements as well as using algorithms based on heart rate variability (HRV) which may provide data comparable to full PSN (www.hypnocore.com). With improvements in biosensor and data acquisition technology, sleep studies have recently becoming more user friendly with companies now offering the possibility of in-home sleep studies and more recently the possibility to perform 'tele-sleep diagnostics' for hotel and resort guests (www.wellnessdiagnostics.com).

Pedometry

While not actually electrophysiological devices, pedometers, which use microelectromechanical inertial sensors systems, can be used to monitor physical activity by providing a measure of the number of steps taken each day. Such devices, which can be simply worn on the belt, are now being integrated into other personal electronic devices such as phones and digital music players and Apple and Nike now offer a kit where a shoe sensor communicates with a wireless iPod receiver to transmit workout information such as elapsed time, distance traveled and calories burned (www.apple.com/ipod/nike).

Bioenergetic testing

In addition to the more conventional wellness assessments, electrical measures can also be applied to less conventional applications that fall under the heading of 'bioenergetic medicine'. Bioenergetic medicine covers a wide range of different therapeutic and diagnostic approaches based on the idea that life is dependent on a subtle form of energy. This subtle energy, often termed 'vital force', 'life energy', 'life force', 'prana', 'chi' or 'Qi', is deemed to flow throughout organisms maintaining both physical and psychological processes. Pain and disease are said to be produced when this energetic flow is disrupted and bioenergetic therapies are aimed at restoring the natural energetic flow (Cohen, 2002).

There is a wide range of equipment designed to monitor the bioenergetic properties of the body with most focusing on electrodermal testing equipment designed to determine a person's energetic balance and draw correlations between the electrical conductivity of various acupuncture points and specific allergies or organ function (Lam et al., 1988). Such equipment includes the 'Mora', 'Vega', 'Dermatron', 'Ryodoraku', 'Electroacupuncture According to Voll (EAV)', 'Biograph', 'Listen' systems and others. These devices, which are mostly based on Russian and German research, have been used around the world since the 1950s in different clinical settings including natural medicine and veterinary practice and dentistry (Voll, 1980) as well as being used by a number of spas.

Direct questioning

Wellness assessment based on direct questioning includes both formal and informal history taking and questionnaires that may be self-administered or administered by practitioners. In this regard the technology refers more to the use of software to record the data and make assessments by comparing it to other normative data.

Direct questioning includes standardized medical history taking that includes questions on current and past symptoms and illnesses, family, occupational, travel, dietary, lifestyle and sexual history, as well as question about allergies, licit, illicit and prescription drug use and organ function. Direct questioning can also include standardized nutritional assessment and food frequency surveys as well as various 'diagnostic questionnaires' used to asses psychosocial issues including stress, anxiety, depression, social networks and quality of life. Such questioning may be useful in spas to help determine any specific health needs, contraindications or other safety issues.

In addition to conventional medical information, direct questioning can also be used to collect information relevant to various complementary and alternative medicine approaches including assessment of 'constitution' according to naturopathy, assessment of 'five element balance' according to traditional Chinese medicine and assessment of 'dosha' according to Ayurveda. Such assessments are commonly used in spas to assist in personalizing treatments including the selection of aromas, herbal teas, colours and massage techniques.

Tissue sampling

Sampling includes the analysis of commonly taken tissue samples such as blood and urine as well as less commonly taken samples such as hair, faeces, sweat, semen, breast milk, ear wax, toe and finger nails and tissue biopsies. Once taken these samples can be subjected to various laboratory tests including biochemical, immunological and genetic profiling, hormonal assays, assessment of anti-oxidant, free radical, cancer and infection markers, as well as toxicological testing that may screen for a range of toxins including heavy metals and organic pollutants such as pesticides and fire retardants.

While many of these tests required advanced technologies available only through highly specialized laboratories, as the technology develops there are an increasing number of tests that can be performed without sending samples to a distant laboratory. Examples of such 'near patient tests' include dipstick urine tests, as well as finger prick blood tests for anti-oxidant and free radical status using the 'Free Radical Analytical System' (FRAS) (www.fras4.com) and the 'determination of Reactive Oxygen Metabolites' (dROM) test (www.diacron.com).

A test that may have particular relevance for spas is hair tissue mineral analysis (HTMA) which involves cutting a small sample of hair which is then sent for analysis of different elements including nutrient and minerals, and heavy metals. The results of these tests can be used to assess toxic exposure to heavy metals and determine the efficacy of detoxification treatments as well as provide information about nutritional status and supplementation requirements (www.traceelements.com).

Functional testing

Functional testing includes methodologies that test various biological functions and performance by assessing the body's ability to respond to a situation or challenge. This includes the testing of lung function, cognitive performance, auditory and visual function as well as fitness assessments, cardiovascular stress testing and nutritional challenge tests.

There are a wide variety of tests used for fitness assessments (www.exrx.net/Testing.html) including tests for aerobic and cardiovascular performance, muscular strength, endurance and flexibility, and there are a large number of technologies used to perform these tests including cycle ergometers and treadmills, direct and indirect calorimetry for measuring metabolic rate and aerobic performance, computerized dynamometry for measuring joint mobility, strength and power, and spirometers for measuring lung function (www.spirometry. com). There are also a wide variety of software programs and calculators for analysing the results of these tests and producing detailed reports (e.g. see www.bsdi.cc, www.bioexsystems. com/TrainerProducts.htm).

In addition to fitness testing there are a range of computerized neurological function tests that can be performed. These include audiometry to test hearing (www.digital-recordings.com) as well as computerized neuropsychological testing that can be used to perform very sensitive cognitive function testing using software that can detect changes in memory, learning and other cognitive tasks (www.cogstate.com). While this type of software has not as yet been widely used by the spa industry, it is currently used in many sports to assess concussive injury and has the potential to be able to document improvements in cognitive function after various spa treatments or wellness programs.

Data analysis and knowledge management

Data analysis and knowledge management involves statistical interpretation and modeling of data so as to compare individuals to populations norms, perform risk assessments and document any decline or improvement. Data analysis generally requires the creation of an electronic medical record and involves a range of knowledge management technologies including the use of bibliographic databases and clinical decision support systems.

Information and communications technology

Information and Communications Technology (ICT) has progressed rapidly over the past few decades so that there is now the possibility that everyone on the globe can be linked via mobile communications technology that infiltrates almost every aspect of society. Similarly information systems have been developed that penetrate into every aspect of business and support standard business functions such as human resources and financial management, reservations, billing, stock management, supply chain logistics, marketing, online retail sales and customer relations management (CRM).

ICT can also be used to support healthcare delivery and the use of electronic health information systems promises to improve patient safety, quality of care and the efficiency of healthcare delivery through the provision of alerts and reminders, diagnostic support, therapy critiquing and planning, prescribing decision support, information retrieval, image recognition and interpretation as well as the discovery of new phenomena and the creation of medical knowledge (Coiera, 2003). However, while there are a number of software packages designed to support spa operations, the use of software to support therapeutic services for spas is still in its infancy.

Electronic health information systems

CRM systems are commonly used to generate individual client records, yet the development of electronic health records in both the medical and spa domain has generally fallen behind other business functions. The poor uptake of electronic health records is due to a number of reasons including poor interoperability between systems making it difficult for different software applications to communicate and exchange data accurately, effectively and consistently, as well as poor human interface design, failure to fit naturally into the routine process of care and reluctance or computer illiteracy of some healthcare workers (Coiera, 2003).

The use of electronic health records also raises many ethical, legal, security and confidentiality issues. If people are to trust their sensitive medical information to a software system, they need to be assured that this information will not be accessed by unauthorised people or used for unauthorised purposes. While these issues are dealt with in medical research by international conventions determined by the International Conference on Harmonisation Good Clinical Practice guidelines (www.ich.org) that specify the use of institutional review boards or independent ethics committees in pharmaceutical research, there is yet to be the equivalent international conventions for medical record management. Despite these challenges there are serious undertakings by governments and the medical profession to address these issues and make electronic medical records a standard part of healthcare. The spa industry can certainly learn from these developments and aim to integrate them into its own operations so as to better provide wellness services as well as better integrate with mainstream health systems.

Knowledge management and bibliographical databases

Knowledge management systems attempt to provide access to the wealth of knowledge that humans have accumulated throughout history. These systems are particularly relevant to heath and wellness domain where knowledge is being integrated from many diverse traditions and systems of thought, as well as being created on a daily basis. Much of this information is freely available via online bibliographical search engines such as Google Scholar (http://scholar.google.com) and PubMed (www.pubmedcentral.nih.gov/) as well as through subscription databases including Embase (www.embase.com/), Thompson scientific (http://scientific.thomson.com/), Science Direct (www.sciencedirect.com) and Scopus (www.scopus.com) which provide access to the latest peer-reviewed medical literature. There are also a number of databases devoted specifically to the natural health and alternative medicine domain as well as to traditional medicine systems and specific therapies or modalities along with 'meta-databases' providing lists of other databases (e.g. see www.rosenthal.hs.columbia.edu/Databases. html). In addition, global academic collaborations such as the Cochrane Collaboration (www.cochrane.org) are attempting to collate, critically review and summarize the wealth of knowledge contained in the world's medical literature.

With such a wide range of information becoming accessible to professionals and consumers alike there is pressure on health professionals to not only keep up-to-date with their own discipline, but also to help consumers interpret information in light of their individual circumstances. This is likely to have increasing relevance to the spa industry as consumers turn to spas to address their health and well-being needs and as research data accumulates documenting the benefits of spa services.

Clinical decision support systems and tele-medicine

The advent of ICT, electronic health records and knowledge management systems has led to the development of computerized clinical decision support systems which aim to integrate medical knowledge with patient data and use an inference engine to generate case specific advice. Such support systems offer the capacity to support the clinical process from diagnosis and investigation through to treatment and long-term care (www.openclinical.org/dss.html).

In the health and well-being domain such systems include the use of online calculators for assessing the risk of various diseases such as heart disease, diabetes and depression, as well as determining the risk of various lifestyle behaviours such as smoking and exercise (e.g. see www.healthcalculators.org or www.mayoclinic.com/health/heart-disease-risk/HB00047). In allowing a person's current risks to be documented, these calculators can provide the basis for providing lifestyle advice and provide motivation for implementing positive lifestyle changes. While many of these calculators are quite simplistic they are likely to become more sophisticated and relevant as further research data accumulates.

While electronic clinical decision support systems are not yet in widespread use, the use of ICT has also led to the development of 'tele-medicine' whereby medical expertise can be accessed remotely through online consultations and prescriptions. This may have particular relevance to spas which may be located in isolated or remote regions or simply wish to provide their guests access to medical expertise without having to employ doctors or other technical specialists on site. Tele-medicine can also include the use of various data collection methodologies allowing for asynchronous, storage and forwarding of data, thus allowing for remote expertise to be accessed without both parties being present at the same time. Such applications are particularly suited to disciplines such as tele-dermatology, tele-radiology and tele-pathology and are applicable to spas that wish to provide access to medical expertise located in differed locations or time zones.

Therapeutic technologies

Therapeutic technologies cover a very wide range of health and medical related technologies including food technology along with fitness, exercise and beauty therapy equipment. It is beyond the scope of this chapter to discuss all these technologies and the rest of this chapter will attempt to merely give an overview and discuss some of the therapeutic technologies related to water, energy medicine and biofeedback that may have relevance to spas.

Water technologies

Hydrotherapy – Spa baths, Jacuzzis and showers

Many people associate spas with spa baths or the 'Jacuzzi'. The Jacuzzi company was originally an engineering firm that became involved in the design of hydraulic pumps. The Jacuzzi whirlpool bath was invented as a personal project of Candido Jacuzzi who developed a small portable pump for placing in a bathtub to provide a hydrotherapy massage to treat his arthritic son. In 1956 the success of this project led to the marketing of the J-300 pump followed by the development and patenting of the first bathtub with a built-in whirlpool system in 1968. Further developments included larger bath sizes and the inclusion of filters and water heaters to create the 'spa' (www.fundinguniverse.com/company-histories/Jacuzzi-Inc-Company-History.html).

In addition to whirlpool baths, hydrotherapy technologies also include various water delivery systems such as the Vichy shower with which a therapist can provide a full body treatment using series of horizontal showers applied to a client lying on water proof table; the Swiss shower which allows water to be sprayed from three or more directions; the Scotch hose which involves using alternating hot and cold water projected through a jet hose from 3 to 4 meters; tropical rain, waterfall and filiform showers; and thermal capsules which encompasses the client providing privacy as well as allowing aromatherapy, steam, infrared sauna, vibrating massage and colour to be included in the experience. Further developments have included pipeless motors and ionisation self-cleaning systems for flushing and disinfecting internal piping as well as reticulated systems that filter, heat and recirculate water in order to conserve water and energy.

Water filters

Throughout the ages imaginations have been captured by stories of the 'fountain of youth' or 'the elixir of life' that would bestow health and vitality to those who drank it. More recently imaginations have been captured by stunning images of water crystals demonstrating strikingly different patterns and properties captured using specialised photography (Imoto, 2004). Today the search for enchanted water has merged with the need for safe water and there is an ever expanding range of technologies that purport to purify, energise and enhance the quality of water used for drinking or bathing.

It is beyond the scope of this chapter to discuss the extensive range of water filters, additives and their related technologies which are based on a range of conventional, esoteric and pseudo science. These technologies include the use of reverse osmosis, activated carbon filtration, ultraviolet radiation, photo-oxidation, electrolysis, ionisers, alkalinisers, anti-oxidants, redox potentials, pH boosters, vortex energies, oxygenators, molecular resonance, far infrared (FIR) emitting ceramics, minerals, volcanic rocks, coral calcium, liquid electrolytes and softeners.

Pure water appears to be a diminishing resource on the planet, yet is an essential element in most spas, the quality of water is likely to become an increasingly important issues for spas these and other water purification and enhancement technologies are likely to become increasingly prominent.

Natural swimming pools/ponds

Natural swimming pools (also referred to as swimming ponds) are a technological innovation that combines landscape design with biotechnology and an understanding of ecosystems. These pools utilize a low volume pump to circulate water from a swimming zone through a shallower zone containing an evolving ecosystem made up of specialized plants and natural water organisms that filter the water and remove nutrients. This creates a living water feature that naturally heats and cleans the water and greatly reduces maintenance while providing naturally clean swimming pool water without the use of chemical treatments (e.g. see www.naturalswimmingpools.com, www.gartenart.co.uk).

Flowforms

Flowforms involve a design technology invented in 1970 by John Wilkes, having been developed from the research work of George Adams and Rudolf Steiner into nature's formative patterns. Flowforms are unique water features whereby water is made to flow rhythmically and fold back upon itself to create aesthetically pleasing lemniscate movements that emulate the swirls and vortices of mountain streams, while at the same time holding a regular heart pulse. Flowforms generally form a cascade of water that is recirculated and as water flows through the flowform it is naturally oxygenated allowing micro-organisms to help break down any waste material (Wilkes, 2003).

Flowforms have many functional uses including the treatment of effluent, grey water recycling, stirring biodynamic preparations, biological purification, farming, food processing, interior air-conditioning as well as having therapeutic and aesthetic uses that include public sculptures, garden features and interior design features. Over 100 flowform designs have been created with installations in over 30 countries (e.g. see www.flow-forms.com, www.livingwaterflowforms.com). It is perhaps surprising that flowforms have not been more widely used within the spa industry as their aesthetic, therapeutic and aquatic nature seems to align well with the values of the industry and it seems likely that their use will become more widespread in the industry as time goes on.

Energy medicine technologies

Environmental electromagnetic activity

Life has evolved bathed in a sea of Electro-Magnetic Radiation (EMR). Over the past 100 years the natural background EMR has been overtaken by man made sources so that we are all currently exposed to artificial EMR of various frequencies from numerous sources including power lines, radio, television, video display units, microwave ovens and mobile phones. Currently there is considerable controversy about the possible harmful effects of EMR as well as increasing research into the potential for beneficial and therapeutic effects (Cohen, 2004).

The study of the biological effects of EMR is an extremely complex and controversial one. Gross effects from EMR are usually attributed to its thermal or ionising properties however, it is now widely accepted that EMR may produce biological effects that are non-thermal. These effects may arise from many factors including the electric or magnetic field components, the energy content, frequency, waveform, amplitude coherence, resonance, or modulation of frequency or amplitude, as well as the length and timing of exposure, the area they are applied to, interference effects with other fields, the presence of existing pathology and the information content of the fields (Presman, 1970; Becker and Seldon, 1985).

While it is clear that humans and other organisms can respond to fields as low as the earth's magnetic field (Bergiannaki et al., 1996), the impact of low-level environmental EMR on health and well-being remains unclear. Proponents of the harmful effects of low-level EMR suggest that EMR may act as a stressor that negatively impacts susceptible individuals as well as having long-term effects on other-wise healthy people (Smith and Best, 1989). There are certainly many reported cases of individuals with so-called electromagnetic sensitivity who present with non-specific ailments or chronic fatigue (Leitgeb et al., 2005) as well as many cases of illnesses occurring in places of heightened EMR exposure due to local geography and/or the position of radio or microwave towers (Becker, 1991).

Reducing environmental electromagnetic activity

The controversy over the potential harmful effects of EMR suggest that the most sensible approach is one of prudent avoidance and exposure minimization, although this may be difficult in the modern world where EMR emitting devices have become part of the social fabric.

Some destination and resort spas have sought to specifically address this issue and have been built to minimize the use of ambient electromagnetic activity (see Chapter 20) and there are also a number of devices that claim to shield the user from electromagnetic exposure or reduce the effects of such exposure. However, these devices, which have received media attention after being endorsed by celebrities, are generally based on esoteric technologies that have not been subject to rigorous scientific testing.

Enhancing environmental electromagnetic activity

While EMR can be hazardous, there are some situations where EMR exposure is necessary or desirable within certain limits. For example while overexposure to the sun is detrimental, adequate exposure is required for vitamin D production. In addition to sunlight there may be other forms of EMR with beneficial effects as suggested by the finding that there are naturally occurring, extremely low frequency electromagnetic waves produced by lightning that travel in the cavity between the ionosphere and the earth's surface. These waves called 'Schumann resonances' have been found to have similar frequency components to the human EEG during meditation (Kenny, 1991) and to correspond to frequencies that propagate along acupuncture meridians (Cohen et al., 1998). This suggests that internal homeostatic processes may be somehow 'tuned' to naturally occurring frequencies which help to support health and well-being.

There is a range of devices designed to induce relaxation and meditative states and improve general well-being by enhancing or mimicking these natural frequencies. The devices include Schumann resonance generators (www.lessemf.com/schumann. html), music CDs that attempt to induce relaxing frequencies using binaural beats (e.g. see www.centerpointe.com and www. binaural-beats.com) as well as meditation trainers that attempt to entrain these frequencies using light–sound devices such as the 'MindSpa' (www.bio-medical.com).

Electromagnetic therapy

The specific use of electromagnetic energy for therapeutic purposes goes back at least as far as ancient Greece where electric eels were used in the treatment of arthritis and ancient China where loadstone was used in healing. Today electromagnetic energy is routinely used for therapeutic purposes within conventional medicine in devices used for electroconvulsive therapy, defibrillation, pacemakers and diathermy. In addition to these applications which are directed at treating pathology, there are a range of technologies that can be directed at enhancing health and well-being. These technologies include FIR saunas, electroacupuncture, micro-current body shaping, transcutaneous electro-neuro stimulation (TENS), LEDs for colour therapy, lasers for microdermabrasion and laser acupuncture, as well as the use of static magnetic fields and pulsed electromagnetic therapy (PEMT).

FIR saunas

Saunas have a long tradition mostly associated with the 'Finnish sauna' or 'dry heat bath' which consists of a wooden paneled room and a radiant heater. While Finnish saunas have become standard offerings in most gyms, fitness centers and hotels, the development of the FIR sauna has made saunas a much more accessible consumer item. FIR saunas use either ceramic or carbon panels to produce FIR radiation which can penetrate the body's surface and produce profuse sweating at lower ambient temperatures than conventional saunas and are therefore better tolerated while requiring less energy.

A review of the research into the health benefits suggests that sauna bathing has benefits for the cardiovascular system and may help lower blood pressure and improve cardiac function as well as having benefits for musculoskeletal conditions (Hannuksela and Ellahham, 2001). This is consistent with recent studies that found that sauna bathing improved symptoms and exercise tolerance in patients with chronic cardiac failure (Michalsen et al., 2003). While there have been few clinical trials specifically on FIR saunas, the benefits of FIR saunas are likely to be similar to those of conventional saunas. FIR saunas are further suggested to be useful for detoxification by mobilising heavy metals and fat-soluble toxins (Crinnion, 2007) and there are suggestions from a number of observational studies that saunas, along with nutritional supplementation, may be effective for detoxification of a number of different compounds as well as reducing the effects of toxin exposure (Cohen, 2007).

Pulsed electromagnetic therapy

PEMT involves the direct application of pulsed EMR of different waveforms and frequencies to various parts of the body to assist in healing. There are a number of companies producing and/or marketing PEMT equipment to promote general well-being and tissue repair as well as to treat pain. While the most thoroughly researched use for PEMT is in the treatment of bone healing (Zhang et al., 2007), there is evidence to suggest that PEMT may be useful for treating a range of other conditions including osteoarthritis (Hulme et al., 2002) and sports injuries (Cohen et al., 2000).

Biofeedback and breath training technologies

Paced breathing therapy

The breath is a vital function that links mind and body and influences every aspect of metabolism. Healthy breathing is emphasised as an important tool for maintaining and enhancing health in traditions such as yoga, tai chi, Ayurveda and naturopathy. The breath is often seen as the link between mind and body and there are a growing number of technologies that aim to modulate respiration to effect positive changes in health an well-being.

RESPeRATE is patented technology the uses an innovative portable electronic device for administering 'paced breathing therapy' for reducing blood pressure and relieving stress (www.resperate.com). This device monitors the user's breath rate and interactively guides the user to reduce their breath rate to below 10 breaths per minute through the use of specially designed music. This device can be used in conjunction with other blood pressure treatments and have found that regular use is a number of clinical trials effective in producing lasting and clinically significant reductions in blood pressure (Elliott et al., 2004).

Respiratory sinus arrhythmia (RSA) biofeedback training is another breath training tool that was developed in Russia, by Alexander Smetankin. RSA biofeedback and involves the monitoring of 'sinus arrhythmia', which is the natural variation in heart rate during inspiration and expiration. Specialised software is used to provide continuous audiovisual feedback so as to allow the user to increase their RSA. This type of biofeedback can be used to enhance parasympathetic nervous system activity and induce relaxation and has been suggested to have benefits for people with asthma (Lehrer et al., 2000).

HRV Training

Heart Rate Variability (HRV) refers to the beat-to-beat alterations in heart rate which is under the control of the autonomic nervous system. HRV may be a marker of well-being as HRV has been found to decline with acute stress, psychological disturbance and the ageing process. In contrast, high HRV has been found to increase with regular physical activity, positive emotional states and during certain relaxation and meditation practices (www.heartmath.org). Over the past two decades HRV has been the subject of extensive medical research which suggests a link between HRV and physical, mental, and emotional health (Malliani, 2005).

The data used for calculating HRV can be easily collected using devices that accurately record the pulse and there are a number of technologies such as nerve-express (www.nerve-express.com), 'biocomm' (www.biocomtech.com), 'emwave' and 'freeze framer' (www.heartmath.org) that integrate simple biosensors with software that enables HRV to be used as a biofeedback training tool to assist in reducing stress, enhancing performance and general well-being.

Intermittent hypoxic training

Intermittent hypoxic training (IHT) is based on research from Russian space and military programs and is primarily used as an alternative to altitude training for enhanced sports performance. There is an extensive research literature on IHT that suggests it is able to enhance sports performance, endurance and recovery (Hamlin and Hellemans, 2007) and IHT is increasingly used to enhance general energy levels, sleep and overall well-being. Modern IHT uses 'hypoxicators' which use a facemask to deliver air with oxygen concentrations between 9% and 15% which is equivalent to air at an altitude between 2700 and 6500 meters. These devices, which are software controlled to provide individualized programs and personalized biofeedback can be easily applied in spas to provide the benefits of a high altitude experience to guests in any location (www.go2altitude.com).

Summary

There is an extremely wide range of diagnostic and therapeutic technologies currently available and existing technologies continue to be refined and become more accessible while new technologies are being continually developed. As yet most of these technologies are not yet widely used within the spa industry, although it seems likely that this use will increase as spas begin to embrace wellness and address the holistic health-care needs of their guests.

It also seems likely that as these technologies become more accessible and available to consumers, there will be higher demands placed on health (and spa) professionals to keep up-to-date and be able to use and understand these technologies as well as to interpret health related information. Thus, there will be an imperative for spas to begin to integrate their services with other healthcare practitioners and providers, raising the possibility for spa services to become seamlessly integrated into mainstream healthcare.

References

Becker, R.O. (1991) *Cross Currents: The Promise of Electromedicine, the Perils of Electropollution*, J.P. Tarcher, New York.

Becker, R.O., Seldon, G. (1985) *The Body Electric: Electromagnetism and the Foundation of Life*, William Morrow, New York.

Bergiannaki, J., Paparrigopoulos, T.J., Stefanis, C.N. (1996) Seasonal variation of melatonin excretion in humans: relationship to day length variation rate and geomagnetic field fluctuations, *Experientia*, 52:253–258.

Cohen, M. (2002) Energy medicine from an ancient and modern perspective. In: Cohen, M. (Ed.), *Prescriptions for Holistic Health"*, Monash Institute of Health Services Research, Clayton, pp. 97–108.

Cohen, M. (2004) Electromagnetic radiation and health, *Journal of Complementary Medicine*, 3(3):52–55.

Cohen, M. (2007) Detox: science or sales-pitch?, *Australian Family Physician*, 36(12):1009–1010.

Cohen, M., Behrenbruch, C., Cosic, I. (1998). Shared frequency components between schumann resonances, EEG spectra and acupuncture meridian transfer functions, *13th International Symposium on Acupuncture and Electro-Therapeutics*, Columbia University, New York, October 1997, published in Acupuncture and Electrotherapeutics Research, 23(1), 92–93.

Cohen, M., Heath, B., Lithgow, B., Cosic, I., Bailey, M. (2000). Pulsed electromagnetic field therapy for exercise-induced muscle injury, *3rd International Conference on the Engineering of Sport*, Sydney, Australia.

Coiera, E. (2003) Clinical Decision Support Systems. In: Coeira, E. (Ed.), *The Guide to Health Informatics*, Arnold, London. , available online at: www.coiera.com/aimd.htm

Crinnion, W. (2007) Components of practical clinical detox programs – sauna as a therapeutic tool, *Alternative therapies in health and medicine*, 13(2):S154–sS156.

Elliott, W.J., Black, H.R., Alter, A., Gavish, B. (2004) Blood pressure reduction with device-guided breathing: pooled data from 7 controlled studies, *Journal of Hypertension*, 22(2):S116.

Erselcan, T., Candan, F., Saruhan, S., Ayca, T. (2000) Comparison of body composition analysis methods in clinical routine, *Annals of Nutrition and Metabolism*, 44(5–6):243–248.

Hamlin, M.J., Hellemans, J. (2007) Effect of intermittent normobaric hypoxic exposure at rest on haematological, physiological, and performance parameters in multi-sport athletes, *Journal of Sports Science*, 25(4):431–441.

Hannuksela, M.L., Ellahham, S. (2001) Benefits and risks of sauna bathing, *American Journal of Medicine*, 110:118–126.

Hulme, J., Robinson, V., DeBie, R., Wells, G., Judd, M., Tugwell, P. (2002) Electromagnetic fields for the treatment of osteoarthritis, *Cochrane Database of Systematic Reviews*, (1):CD003523.

Imoto, M. (2004) *The Hidden Messages in Water*, Beyond Words Publishing, Hillsboro. Thayne, D. (translator)

Kenny, J. (1991) Resonances of interest; EEG and ELF, *Speculations in Science and Technology*, 15:50–53.

Lam, F.M.K., Tsuei, J.J., Zhao, Z. (1988) Bioenergetic regulatory measurement instruments and devices, *American Journal of Acupuncture*, 16(4):345–348.

Lehrer, P., Smetankin, A., Potapova, T. (2000) Respiratory sinus arrhythmia biofeedback therapy for asthma: a report of 20 unmedicated pediatric cases using the Smetan-kin method, *Applied Psychophysiology and Biofeedback*, 25(3):193–200.

Leitgeb, N., Schröttner, J., Böhm, M. (2005) Does 'electromagnetic pollution' cause illness? An inquiry among Austrian general practitioners, *Wiener Medizinische Wochenschrift*, 155(9–10):237–241.

Malliani, A. (2005) Heart rate variability: from bench to bedside, *European Journal of Internal Medicine*, 16(1):12–20.

Mattsson, S., Thomas, B.J. (2006) Development of methods for body composition studies, *Physics in Medicine and Biology*, 51(3):R203–R228.

Michalsen, A., Lüdtke, R., Bühring, M., Spahn, G., Langhorst, J., Dobos, G.J. (2003) Thermal hydrotherapy improves quality of life and hemodynamic function in patients with chronic heart failure, *American Heart Journal*, 146:e11p1–epe11p6.

Noreen, E.E., Lemon, P.W.R. (2006) Reliability of air displacement plethysmography in a large, heterogeneous sample, *Medicine and Science in Sports and Exercise*, 38(8):1505–1509.

Presman, A.S. (1970) *Electromagnetic Fields and Life*, Plenum Press, New York.

Smith, C., Best, S. (1989) *Electromagnetic Man: Health and Hazard in the Electrical Environment*, Dent, London.

Voll, R. (1980) The phenomenon of medicine testing in Electroacupuncture According to Voll, *American Journal of Acupuncture*, 8(2):97–104.

Wilkes, A.J. (2003) *Flowforms: The Rhythmic Power of Water*, Floris Books, Edinburgh.

Zhang, X., Zhang, J., Qu, X., Wen, J. (2007) Effects of different extremely low-frequency electromagnetic fields on osteoblasts, *Electromagnetic Biology and Medicine*, 26(3):167–177.

Spa marketing

Pete Ellis

Introduction: The global spa industry – unique marketing challenges

The spa industry has witnessed continuous and explosive growth over the last decade. To put the current state of the industry in some perspective: there are now far more spas than there are Starbucks. At year-end 2007, there were just over 15,000 Starbuck locations worldwide, but according to SpaFinder, there were 16,000 spas in the USA alone, and over 50,000 spas around the globe.

Unlike Starbucks, however, which has a tightly controlled corporate franchise system, there are many different types of spas, most independently owned with unique business models and offerings. The day spa sector, which is comprised of spas that offer spa and beauty treatments without providing accommodations, is by far the largest industry segment. There are also medical spas, club spas, destination spas, hotel spas, resort spas, spa residence communities, etc. – all with unique approaches to the business.

A large, fragmented industry consisting of small stand-alone businesses

While the spa market is a vast, growing $40 billion global industry (SpaFinder, 2007) it is critical to keep in mind that it is also a deeply fragmented one. Day and medical spas, represent roughly nine out of ten spa properties overall in the USA, and this dominant spa sector is essentially a disconnected network of small, stand-alone enterprises.

Recent SpaFinder industry research (Spafinder, 2007) conducted with owners of day spas in North America reveals that 85% of day spa businesses have just one location (with only approximately 8% having three locations or more). The majority of these facilities measure less than 2000 ft^2, or approximately 186 m^2, and more than one out of three day spas report gross annual revenues under $200,000, with 56% (the majority) reporting gross revenues falling under $400,000. These small operations are also young: a third of day spas in the USA have been fully operational for only 2 years, and the majority for less than four.

Data also suggests that for an average day spa, it takes 9 years to cross the $1 million revenue mark (Figure 15.1).

As with most small businesses, payroll takes its toll, swallowing a significant part of gross revenue: a majority of day spas report that payroll accounts for more than 40% of their annual revenue.

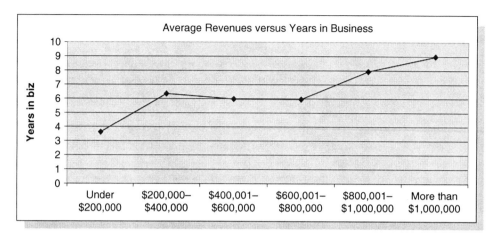

Figure 15.1
Average day spa revenue versus years in business

While the SpaFinder study looked at day spas, which comprise an estimated four out of five spa businesses, in recent years the industry has also seen a rise of larger spa brands, such as ESPA, Mandarin Oriental, Fairmont, and Hyatt. These global companies employ cutting edge marketing strategies and techniques that are extensively reviewed in numerous marketing and business texts. However, the larger spa companies can learn from the findings of the Day Spa Study. 'Spa', by its nature, is a business comprised of personal services and programs and larger spa brands should take note that more personalized, one-to-one marketing techniques are reported to be the most effective.

Marketing with small budgets: targeted strategies trump traditional advertising

It is understandable that many of these young, revenue-restricted, stand-alone businesses have modest marketing budgets. Therefore, a key goal of the SpaFinder study was to determine which marketing strategies are being utilized and, of those strategies, which demonstrate the most effective results.

While the report was limited to analyzing the marketing realities and strategies of the day spa universe, (representing 80% of the spa world as mentioned above), the findings are likely to be proven relevant for other industry sectors – such as resort, hotel and destination spas. The study revealed that for the vast majority of day or stay spa operations, traditional, mass-media, 'spray and pray' marketing tactics like television and radio, even often at the local level, are too expensive and are not the most effective components of a targeted, efficient spa marketing plan.

However, the study found that many spas are still embracing traditional 'old media' marketing methods. Those techniques include magazine and newspaper advertisements in non-targeted publications, mass mailings, ads in directories and non-targeted broadcast commercials. But more critically, the effectiveness ratings clearly indicate that it is the more targeted marketing methods that are delivering the significantly higher return on investment.

For instance, while magazine ads, directories and news-papers were found to have some positive effect for spas pro-motions, direct mail/coupons and targeted newsletters were much more effective. Thus, when apportioning marketing budgets, it is advisable for spas to dedicate more dollars to tar-geted, one-on-one campaigns, or to outlets used by consumers specifically looking for spa services, such as internet referral sites and online search programs.

While reaching new customers and generating incremental business is paramount, marketing to, and retaining, return-ing customers is even more important. However, the study found that while a majority of spas do utilize special events and loyalty programs effectively, many are still not using these targeted techniques. Spas are reporting that outreach to exist-ing clients and retention strategies boast some of the highest effectiveness ratings overall, significantly outperforming tradi-tional marketing, like print ads. These strategies need to be re-considered as part of a savvy marketing mix.

Disconnect between online marketing adoption and high effectiveness

While the study revealed that spas have taken steps to embrace the virtual world of online marketing, with almost all surveyed (95%) having invested in a website, few spas were promoting their online presence or expanding their web-gen-erated business. This is surprising – especially given the very high effectiveness ratings online marketing received from spa adopters. For example:

- 74% of the spas that purchase 'keywords' through major search engines, such as Google or Yahoo!, report that a search marketing strategy is effective, yet over 50% of day spas studied were not using any search marketing programs.

- Over 80% of spas using referral programs that generate customers from large consumer spa portals (such as SpaFinder. com) report these programs are effective, yet roughly one in four spas do not embrace this option.
- 85% of spas report that outbound email newsletters are effective, and yet 30% are not utilizing this communication method.

So, while days spas rated their own website as their most important online marketing investment (92% rank it as effective), it is important to consider that many are doing far too little to drive traffic to the website, or explore the spectrum of online tactics that can generate new business.

It is evident then, that spa marketers should consider the high effectiveness ratings that online referral programs, email marketing/newsletters and search marketing are receiving from their adopter brethren, and invest accordingly in these targeted, efficient internet tactics.

The spa website: they have built it ... but not much more

It appears that many day spas are not investing in the content, tools and user-generated features that help create a more compelling, 'sticky', interactive consumer resource. For example:

- 56% of day spa websites do not offer consumer reviews, but 80% of those that do report they are effective.
- 77% do not offer message boards, despite a reported 58% effectiveness rate.
- 68% do not offer social networking/user groups, despite a 70% effectiveness rate.
- Few spas embrace sophisticated visuals and new media at their sites that would greatly help them showcase their spa: 38% do not offer photos, 80% do not offer streaming video and 77% do not offer virtual spa tours, despite being ranked as effective strategies by roughly four out of five spas who do use these tools. Thus, while advanced website features are highly effective, less than 30% of day spas use most options (Figure 15.2).

There is good news for small businesses set on expanding their marketing presence and investing in new, targeted media: consumer spa adoption keeps growing, and 60% of day spas reported an increase in revenues last year, with an impressive

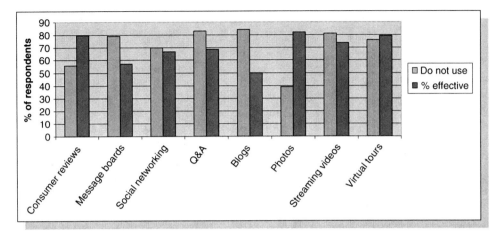

Figure 15.2
Advanced website features and their utilization

average increase of roughly 32%. Furthermore, as a young day spa matures, revenues follow suit.

Spas reporting revenues at the one million mark or above have been in business for at least 9 years. In many ways, the day spa world is becoming somewhat of a 'tale of two cities' in terms of revenue: one in five spas now report gross annual revenues over $1 million, signaling some key industry developments – both the rise of a larger day spa operation (the 'day resort' model) and multi-unit day spa chains.

The SpaFinder study found that as revenues increase, so do marketing budgets, but interestingly, the relationship is not simply linear. Bigger spas, generating higher revenues, are not turning wholesale to expensive traditional marketing, but are choosing to focus their larger budgets on more targeted marketing strategies, both on- and off-line.

Overall, research reveals that despite day spas' persistent high usage rates of traditional print advertising (magazines, newspapers, directories), internet marketing methods (search, referral programs, email newsletters, etc.) are now trumping traditional media like print in effectiveness ratings by significant margins. Thus, it is important to consider that spas, large and small, would be well served to invest more of those precious marketing dollars in both targeted traditional campaigns (promotions, direct mail, etc.) as well as testing, and investing in, the full spectrum of online marketing options. These include referral programs, email campaigns and newsletters, website improvements, search and site optimization, and online marketing at appropriate local or niche travel and lifestyle sites.

Marketing experts agree that no medium in history has delivered the reach, precise targeting abilities and cost efficiencies of the internet, allowing smaller businesses, like spas, to cast far wider and more precise marketing nets. Whether it is a spa employing three people in Toronto, Canada, or a destination spa in rural Ireland, global internet platforms like search engines – or large travel and spa consumer websites/aggregators – let the consumers find the spa, rather than the spa spending marketing money, they do not have, to find their customers.

The same marketing lessons apply to the 10% of the spa industry working with large corporate marketing budgets (those roughly 1800 destination, resort and hotel spas across the globe): select targeted marketing campaigns are more effective that mass, untargeted campaigns. If able to afford traditional media (TV, print, radio), the strategy would be to isolate those outlets that deliver precisely targeted, appropriate, niche audiences over sometimes sexier, mass demographics.

Spa – a customer magnet for resorts and hotels

For resort and hotel spas, independent research (Yesawich et al., 2007) indicates a key element of marketing the overall property should be to put the spa front-and-center, and showcase the spa component and offerings in all marketing communications:

- 58% of affluent travelers report that a full-service spa is now their number one, most preferred hotel / resort amenity.
- There are now twice as many adults interested in a spa vacation as there are adults interested in playing golf.

It is of relevance to all segments of the spa industry, but particularly to resort and hotel spas, that as 'spa' evolves from its once-narrower association with pampering to a global preoccupation with wellness in all its forms, the profile of the spa-goer is broadening beyond just the women and the affluent.

Therefore, it is critical that audience targets are widened accordingly. For example, men now represent 30% of spa-goers in the USA and UK, but at resort spas that number jumps to 40%, and in other regions, such as Japan, men represent the majority of spa visitors (SpaFinder, 2007).

Applying lessons learned from research

The global spa industry has its own unique set of challenges. If a resort or destination spa is in Mexico, its customers could be from anywhere in the world. How can it possibly cast a global marketing net on a limited budget? Or if a day spa is in London, how does it bring in new business and elevate itself amidst an increasingly competitive marketplace? And no matter what kind of spa it is, how does it market a 'product' (the expert touch of a skilled therapist, or a feeling of utter relaxation) that words, and even images, simply cannot convey?

Getting started: marketing basics

Marketing can be simply defined as everything an enterprise does to build its business and drive sales. In other words, marketing is the bucket that includes all sales and communications activities, including: advertising, customer relations, internet marketing (including websites) public and media relations, direct and database marketing, sales strategies, as well as internal and external communications. In fact, many experts suggest that marketing strategies should be a factor in everything that touches a spa's business, from how the staff says 'hello' to customers, to the typeface used on the business card, to the location of the business, to the type of equipment selected for the massage rooms.

Marketing plans and budgets

There are many excellent examples of marketing plans online, many of which contain four elements:

1. *Objectives*, or what the marketer wants to accomplish. An objective might be to increase sales by 35% and revenues by 15%.
2. *Strategies* – how the objectives will be accomplished. For example, increasing sales by 35% might be realized by adding facials to the treatment menu.
3. *Tactics*, which describe how the strategies will be executed. Using 'adding facials to the treatment menu' as an example, tactics might include: hiring a facialist with an existing clientele; designing the facial treatment area and menu; informing existing customers about the new service via a special email; announcing the new facials on the spa's website and at the spa (window signs and posters); offering special discounts to existing customers; and inviting a local reporter to try a facial in the interest of promoting press coverage.
4. *Timeline* – this can be part of the tactics or a separate calendar that tracks activities.

The plan can be formal or informal but the objective is to think through marketing goals.

Budgets

Budgets can also be formal or informal, but are often developed after a plan is in place. Here the reverse is recommended: it is important to first consider what needs to be accomplished then the budget can be developed accordingly. This method is designed to keep creativity and new ideas in the mix.

Responsibility

At larger resort and stay spas or at hotel chains with spas, responsibility for the spa's marketing may be assigned to the property's marketing department. At smaller stay spas and the majority of day and medical spas marketing activities are supervised by the spa owner or spa director. In some cases, the spa may have a dedicated marketing director who oversees sales and communications or an outside firm may be hired to help execute marketing strategies.

In most instances, however, the spa owner is ultimately responsible for establishing the marketing budget, developing marketing plans and ideas and overseeing the successful execution of all marketing activities. For that reason, much of the information presented in this chapter is directed to entrepreneurs who own and operate spas. It is that person's responsibility to stay informed about new marketing opportunities and keep abreast of trends in the industry.

Marketing basics and branding

The spa industry is experiencing breakneck growth and all sectors of the spa industry are headed toward increased competition and, in some areas, market saturation. For instance, 39% of high-end hotels now in development plan to include spas, more than double the number just 5 years ago. It is important to consider that just to stay in business, a spa will need to identify a range of targeted, cost-efficient, attention-grabbing marketing strategies that bring new spa consumers into their business and, at the same time, retain its core clientele.

The importance of branding

Branding is defined as a 'name, term, sign, symbol or design, or a combination of them, intended to identify the goods or services of one seller or group of sellers to differentiate them from those of competitors' (The American Marketing Association,

2007). In other words, a brand differentiates the product or service from other products or services in some distinct way. (see Chapter 15) For greater impact, spas should focus on specializing and differentiating their brand and spa offerings – and sound that unique message clearly across all marketing communications (PriceWaterHouseCoopers Research, 2006; Kotler and Keller, 2007)

That differentiation is known as building a brand identity, arguably one of the most important aspects of marketing. A brand is much more than a name or logo; it represents the core qualities of the company, people or service it symbolizes (e.g. the Nike swoosh, known around the globe). To be recognized for its talented, nurturing staff, a spa must consider every aspect of its brand identity from appealing colors to a friendly typeface to engaging photographs.

How to begin

The first step: research

First, it is important to consider market research and acquiring data on every aspect of the spa's existing and target customers (age, gender, income, education, lifestyle habits, etc.). Understanding existing customers, and the customers the spa hopes to attract, is the foundation of sound marketing decisions that include everything from advertising, to hours of operation, to staffing.

Next, undertake a basic analysis of the competition to understand how successful spas in the area and across the world are marketed. Simple observation, talking with other spa owners and gaining knowledge from professional associations and industry marketing experts are practical and cost-effective ways to gather this information.

Once research has been completed, the target audience identified, the plan has been written and the budget established, a successful marketing campaign or promotion requires consistent creative elements in each marketing activity.

Remember the basics

Marketing experts agree: Good design and good photography are key. These elements, typically on the spas' website and signing, are the first impression most customers will have of the business.

It is also important not to make the mistake of implementing too many ideas – and spreading the budget too thin.

When choosing a marketing strategy for a spa, there are a wide variety of options that can be exciting as well as overwhelming. To simplify decision-making, three broad reference questions can be utilized: (1) who are the customers? (2) what are the unique offerings? (3) how will the spa brand be perceived?.

A spa's location should also influence marketing decisions. A day or medical spa relies on repeat business and needs to attract people in the immediate area so it is important to choose campaigns that both stand outs and are relevant to fits into the local community. For 'stay' spas, the community can be the world.

Finally, it is important to consider the unique services and programs the spa offers compared to direct competitors – and to focus on those services. For example, if the spa is the only one to offer hot stone massage or custom facials in a 25-mile radius, those services should be the key selling points.

Marketing options

The results of the Day Spa Study indicate that important marketing considerations are word-of-mouth or customer satisfaction, internet or web marketing strategies and public and media relations. A number of excellent marketing books and papers focused on these techniques are included in the reference list at the end of the chapter.

Word-of-mouth: If a spa is well run, referrals through word-of-mouth should be the biggest source of new business. Word-of-mouth referrals may be driven by the spa's location, staffing, aesthetics and customer communications. Customer communications include everything from how a customer is greeted to sending 'thank you' notes,' to handling billing or service questions, to written communications, such as regular email newsletters.

Internet marketing: The SpaFinder marketing study demonstrates that platform delivering the highest return on investment today is the internet. To compete in today's market, all spas must consider an attractive and accessible website along with numerous other online marketing opportunities such as web promotions, email newsletters and advertisements, gift certificates, search marketing and web partnerships.

Public and media relations: Public relations, or 'PR', fosters positive relationships with the 'public' (customers, prospects and community) to build business. Face-to-face marketing is part of PR. This includes special events, trade shows, support for community and charities, workshops, and demonstrations. Media relations, on the other hand, consist of developing a working relationships with the media in order to generate positive press about the spa. Every spa should have a public and media relations strategy and plan. See 'Public and media relations section' at the end of this chapter.

Brochures and targeted mailers, online and print: Creating a visually engaging brochure is part of customer communications and can excite an audience, but it is important to consider how the brochure is going to be distributed and how people are going to perceive it. According to the Day Spa Study, a website (which serves as an online 'brochure') and targeted emails are the most effective tools.

Promotions and gift certificates or vouchers: These are an excellent means to encourage people who would typically not go to a spa for treatments. Promotions can highlight a spa's slower the days and hours and be reinforced by a gift certificate/voucher program. There are excellent companies that provide turnkey solutions for website gift certificates and vouchers and internet companies that use sophisticated strategies to drive gift certificate customers to the spa.

Next: test, track and fine-tune

With so many marketing possibilities competing for the attention of consumers, it is important that spas evaluate each marketing campaign they launch. Media planners and buyers use sophisticated research and tracking tools to test and fine-tune marketing and advertising campaigns before they are launched, as well as evaluating the impact on sales after they are implemented. Many firms offer these services but if the spa cannot afford this cost, common sense and internet sales tracking techniques can be used to evaluate results.

For example, customers can be asked how and where they heard about the spa. Careful attention needs to be paid to special promotions, such as discounts and coupons, by tracking the return compared to the spa's investment. Evaluation would focus on which services and which staff members generate the most profits so there can be a focus on those profit centers.

Before money is spent on marketing or advertising, staff should be taught how to turn inquiries into sales – and how to provide outstanding customer service. They should be aware of marketing strategies and activities and be able to turn prospects into paying customers.

The importance of word-of-mouth

Word-of-mouth is a spa's most valuable marketing tool because it is a persuasive advertisement at no additional cost.

269

The spa must be sure each customer is always happy and that the spa achieves to expected quality standards of cleanliness, friendliness, responsiveness and quality. Spas promote a better life, so it is important that customers experience a taste of that life whenever they visit.

It is vital that spas remember that today's consumers are also online reviewers and critics. Anyone can post an opinion on websites like CitySearch where consumers notice and listen to the thoughts of their peers. If a spa is getting low ratings in a certain area, it is important that the marketing team focus on that area of the business and avoid the desire to argue and be defensive.

Repeat business

It is much easier and more cost efficient to keep a customer than to bring in new ones, so it makes good sense for a spa to focus on providing an experience that an individual would want to repeat and recommend to friends.

Earlier, the chapter discussed creating a database for an email newsletter. Used effectively, this can be a great tool to draw attention to new features, discounts and information. This can be implemented by asking for customers' email addresses when they visit the site, however; they should be given an option to click yes or no on whether they would like to receive special offers by email.

Today, marketers need to make email campaigns valuable to the reader. For example, a spa offering a two-for-one massage special can encourage regular customers to bring in friends or family – and create new customers. Similarly, a referral policy may reward clients who refer new customers.

Web-based marketing: a must for successful spas

With the proliferation of media and technology, media audiences are fragmented and more difficult to reach. Television may deliver hundreds of channels but audiences are spending more time online, and research shows that newspaper Circulations, 2008 are shrinking (Audit Bureau of Circulations) while consumers flock to the web in droves.

With unlimited media options, audiences are spread out, a phenomenon called the long tail theory (Anderson, 2006). This means advertisers must spread their messages across even more channels in order to reach the same number of people as when television, newspaper and radio audiences delivered a captive audience. The good news is that internet advertising and marketing is so cost efficient, that while; a spa may have to be present in more places to reach a shrinking customer base, it costs significantly less to reach them online.

Keep websites simple – and attractive

Experience shows that site visitors who feel overwhelmed by the number of choices because of poor site design simply leave. With search engines like Google and Yahoo! Search, web users today have almost unlimited choices, and if a competitor makes it easier for customers to find what they need, that spa will win.

Cover the basics online

An effective website needs to be clean, simple and easy to navigate. Visitors to the site need to immediately understand what the business does and how they can buy or book services. Location and address, phone number and email address, a menu of services, hours of operations and specials or promotions must be easy to find. A simple, attractive design is best. Complicated 'flash' animation can be confusing, time consuming for visitors and actually make it harder for search engines to find the site.

How will they find the spa?

Once a clean, simple and easy-to-navigate website has been created, how can a spa drive customers to it? Often, first time visitors will find a spa through an online search engine, such as Google, where web-users enter 'key words' like 'spas' or 'spa gift vouchers' or 'facials in Brazil' or 'massage in Hong Kong'. A site's 'google-ability' can be tested by entering certain key words such as 'Melissa's Day Spa' or 'massage in Manchester'. The spa should aim to be in the top results.

If the spa cannot be easily found, search engine optimization can be performed by adding key words to the spa's webpages. For example, text that gets good search results might read: 'Jasmine Day Spa is the number one place to find relaxing spa treatments in Dubai, from facials, massages, manicures and pedicures to wraps and scrubs. Jasmine Day Spa offers an exciting and relaxing spa experience for men and women.' All the keywords that describe the company are covered in just a few sentences.

In addition to search engine optimization, if the marketing budget allows, a spa can purchase a presence on the web. Search engine sponsored links that generate an ad next to the organic listings can work well. The spa can also consider purchasing banner ads or links on relevant sites where potential customers might be visiting. With new technologies, it is possible to create these within minutes, specifying the target consumer and the budget.

Database marketing

Websites are an excellent way to build a customer database. Visitors can register for news about special offers and promotions, enter a contest to win a spa experience or receive an e-newsletter. This online database must be combined with the spa's customer file and be maintained diligently, as it provides a foundation for one of the most effective marketing tools – email campaigns. To assist with this there are highly effective customer management software systems that not only manage the spa's business, but also provides easy-to-use templates that can be customized for new promotions and offers.

Consistency is the key to effective email marketing – sending a new email every 6 weeks is often recommended. A day spa in Toronto, for example, reports great success in regular one-page emails to announce seasonal specials, promotions to introduce new therapists and aestheticians and product specials.

Summary: The key to effective web marketing is for the spa to keep it simple; to enlist the help of a web professional; to be consistent; to keep track of new trends, such as online appointment booking technology that drives new customers to a spa; and to experiment.

Public and media relations – a marketing essential

The public and media relations plan should include every aspect of how the owner and staff interact with customers and the general public – from greeting customers to 'thank you' communications to participation in community and neighborhood events to communications with the press. While it is not necessary to write a 'formal' document, it is recommended that the plan include how the spas will handle emergencies or a crisis that may affect customers or staff.

Essential PR and media relations tools include a press kit, which typically contains basic information about the spa (often called a 'backgrounder'); biographies of key staff; the service menu and descriptions of special treatments; photos of the spa and key staff; and recent press releases. The kit can be printed but is most useful when posted on the spa's website.

Press announcements (press releases) should contain *real* news. It is also best not to overwhelm reporters with releases and calls, but rather to keep contacts friendly and respect reporters' busy schedules.

Finally, spas should develop a good media contact list and update it regularly. Many large beauty and travel magazines also spotlight local spas in their 'best of' features. When calling the press, it is always advisable to speak knowledgeably and specifically to the reporter about the subjects he or she writes about.

Conclusion

To be successful in the global spa industry, exceptional customer service and highly targeted marketing strategies are essential. A spa marketing plan should include techniques to:

- Raise the bar on customer service
- Build a unique brand
- Employ research that helps the spa understand the customer and the competition
- Build a customer database which is used to maintain consistent communications with the spa's most valuable asset – its existing customers
- Take advantage of proven online and web marketing strategies and resources
- Maintain a consistent and effective public and media relations campaign
- Include a budget for professional photography, graphics, and web design.

Many businesses do not succeed because they invest time and money in property, equipment and design, but do not put the same effort and resources into marketing. The successful spa marketer will combine these proven techniques with his or her own creativity to build a unique and profitable brand.

References

American Marketing Association (2008). Marketing and advertising articles and tips www.marketingpower.com (site accessed 28 March, 2008.)

Anderson, C. (2006) *The Long Tail: Why the Future of Business is Selling Less of More*, Hyperion Books, New York, NY.

Audit Bureau of circulation (2008) *Non-profit association of advertisers and publishers*, www.accessabc.com (site accessed 28 March, 2008).

Kotler, P., Keller, K.L. (2007) *A Framework for Marketing Management*, Prentice Hall, Upper Saddle River, New Jersey.

PricewaterhouseCoopers (2007) Trends and outlook for the luxury hotel sector; Hospitality Directors Series.

SpaFinder (2007) Day Spa Industry Report including data on business performance and revenue, operations, facilities, marketing, personnel management, treatment offerings, retail business, technology adoption, trends in spa clientele, etc.

Yesawich, Pepperdine, Brown, Russell (2007) The Travel Monitor.

Suggested reading & bibliography

Battelle, J. (2006) *The Search: How Google and Its Rivals Rewrote the Rules of Business and Transformed Our Culture*, The Penguin Group, Seattle, WA.

Cialdini, R.B. (2007). Influence: the psychology of persuasion. In: Cialdini, R.B. Collins Business Essentials.

Cristol, S., M., Sealey, P. (2000) *Simplicity Marketing: End Brand Complexity, Clutter and Confusion*, Free Press, Detroit, MI.

David, M.S. (2007) *The New Rules of Marketing and PR: How to Use News Releases, Blogs, Podcasting, Viral Marketing and Online Media to Reach Buyers Directly*, John Wiley & Sons, Inc, Hoboken, NJ.

Gladwell, M. (2000) *The Tipping Point, How Little Things Can Make a Big Difference*, Little Brown & Co., London, UK.

Gillin, P. (2007) *The New Influencers: A Marketer's Guide to the New Social Media*, Quill Driver Books, Sanger, CA.

Godin, S. (2003) *Purple Cow: Transform Your Business by Being Remarkable*, Penguin Books, Seattle, WA.

Godin, S. (2006) *Small Is the New Big: and 183 Other Riffs, Rants, and Remarkable Business Ideas*, The Penguin Group, Seattle, WA.

Imbriale, R. (2007) *Motivational Marketing: How to Effectively Motivate Your Prospects to Buy Now, Buy More, and Tell Their Friends Too!*, John Wiley & Sons, Inc, Hoboken, NJ.

Jaffe, J. (2007) *Join the Conversation: How to Engage Marketing-Weary Consumers with the Power of Community, Dialogue, and Partnership*, Wiley & Sons, Inc, Hoboken, NJ.

Jantsch, J. (2007) *Duct Tape Marketing: The World's Most Practical Small Business Marketing Guide*, Thomas Nelson, Nashville, TN.

Joyner, M. (2005) *The Irresistible Offer: How to Sell Your Product or Service in 3 Seconds or Less*, John Wiley & Sons, Inc, Hoboken, NJ.

Kaushik, A. (2007) *Web Analytics: An Hour a Day*, Sybex, Hoboken, NJ.

Kotler, P., Kevin, L.K. (2007) *A Framework for Marketing Management*, Prentice Hall, Upper Saddle River, NJ.

Livingston, G., Solis, B. (2007) *Now Is Gone: A Primer on New Media for Executives and Entrepreneurs*, Bartleby Press, Laurel, MD.

Lee, K., Baldwin, S. (2007) *The Eyes Have It: How to Market in an Age of Divergent Consumers, Media Chaos and Advertising Anarchy*, Easton Studio Press, New York, NY.

Levinson, J.C. (2007) *Guerrilla Marketing, 4th edition: Easy and Inexpensive Strategies for Making Big Profits from Your Small Business*, Houghton Mifflin Company, Boston, MA.

Marshall, P., Todd, B. (2006) *Ultimate Guide to Google AdWords*, McGraw-Hill, Columbus, OH.

McConnell, B., Huba, J. (2007) *Citizen Marketers: When People Are the Message*, Kaplan Publishing, New York, NY.

Port, M. (2006) *Book Yourself Solid: The Fastest, Easiest, and Most Reliable System for Getting More Clients Than You Can Handle Even if You Hate Marketing and Selling*, John Wiley & Sons, Hoboken, NJ.

Sernovitz, A. (2006) *Word of Mouth Marketing: How Smart Companies Get People Talking*, Kaplan Publishing, New York, NY.

Stowe, S., Lewis, R., Yesawich, P. (2006) *Marketing leadership in hospitality and tourism: Strategies and tactics for competitive advantage*, Prentice Hall, Upper Saddle River, NJ.

Vitale, J. (2007) *Hypnotic Writing: How to Seduce and Persuade Customers with Only Your Words*, Hypnotic Marketing, London, UK.

275

Weber, S. (2007) *Plug Your Business! Marketing on MySpace, YouTube, blogs and podcasts and other Web 2.0 social networks*, Weber Books.

Weber, K.L., Steve, B. (2006) *The Eyes Have It: How to Market in an Age of Divergent Consumers, Media Chaos and Advertising Anarchy*, Easton Studio Press.

Weinberger, D. (2007) *Everything is miscellaneous: the power of the new digital disorder*, Hendry Holt & Company, Bristol.

Yesawich, Pepperdine, Brown, Russell, The Travel Monitor, 2007.

Textbooks

Kotler, P., Keller, K.L. (2006) *Basic Marketing Management, 12th, 16th Edition*, Pearson Prentice Hall, Englewood Cliffs, NJ.

Mason, C.H., Perreault, W.D. Jr (2007) *The Marketing Game*, McGrawHill/Irwin, Columbus, OH.

Perreault, C., McCarthy, S. (2007) *Basic Marketing, 16th Edition*, McGraw Hill/Irwin, Columbus, OH.

Suggested web resources:

Kotler, P., Keller, K.L. (2006) *Marketing Management, 12th Edition*, Pearson Prentice Hall, Englewood Cliffs, NJ.

Marketing, online marketing & research

MediaPost Media, marketing and advertising news, expert analysis and professional resources http://www.mediapost.com

Internet Advertising Board& Daily Newsletter **IAB Informer** International community for online advertising issues, news, expert analysis and insight, resources http://www.iab.net-www.iab.net

eMarketer E-Business and online marketing research & analysis www.emarketer.com

The Wise Marketer Customer loyalty and retention marketing: news, analysis, research and resources for loyalty marketers www.thewisemarketer.com

Marketing Vox Internet marketing and e-marketing resources, research and news www.marketingvox.com

Spa Industry

SpaFinder Inc. Consumer and industry global spa resource, including SpaFinder Insider newsletters for spa professionals on latest industry trends and news, as well as blogs by industry experts. www.spafinder.com www.spafinder.com/spalifestyle/insider/newsletter/index.jsp

International Spa Association Largest professional, global organization of the spa industry (75 countries), site features education and business tools and resources www.experienceispa.com/ISPA/

Day Spa Association Primary business resource for day spa professionals, with news, resources, educational and business tools http://www.dayspaassociation.com

Spa Business Numerous magazines/websites for spa and leisure industry professionals – newsletters, diverse industry news, professional resources, etc. http://www.spabusiness.com

Spa Business Association UK Portal for spa business professionals in the UK and Ireland. News, education, business resources http://www.britishspas.co.uk

BISA – British International Spa Association News and educational resources for spa professionals/therapists in British Isles http://www.spaassociation.org.uk/2.html

Spa Trade Publication/website for spa professionals: multimedia content, news, expert discussion forums, product and service guides, etc. www.spatrade.com

About.com's Spa Section Consumer-focused spa portal/resource, but with updated industry news, research, etc. http://www.spas.about.com

SpaMarketing Tools Blog/news site supporting spa and salon marketing efforts and trends http://www.spamarketingtools.com/blog

Australasian Spa Association (ASpa) Website/resource for members of Australasian spa and wellness industry--news, resources, etc. www.australasianspaassociation.com

PART 4

Planet

Built environment–spa design

Peter Remedios

The global spa industry is an ever-fluctuating entity that is highly influenced by societal and global pressures. Growing technology and the increase of international travel has contributed to increased stress levels and has raised the bar for design as a whole. People are being exposed to different experiences and good design which creates a unique, exotic experience that appeals not only to the visual sense but evokes a profound physical and emotional response. As a result, there is a heightened level of expectation which designers and the spa industry must respond to. The intention of spa design is to meet the demands of these drivers through research, calculated planning, and execution. Current spas must respond appropriately to these demands and create a comforting social atmosphere and sanctuary. This is achieved by creating a visually dynamic design which generates a refuge for the stress riddled spa patron. Creating a total sensory experience is fundamental in crafting a sense of place that is wholly separate from the world beyond its walls.

Historical and cultural influences on spa design

Roman baths

The need for physical and mental relief is not a new, it has been present throughout human history. The ancient Roman Empire regarded bathing as one of the most important leisure activities to be indulged in. The act of bathing became a daily ritual for both men and women, and this tradition was carried with them everywhere they traveled. Spas were so important that they often became massive monument-like spaces that defined the social structure and displayed the wealth of the leadership of the time. They were classical in architecture and used the naturally occurring marble and stone of the regions they inhabited. The space was primarily lit by natural light and built over natural occurring hot springs where possible. These public baths were often very large and housed hundreds of people. Although the privileged often had a small private facility in their home, the Romans saw a visit to the public baths as an important social event in which to meet friends, conduct business, and have an uplifting social experience. (Glancey, 2003)

The Roman baths were constructed around a regular bathing ritual which demonstrated a highly refined and efficient use of space (see Figure 16.1).

First, the bather would enter the apodyterium, or changing room. Men and women were separated at this time and went

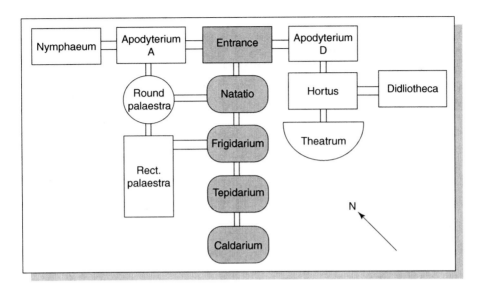

Figure 16.1
Typical area plan for a Roman Bath

into their own gender specific 'locker' rooms equipped with niches to place ones street clothes. Typically the men would then proceed to the fitness area prior to bathing, where they would lift weights, play ball games, run, and swim prior to initiating in the bathing experience. As the floors were heated through a sophisticated underground heating system, spa goers would don sandals to protect their feet. They then progressed down the warm hallways flooded with natural light, to their next destination which was generally the tepidarium. This warm, dry room initiated the relaxation process prior to proceeding to the caldarium which was a hot bath. This room had a small pool filled with very hot water, and a cold water tap in which to refresh. The Roman bather could then choose to return to the tepidarium or proceed to the laconium, or dry sauna. Additional rooms that offered steam or oil massage were not uncommon in ancient Roman baths. The bathing experience was finished off in the fridgidarium, where one could take a dip in an ice cold pool. Other amenities were offered such as libraries, food areas, and other areas in which to gather and socialize. The Roman baths ushered their patrons through a series of treatments that not only served to cleanse the body but also offered therapeutic means to relax and take part in the social energy around them.

Turkish hamam

The Turkish hamam, meaning spreader of warmth, can trace its roots back to this earlier Greek and Roman bath ritual. The Turkish spa tradition transitioned from bathing in cold running water, to 'sweat' bathing around 600AD when the Arabs encountered both Roman and Greek baths in Syria. They tailored the foreign bathing habits to accommodate their own cultural needs. The Hamam evolved into a quiet retreat, with an atmosphere of half-light, tranquility, and seclusion. Architecturally modest and intimate, there was an extensive use of mosaic which was accentuated by a filtered ambient light, with careful attention paid to the functionality of each space. The individual hamams were relatively small but held a significant presence as their numbers were numerous throughout the towns and cities. (Sansal, 2007; Aaland, 1997)

Like the Roman baths, the hamam became a social hub and was an intrinsic part of the communal fabric for the upper and lower classes alike. The Turkish spa tradition was a complex and varied sensory experience which was achieved through the use of multiple bathing experiences, music, oil massage, and personal beauty treatments that were administered by 'professional staff'. The Turkish hamam acquired certain characteristics of the Roman spas and adapted them to fit within their cultural and geographical context.

Japanese onsen

Much the same can be said about the Japanese spa experience and the ways in which their particular spa culture derived from its geological location and the societal demands of their civilization. Being a volcanic region, the geology of Japan is instrumental in the cultural development of the onsen, or hot spring bathing experience. A variety of onsen developed around the numerous geothermal springs. The types ranged from the outdoor 'rotenburo' to the indoor 'notenburo' where the baths were often incorporated into an inn serving the weary traveler. People traveled considerable distances to visit the hot springs, establishing the need for the traditional 'ryokan' or inn at the onsen location. Historically, the onsen also served the needs of the warriors and monks traveling through the area, and offered them refuge and rest from the demands of travel.

The design of the onsen was not only driven by the geothermal springs but also by a cultural appreciation of the natural environment. Due to this connection, a garden element was essential to the space. The use of natural and indigenous materials such as granite and wood, typically Japanese Cyprus because of its clean scent and anti-mildew characteristics, became inherent to the onsen design. The spaces were designed for mixed gender bathing as nakedness was culturally acceptable. The ritual act of bathing became a means of breaking down gender and hierarchical barriers in a comforting natural environment. (Martin-Wurwand, 1998; Farnay, 2007)

Nordic spas

Just as the Japanese onsen was highly influenced by its relationship to the natural world and the demands of the people they served, the Nordic spa culture developed in much the same way. The Scandinavian region is legendary for its extremes; extreme climate, daylight, and physical activities. The same can be said for the Scandinavian spa experience which originated around 1000 AD along the Baltic Sea when nomadic tribes settled in the region and became agriculturally centered. The cornerstone of this particular spa practice is the sauna and focuses on the vacillation between hot and cold experiences. The structure of the sauna is generally a simple wood room with benches, typically birch due to its natural abundance in the region and aromatic qualities, with a central heating system that is either driven by fire or electric coils. This room is meant to provide a low humidity heat to promote cleansing and relaxation through perspiration. Because of their northern location, Scandinavian spas prefer to use natural means to provide the cold treatment after the sauna experience. Rolling in snow or swimming in a cold lake is the preferred manner in which to cool the body.

The original sauna was a place of ceremonial revere and was the location in which religious ceremonies, medicinal practices, social activities, community work, relaxation, and body cleansing occurred. Swedish massage was incorporated into the Scandinavian spa repertoire in the 19th century. This deep therapeutic massage was developed to loosen tight muscles, stimulate blood circulation, and promote wellness and mental relaxation. Currently, saunas remain an essential element to daily life in those living in the Nordic regions where the amount of saunas outnumbers that of cars. The sauna has spread throughout the world and is most often associated with fitness centers and resorts. Modern Scandinavian spas have incorporated various treatments from other cultures to compete in the growing spa industry, but their philosophy remains the same: improve circulation and mental clarity, decrease stress, and improve the quality of life through perspiration and alternating hot and cold treatments. (The Finnish Sauna Society, 2006; Hambraeus, 2006)

Native American sweat lodge

The native American culture also sought mental and physical balance through the practice of sweating. The sweat lodge tradition of the nomadic native Americans was based upon the discovery of natural hot springs and steam. The sweat lodge was a temporary structure built from tree branches, tied together to form domes, covered in animal skins and sealed with mud. The structure trapped heat inside and became a center for ritual cleansing of mind, body, and spirit through sweat. (Strauss, 2007; Baldwin, 2007)

Ayurvedic spa

The ceremonial approach to treatment is also fundamental in the Indian spa practice. Their practice is a traditional form of holistic medicine, derived from the word ayurveda, meaning the science or knowledge of life. The Indian spa experience differs most greatly from other spa traditions in that water is not a key element. Water has a religious significance and therefore is limited in this particular spa experience and oil is used in its stead. This tradition evolved around 600 BC with a focus on achieving equal balance of mind, body, and spirit. It is not a bathing experience, but a more hands-on touch based treatment with the use of warm oils, massage, and other applied treatments. It is an extremely private experience with dimly lit, locked treatment rooms which afford the sensation of being in a sacred space. Wood is the primary material throughout with some stone used to create an uncomplicated sanctuary. With these modest surroundings as a back drop, gold accents and gold utensils are used to further emphasize the sacredness of the treatment. (Martin-Wurwand, 1998; Ayurveda Travel Mall, 2007)

The Indian ayurvedic methods heavily influenced the southeast Asian spa. Buddhist monks traveled through the east bringing with them the ayurvedic techniques. These traditions merged with the indigenous folk wisdom and healing methods, forming the southeast Asian experience known today. Kindness, compassion, and the act of comforting, are intrinsic components of East Asian treatments, particularly in Thailand.

It is believed that through compassionate human touch, a person can be cured of ailments, release physical tension, and achieve mental clarity. This spa experience, unlike Indian ayurvedic, is often performed outdoors, negating the ritualistic privacy that is so revered in the Indian tradition. Having adapted to the location, often in close proximity to the sea, the use of leaves, kelp, and salts are common. (Thai Spa and Massage, 1999; Thailand Spas, 2006)

Modern spa design

Modern spas and traditional design sources

Just as many of the historical spa traditions influenced and transformed one another, the modern spa industry has used these bygone traditions as ingredients for current spa design and practice. The intrinsic use of water remains a fundamental element in spa design and can trace its origins back to the Roman bath tradition, through the Turkish hamam, Japanese onsen, Scandinavian tradition, and a myriad of other healing practices. While many former customs concentrated their spas around natural occurring springs, spas today strive to recreate this natural experience and still incorporate naturally occurring sources where possible. Many modern spas located in rural terrain remain focused around these natural resources while urban spas recreate this feeling within the confines of today's urban and industrial environments.

The therapeutic nature of human touch has also traveled through time and has become a cornerstone of the spa experience. One can argue that the historical hamam is a true forerunner of today's modern spa experience; utilizing multiple bathing experiences, music, oil massage, and other healing and beautification techniques. The essential use of human touch was also crucial for the Indian and southeast Asian spa movements, and current design has reacted to this key element by creating a variety of treatment room experiences to enhance and promote the healing properties of each individual treatment. The environment of the modern treatment room can be traced back to the Turkish hamam, Indian ayurveda practice, and southeast Asian spa tradition and the private sanctuaries they cultivated. Privacy levels may vary depending on cultural context, just as it did in historical times, but the chief principle of a treatment room as a sacred space for healing remains.

A primal connection to nature, which was prevalent throughout the historical traditions, permeates into current spa design through the use of natural materials. Spa materials should center on the clean, simple, beauty of the materials themselves, and, just as in the Indian practice, serve as a modest back drop to the healing nature of the space. Current spa design also draws from the Japanese incorporation of a garden element and the idea of bringing the natural world into a man made space. The Asian aesthetic is a favorable form of design and the sheer simplicity of the Japanese design and its natural use of materials intrinsically captures a Zen-like quality which promotes calmness. The southeast Asian aesthetic also fits naturally into a spa design as it is innately exotic to the typical spa patron and its rustic use of materials naturally transports people to distant a sanctuary.

Good design successfully captures these historical references and creates a total sensory experience for the spa patron. It is also important that the design creates a sense of place that becomes an exotic individual experience for the guest. High quality design also understands the intimate nature of the treatment rooms and crafts a comforting and inviting space to allow for total relaxation. This is achieved through the use of natural materials, intimate lighting, and a soothing palette. Also, a well designed spa incorporates water into the design to create a cleansing experience which is both functional and aesthetically pleasing. Despite the countless variables in the world of spa design, there are nevertheless many commonalities in the approach to planning a successful spa. Some of these commonalities include creating a sense of space, essential use of water and use of natural materials.

Shortcomings in contemporary spa design

As there is a proliferation of the spa industry, there are many spas being built that do not understand or develop these key ingredients from the past. Many spas are often built with a primary focus on the treatment and little attention is paid to the overall environment. The design of the space should serve to enhance the treatment by creating a total sensory and emotional experience which allows the guest to fully submit to, and benefit from, the treatments without any outside distractions, unless of course the environment adds to the 'exotic' experience. The design of the space ultimately impacts the lasting impression of the spa and the complete experience of the spa client. This being said, spa design fails when a total sensory experience is not achieved and the spa does not create a refuge for the spa patron. Often times, this is due to under-design and little attention being paid to the use of materials. It is important to have a balance between hard and soft materials and warm and cold tones. Otherwise, the overall feel will be clinical, cold, or dull.

Spa design is also unsuccessful when the historical references such as Japanese or southeast Asian spa aesthetic are misinterpreted. When creating an exotic space, many spas do not realize the pitfalls of an over-designed space. Rather than creating a comforting environment that enhances the spa experience, the space becomes a false imitation, theme environment that is too artificial and fabricated to give a realistic sense of place.

Spas today often fall short in creating individual experiences depending on the function of the space. For instance, the reception is a public area that is an important retail space, but it is crucial that the reception experience is not entirely focused around the retail aspect. The retail items should be displayed in an enticing manner which allows the patron to view the items but not be too obtrusive. The reception experience is shattered if the retail aspect is too aggressive and prominently displayed, making the patron feel uncomfortable and pressured. Often times, the reception is too far forward in the space and the staff too eager, destroying the entrance experience and subsequently turning away potential clients. Many spas also fail to realize the intimate nature of the treatment rooms, and create overly large, cavernous rooms that lose all sense of sanctuary and leave the guest feeling cold, exposed, and vulnerable. It is also important in these treatment areas to keep in mind the sound qualities of the space, as sound leakage from the public areas or other treatment rooms can ruin the tranquil sense of the environment. A leading problem in spa design is that many periphery areas are not included or well designed. Insufficient attention is paid to areas such as locker rooms, relaxation rooms, and corridors. Albeit these areas are not the primary spaces, they are important areas that work to create the overall experience. The design should be carried into all of these areas and should be considered to have equal significance as other areas such as reception and treatment rooms. If these areas are not well designed and planned, it can detract from what may be a good design elsewhere. It is also imperative to pay attention to detailing, installation, and execution with an appropriate use of materials. If items are not well detailed and executed, the overall space begins to look inexpensive and substandard, no matter how expensive the materials may be. Good planning, research, and attention to detail are ways to avoid creating these design pitfalls.

Designing a successful spa

In planning a spa, it is essential to identify the team that will be operating the facility. As each operator or spa consultant has varying philosophies regarding the types of treatments offered and the level of luxury, it is important for them to be brought in from the start to define an area program. This program will take into consideration the demographics of the location as well as the demands of the space, in order to create the philosophy that will ultimately drive the overall planning of the spa. This will provide a common foundation for not only a business plan but provide the design team with the necessary criteria to work with. If an operator or spa consultant is brought in early, they can understand and manage the multitude of variables that are inherent in any design, and allow all consultants to begin with the same guidelines. After the area program is established, a bubble diagram of the space should be created to locate the necessary areas and to then create a flow chart and adjacencies to pinpoint where each space should be located. This will give a preliminary view of where the individual spaces will be, what they will be near and how the guests and employees will interact with and move through the space.

When beginning a spa design, it is important to recognize that a spa patron is looking for a unique experience that will transport them to another location. This sense of place can vary depending on indigenous culture, geographical location, and operational intent, and this is where it is necessary for the operator to define the needs of that particular locale. In the case of a resort, the aim may not be to create a different sense of place but to capture the innate exotic qualities of that particular region. However, when dealing with urban spas, it is important to set the stage for a unique and sometimes exotic experience that is entirely separate from the city outside. It is within the varying geographical regions, and the multitude of design opportunities in the urban settings, that design can take several variations.

As was demonstrated earlier in the chapter, historical references have carried through most spa cultures and remain a common thread in the visual aesthetics and sensory experience of current spa design. As with the Roman baths, Turkish hamam, Japanese onsen, Scandinavian treatments, Indian and southeast Asian traditions, the spa experience can be broken into a series of individual moments which combine to create a complete and intriguing experience.

Designing for the spa experience

The arrival experience

The arrival experience is the first impression the spa patron has of the facility. The aesthetic expression of the spa is set forth at this point, and its impact is paramount throughout the entire environment. Often times the spa is not located near the drop off point or entrance to the space. Rather than a hindrance, this situation should be regarded as an opportunity to create an arrival experience that prepares the guest for the spa itself. The arrival experience can and should be transformed into a journey which begins at the drop off point and continues as the guest perhaps meanders through tranquil gardens, for instance, before arriving at the reception area.

The reception experience

The reception experience should welcome the guest and provide a sense that from this point forward; they will be taken care of. This is the zone in which the traveler, guest, or everyday patron can begin to hand over the stress of their lives into the competent hands of the spa staff. This sense of safety is achieved through natural materials, soothing lighting, and a well organized space. The space should be functional and intuitive to the needs of the patron to create a space that is stress free and aesthetically pleasing. The reception counter itself has to be visible, functional, and at the same time visually attractive. One to one and a half meters should be allowed per attendant. A small seating area should be placed adjacent to this allowing relief for waiting patrons. As impulse buys are often made in this area, the reception space also serves as an important location for the display of retail products which is a lucrative part of the spa industry. We generally advocate incorporating this element throughout the entire reception area. The waiting lounge is often near the reception space and should allow for guests to be received and welcomed. An area for shoe removal and storage should be provided and can be a function of the waiting area. An area for a welcome tea service should also be incorporated into the reception area. It may be desirable to have a food and beverage component which serves specially prepared items to the waiting guests. This can either be an element of the waiting area or a spa café can be added adjacent to this space and allow for sit down dining and take out.

Wet and dry areas – flow

After proceeding through the arrival and reception experiences, the guest moves into gender specific locker rooms. It is important that an appropriate locker count is established and includes both full and half size lockers. The function and location of the spa should be taken into account when formulating the locker count. If the spa is for day use only or is located in a hotel, the locker count can be lower as the guest may change in his or her room and there will not be designated lockers. If the spa is member based, there may be designated lockers, increasing the need for a higher number of general use lockers. Within the locker rooms, there are often amenities offered which involve the use of water and other heat treatments. These treatments could include vitality pools, Kneip or Rassoul treatments, hot and cold showers, steam baths, and saunas.

The type of amenities, which are discussed largely in other chapters, should be set forth by the operator or spa consultant. In planning for these, it is once again necessary for the exact amenities to be established from the onset as each treatment requires different space and equipment needs and are difficult to add later.

As a large amount of the budget will be spent in infrastructure costs, it is necessary to have a clear and realistic grasp of the amenities and the costs involved in each. Typically the flow through the locker rooms follows a well ordered sequence which takes you through the common entrance, to the locker rooms and dry grooming areas, through the semi-wet toilet and shower areas, finally ending in the wet areas which include the spas, pools, and other amenities.

It is important to keep in mind the privacy of the changing areas so they are not too close to the entrance and are perhaps clustered into more private areas. In more luxurious spas, showers often have a self contained private changing area. There needs to be a clear separation between the dry, semi-wet, and wet areas. Occasionally, these wet areas will also lead to a lap pool. If a hair salon, manicure or pedicure area is to be provided, it should be situated near the women's locker room and be in close proximity to the reception or waiting lounge, preferably with direct access from the reception area as well. Within the locker areas, it is also important to pay attention to the material choice. Natural, comforting and warm materials are preferable. Slip resistance and porosity of materials also need to be taken into consideration as well, especially in the wet areas.

The treatment experience

The locker rooms should exit close to the treatment rooms. This zone is usually a unisex space; therefore patrons generally wear robes and slippers. Treatment rooms run the gamut from the fairly straightforward massage room, to rooms offering highly specialized signature treatments. In planning a treatment room, it is important to know that the treatment tables require 360° access for the therapist to operate properly. In addition, there needs to be some work counter space and storage for equipment and supplies. Consideration for out of site cart storage should also be taken into account, to eliminate clutter and allow easy access throughout the room. Occasionally, a shower and changing area may be included, as well as a space to receive a foot massage prior to the treatment. The minimum size for a basic treatment room is approximately 3 meters by 4 meters. This does not allow any space for additional amenities such as foot massage, showers, changing area, etc. In addition to single treatment rooms, couple suites and specialty suites are offered in many spas and are becoming more popular. These large suites can be very luxurious and operate as a self contained personal spa, allowing the patron to enter and exit in their street clothes. As such, each room needs to have self contained private quarters with a changing area, toilet, and shower facilities. More luxurious spas will offer added amenities such as vitality tubs and steam rooms, as well as personalized lounging areas for post-treatment relaxation.

These private rooms will also have sophisticated lighting and sound systems to create a specific ambiance.

The post-treatment experience

Often a post-treatment relaxation lounge is provided which should be in close proximity to the treatment rooms. This area needs to have tea making and other service facilities in close adjacency. The relaxation lounge should incorporate numerous chaise lounges that are often motorized to allow users to adjust them according to their specific needs. The chaises often include small reading lights and/or headphones, and a small TV screen. The lighting in these lounges is generally quite dim and should be designed to emanate a calming effect. A screening element between the chaises should be considered for added privacy.

Service areas

In addition to the 'front of house' spaces outlined above, there needs to be adequate facilities for the necessary 'back of house' or service elements. These areas include store rooms for products, linens, and equipment, as well as preparation areas. A laundry facility, or holding facility if laundry is done off premises, needs to be incorporated as spas generate a large amount of dirty towels, robes, etc. A space for the laundry carts needs to be allowed for and service entrances and elevators should be incorporated so the spa patron does not witness the back of house operations. Within these back of house areas, a staff facility is also required along with mechanical rooms for the equipment necessary for the spa. Access to the mechanical rooms needs to be taken into consideration and should occur along a service corridor away from the public spaces of the spa. The mechanical engineer should determine these requirements once the operational brief is established and the specialized treatments are determined. In addition, local planning codes, exiting requirements and disabled access needs to be addressed during the early planning stage.

The overall flow of the space as it relates to guest traffic and staffing patterns, is one of the most critical issues necessary for a spa to function successfully. The diagram below demonstrates the requirements for ideal flow and adjacencies within a typical spa.

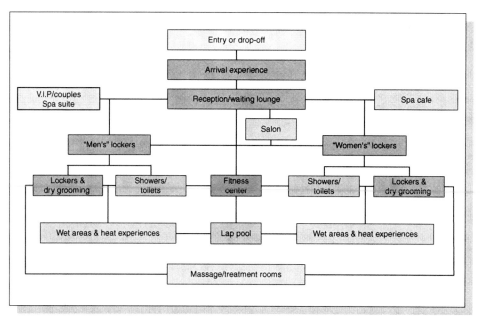

Figure 16.2
Spa flow chart and adjacencies

As is demonstrated above, the separation of wet and dry areas needs to be carefully considered. The question of privacy should also be given consideration through all the spaces, even in the gender specific areas such as locker rooms. As attitudes regarding nudity are dependent on region and cultural acceptance, the varying levels of privacy should be analyzed on a case by case basis. In some cultures, it is socially acceptable to have open showers where nudity is a non-issue, while other cultures may require individual showers with secluded changing areas to respond to the cultural need for privacy.

Conclusion

Just as the global spa industry is a growing industry, the design field is an ever fluctuating and evolving field that is expanding to meet the demands of a growing affluent market. It is the job of a designer to use the historical references and demands of the current society to create a fulfilling and serene environment to contrast and soothe today's hectic and demanding lifestyle.

Reference list

Martin-Wurwand, J., comp. *Spa Treatments: an Ancient Legacy.* The International Dermal Institute. March 1998. 11 June 2007 <http://www.dermalinstitute.com>.

Farnay, R., (2007) *Soaking up Japan's Hot Springs.* 7 June 2007 <http://www.anatol.org/projects/rachel/springs.html>.

Thai Spa and Massage. Tourism Thailand. 1999. June–July 2007 <http://www.insitethailand.com>.

Thailand Spas. Thailand Paradise. 2006. June–July 2007 <http://www.thailandparadise.com>.

Martin-Wurwand, J., comp. *Spa Treatments: an Ancient Legacy.* The International Dermal Institute. March 1998. 11 June 2007 <http://www.dermalinstitute.com>.

AyurvedaTravel Mall. 7 January 2007. 7 June 2007 <http://www.ayurvedatravelmall.com/treatement.htm>.

Strauss, L. *The Bishop's Lodge Ranch Resort & Spa.* 12 January. 2007. 10 July 2007 <http://www.bishopslodge.com/>.

Baldwin, B.L. *Spa at Sundance.* 7 May 2007. 7 May 2007 <http://www.dayspamagazine.com>.

The Finnish Sauna Society (2006) *Introduction to Sweat Baths*, available at: http://www.sauna.fi/englanti/englanti.html (last accessed July 10, 2007).

Hambraeus, T.O. (2006). *Spas in Sweden: And Adventure in Wellness*, available at: www.sweden.se/templates/cs/article_12317.aspx (last accessed July 10, 2007).

Glancey, J. (2003). *In Hot Water*, available at: http://arts.guardian.co.uk/print/0,,4753518–110428,00.html (last accessed August, 2007).

Sansal, B. (2007). *Turkish bath (Hamam)*, available at: http://allaboutturkey.com/hamam.htm (last accessed October 26, 2007).

Aaland, M. (1997). *Mediterranean Baths; The Islamic Hamam is Born*, available at: http://www.pureinsideout.com/roman-bath.html (last accessed October 26, 2007).

Environmental responsibility in the spa industry: a business perspective

Russell Arthur Smith

Global focus for sustainability

Environmentally responsible spa operators have for some time acknowledged the principles of 'reduce, reuse and recycle'. These principles are central to the conservation of resources for a sustainable future. Recently the consequences of global warming have brought environmental responsibility into sharper focus. The need to limit greenhouse gas emissions has gained global prominence where the reduction of carbon dioxide generation is the primary target.

The hospitality and tourism sector has been subjected to high-profile criticism for failure to properly address environmental and global warming issues. Airlines have been targeted as with the protest demonstration at Heathrow Airport in August 2007 (The Camp for Climate Action, 2007). To address global warming concerns, some airlines have sought to redress their contribution to global warming through carbon-offset programs. The air carrier, Virgin Blue, encourages passengers to add the cost of a carbon-offset to their airline tickets at the time of purchase (Virgin Blue, 2007).

Other segments of the hospitality and tourism sector are also seeking viable ways of addressing the heightened environmental concern. Many spas and their closely associated businesses, such as hotels and serviced apartments, now seek to improve their operations environmentally. Support is found in a multitude of organizations; international (e.g. World Green Building Council), industry (e.g. EC3 Global) and government (e.g. Japan Sustainable Building Consortium; National Environmental Agency, Singapore). Many of these organizations provide advisory, benchmarking and audit services for companies seeking to certify that they are environmentally sustainable.

Operation alone is insufficient to achieve environmental sustainability. The physical development of the building – its site, its form and its construction – impacts the environment. These impacts may be positive or negative and they may also significantly influence how spa operation is subsequently conducted.

Sustainability in practice

A number of exemplary spa projects have been recognized for environmental preeminence. One case is the Evason Phuket and Six Senses Spa at Rawai Beach, Phuket, Thailand, which has 260 guestrooms on a 26 ha rural coastal site. This spa developer and operator was Green Globe Certified in 2007 at the Silver Level. To achieve this certification, Six Senses developed a Corporate Environmental and Social Sustainability Policy and then proceeded to implement it. Subsequently, the Rawai-based operation was evaluated using the Earthcheck Benchmarking System (see Chapter 18). In addressing the Earthcheck indicators, Six Senses sought to reduce greenhouse gas emissions through energy efficiency, to reduce water consumption, to preserve the ecosystem, to involve and to contribute to local communities, to preserve the natural habitat for wildlife and vegetation, to protect air quality, to control noise pollution, to treat waste water and to minimize waste (Six Senses, 2007).

Environmental sustainability is also achievable in highly urbanized settings. The Shiodome Tower is an outstanding example. This high-rise urban tower with 38 floors has a 0.6 ha site in downtown Tokyo, Japan. Its upper levels contain a Royal Park hotel, with 490 guestrooms, which operate a Mandara Spa. The lower levels are devoted to single-tenant offices with limited retail uses. The Japan Sustainable Building Consortium certified this project with its Comprehensive Assessment System for Building Environmental Efficiency. This assessment system incorporates tools that evaluate environmental quality and loads, such as energy use, materials recycling and water conservation (Royal Park, 2007; World Green Building Council, 2007).

The Shiodome Tower incorporates many environmentally sustainable features. For example, the building's external appearance is unlike that of many other inner-city high-rise buildings which have extensive external glazed fenestration with aluminum framing. The limited use of external glazing in the Shiodome Tower's building façade contributes to energy efficiency. In addition the façade was clad with terra cotta tiles which incorporate 40% recycled material. These tiles also reduce glare.

The building incorporates a Building Energy Management System (BEMS) that enhances energy efficiency during operation and verifies performance, for lower running costs. Natural ventilation is used to supplement mechanical air conditioning throughout the building. Energy efficient lighting is also installed. Energy is conserved indirectly through the location of the project near urban mass transit services thus reducing the reliance on road transport for guest and staff access. Other sustainable measures relate to water. Kitchen wastewater is treated on-site and rainwater runoff is collected and utilized.

Business implications

An important business operational issue is the cost of inclusion of these environmental measures in new or existing spas. The India Green Building Council has generally found that the cost of including environmental measures needed to achieve its platinum rating can increase overall development costs by 8–20%, yet the energy and other savings result in sharply reduced costs of operation. The payback period for these projects is between 5 and 7 years, beyond which the savings go directly to improve the business's financial bottom line.

Energy efficiency has been recognized as a major driver for environmental sustainability in the hospitality industry. Gaglia et al. (2007) surveyed 14 types of energy conservation measures in Hellenic hospitality businesses. Of these, the most effective were the use of a BEMS followed by solar collectors for sanitary hot water, energy efficient lighting and installation of ceiling fans.

In Singapore, energy efficiency has been a driver for reduction of greenhouse gas emissions. Recognizing that hotels currently account for 2% of the total national greenhouse gas emission, the National Environmental Agency (NEA) has developed an 'Energy Smart' program which will recognize energy efficient excellence in hospitality businesses. Under is program, accredited energy service organizations audit hospitality companies for established benchmarks which reflect a range of criteria that include the building's physical features, the operational characteristics and energy use. The audit recommends improvements that will include improving energy efficiency. Only the top 25% of hospitality businesses that meet the criteria qualify for award of the certification.

One recipient of the Energy Smart label is The Regent Singapore. This centrally located urban hotel has 439 guestrooms, spa, swimming pool, gymnasium and other features. An energy audit was conducted where a key recommendation was to replace the existing diesel boilers with a heat recovery system. Overall energy reduction of 26% in kWh terms was achieved. The payback period was only one and a half years, after which the savings on energy significantly reduced operating costs.

The paradigm for the NEA is grounded in pragmatic principles. It is a government devised and operated program, although participation is voluntary, not statutory or obligatory. The program is focused solely on the hospitality industry. The program is business oriented and avoids idealism. There are financial incentives in the form of government subsidies to help cover half of the audit costs. There are rising energy standards which are industry driven by the cap of top 25% best performers. Program outcomes are targeted with immediate energy cost savings for hospitality operators as well as national greenhouse gas emission reduction.

Conclusion

Spa owners, developers and operators generally acknowledge the challenge of global warming and the need for environmental sustainability. Ways of achieving this must contribute positively to their business operations' outcome. There is likely to be little business acceptance of idealism or solutions that increase costs or reduce business competitiveness. While many actions can certainly contribute to sustainability and help to reduce global warming, energy conservation is a leading strategy for spas as this will reduce energy operating expenses as well as carbon dioxide production.

Large operators and chains or those partnered with other hospitality operations, such as lodging, may have more scope for immediately implementing a program for sustainability. Smaller operators, however, may lack the resources to plan and implement environmental solutions within a short timeframe. In such cases, the first priority would be to conduct an environmental audit and to then prepare a plan for achieving sustainability that is within the capabilities and resources of the company. Realistic targets for implementing the plan over time can then be set and incremental progress can be shown in moving the spa operation towards sustainability.

Global warming is a new concept that spas need to address. The full business implications of this for spa development and operation are evolving. That there are major environmental implications is obvious, though what is expected of spa managements by their clients in terms of environmental actions is not certain. It is clear that customers want to feel comfortable that their spas are environmentally attuned. The danger for spa businesses is turning customers away through too little, too much or too expensive sustainable actions. Deciding how to proceed is not easy. What is certain is that spas need to be seen to be striving for sustainability and to demonstrate unambiguously that they are taking positive actions that are desired by their clients.

References

Gaglia, A.G., Balaras, C.A., Mirasgedis, S., Georgopoulou, E., Sarafidis, Y., Lalas, D.P. (2007) Empirical assessment of the Hellenic non-residential building stock, energy consumption, emissions and potential energy savings, *Energy Conservation and Management*, 48(4):1160–1175.

Royal Park (2007) Mandara Spa available at: http://rps-tower.co.jp/english/mandara/ (site accessed 09 December 2007).

Six Senses (2007) Environmental and Social Sustainability Policy available at: http://www.sixsenses.com/evason-phuket/social_policy.php (site accessed 09 December 2007).

The Camp for Climate Action (2007). Camp for Climate Action 2007 is a resounding success! available at: http://www.climate-camp.org.uk/ (site accessed 09 December 2007).

Virgin Blue (2007). Fly Carbon Neutral Available at: http://www.virginblue.com.au/carbonoffset/ (site accessed 09 December 2007).

World Green Building Council (2007) Shiodome Tower available at: http://worldgbc.org/docs/ShiodomeTower.pdf (site accessed 09 December 2007).

Environmental and Social Benchmarking

Melinda Watt and Ben Bayada

Introduction

Travel and tourism is like no other industry sector in terms of both the intimacy and time it directly spends with its customers. The growing customer awareness of, and demand for, good environmental practices exposes the long-term market share of this industry to heightened risk of the consequences of environmental deterioration and poor environmental practices. Drawing on the work of Scott (2007a), a set of position points can be identified for orienting the spa industry to some core environmental and social responsibilities.

Within travel and tourism, the spa industry is at the forefront of direct customer contact and holds a key position by which to demonstrate good environmental stewardship. In basic terms, it consumes and disposes of energy, water and materials, and how it approaches these actions will determine not only its own long-term economic viability, but also the messages that customers and staff take away with them.

Reducing water usage and energy consumption not only makes economic sense, it also contributes to the urgent need to reduce the impact on the world's rapidly dwindling natural resources and addresses the need to decrease greenhouse gas emissions by, where possible, accessing renewable sources (such as solar, hydro or wind).

Equally important, for the spa industry to consider is appropriate choice and application of chemical products, not just for personal use, such as cleansers and oils, but also for surface cleaning, laundry and water purification. The first step should always be to re-examine and challenge existing housekeeping and other practices to ensure that the frequency and quantities of application are not excessive. In almost every instance where this has occurred, considerable environmental and economic savings have been made without comprising cleanliness, safety or customer satisfaction. At the same time, this provides the ideal opportunity to look for products that are biodegradable, obtainable locally wherever possible and can be bought in bulk to avoid excessive packaging.

However, despite the actions that are taken, it is vital that interest amongst the staff and customers is maintained on an ongoing basis to avoid complacency. The most effective method to ensure this is to benchmark progress through annually recording, the outcomes of resource savings, product replacement and general good house-keeping with practices, and using this information to set and reward the achieving of realistic targets for the following year.

With the current emphasis in the world community on 'climate change' and how the global community should respond to this call to action, the need to benchmark not only spa operations but all travel and tourism operations is exacerbated. Benchmarking gives the tourism industry the opportunity to quantitatively demonstrate to its clients that it is taking action and responding positively to help address this global problem.

What is benchmarking?

Benchmarking is a means by which an operation can assess and improve its environmental, social and economic performance quantitatively. Benchmarking indicators establish the measures that need to be recorded by an operation. It is essential that collecting benchmarking data is a straightforward process. Environmental benchmarking should involve practical, everyday measures such as the volume of water used in a year as shown by an operation's water bills and the amount of electricity used, as shown by an operation's electricity bills (EC3 Global, 2007).

Activity Measure

To facilitate comparison of results across the sector it is necessary to include an 'Activity Measure' in the data analysis. An Activity Measure reflects the key activity of an operation, taking into account the type of impact. Energy consumption, water consumption and waste sent to landfill, etc. can then be benchmarked against the Activity Measure. For example, in the accommodation sector, the Activity Measure is 'guest nights'. Energy consumption, water consumption and waste sent to landfill are benchmarked per 'guest night'. Within the spa sector, the 'Activity Measure' is 'guest treatment hours', with energy consumption, water consumption and waste sent to landfill reported as 'per guest treatment hour' (Table 18.1).

Benefits of benchmarking

Environmental and social benchmarking will:
- demonstrate contribution to protection of local and global environmental quality;
- retain existing customers and attract ones;
- improve profitability through greater efficiency and less waste;
- provide a sound basis for environmental reporting to stakeholders;

Table 18.1 Company standard

Sector	Activity measure
Accommodation	Guest Nights Area Under Roof (m^2)
Administration Office	Area Under Roof (m^2)
Aerial Cableway	Revenue Passenger Kilometres (RPK)
Cruise Vessel	Revenue Passenger Kilometres (RPK)
Visitor Centre	Total Visitors
Spa	Guest Treatment hour

- attract ethical investment;
- improve business-to-business opportunities and outcomes;
- improve relations with government regulators;
- enhance relations with local communities;
- motivate employees.

Current benchmarking programs

Ideally, benchmarking is carried out on a sectoral basis allowing comparison of numerous operations within the sector. Since 2001 Green Globe (www.ec3global.com/products-programs/green-globe/) in conjunction with the Sustainable Tourism Cooperative Research Centre (STCRC) (www.crctourism.com.au) – the peak body for Travel and Tourism Research globally – has developed, environmentally responsible benchmarking for over 25 travel and tourism sectors including accommodation, administration offices, restaurants, resorts, aerial cableways, cruise vessels, golf courses and tour operators. The Green Globe program is based on the Agenda 21 principles for Sustainable Development endorsed by 182 Heads of State at the United Nations Rio De Janeiro Earth Summit in 1992. Green Globe is managed by EC3 Global, a subsidiary of the STCRC.

The Earthcheck Benchmarking system

The Earthcheck Benchmarking system is a simple web-based application (www.ec3global.com/products-programs/earthcheck/) which empowers operators to input data needed to carry out the assessment and reporting process and which allows the operator to track their performance annually in relation to baseline and best practice within the sector and implement improvements accordingly. The Earthcheck system, which was developed by the STCRC in March 2001 to simplify and standardise environmental and social benchmarking, offers a low-cost entry point in the journey to become sustainable. To do this the STCRC drew on a research team from over 17 universities to compile case studies and national reference data to create an adaptable tool that can be plugged in or purchased to allow an organisation to monitor and reduce its environmental impact.

The Earthcheck Benchmarking system can assist an organisation to reduce costs in areas like energy consumption, waste production and resource conservation by monitoring and reporting outputs. It also demonstrates to consumers that the spa is serious about its environmental, social and economic performance, and can help with implementing better management practices while improving the quality of the environment in which the spa operates.

Sector benchmarking indicator development for the spa sector

It is essential in the development of sector benchmarking indicators (SBI) to work in close consultation with the industry group to ensure details specific to the sector are included and determine sector-specific baseline and best practice data. Before 2008 there were no international benchmarking programs for the spa sector. Traditionally any benchmarking has been linked with the resorts and hotels in which spas operate. However, in light of the rapid expansion of the spa industry, Green Globe, in conjunction with the STCRC, has collaborated with Six Senses Resorts and Spas, a driving force in environmentally friendly spa development and operations, to develop SBI for spa operations worldwide, using the Earthcheck Benchmarking system.

Methodology

In December 2006 Green Globe was requested by Six Senses Spas to develop indicators and benchmarks for the spa sector. Six Senses Resorts and Spas are at the forefront of the spa sector's growth, operating several award-winning properties in Thailand, Vietnam and the Maldives. The group has demonstrated their commitment to the environment by assisting Green Globe to establish a spa sector within the Green Globe program and they have committed to initially benchmark all of their spa operations and ensure all of their future developments participate in the Green Globe program.

The project involved working with the current Earthcheck Benchmarking system using the existing core indicators and expanding the indicator set where necessary to include sector-specific indicators as they relate to spa operations. A draft indicator set was developed by EC3 and submitted for industry review by Six Senses. Following this, any recommendations made from the industry sector were taken on board and the final indicator set was then distributed to each of the 14 operations globally, with each participant selected by Six Senses Group Management. Individual operations submitted data for each indicator which was then analysed by EC3 to determine appropriate benchmarks. These benchmarks were categorised specifically to region and climate variables relative to the sample dataset.

Each participating operation was issued with a benchmarking assessment report which confirmed their status as an operation committed to monitoring environmental performance and achieving benchmarked status as part of the Green Globe global benchmarking and certification program. To ensure adherence with the Green Globe Standard, benchmarking is carried out annually.

Determination of baseline and best practice levels

For the Earthcheck Benchmarking system, the values for the baseline and best practice levels for each indicator are derived from extensive worldwide research into available and appropriate case studies (Six Senses Spas industry surveys, engineering design handbooks, energy, water and waste audits, and climatic and geographic conditions).

National and regional data for per capita energy use, greenhouse gas and other emissions, wastes to landfill and water consumption, where available provide background data for normalisation of the expected performance values for customers or employees, and/or overall performance of an enterprise being benchmarked. They are used to gauge the regional or national situation and environmental performances that an enterprise is based in, and hence, the levels of achievement that the enterprise is expected to achieve.

A benchmarking result at, or above, the baseline level demonstrates to all stakeholders that the enterprise is achieving above average performance. A result below the baseline level indicates that an enterprise can and should carry out actions that will make beneficial improvements in performance.

Context

It Is recognised that spas can vary significantly, not just in size and location, but also in the number and type of facilities offered. As a consequence, a detailed analysis of the on-site facilities is requested in order to ensure that when benchmarking is done, a reasonable comparison between operations is made. Examples of facility types include saunas, spa baths, treatment beds, hammams, swimming pools, etc. (Scott, 2007b).

Sustainability policy

The Sustainability Policy is an operation's statement with respect to its assessment, control and, where appropriate, continual improvement of environmental and local social impacts. As part of the benchmarking process an operation must compile and submit their Sustainability Policy. Templates are available for use via the Earthcheck system.

Core indicators

The Earthcheck Benchmarking system has a number of core indicators which are applicable to all travel and tourism sectors undergoing benchmarking including the spa sector which are:

- energy consumption;
- greenhouse gas emissions;
- water consumption;
- waste sent to landfill;
- community commitment;
- paper products;
- cleaning products;
- pesticide products.

Energy consumption

Energy can be obtained from a variety of sources (e.g. grid electricity, natural gas, gasoline, diesel) and significant levels of energy can be consumed by a spa's infrastructure (e.g. lighting, saunas, pools), and spa operated transport (e.g. for customer and staff transfer, on-site maintenance and delivery). An overall reduction in energy consumed can have major economic and environmental benefits, the latter primarily through conservation of natural resources and lowering associated greenhouse gas emissions.

Greenhouse gas emissions

It is essential to ensure that the SBI address the emission of greenhouse gases from the operation. This is delivered within the Earthcheck system via a purpose built energy calculator which calculates the amount of CO_2 emissions using initial energy data (including energy sources and quantities) entered by the operator.

Water consumption

Potable water resources (water suitable for drinking) are typically treated to remove harmful elements). This water can be consumed by a wide range of activities, including cleansing treatments (including saunas), services (e.g. kitchens, laundries), recreational facilities (e.g. pools, decorative ponds), surface cleaning and watering of grounds. Furthermore, many operations are located in regions where year-round access to fresh water is a significant concern. Actions leading to an overall reduction in water usage (from lowering demand, and increasing reuse and recycling) will be a major contribution to the long-term sustainability of both the local environment and the operation.

In addition to measuring water consumption, and itemising the various sources of water used, the Earthcheck Benchmarking system also includes an indicator checklist which itemises various ways by which water is conserved within an operation.

Water saving checklist

- Check for leaks
- Use of low/dual flow toilets
- Use of low flow faucets
- Use of low flow shower fittings
- Use of water sprinklers after dark
- Use of minimal irrigation landscaping
- Use of recycle/grey/rain water

Waste sent to landfill

Used or waste materials sent to landfills not only creates a negative environmental impact from the transportation used, but also results in a loss of resources and the risk from leaching of contaminants and greenhouse gas emissions from the breakdown of organic materials. Replacement of materials landfilled will also increase greenhouse gases from their production and transport. To reduce these impacts, the first step for the operation should be to look to reduce quantities of materials consumed including packaging (e.g. consider where possible to buy in bulk), to then consider reuse, or if not possible, recycle, including use of designed composting of green wastes (e.g. from any kitchens, gardens, etc.).

The assessment of waste sent to landfill also includes an Earthcheck indicator checklist which itemises various ways by which waste levels can be reduced.

Waste recycling checklist

- Glass
- Paper/card
- Iron and steel
- Other metals
- Plastics
- Rubber
- Green waste

Community commitment

A key issue in achieving sustainability is to consider the social as well as environmental impact of the operation on local communities. Respecting where appropriate, local traditions and customs, and purchasing where possible local goods and services are positive contributions that can be made, and should be incorporated into the operation's Sustainability Policy. Other considerations should include active participation in local committees and organisations.

In recognition that the nature of the operation may rely on seasonal labour, an indicator that monitors the number of owners, managers and/or employees that live close to where they are based within the operation is used (for remote operations, such as on small low-populated islands or wilderness regions, the nearest permanent township can be used instead of the operation). This highlights and encourages local employment, and thereby economic contribution to the local communities, and also minimises environmental impacts due to personnel transportation. Another measure, which reflects the amount of monetary support which is given to the local community, shows that the operation is responsive to community needs. In addition to the above, the assessment of community commitment also includes the various ways by which the operation contributes directly to their local communities.

Paper products

An active policy of purchasing supplies of materials from sources using environmentally sound ingredients and processes can be a major contribution to resource conservation and biodiversity through less impact on the local ecosystem.

Community contributions checklist

- Net income spent on sustainability programs
- Perishable goods of local origin
- Service contracts given to local contractors
- Staff received training on sustainability issues

A strategy of reuse and recycle where possible, coupled with the use of products proven to be environmentally friendly (such as those carrying credible ecolabels), should be adopted. For paper products, desirable qualities include avoidance of chlorine-based bleaches, use of biodegradable inks and dyes, and use of wood from sustainable plantations. Benchmarking paper products not only includes listing the source of paper, but also the various ways paper can be used.

Paper products checklist

- Office paper used
- Product packaging used
- Serviettes and tissues used
- Toilet tissue used
- Towels used

Cleaning products

The active (non-water) chemical ingredients of treatment and cleaning products (e.g. lotions, hand and body soaps, shampoos, laundry detergents, surface degreasers and cleansers, etc.), and those used to condition water facilities (e.g. in pools to control bacteria, additives to soften water, etc.) can end up in wastewater (from cleaned toilets, washbasins, washing machines, kitchen sinks, etc.), as well as the ground- and stormwater systems (e.g. from pool draining, run off from roofs, windows, driveways, etc.). They can represent a significant source of environmental contamination in terms of toxicity and disturbance of the natural balance of ecosystems (e.g. phosphates contributing to eutrophication (a build-up of excess nutrients)). Benchmarking cleaning products includes measuring the types and quantities of cleaning products as well as itemising the various ways they are used.

Cleaning products checklist

- Used on hard floors
- Used on carpets
- Used on interior surfaces
- Used on exterior surfaces
- Used on glass
- Used for laundry (detergents)
- Used for personal hygiene

Pesticide products

A reduction in the ecological impact of pesticides can be achieved by greater use of biodegradable products (usually based on natural plant extracts) and alternative practices including integrated pest management programs (programs that develop locality specific solutions and can include practices such as using grass species suited to the locality and avoiding over-application of chemicals). Similar to the benchmarking of cleaning products, the benchmarking of pesticide products includes measuring the types and quantities of product as well as itemising the various ways they are used.

Pesticide products checklist

- Weed killers used
- Fugal killers used
- Rodent killers used
- Insect killers used

Sector-specific indicators for the spa sector

In addition to the core indicator set used by the Earthcheck system, it may be necessary to include additional sector-specific indicators.

Vehicle management

The type and number of any vehicles used (e.g. car, truck, boat, coach, 4WD, small plane, helicopter) and their purpose (e.g. maintenance, staff/customer transport) will be dictated by the activity type and location. The operation can, however, contribute to minimising energy consumption and any associated emissions through ensuring regular vehicle maintenance of its vehicles as per the manufacturer's schedule. As part of the service, each vehicle should, where appropriate, have its engine's exhaust emissions tested and pass local regulatory standards. Exhaust emissions are a good guide to the efficiency of combustion, and hence fuel consumption and level of harmful exhaust gases. The indicator is the ratio of total vehicle services completed to the total number of services required, as per the original vehicle manufacturer's maintenance schedule and specifications.

Wellness indicator

An active policy to provide humane and responsive services and benefits to staff to maintain a safe and healthy work environment promotes a beneficial working relationship for both staff and management (see Chapter 21). A wellness indicator itemises various conditions applied to staff.

Consideration of climate

A major determinant of energy consumption in some sectors, primarily those centred on buildings such as accommodation, visitor centres and administration offices will be the dominant climatic conditions in which the enterprise is located. In general, to maintain the same level of indoor comfort, enterprises operating in hot or cold climates will consume more energy than those in temperate climates.

Similarly, it is recognised that in certain sectors a major determinant of potable water consumption will be the climate in which an enterprise is located, in particular those with large grounds and/or significant water-based facilities or activities. That is, enterprises located in hot climates are more likely to consume more potable water than equivalent ones located in cooler climates. Factors that are likely to lead to a higher level of potable water consumption, for example in the accommodation sector, include increased evaporation rates of swimming pools, personal bathing and irrigation demands of grounds. In consideration of this factor, it is natural for baseline and best practice levels to vary in relation to country and location.

Review of performance levels

The baseline and best practice performance levels for Earthcheck indicators are continuously reviewed and are likely to change over time. This review by a team of international experts takes into account 'business-as-usual' changes in practices, equipment and facilities, as well as regulations and general improvement trends in performance and procedures. This review is used to update the levels of baseline and best practice for individual sectors, and provides useful feedback to the user of the indicators.

The list below summarises the basic generic rules used to determine baseline and best practice levels for Earthcheck indicators:

- If relevant enterprise sector-specific case studies are not available for a type of activity in a designated region, then national averages will be used to ascertain the baseline level. In this case, the best practice level will be set at a minimum of 30% better performance than the baseline.
- If case study or national data are not available for a specific indicator, then the first enterprise that benchmarks will have its results set as 15% better than baseline (i.e. half way between baseline and best practice).

Performance reporting

Once the baseline and best practice levels have been established and an operator has submitted their data, it is then possible to report on the operations performance. This is typically done via a comprehensive report which includes graphical representation of performance per indicator, a summary of data inputs, as well as conclusions and recommendations to the operation on how they can improve their performance.

Conclusion

To date there have been no international benchmarking programs for the spa sector, with any benchmarking being linked with the resorts or hotels in which spas operate. With nearly 100 million active spa users globally, the need for an international benchmarking program, specific to the spa industry, has never been more paramount.

The introduction of the spa sector to the Green Globe program is an alignment of philosophies. The spa industry promotes health and well-being and this philosophy is based on environmentally conscious roots. As a consequence, this sector lies at the forefront of groups tapping into the market of the environmentally aware consumer.

References

Bayada (2007) *The Effects of Peak Oil on the Travel/Spa Industry*, The Leisure Media Company Ltd, London.

EC3 Global (2007) Earthcheck [Online], available at: http://www.ec3global.com/products-programs/earthcheck/ (site accessed 30 October 2007). Earthcheck Pty Ltd: Brisbane.

Scott, J.A. (2007) *Spa Industry*, Earthcheck Pty Ltd, Brisbane.

Scott, J.A. (2007) *Sector Benchmarking Indicators for Spas*, Earthcheck Pty Ltd, Brisbane.

Websites

Green Globe: http://www.ec3global.com/products-programs/green-globe/
EC3 Global: http://www.ec3global.com/
Earthcheck: http://www.ec3global.com/products-programs/earthcheck/ Community contributions checklist

Water requirements, water quality and related technologies

Daryl P Stevens and
David Cunliffe

Introduction

Globally the spa and wellness industry is experiencing rapid growth, with the development of new spa resorts and hotels and the refurbishment and upgrade of existing spa facilities. In some instances entire spa towns have been upgraded as a direct result of the growing demand for spa and wellness experiences. The spa and wellness businesses must also be encouraged to adopt environmentally sustainable principles, including responsible use of water and energy efficiency and waste management (Victoria's Spa and Wellness Action Plan, 2005–2010).

Spa facilities can utilise water from a variety of sources (e.g. mains water, ground water, sea water). Many spa treatments involve a high level of human exposure to water directly (e.g. plunge pool) or indirectly (aerosols) from the water (e.g. shower-based treatments). Consequently, from a human health (pathogen) perspective, the water quality must be to a standard considered to be fit for drinking.

As the world's populations grow there is an increasing demand on our limited drinking water resources (UN GIWA, 2006). At the same time our water resources are being threatened by climate change and changing weather patterns (e.g. CSIRO, 2007). In many countries, a wide range of industries that use water are under constant threat of water restrictions or increased supply costs impacting their demand for water. The spa industry is no different; it must take on the social responsibility of efficient water use and be recognised as environmentally responsible. This is especially true in many parts of the world (e.g. Australia, California, Israel, Spain and Sub-Saharan Africa, as well as arid zones in India, such as Rajasthan) where water supplies are limited and many industries and people are already suffering due to restrictions placed on their water supplies.

This chapter outlines the major sources and uses of water in the spa health and wellness industry. It also considers opportunities for management and reuse of wastewater; and measures that can be taken to ensure water is used efficiently and is fit for the purpose it is intended ('fit for purpose') from a human health and environmental protection perspective.

Water requirements for spa facilities

Water quality requirements

Risk management

Risk management approaches are now being used across the world for ensuring water quality for drinking, recreational and recycling water (e.g. NRMMC, EPHC 2006; WHO 2006a). The core of the risk management system is proactive management of any risk by identifying the likelihood of an event (a hazard being exposed to a receptor) and the impact of the event on human health or the environment (Standards Australia, 2004a). Risks are managed through critical control points and implementation of appropriate control measures in conjunction with the appropriate monitoring, auditing and reviewing.

Water supplied to the spa, used in the spa and disposed of or recycled from the spa, should be managed via a risk management system which is audited and reviewed yearly.

Human health impacts

There are three main components of water use in the spa health and wellness industry that can potentially pose risks to human health:

1. Water supplied to the spa
2. Water when used in the spa (contamination in-house)
3. Disposal or recycling of spa wastewater

There are two major hazard (contaminant) groups within each of these major water components. These are pathogens (e.g. microbe, bacteria and viruses) and physical and chemical hazards (e.g. chlorine, bromide, pH, temperature).

From a human health perspective, it is a reasonable precautionary approach to ensure that the quality of water supplied for use in spas should meet drinking water standards from a pathogen perspective (e.g. NHMRC, NRMMC, 2004; WHO, 2006a). From a physical/chemical hazard perspective, drinking water standards should also be met. However, there will be a number of specific cases for destination and natural bath spa facilities where, for example, contaminants in the water are above guidelines for drinking water (e.g. the hazard salinity of seawater would prevent it from being suitable for drinking water), yet there would be low risks to human health from this hazard in the water quality.

Spa water (communal-use public water) is also susceptible to contamination with pathogens from people exposed to the water (Table 19.1). It should also be noted that changes in environmental conditions of a water supply (e.g. increases in temperature) can make the water sources susceptible to contamination with an amplification of thermophilic pathogens (e.g. *Pseudomonas* and *Legionella*) that naturally occur in the environment (Dziuban et al., 2006). Spa pools, baths and treatment facilities must be maintained appropriately to ensure there are no significant risks to human health particularly from pathogenic microorganisms.

These organisms can lead to illnesses ranging from mild to severe skin, eye and ear infections to gastrointestinal infections, hypersensitivity, pneumonitis and in extreme cases death from organisms such as Legionella (Dziuban et al., 2006)(Table 19.2).

Table 19.1 Potential microbial hazards found in water sources

Pathogen type	Examples	Source	Illness
Protozoa	*Cryptosporidium*	Fecal	Gastroenteritis
	Giardia	Fecal	Gastroenteritis
	Naegleria fowleri	Free living	Amoebic meningitis
Bacteria	*Salmonella*	Fecal	Gastroenteritis, reactive arthritis
	Campylobacter	Fecal	Gastroenteritis, Guillain–Barré syndrome
	Pathogenic *Escherichia coli* including enterohaemorrhagic strains	Fecal	Gastroenteritis, haemolytic uremic syndrome
	Shigella	Fecal	Dysentery
	Atypical *Mycobacteria*	Free living	Respiratory illness (hypersensitivity pneumonitis)
	Legionella spp	Free living	Respiratory illness (pneumonia, Pontiac fever)
	Staphylococcus aureus	Free living	Skin, eye, ear infections, septicaemia
	Pseudomonas aeruginosa	Free living	Skin, eye, ear infections
Viruses	Enterovirus		Gastroenteritis, respiratory illness, nervous disorders, myocarditis
	Adenovirus		Gastroenteritis, respiratory illness, eye infections
	Rotavirus		Gastroenteritis
	Norovirus		Gastroenteritis
	Hepatitis A		Infectious hepatitis

Table 19.2 Potential health problems associated with spa pools[1]

Health problems	Causative organisms/ agent	Predisposing factors to infection
1. Follicular dermatitis	*Pseudomonas aeruginosa*	High numbers of microorganisms
		Long exposure time or high temperatures
2. Skin, ear and eye infections	*Pseudomonas aeruginosa, Pseudomonas cepacia, Mycobacterium marinum*, Papilloma viruses, *Acanthamoeba Staphylococcus aureus* – otitis externa and media	Injury
		Spa environs and materials
		Skin lesions from recent trauma or immune deficiency
		People with corneal abrasions
3. Skin irritation	Chloramines	Inadequate dumping frequency
		Low chlorine disinfectant levels
4. Dermatitis – irritant or allergic	Choice of disinfectant, e.g. bromine	Sensitivity to disinfectant or excessive exposures
5. Respiratory infection	*Legionella, Pseudomonas* spp.Enterobacteriaceae, aerobic amoebae, adenoviruses *Mycobacterium avium*	Aerosol dispersion of contaminated water, Poor disinfection practice, Immersion of the head
		Pre-existing respiratory disease
		Can occur in immuno-suppressed people
6. Gastrointestinal infection	*Giardia, Cryptosporidium,* Enterobacteriaceae – *Klebsiella, Yersinia*	Ingestion of fecally polluted water
7. Heat stress (hyperthermia)	Hot water	Excessive exposure to heat High temperature, especially above 40°C (or above 38°C for those at risk such as the elderly or those with heart conditions)[2]
8. Central nervous system infections (Amoebic meningoencephalitis, Granulomatous encephalitis)	*Naegleria fowleri Acanthamoeba* spp	Can occur in immuno-suppressed people after exposure to contaminated fresh or sea water. (Almost invariably fatal)
9. Liver or renal disease	*Leptospira* spp	Skin contact with water contaminated with animal (especially rodent) urine in warmer climates.

Source: NHMRC, 2006,Broadbent, 1996.
[1]This could also include any spa treatment involving water.
[2]In some studies hyperthermia of pregnant women in early pregnancy has been associated with an increased risk of birth defects in their offspring.

Cause of illness, route of entry and predominant illness data for recreational water in the USA and human health outbreaks indicate:

- the most common cause of illness is infection by pathogens (76%), with bacteria as the leading cause of infection (Figure 19.1a);
- route of entry is predominantly through ingestion, yet contact and inhalation are also significant entry points (Figure 19.1b); and
- the most common illness suffered is acute gastrointestinal illness, followed by dermatitis and acute respiratory infection (Figure 19.1c).

Microorganisms that represent hazards and potential risks for operators and clients of spa treatments can be divided into two groups, fecal pathogens (from feces) and free-living pathogens (found commonly in the environment). Fecal pathogens include microorganisms that represent risks through ingestion of water. The common form of illness caused by these microorganisms is a gastrointestinal infection resulting in mild to severe cases of diarrhea illness in the normal population (Figure 19.1). However, a number of organisms can cause more severe outcomes in a subset of cases. Vulnerable groups such as the severely immuno-compromised can experience more debilitating illness.

Algae growth in some water sources can also produce toxins that cause skin rashes, swollen lips, eye irritation and redness, ear ache and itchiness if exposed to humans. (CRC Water Quality and Treatment 2002). If the water sources used are susceptible to algae bloom appropriate control measure should be sought (e.g. aeration, lower nitrogen and phosphorus levels, shading of water storage).

There are also human health risks associated with pollution from animal excreta, and some pathogens, such as *Cryptosporidium parvum*, *Campylobacter spp* and *E. coli* O157:H7 can be transmitted through this route (NHMRC, 2006). These risks are most relevant for untreated water sources from rainfall, storm water and surface water (i.e. not mains water) and should be considered in the risk assessment if these sources of water are used.

Environmental impacts

Environmental impacts from the water used in health and wellness spa facilities can be grouped into three components of the environment:

1. Where the water was taken from
2. The spa infrastructure
3. Where the wastewater is returned to the environment.

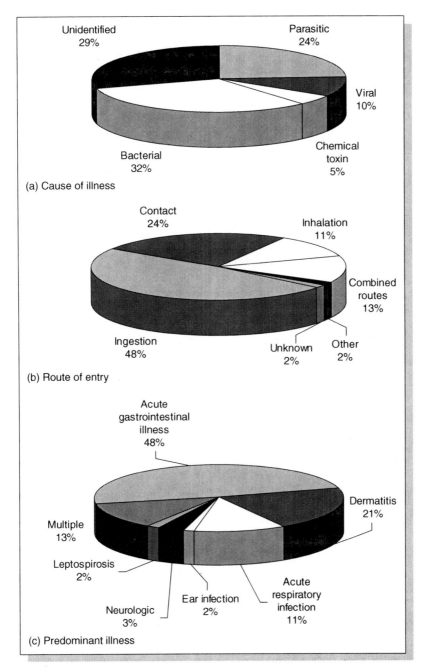

(a) Cause of illness

(b) Route of entry

(c) Predominant illness

Figure 19.1
Recreational water-associated human health outbreaks ($n = 62$) by cause of illness (a), route of entry (b) and predominant illness (c) USA 2003–2004. Modified from Dziuban et al., 2006.

In most cases spa facility water use will be insignificant compared to the water used in the district (see Section 'Water volumes'). However in situations where use of water by a spa operation removes significant volumes of water from the environment the impact on that environment should be considered. This is generally considered through water resource allocation and entitlement systems and should be the first check made prior to developing a spa that relies on a specific water source (i.e. do you have a right to use the water?).

The physical environment within the spa facility may also be impacted by the quality of the water used in the spa. For example, seawater is very corrosive to many metals; mineral water high in iron can cause red discoloration of hydrotherapy equipment and some natural spring waters release hydrogen sulphide with an offensive odour.

Consideration should also be given to the products and chemicals (operational or treatment) added to the water when the water is used in the delivery of spa treatments, and other operational uses such as cleaning and laundering. Eventually these contaminants enter the wastewater system(s) for disposal or recycling and eventually enter the environment external to the Spa facility. Potential impacts on the environment and management strategies of the major hazards (contaminants) are discussed further in Section 'Managing waste water – disposal or recycle'.

Water volumes

The three general areas (Table 19.3) where water is used in spa facilities are:

1. Treatments;
2. Operation; and
3. Landscape and aesthetics.

Water use for treatments

The volume of water used in spa facilities varies considerably depending on the number of clients visiting the spa and the types of treatments delivered. For example, a recent study in Victoria, Australia, sampled a subset of the spa industry in this state and found that water use per single treatment ranged from 1–2 L to 800 L (Figure 19.2). The higher water use treatments included Vichy treatments, Capsules, Tubs and Spa baths.

Table 19.3 Examples of major water use categories and specific uses

Spa treatments		Operational	Landscape
Spa	Salon hair basin	Client basin/shower	Fountain
Tub	Manicure bowl/basin	Laundry	Pond/lake
Capsules/Flotation tank	Foot soak/Pedicure bowl/basin	Toilets	River/stream
Vichy	Stone heater	Staff basins/shower	Garden
Hydrostorm	Facial bowl	Dishwasher	Dust suppression
Pool	Spray booth	Kitchen sink	
Plunge pool	Treatment shower	General cleaning	
		Drinking	
		Cooling	

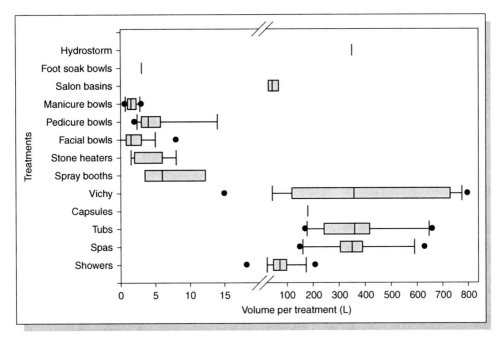

Figure 19.2
Water used in different water treatments practiced in the 20 spas audited in Victoria (Stevens and Smolenaars, 2007). Line in middle of grey box = median; ends of grey box = 25th and 75th percentiles; end of T is 5th and 95th percentile; filled circles are outliers. (*Note:* in some cases due to the data distribution only the median, 25th or 75th percentiles are shown)

Water use in the Vichy treatments varied due to the number of shower heads (1 to 18), the flow rate (4–25 L/min), and the treatment method/time (operator dependent).

Often the type of spa facility influences the types of treatments offered and therefore the volume of water used (e.g. Hot springs – A destination spa based predominantly on water treatments will use a lot more water). There are a number of other psychological factors that can influence water use. These factors included:

- Water awareness (e.g. water restrictions, droughts, staff training)
- Water sources (see Section 'Water sources, treatment and management').

Given the factors discussed above that influence water usage in spa facilities, estimates of water use per client visiting a spa vary considerably. Stevens and Smolenaars (2007) found that the average use of water across the total number of clients to the spa facilities audited was 79 ± 39 L/client, or use of water per water treatment was 176 ± 104 L/treatment (Errors are one standard deviation from the mean). The volume per client was much lower as many clients did not have water-based spa treatments (e.g. massage, manicure). This usage is at the lower end of world wide water use in hotels which can range from approximately 90–3200 L/room/night, averaging approximately 250 to 1000 L/room/night (Table 19.4).

Operational water requirements

Operational water requirements include toilets flushing, cooking, staff showering, equipment washing and cleaning of buildings. The largest single use of water for operation water requirements is the laundering of towels and garments.

The volumes of water required to launder towels and garments used as part of the spa experience can also add considerably to the total volume of water used by spa facilities. For example, $22\% \pm 9\%$ of total water used for treatment and operation of the spa could be used in the laundry (Stevens and Smolenaars, 2007). The laundry can be washed on or off-site. In many instances an off-site laundering option can provide a cost effective water efficient solution as a result of increased focus on water and resource efficiency by large commercial laundries. Spas should consult their local suppliers and water

Table 19.4 Average water consumption for hotels worldwide, L/room or L/guest-night

Country (data for the year)	Average water use, L/room/day, unless specified otherwise
Philippines (2000)	1499
Jamaica (1999)	527–1595.7, average 981.9 L/ guest-night
Hong Kong (1996–1997)	336–3198, average 939.2
Zanzibar (2000)	200–2000, average 930.9 L/guest-night
Thailand (1990s)	913–3424
USA (2000)	382–787, average 583
	Forecast for 2010: 1798
Australia (1993)	750
Spain (2000)	440–880 L/guest-night
Sweden Sanga Saby Course & Conference Centre (2002)	314 L/guest-night
Germany (1990s)	90–900, average 342 L/guest-night

Source: Bohdanowicz and Martinac, 2007.

authorities for advice, as water efficiency and costs may vary significantly depending on the supplier.

All staff should be made aware that laundering is one of the spa's biggest use of water and towels should be used wisely, but without compromising the spa experience.

Landscape and aesthetic water considerations

Water requirements for landscapes will vary considerably relative to the plants grown, local climate and area irrigated. A simple definition of irrigation requirements is that the irrigation requirement is equal to the difference between the plant water requirement and the depth of rainfall at a location. While rainfall can be measured using standard meteorological equipment, the plant water requirement is more complex, but ultimately linked to evaporation. For plant requirements to be met, additional water is also required to overcome inefficiencies in irrigation methods and provide leaching requirements for removal of salts from the root zone.

More detailed information should be sourced from a horticulturalist familiar with the local area.

Water sources, treatment and management

Sources of water for use in spa facilities

Water can be supplied from a variety of sources. These include:

- *Mains water* – from the tap and usually of potable or drinking water quality
- *Ground water* – from an aquifer or bore, springs and thermal springs
- *Rainwater* – usually stored in a tank and captured from roof structures
- *Surface water* – i.e. lakes, rivers, streams, dams and reservoirs
- *Stormwater* – water captured from man made structures, like roads and other hard surfaces at ground level in the urban environment
- *Seawater* – water collected directly from the sea
- *Recycled water* – any of the above sources which have previously been used for other purposes, then treated to be suitable for another use.

Recent observations by Stevens and Smolenaars (2007) indicate that the source of water used in spa facilities influences water use. In Victoria, Australia, spas experiencing water restrictions, or that have limited water supply, tended to use less water per treatment than spas with unlimited water supply (e.g. sea water, plentiful groundwater or located in high rainfall areas). Spa facilities where water resources are plentiful often have signature types of treatments based on these water sources.

Mains water, ground water, rain water, surface water, storm water and seawater are more traditional sources of water where, in many cases, little water treatment is required to make the water fit for use in the spa. For water from these sources, the water quality can be improved considerably by managing the resource at the catchment scale. In contrast, for recycled water, the level of treatment required is usually higher relative to other sources and ultimately determines the quality of the water – hazards entering the wastewater can be managed to some degree. Recycled water is discussed in more detail below as it offers specific opportunities for spas, which create significant volumes of wastewater, to use water efficiently by recycling water in the landscape or in operational aspects of the spa facility.

Recycled water

Reclamation and reuse of water going to waste (recycled water) is becoming a solution to water shortages in many countries around the world (Bixio et al., 2006, Asano et al., 2007). Recycled water is generally used and is publicly accepted for non-drinking purposes, e.g. watering landscapes (Asano et al., 2007). However, some countries do use water recycled indirectly for supplementing drinking water resources, e.g. reservoirs (Radcliffe, 2004). The costs and extensive risk management program associated with treating wastewater to a level where it is fit for drinking usually prevents individual operators from undertaking potable reuse options.

Recycling of water for use in the spa treatment process would also need to overcome the 'yuck factor' often referred to in terms of drinking recycled water. Research across the world has highlighted the fact that the closer recycled water comes to direct exposure to the individual the more apprehensive they become with respect to the proposed use of the recycled water (Asano et al., 2007; Marks et al., 2006, p. 30). Spa treatment use of recycled water would be considered similar to swimming in, or drinking recycled water, and therefore have limited acceptance in most communities for spa treatment use.

However, there are many cost effective alternatives for using spa treatment wastewater for irrigation of landscapes or some operational uses such as toilet flushing. Wastewater from spas can be recycled from the greywater systems (non-fecal – shower, laundry, bath, kitchen (not usually recommended) and sinks) and/or the blackwater system (fecal contaminated water – toilet) (Figure 19.3). Greywater use from public facilities is often controlled differently to single residential houses (NRMMC, EPHC, 2006), so spas should check with their local authority (health and environment) to determine if this is a viable option.

Treatment to ensure appropriate source water quality

The quality of the water will primarily be influenced by its source (see Section 'Sources of water for use in spa facilities'). Mains water is usually fit for the purpose of drinking and will not required further treatment for use in a spa (always check and confirm this with the supplier). All other water sources should be tested and confirmed as suitable for use in a through an appropriate monitoring program, and if required treated. Without limited treatment, the human health risk is usually highest for recycled water (especially if sourced from sewage

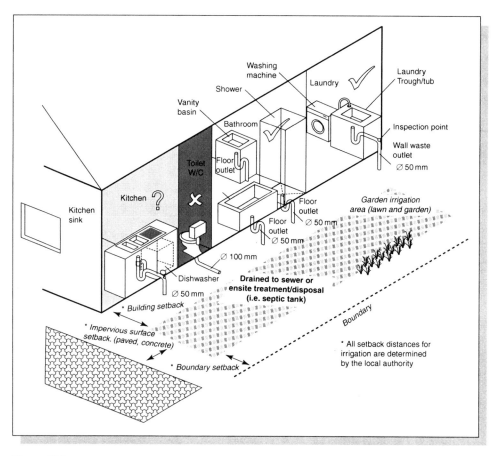

Figure 19.3
Wastewater sources found in spas that could be recycled as greywater for use in the landscape with limited treatment if subsurface irrigation is practiced

effluent) followed by stormwater, surface water, rainwater, groundwater and seawater (in order of highest to lowest risk; Table 19.5). However, this is dependent on the specific catchment or water body and the factors which impact on it.

There are many ways to treat water to ensure its microbiological, chemical and physical quality is suitable for the intended use. These methods can be a combination of chemical and/or mechanical means (Table 19.6).

It is technically possible to treat any water to a level that would be safe for use in a spa treatment. However, the greater the treatment required the greater the cost of producing the recycled water (Table 19.6). Any water source used should be checked for its pathogen load and the appropriate authority

Table 19.5 Estimates of risk levels associated with different water sources for human health and the environment

	Estimate of risk level	
Water source	Human health	Environment
Mains water (Reticulated for drinking purposes)	Low	Low
Rainwater (roof collection)	Moderate	Low
Ground water (springs, aquifers)	Moderate	Moderate
Surface water (lakes, rivers)	Moderate	Moderate
Storm water (Urban catchments)	High	Moderate
Sea water	Low	High
Recycled water (limited treatment)	Very high	Moderate to very high
Recycled water (extensive treatment)	Low	Low

Estimates of risk have been determined for landscape irrigation and toilet flushing under conditions in Australia using Standards Australia, 2004b.

Table 19.6 Ranking of technical complexity and cost of water

Ranking[1]	Examples of treatment processes
1	Simple chlorination Plain filtration (rapid sand, slow sand)
2	Pre-chlorination plus filtration Aeration
3	Chemical coagulationProcess optimisation for control of DBPs
4	Granular activated carbon (GAC) treatment Ion exchange
5	Ozonation
6	Advanced oxidation processes Membrane treatment

Source: WHO, 2006a.
[1]Lowest complexity and cost = 1.

guidelines should be consulted to determine if it is suitable for use in the spa treatment, operation and/or landscape. Many countries or states/regions have guidelines that should be checked (e.g. www.recycledwater.com.au).

Spa hygiene: Maintaining water quality in the spa

Where any communal water-based treatments or facilities are used in the spa operation, human health risks are much greater than single-use treatments. For single-use systems equipment should be washed and sterilised appropriately between clients. Equipment should be maintained as per hygiene standards provided. For communal-use facilities (i.e. spa pools and swimming pools), control measures must focus on the management of the water quality within that system and on regular maintenance of the system as defined by local health requirements and by the manufacturers of the equipment.

Successful implementation of measures to control hazards and minimise risk to human health must be multifaceted and address spa equipment design, operator and inspector training, maintenance, hygiene (staff, client, equipment and premises), as well as public awareness.

Those responsible for manufacturing or supplying spa baths and treatment systems (HSE 2007 (accessed)), should:

- ensure these are designed and constructed so that they are safe to use;
- give the user adequate information about the risks of the product and, importantly, keep them updated if any of the information changes.

Those responsible for managing spa baths and treatment systems need to identify and assess any potential sources of Legionella (and any other pathogens), and consider who and how these people could be exposed; in other words conduct a risk assessment which involves:

- preparing a plan to prevent or control any risks that have been identified
- implementing, manage and monitor the control measures that are put in place
- keeping records of this work
- appointing someone to manage this responsibility
- training staff to correctly operate the spa bath or treatment system – giving them appropriate information about the risks and the plan to manage these.

Most countries have health and safety laws and guidelines for spa equipment (or similar products) and associated guideline or information sheets. For example, the Health and Safety

Executive in the United Kingdom (UK) has produced an information sheet providing guidance for people who supply spa baths or manage premises where they are used. It includes the responsibilities under health and safety law to manage risks associated with use of their equipment and the spread of Legionella bacteria (http://www.hse.gov.uk/pubns/spalegion.pdf).

Single-use systems

For smaller hydrotherapy treatments where water is run directly to waste and renewed with fresh water for each client, recommendations for maintaining hydrotherapy equipment (MMWR, 2003) are:

- Drain and clean hydrotherapy equipment after each client's use
- Disinfect equipment surfaces and components by using an approved product in accordance with the manufacturer's instructions.

Pedicure Spas are discussed below as an example of single use smaller hydrotheraphy equipment.

Outbreaks of skin infections on the legs and feet of patrons following spa pedicures have caused concern about spa safety in the USA (www.epa.gov/pesticides/factsheets/pedicure.htm). Surveys have indicated that potentially pathogenic mycobacteria are widespread in many foot spas across California (Vugia et al., 2005) and probably throughout the world. The bacterium can cause prolonged boils on the lower legs that leave scars when healed. Mycobacterium species are ubiquitous in the environment and are found worldwide (Lumb et al., 2004) and are commonly associated with lung disorder (Lumb et al., 2004). These infections can sometime increase in severity over time, and potentially result in pus and scarring (US EPA, CDC, 2006). Some incidents of foot spa infections have been caused by *Mycobacterium fortuitum* and several other organisms. Many which occur naturally in water and soil. The screens and tubes of foot spas are where bacteria collect and grow often form dense layers of cells and proteins (biofilms) which can be very difficult to remove.

Consequently the US Environmental Protection Agency (EPA) and the Centers for Disease Control and Prevention

(CDC) have provided guidance for foot spa owners, operators and workers. This includes:

- Microorganisms in foot spas can enter through the skin; so broken skin (e.g. cuts and abrasions) should not come into contact with foot spa water.
- Clients should not shave, use hair removal creams, or wax their legs during the 24 hours before receiving treatment in a foot spa.
- Clients should not use a foot spa if their skin has any open wounds such as bug bites, bruises, scratches, cuts, scabs, poison ivy, etc.

A foot spa should be disinfected between each customer, and nightly. The disinfectant needs to work for the full time listed on its label, typically 10 minutes, depending on the type of disinfectant. Proper cleaning and disinfection can greatly reduce the risk of getting an infection by reducing the bacteria that can build up in the foot spa system.

The information provided above is discussed in general terms of best management practice. However, spa operators should always seek advice from their relevant human health department or water authority.

Communal-use systems

Spa pools have been associated in *legionellosis* outbreaks across Europe. Health authorities around the world have produced guidelines for the maintenance and design of spa/whirlpools in order to reduce the risk of these types of incidents (e.g. HSE 2007). This type of guideline would be appropriate for maintenance and use of all water treatment systems in spas where the water is not changed between clients (communal-use compared with single-use).

Spa baths are also known as spa pools, whirlpool spas, hot tubs, hot spas, portable spas and Jacuzzi (a brand name). Public awareness about the proper maintenance of private (residential) spa pools or similar spa treatment equipment must be promoted by health departments in partnership with spa treatment equipment manufacturers (Lumb et al., 2004).

A typical maintenance program for maintaining public or communal-use spa (Table 19.7) indicates the diligence required to maintain water quality fit for the purpose of use in the spa industry. The relevant local health department (or its equivalent)

Table 19.7 Example of a monitoring/maintenance program for a spa bath

Interval	Check
Every 2 hours	Residual disinfectant levels and pH – after the initial test
Three times a day	Water treatment, if not continual or water is renewed for each client
Weekly	Drain, clean and disinfect whole system and clean strainers (if not done in shorter time frame)
Monthly	Bacteriological test, clean input air filter, clean pipes, and all automatic systems.
Every 3 months	Filters (thoroughly), replace if required.
Annually	Written procedures are up-to-date, sand filter effectiveness.

should always be consulted to ensure the spa is complying with requirements in its country or region.

In the absence of an EPA-registered product for water treatment, sodium hypochlorite should be added to the water (MMWR, 2003):

- Maintain a 15 mg/L chlorine residual in the water of small hydrotherapy tanks.
- Maintain a 2–5 mg/L chlorine residual in the water of whirlpools and whirlpool spas.
- If the pH of the municipal water is in the basic range (e.g. when chloramine is used as the primary drinking water disinfectant in the community), consult the facility engineer regarding the possible need to adjust the pH of the water to a more acidic level before disinfection, to enhance the biocidal activity of the chlorine.
- Conduct a risk assessment of clients before their use of hydrotherapy equipment, potentially deferring patients with open cuts or who are immuno-compromised until their condition resolves.
- For large hydrotherapy pools, use pH and chlorine residual levels appropriate for an indoor pool as provided by local and state health agencies.

Commonly accepted good hygiene practice for clients entering communal-use water facilities should also be encouraged. For example, clients should shower before entering communal-use pools and spas, and hands should be washed after using the toilet or changing diapers.

Managing wastewater – disposal or recycle?

The water used in a spa facility ultimately enters the drainage or sewer systems utilised by the business. Where sewerage systems are available the treatment of wastewater is usually undertaken by a water treatment authority/company where the treated water is returned to the water cycle via disposal into water bodies (marine or freshwater) or through recycling.

Recycling can also be undertaken on-site at the spa facility by utilising on-site treatment systems which may tap into the spa's drainage system before it enters the public sewer. Wastewater can be treated through a variety of systems publicly available for treating greywater, black water or a combination of both (see Section 'Sources of water for use in spa facilities') to treat the wastewater (e.g. reed beds, sand filtration, engineered aerobic/anaerobic systems with disinfection).

If water is recycled at the spa, relevant guidelines to protect human health and the environment will need to be followed. This should be checked with local authorities.

Human health requirements

Guidelines that ensure risks posed to human health are low (acceptable) when recycling water usually focus on lowering the pathogens levels (hazard removal by treatment) and minimising human exposure to the recycled water (end use restrictions).

Pathogens found in recycled water that require treatment fall into four major categories:

1. Bacteria
2. Virus
3. Protozoa (single celled microbes)
4. Helminths (parasitic worms).

Installation and operation of systems to recycled water should be undertaken with expert advice and appropriate approvals obtained. Background information and guidelines (EPA US, 2004; NRMMC, EPHC, 2006) can be sourced from www.recycledwater.com.au.

Environmental requirements

Key environmental hazards (NRMMC, EPHC, 2006; WHO, 2006b;) found in wastewater include:

- Boron
- Cadmium

- Fats and oils
- Nitrogen
- pH
- Phosphorus
- Salts
- Sodium and chloride
- Suspended solids.

The most effective way to manage the hazards listed above is to minimise their addition to the wastewater if it is to be recycled. However, it is often difficult to determine the concentration in many domestic products (i.e. detergents) used for operation of the spa or for spa treatment product. For some hazards (e.g. sodium and phosphorus) in detergents, information is available from independent research (e.g. www.lanfaxlabs.com.au/greywater.htm) and some products do indicate they are environmentally friendly. However, to-date there is no comprehensive standard to assess the environmental friendliness of products.

There seems to be limited information on spa products regarding the hazards they may contain and their impact on the environment if wastewater is recycled for irrigation of the surrounding landscape. Consequently, treatment may need to be relied on to ensure recycled water is fit for operational and landscape uses in the spa.

The type of spa can also influence the wastewater quality. For example, natural bathing spas, which included hot springs, natural springs, natural mud and sea water will impact significantly on the quality of wastewater produced in spas. It could be high in salinity. Sea water total dissolved salts (TDS) is approximately 40 000 mg/L, where most drinking water usually has TDS less than 300 mg/L.

To ensure these risks are managed and the recycled water is fit for the intended purpose, relevant authorities and guidelines should be checked and complied with if any recycling is to be undertaken.

Developing and operating a water efficient spa

Operational considerations

A number of considerations should be made when considering the operation of a water efficient spa facility. A key consideration is finding the right balance between customer experience and best practice water efficiency. As shown previously (Figure 19.2) there is a great variation in water used by different spa facilities for water treatments; illustrating that similar treatments can be given with greater water efficiencies if required. This said, the treatment quality and customer experience should not be compromised. Some operational aspects to consider include:

- Laundering – Spas should evaluate whether laundry volumes could potentially be lowered by reducing the number of garments and towels used or types of towel (size and weight of wash load influences the water requirements to wash). In many spa facilities towels are used for soaking up water and then discarded. One example of improving water efficiencies is the discrete use of mops on floors, helping to minimise laundry loads (water use), while having negligible impact on the spa experience. Other areas for consideration include: full wash loads versus partial loads, selection of environmentally friendly detergents (see Section 'Environmental requirements') to minimise impact on greywater. Consider the option of external laundering. Laundries that recycle their water or that minimise water use per weight of laundry should also be considered.
- Client & staff education can be used to promote your endeavours to achieve water efficiency and ask for their support. For example, clients can be invited to minimise towel usage (as seen in many hotels), advised on water volumes utilised per treatment to enable clients to select treatments they are comfortable with. Input should be sought from spa staff for other suggestions on water efficiency options.
- Use of geothermal water for hydronic heating systems may be possible.
- Loss of water in water features through mist and evaporation should be minimised.
- Evaporation of water from pools should be minimised by covering them when not in use.

Equipment choices

Equipment, fixtures and fittings selected should be of a high quality for the purpose intended and have the best possible water efficiencies. The Water Efficiency Labelling and Standards (WELS) system utilised in Australia (www.waterrating.gov.au/) offers some guidance on water efficiency through its star rating and water consumption in litres per minute. Alternatively, product efficiencies can be compared to find the best product for the spa's requirements.

For showers (client and staff), the most sensitive variable that contributes to water use is the length (time) of the shower, rather than the flow rate of the shower head (Stevens and Smolenaars 2007). However, if the length of a shower is restricted this could impact significantly on the spa experience. Therefore shower heads that still maximise the spa experience, but minimise water use, offer the best solution for conserving water.

There are a number of shower heads on the market which claim low water usage with good perceived water flow/pressure through oxygenation of the water in the shower head. Another innovative approach is a reticulating shower, where the initial wash water might go to the drain and then the water within the shower re-circulated saving on water and energy required to heat the water (e.g. www.quenchshowers.com/shower/overview.asp).

Most spa facilities should already have low volume toilet flush systems. If not, they should be installed. Waterless toilets may also be an option in some areas. Other considerations include fixing of all leaks (no matter how minor), utilisation of high pressure hoses for cleaning and low water usage cleaning systems for pumps and reticulation systems.

Product choices

The range of products available for treatments in spas is enormous. These products should be chosen wisely from a treatment perspective and a disposal perspective (full life cycle). What goes into a spa's wastewater will ultimately require treatment (on or off-site) before re-entering the environment.

Natural/organic products may be good for the client/treatment, but may not be as good for the environment. Many products used in the spa facility have been concentrated to much higher levels than those found in the environment and when they end up in wastewater that is recycled the environment may be exposed to much higher concentrations than normal. Some key things to consider when evaluating product choices include:

- What are the concentrations of key environmental hazards?
- Are they degradable during wastewater treatment processes?
- Should salts, mud & clay, organic materials (i.e. herbs and petals) food products (i.e. fruit, milk) be excluded from the wastewater system?

339

Treatment selection

As discussed above in Section 'Water volumes' the type of spa treatment offered by the spa facility will influence the water usage per treatment. Some spa treatments rely on ample quantities of water to give the client the ultimate in spa experiences. Changing the delivery of a treatment can often provide a more fulfilling spa experience while at the same time reducing water consumption. For example when providing a Vichy shower experience, a systematic rotating of the shower heads over the body rather than all shower heads on full pressure for the duration of the treatment may provide a more pleasurable experience. Practitioners should ensure that the Vichy shower is turned of when not in use rather than simply being pushed aside while still running.

Spa facilities can also review treatment menus with a view to including a variety of experiences that utilise minimal, or at least less, water.

Summary

The spa industry is dependent on water for its survival. The water source must be suitable for use in the spa facility from a human health (drinking water) and environmental perspective. If not, treatment will be required to ensure risks to human health and the environment are controlled to acceptable standards. Any water source can be treated to be fit for the purposes required in the spa industry, however, the more treatment required the greater the cost. Regulations and guidelines across the world vary considerably for the quality of water entering spas, maintaining water quality and hygiene standards in the spa, and for disposal or recycling of the wastewater. Local and national requirements for each spa should always be checked with the appropriate government departments. Good practice is to use an accepted risk management system to proactively minimise any risk to human health or the environment.

In the current climate of limited water supplies in many countries, as populations grow and climates change, the spa industry should be proactive in acting on and presenting an image of responsible and sustainable use of water. While undertaking this, any changes implemented to improve water efficiencies should not compromise the treatment or the spa experience. Several opportunities for achieving this have been identified in this chapter, ranging from treatment/equipment selection to recycling of wastewater for operational and landscape aspects of the spa operation.

Acknowledgements

Jodie Hannaford, Junglefish Pty Ltd – research assistance and proofing.

Board of Directors of the Australasian Spa Association Ltd for their guidance and direction in initiating a Victorian Spa Water Audit funded by the Smart Water and prepared by Arris Pty Ltd.

References

Asano, T., Burton, F.L., Laeverenz, H.L., Tsuchihashi, R., Tchobanoglous, G. (2007) *Water Reuse. Issues, Technologies and Applications. Metcalf and Eddy*, McGraw Hill, New York, USA.

Bixio, D., Thoeye, C., De Koning, J., Joksimovic, D., Savic, D., Wintgens, T., Melin, T. (2006) Wastewater reuse in Europe, *Desalination*, 187:89–101.

Bohdanowicz, P., Martinac, I. (2007) Determinants and benchmarking of resource consumption in hotels – Case study of Hilton International and Scandic in Europe, *Energy and Building*, 39:82–95.

Broadbent, C. (1996) Guidance on water quality for heated spas. In: NEHFMWSN 2 (Ed.). National Environmental Health Forum, Adelaide, Australia.

CRC Water Quality and Treatment (2002) Blue-green Algae. There significances and management in water supplies. CRC Water Quality and Treatment, Occasional Paper 4, Adelaide.

CSIRO (2007) Climate Change in Australia – Technical Report 2007. *Commonwealth Scientific Industrial Research Organisation*, Canberra.

Dziuban E.J., Liang J.L. et al. (2006) Surveillance for Waterborne Disease and Outbreaks Associated with Recreational Water – United States, 2003–2004. *Morbidity and Mortality Weekly Report, Centers for Disease Control and Prevention, Department of Health and Human Services, USA Government*, Atlanta, GA, USA.

EPA US (2004) 'Guidelines for Water Reuse. *Environmental Protection Agency, Municipal Support Division Office of Wastewater Management Office of Water Washington, DC. Agency for International Development* Washington, DC, EPA/625/R-04/108, Cincinnati, OH U.S.EPA/625/R-04/108.

HSE (2007 (accessed on 17/12/2007)) 'Legionnaires' Disease: Controlling the risks associated with using spa baths. Health and Safety Executive, UK Government.

Lumb, R., Stapledon, R., Scroop, A., Bond, P., Cunliffe, D., Goodwin, A., Doyle, R., Bastian, I. (2004) Investigation of spa pools associated with lung disorders caused by *Mycobacterium avium* complex in immunocompetent adults, *Applied and Environmental Microbiology*, 70:4906–4910.

Marks, J., Martin, B., Zadoroznyj, M. (2006) Acceptance of water recycling in Australia: National baseline data, *Water*, 33:151–157.

MMWR (2003) Guidelines for Environmental Infection Control in Health-Care Facilities. Recommendations of CDC and the Healthcare Infection Control Practices Advisory Committee (HICPAC). *Morbidity and Mortality Weekly Report, Centers for Disease Control and Prevention, Department of Health and Human Services, USA Government*, 52. (No. RR-10), Atlanta, GA, USA.

NHMRC, NRMMC (2004) Australian Drinking Water Guidelines. National water Quality Management Strategy. *National Health and Medical Research Council. Natural Resource Management Ministerial Council*, Canberra.

NHMRC (2006) Guidelines for Managing Risks in Recreational Water. *National Health and Medical Research Council, Australian Government*, Canberra, ACT, Australia.

NRMMC, EPHC (2006) Australian Guidelines for Water Recycling. Managing Health and Environmental Risks. Phase 1. National Water Quality Management Strategy 21. *Natural Resource Management Ministerial Council. Environment Protection and Heritage Council Australian Health Ministers' Conference*, Canberra, Australia.

Radcliffe, J. (2004) *Water Recycling in Australia*, Australian Academy of Technological Sciences and Engineering, Parkville, Victoria: Melbourne, Australia.

Standards Australia (2004a) Australian/New Zealand Standard. AS/NZS 4360:2004. Risk Management. *Standards Australia and Standards New Zealand, AS/NZS 4360:2004*, Sydney and Wellington.

Standards Australia (2004b) Risk Management Guidelines. Companion to AS/NZS 4360:2004. *Standards Australia and Standards New Zealand*, Sydney and Wellington.

Stevens, D.P., Smolenaars, S.P. (2007) *ASPA Water Wise Project. Physical Audits*, Australian Spa Association, Carlton South, Victoria, Australia.

UN GIWA (2006) Challenges to International Waters. Regional Assessments in a Global Perspective. *United Nations Global International Waters Assessment.*

US EPA, CDC (2006) *Preventing Pedicure Foot Spa Infections.*, Environmental Protection Agency, Washington, DC, USA.

Vugia, D.J., Jang, Y., Zizek, C., Ely, J., Winthrop, K.L., Desmond, E. (2005) Mycobacteria in nail salon whirlpool foot-baths, California, *Emerging Infectious Diseases*, 11.

WHO (2006a) *Guidelines for drinking-water quality [electronic resource]: incorporating first addendum. Vol. 1, Recommendations,* 3rd ed., World Health Organization, Geneva, Switzerland.

WHO (2006b) *Guidelines for the Safe Use of Wastewater, Excreta and Greywater,* World Health Organization, Geneva, Switzerland.

Internet links

www.recycledwater.com.au.

www.who.int/water_sanitation_health/wastewater/gsuww/en/index.html.

www.lanfaxlabs.com.au/greywater.htm.

www.cdc.gov/healthyswimming/hydrotherapy.htm.

www.cdc.gov/ncidod/dhqp/dpac_footspa.html.

www.worldwidestandards.com/.

Spas and sustainability

Marc Cohen and Sonu Shivdasani

Spas and sustainability

Sustainability has become the buzzword of the new millennium. As the graphs that define humanity in terms of population, energy consumption, environmental degradation and pollution continue to increase, seemingly unabated, there is a growing realisation that within the next century humanity will have to radically change the way it operates and embrace sustainable practices or suffer significant environmental degradation and economic loss.

The issue of sustainability has ecological, social, economic and cultural dimensions and therefore impacts on all human activity. Yet despite the growing awareness that we must constrain our activities to the limitations and regenerative capacities of our planet's finite resources, there is also an increasing expectation amongst the world's growing population of material wealth, well-being and quality of life.

In a compelling essay titled 'The World in Context: Beyond the Business Case for Sustainable Development', Jonathon Porritt, Co-Director of HRH The Prince of Wales Business & the Environment Programme (BEP), Co-Founder and Programme Director of Forum for the Future and Chairman of the UK Sustainable Development Commission, outlines the sustainability issues facing humanity and expresses the concern that: 'Many environmentally destructive activities and products seem to remain deeply attractive to the majority of consumers. At the glamorous end of 'conspicuous consumption', which does so much to fuel mass consumer aspirations, environmentally friendly technologies are not going to find it easy to deliver the ever-expanding choices involving speed, fashion, change, variety and luxury which the globalised affluent middle classes increasingly expect' (Porritt, 2004, p7).

The spa industry certainly encompasses 'conspicuous consumption'. Attending spas is an aspiration and while in the past frequenting spas has been the privilege of the wealthy, mobile, educated consumer, spas are now becoming increasingly accessible to a global market. Yet, as spas begin to embrace personal wellness, which cannot be separated from the wellness of the planet (see Chapter 1), they take on a responsibility to demonstrate how environmentally friendly technologies can be used to deliver the experience of well-being in a sustainable manner.

Spas have the potential to make sustainability an aspiration and significantly advance the global sustainability agenda. However, while recent moves towards defining 'barefoot luxury' appear to be one step along this track, the great challenge for the global spa industry will be to embrace sustainability, yet still deliver on its promise of delivering the almost universal aspirations of luxury and wellness.

What is sustainability?

Sustainability refers to a process that can be maintained indefinitely. Within the business context, sustainability is also linked to progress and sustainable development which the World Commission on Environment and Development defines as; 'forms of progress that meet the needs of the present without compromising the ability of future generations to meet their needs' (Brundtland Commission, 1987). Yet another definition put forward by the Forum for the Future suggests that sustainable development is: 'A dynamic process which enables all people to realise their potential to improve their quality of life in ways which simultaneously protect and enhance the Earth's life support systems' (www.forumforthefuture.org.uk).

Sustainability embraces all aspects of environmental, social, economic and cultural activity and includes the concept of Corporate Social Responsibility (CSR) (see CSR chapter), however CSR and sustainability can be vague terms and as Porritt points out, the terminology may not be helpful as: 'Only rarely are issues of sustainable development properly connected back to the much harder-edged science of sustainability (based on the laws of thermodynamics, evolutionary biology and systems thinking)' (Porritt, 2004, p13).

Over the past two decades there has been much thought and effort applied to defining metrics for how sustainability can be assessed and measured. Concepts such as; *'ecological rucksack'* which measures the sum of all materials needed for for manufacturing, marketing, buying and using a product; *'material intensity per service unit'* (MIPS) which refers to the total weight of materials moved to make a product or provide a service, and is used to calculate a *'materials flow analysis'* which is used to trace the flow of different materials such as toxic or recyclable substances through a region; (Yencken and Wilkinson, 2000) *'ecological footprint* which estimates the area required to support a person in terms of their food, energy and space requirements along with the surface needed to absorb their waste (the earth's ecological carrying capacity is estimated to be 1.9 ha/person (Bond, 2002) whereas countries such as the US and Australia have a footprint' greater than 4 times this (Yencken and Wilkinson, 2000); and *'lifecycle cost'*, which comprises all costs attributable to a product from conception, to those customers incur throughout the life of the product, including the costs of installation, operation, support, maintenance and disposal (Dunk, 2004).

In a project that engaged 60 academics and practitioners, the Forum for the Future (www.forumforthefuture.org.uk) developed a model for sustainability based on 'Five Capitals' that define human activity. These five capitals are: *natural capital*, which includes both renewable and non-renewable resources use to produce goods and services, sinks that absorb, neutralise and recycle wastes and processes such as climate; *human capital*, which consists of people's health, knowledge, skills and motivation; *social capital*, which concerns institutions that help maintain and develop human capital such as families, communities, businesses, trade unions, schools and voluntary organisations; *manufactured capital*, which comprises material goods or fixed assets which contribute to the production process rather than being the output itself – for example, tools, machines and buildings; and *financial capital*, which enables the other types of Capital to be owned and traded.

This model which is elaborated on in Jonathon Porritt's book 'Capitalism as if the World Mattered', suggests that we are facing a sustainability crisis because we're consuming our stocks of natural, human and social capital faster than they are being produced. Thus, sustainability can be achieved by maintaining and trying to increase stocks of these capital assets, thereby allowing us to live off the income without reducing the capital itself. This model also recognises that ultimately we are dependent on the environment, as manufactured and financial capital are essentially products of, and dependent on, human and social capital, which in turn are products of and dependent on natural capital (Porritt, 2005).

The greatest threat to sustainable development world wide is climate change. Former Chief World Bank Economist Sir Nicholas Stern commissioned to deliver the UK report on the economics of climate change suggests that climate change is currently costing 1% of GDP and if business continues as usual, the economic impact would be between 15% and 20% of the GDP. This is predicted to disrupt economic and social activity on a similar scale to that of the great wars and the economic depression of the first half of the 20th century combined, and be difficult or impossible to reverse (Stern, 2006).

Recognising the importance of the environment as the basis for sustainable human development, Australians Bill Mollison and David Holmgren coined the term 'permaculture' in the 1970s to embrace the ideals of permanent culture and permanent agriculture. Permaculture, which recognises that without permanent agriculture there is no possibility of a stable social order, is defined as; 'the conscious design and maintenance of agriculturally productive ecosystems which have the diversity, stability and resilience of natural ecosystems. It is the harmonious integration of landscape and people providing their food, energy, shelter and other material and non-material needs in a sustainable way' (www.permaculture.org).

While originating as an agro–ecological design theory, permaculture has developed an international following and has become both a design system as well as a loosely defined philosophy or lifestyle ethic. While permaculture philosophy has not yet been seriously embraced by the corporate sector, the momentum towards a sustainability agenda for the corporate world is mounting as the business case for sustainable practices is articulated and expanded.

Why be sustainable?

The business case for sustainability was originally articulated by the World Business Council for Sustainable Development (www.wbcsd.org) based on eco-efficiency, risk management and stakeholder engagement; however, more recently the case has been extended to a range of tangible and intangible benefits as outlined in Table 20.1.

The benefits to businesses of embracing sustainability are indisputable and profound, yet it seems that the sustainability agenda is still in its infancy in the corporate world. In their preface to 'Facing the Future: Business, Society and the Sustainable Development Challenge' Courtice and Porritt point out that: 'It is difficult not to be perturbed at how relatively few companies are engaged strategically and systematically in the sustainable development agenda and how many are still testing the ground in a somewhat apprehensive way' (Courtice and Porritt, 2004, p8).

A similar sentiment could be applied to the global spa industry. However, initiatives such as the recent development of social and environmental benchmarks for spas by GreenGlobe (see Chapter 18), the recent establishment of the Green Spa Network (greenspanetwork.org) to provide environmental education for spa professionals and encourage best practice (Ullman, 2008) and recent attempts by some operators to embrace sustainable practices, suggest that the spa industry is poised to begin embracing sustainability principles.

It would seem, however; that in purporting to deliver 'wellness', the spa industry should be taking up a leadership role in

---

Table 20.1 The business benefits of sustainable development (from Porritt, 2004, p4)

Ecoefficiency
  1. Reduced costs
  2. Costs avoided (design for environment, eco-innovation)
  3. Optimal investment strategies

Quality management
  4. Better risk management
  5. Greater responsiveness in volatile markets
  6. Staff motivation/commitment
  7. Enhanced intellectual capital

Licence to operate
  8. Reduced cost of compliance/planning permits/licences
  9. Enhanced reputation with all key stakeholders
 10. Influence with regulator

Market advantage
 11. Stronger brands
 12. Customer preference loyalty
 13. Lower costs of capital
 14. New products/processes/services
 15. Attracting the right talent

Sustainable profits
 16. New business/increased market share
 17. Enhanced shareholder value

---

furthering a sustainability agenda rather than merely following other industry sectors. Currently though, spas are being led by the hospitality industry where there has been a growing interest in what is now termed 'eco-tourism' in response to increased consumer awareness of environmental issues. Travellers and guests now expect hotels, resorts and spas to have policies and practices that; promote sustainable waste management; reduce energy use; encourage sustainable purchasing; use local produce and products; minimise carbon emissions and provide support for local community projects.

While consumers have growing expectations for companies to embrace sustainability, they are also sceptical of 'greenwashing' whereby companies pay lip service to sustainability as a marketing ploy without truly embracing sustainable practices. It is apparent that such scepticism is warranted. A recent report on 'the Six Sins of Greenwashing' concluded that the overwhelming majority of environmental marketing claims in North America were found to be inaccurate, inappropriate or unsubstantiated. This report, which examined 1018 consumer products bearing 1753 environmental claims, found that all but one made claims that were either 'demonstrably false or that risk misleading intended audiences' (TerraChoice, 2007).

Sustainability in business

Since the 1992 Earth Summit, when many hundreds of companies signed up to the Business Charter for Sustainable Development, sustainable development has become a guiding principle for governments, businesses, Non Government Organisations (NGOs) and the public sector (International Chamber of Commerce Working Party for Sustainable Development, 1991[*]).

The Prince of Wales Business & the Environment Programme, which is considered one of the premier international forums for executive learning and leadership on sustainability, has commissioned a series of background briefings focusing on critical aspects of sustainable development from a business perspective. One of these titled; 'The State of the Planet and its People', (Hanks, 2003a) outlines the current status and recent trends regarding the planet's five main capital stocks, while the 'Reference Compendium on Business and Sustainability' highlights the extraordinary profusion of new initiatives, new thinking and new practice (Hanks, 2003b).

More recently a US report on; 'The State of Green Business 2008' (Makower, 2008), reviewed environmental initiatives in business and concluded that: 'the greening of business practices has reached a tipping point…The state of green business is improving, slowly but surely, as companies both large and small learn the value of integrating environmental thinking into their operations in ways that align with core business strategy and bottom-line goals. Green business has shifted from a movement to a market. But there is much, much more to do' (Makower, 2008, p3).

This report goes on to conclude; 'The quantity and quality of data on business and the environment is wanting, to say the least. Government agencies, non-profit groups, academic institutions and companies themselves have done relatively little

*The Reference Compendium provides executives with a ready reference source of the many tools and concepts associated with corporate sustainability, and reviews the growing number of international agreements on sustainability issues. For each element of the Briefing, a short definition and useful web reference is supplied at the end of this chapter.

to quantify, let alone assess, simple measures of business environmental impact' (Makower, 2008, p13).

Reporting on sustainability

The concept of reporting on the sustainability of businesses came to prominence in the 1990s with the idea of 'triple bottom line' (TBL) reporting. This phrase, which was first coined by John Elkington in 1994, has a definition that combines an accounting concept with a philosophy (Elkington, 1994).

'At its narrowest, the term 'TBL' is used as a framework for measuring and reporting corporate performance against economic, social and environmental parameters.' At its broadest, the term is used to capture the whole set of values, issues and processes that companies must address in order to minimise any harm resulting from their activities and to create economic, social and environmental value. This involves being clear about the company's purpose and taking into consideration the needs of all the company's stakeholders'(www.sustainability.com/downloads_public/news/TBL.pdf).

More recently there have been moves to extend the concept social, environmental and financial reporting to a 'quadruple bottom line' through the addition of governance as a fourth dimension (Woodward et al., 2005). While the principles of TBL reporting is gaining acceptance throughout the world, there are many problems in its implementation. There is a truism in business that says; 'if you don't measure you can't manage', and currently quantifying social and environmental bottom lines is relatively new, problematic and often subjective, making the management of sustainability challenging.

This challenge is the subject of the field of environmental and social 'impact assessment' which is a discipline that attempts to predict or estimate the consequences of any current or proposed action. Impact assessment aims to 'bring about a more sustainable and equitable biophysical and human environment' and the International Association for Impact Assessment (www.iaia.org) has articulated a set of core values and principles as well as a formal definition that provides an overarching academic framework, yet there is still little agreement on how to define and measure 'social issues' (Vanclay, 2004).

While as yet there is no firmly established accounting systems for sustainability issues, there are a number of new global initiatives that have recently been launched to facilitate corporate sustainability reporting. These initiatives aim to provide quality information to investors and shareholders, many of who are showing heightened interest in sustainability after a series of high pro-file corporate environmental and social scandals and corporate collapses.

The Global Reporting Initiative (GRI), which produces the world's de facto standard in sustainability reporting guide-lines, aims to make sustainability reporting by all organisa-tions as routine and comparable as financial reporting. The 'third generation guidelines' launched in 2006 provide univer-sal guidance for reporting on sustainability performance and include principles such as materiality, stakeholder inclusive-ness, comparability and timeliness and disclosure items, which include disclosures on management of issues as well as spe-cific performance indicators (www.globalreporting.org).

Another global initiative that aims to facilitate reporting on environmental impacts is the Carbon Disclosure Project (CDP). The CDP is an independent not-for-profit organisation that aims to create a lasting relationship between shareholders and corporations by seeking information on the business risks and opportunities presented by climate change and greenhouse gas emissions data from the world's largest companies: 3000 in 2008. The CDP has become the gold standard for carbon disclosure methodology and process and currently provides a service to institutional investors with a combined $57 trillion of assets under management (www.cdproject.net).

Perhaps the greatest push towards sustainability will come from the investment community which is beginning to come to terms with its responsibility for promoting responsible envi-ronmental stewardship and socially responsible development. This is demonstrated by the fact that nearly all big banks have now signed the Equator Principles, aimed at assessing and managing the environmental and social risks associated with project financing (www.equator-principles.com).

The power of the corporate community to drive a sustainability agenda is recognised by 'The Global 100' project (www.global100.org), which attempts to demonstrate the correlation between sus-tainability and financial performance and announces a list of 'The Global 100 Most Sustainable Corporations in the World' each year at the World Economic Forum in Davos. The 2008 list was dominated by the financial sector, although the hospitality indus-try was notably represented by Accor (Heaps et al., 2008).

As yet there are no spa companies listed on the Global 100 and it is uncertain how many spas (if any) currently provide transpar-ency on their social and environmental performance or report into the GRI or other initiatives such as the Corporate Responsibility Index (www.corporate-responsibility.com.au). As the spa indus-try matures and begins to attract institutional investors, and as sustainability reporting becomes more prevalent and robust, it is likely that the spa industry will begin to take such indices more seriously. A significant step in this direction has recently been taken with Green Globe in conjunction with Six Senses Resorts & Spas developing a social and environmental benchmarking and certification scheme for the spa industry (see Chapter 18).

Sustainability as a core purpose

While corporate sustainability reporting is likely to become a standard for corporations in the new millennium, it is widely acknowledged that sustainability must be integrated into all the ways companies interact with their various stakeholders. Thus to be effective and authentic, sustainability and CSR must be ingrained into the 'corporate psyche' and become part of the corporate business strategy. Sustainability cannot be simply 'bolted on' to previous ways of doing business.

Lord Michael Hastings currently the Global Head Corporate Citizenship KPMG and Former Head BBC's CSR who helped establish the CSR Academy in UK suggests that CSR needs to be part of the corporate business strategy stating: '...that's the key ... the business strategy. A contract between the corporation and civil society founded on principles of trust with integrity delivered through integrated business strategy – now that's a real CSR that will make a difference. Not just philanthropy; not just volunteering; not just compliance; not just good community activity; not even sustainable environmental practices at their best or human rights evident in employment and customer service. All of it – and more – as a central business strategy and not a bolt on benefit. Deny it at your peril. Embrace it to your benefit' (Hastings, 2006, p38).

Towards sustainable spas

One company that has attempted to make sustainability a central business strategy is Six Senses Resorts & Spas which has defined its core purpose: 'To create innovative and enriching experiences in a sustainable environment' (www.sixsenses.com). Six Senses focuses on destination and resort spas rather than urban day spas and has instigated a number of innovative approaches to sustainability that includes projects that are designed to showcase what is possible and serve as a model and an inspiration to guests and future spa developers.

Six Senses demonstration projects include Soneva Fushi's Zero Emission Project in the Maldives which aims to replace fossil fuels with renewable energy sources such as solar, wind and tidal power and reduce energy consumption through the use of efficient energy, cooling, lighting and water systems so that by 2010 it will use no fossil fuels and have zero carbon emissions. A Deep Sea Water Cooling System (DSWS) that makes use of 10°C water from 300 metres below the tropical surface waters will be used to provide air conditioning. The cold water will also be used to cool a greenhouse in order to grow herbs, vegetables and fruits.

Where diesel fuel is required, such as for the fleet of water craft and back up purposes, it will be supplied by bio-diesel produced from waste cooking oil and coconut meat (Gerpen, 2005). At a test run of a bio-diesel plant at the Evason Phuket & Six Senses Spa, Thailand, 380 litres of used cooking oil was turned into 300 litres of bio-diesel and it is expected that bio-diesel will be able to replace all of the resort's diesel consumption and therefore reduce its greenhouse gas emissions by 220 ton per year or 5% of total emissions.

Another demonstration project is Soneva Kiri in Thailand, where guest transportation around the site and the island will be provided by electrical vehicles powered by integrated solar panels (www.venturi.fr) as well as generated through wind and mini-hydroelectric turbines that run off waste-water flowing down hill from the hillside villas (www.microhydropower.net).

The Eco Suite project at Soneva Kiri in Thailand is another prototype zero emissions project that showcases of a range of environmental technologies incorporated into a bio-climatically designed structure. Buildings will be made from low embodied energy materials, including locally sourced building materials, that will demonstrate it is possible to provide the same levels of service and comfort as a five star luxury hotel room using sustainable technologies and modern building techniques combined with indigenous skills and knowledge.

As well as having zero emissions, the Eco Suite will also have a range of features that may enhance the guest experience such as natural lighting, passive cooling systems that allow fresh air ventilation, a rainwater harvesting system linked to the natural swimming pool which acts as both a rainwater storage system, a wildlife magnet and a swimming pool that does not require the use of chemicals (see Chapter 14), landscaping that utilizes a combination of endemic plants for aesthetics such as epiphytic ferns and edible plants such as banana, papaya and herbs grown for guest consumption as well as using non-toxic adhesives and wood treatments and little or no artificial electromagnetic radiation so as to be suitable for guests with allergies or sensitivities to electromagnetic fields.

Each Six Senses resort and spa will also place a focus on a holistic approach to nutrition, meditation, physical wellness activities and the use of natural products and organic locally sourced food with some organic herbs and vegetables grown onsite and used throughout the food and beverage menus. Spa treatment products will also be organic and biodegradable so as to be healthy for the body and the environment.

In addition to environmental initiatives, Six Senses has committed to a social sustainability agenda with 0.5% of total revenue and 100% of total guest laundry revenue donated to social and environmental projects. These include projects initiated by various partners such as Converging World which generates clean energy in developing countries and invests the profits back into renewable energy and community development (www.theconvergingworld.com) and Care for Children which places abandoned and orphaned children into foster families (www.careforchildren.com.cn). Furthermore, recognising that the local community plays a key role to the achievement of sustainable development, 40% of the contribution will typically be spent at the local level. Six Senses also supports the local community through a local employment policy as well as through a range of social and community activities that attempt to protect the local environment and enhance local social and cultural activities.

These projects not only aim to provide outstanding guest experiences and establish Six Senses in a leadership position with regard to spas and sustainability, they will also provide a first to market brand advantage along with all the tangible and intangible advantages associated with sustainability as outlined in Table 20.1.

In December 2006 Six Senses Spas began collaborating with Green Globe to develop indicators and sustainability benchmarks for the spa sector and has since committed to benchmark all of its spa operations using the Green Globe program. This program promises to enable the entire spa industry to develop benchmarks and establish best practice in social and environmental performance (see Chapter 18).

The sustainable future

While the above projects and initiatives currently represent the state of the art in sustainable luxury developments, the landscape is shifting rapidly and new developments and new technologies are continually being created. There is a vast array of innovative sustainable technologies available with new ones being developed on a daily basis. All commentators agree, however; there is still a long way to go and that sustainable development will remain by far the biggest challenge all the way through to the end of this century. As Porritt states; 'If

355

we get it right, the genius and technological virtuosity of the human species will enable us to fashion elegant, regenerative and genuinely sustainable ways of meeting human needs and aspirations. If we get it wrong, the consequences could indeed be dire' (Porritt, 2004).

The spa industry is only just emerging as a significant global industry and its business practices, products and services as well as its sustainability agenda is still evolving. However; the spa industry not only has a responsibility to embrace sustainable practices for their own sake, it also has an opportunity to apply human genius and technological virtuosity and demonstrate that sustainable technologies can not only save money and the environment, they can also facilitate luxurious experiences and sustainable well-being. Thus spas have the potential to not only deliver on the basic human need of wellness, they can also transform 'conspicuous consumption' from being a burden on the planet to being a sustainable aspiration.

Acknowledgement

Anne-Maree Huxley, CEO, Models of Success & Sustainability (www.moss.org.au) provided valuable assistance for this chapter by way of reference materials. Her generous contribution is greatly appreciated.

References

Bond, S. (2002) Ecological Footprints: A guide for local authorities, WWF-UK, Surrey, available at: http://www.gdrc.org/uem/footprints/wwf-ecologicalfootprints.pdf

Brundtland Commission, (1987) Report of the World Commission on Environment and Development: Our Common Future, Oxford University Press, available from; www.un-documents.net/wced-ocf.htm

Courtice, P., & Porritt, J. (2004) Facing the Future: Business, Society and the Sustainable Development Challenge. The University of Cambridge Programme for Industry, available at: www.cpi.cam.ac.uk/pdf/Facing%20the%20Future.pdf

Dunk, A.S. (2004) Product life cycle cost analysis: the impact of customer profiling, competitive advantage, and quality of IS information, *Management Accounting Research*, 15(4):401–414.

Elkington, J. (1994) Towards the sustainable corporation: Win-win-win business strategies for sustainable development, *California Management Review*, 36(2):90–100.

Gerpen, J.V. (2005) Biodiesel processing and production, *Fuel Processing Technology*, 86:1097–1107.

Hanks, J. (2003a) The State of the Planet and its People, Business & the Environment Programme University of Cambridge Programme for Industry http://www.cpi.cam.ac.uk/PDF/The%20State%20of%20the%20Planet.pdf

Hanks, J. (2003b) The Reference Compendium on Business and Sustainability, Business & the Environment Programme University of Cambridge Programme for Industry http://www.cpi.cam.ac.uk/programmes/sustainable_development/business__the_environment_pro/bep_network/reports_and_newsletters.aspx

Hastings, M. J. (2006) A New Social Contract for Sustainable Competitiveness – CSR and Smart Business In: Social Innovation in the 21st century: A Dialogue p 36–44, available at: http://www.macquarie.com.au/au/acrobat/social-innovation/researchpaper.pdf

Heaps, T., Shin, M., Wilkes, P., McCulloch, M. (2008) Corporate Knights Global 100 Most Sustainable Corporations Announced In: Davos Corporate Knights Media release Available at www.global100.org/PR_Global_2008.pdf

International Chamber of Commerce Working Party for Sustainable Development. (1991) Business Charter for Sustainable Development International Chamber of Commerce, available from: www.iccwbo.org/home/environment_and_energy/charter.asp

Makower, J. (2008) The State of Green Business, Greener World Media, available from: http://www.greenbiz.comwww.greenbiz.com

Porritt, J. (2005) *Capitalism As if the World Matters*, Earthscan.

Porritt, J. (2004) The World in Context: Beyond the Business Case for Sustainable Development, HRH the Prince of Wales Business & the Environment Programme, University of Cambridge Programme for Industry

Stern, N. (2006) *The Economics of Climate Change*, H. M. Treasury, London.

TerraChoice (2007) *The "Six Sins of Greenwashing" A Study of Environmental Claims in North American Consumer Markets*, TerraChoice Environmental Marketing Inc.

Ullman, R. (2008) The Green Spa-Part 1 Renew Professional. com Wellness, Posted On: 1/24/2008

Vanclay, F. (2004) Impact assessment and the triple bottom line: Competing pathways to sustainability?. In: Cheney, H., Katz, E., Solomon, F. (Eds), *Sustainability and Social Science Round Table Proceedings,,* The Institute for Sustainable Futures, Sydney & CSIRO Minerals, Melbourne.

Woodward, D.G., Woodward, T., Rovera Val, M.R. (2005) Towards Comprehensive Reporting: A Quadruple Bottom Line Approach, First International Conference on Environmental, Cultural, Economic & Social Sustainability, available at: http://s05.cgpublisher.com/proposals/150/index_html

Yencken, D., Wilkinson, D. (2000) *Resetting the Compass: Australia's journey towards sustainability,* CSIRO Publishing Collingwood.

Websites

www.permaculture.co.uk – general permaculture information

www.greywaterguerillas.com – greywater filtration and rain-water harvesting

www.gaiamovement.org – information on green technologies

www.treehugger.com – general environmental news and information

www.neco.com.au – specialized eco-products shop

www.gaiam.com – eco-products shop

www.usgbc.org – United States green building council (LEED certification)

www.quantumenergy.com.au.

www.uridan.com.

www.siamgpi.com – Siam Green Power International

www.greenglobe.org.

www.sixsenses.com.

www.careforchildren.com.cn – Care for Children

www.theconvergingworld.com – The Converging World

www.phuket-lions.com.

www.lifehomeproject.org.

Business and Sustainable Development
This site explains the strategies and tools that companies can draw on to translate an spiration of sustainability into practical, effective solutions. Case studies from around the world are provided as an example of each measure. http://www.bsdglobal.com

Business for Social Responsibility
Business for Social Responsibility is a non-profit global organisation that provides information, tools, training and advisory services to make CSR an integral part of business operations and strategies. ttp://www.bsr.org

Business in the Community
Business in the Community UK, is an independent business led charity whose purpose is to engage and support companies, to continually improve the impact they have on society. With a current membership of over 750 companies, Business in the Community members employ 12.4 million people in over 200 countries worldwide. http://www.bitc.org.uk

CSR Europe
CSR Europe is a non-profit organisation that promotes corporate social responsibility. It is a European business network of CSR professionals based upon the sharing of CSR solutions and shaping the modern day business and political agenda on sustainability and competitiveness. www.csreurope.org

Global Reporting Initiative
The Global Reporting Initiative is a multi-stakeholder process and independent institution whose mission is to develop and disseminate globally applicable sustainability Reporting Guidelines. www.globalreporting.org

Society and Business UK
The UK government's gateway to Corporate Social Responsibility. www.societyandbusiness.gov.uk/

World Business Council for Sustainable Development
The World Business Council for Sustainable Development brings together some 180 international companies in a shared commitment to sustainable development through economic growth, ecological balance and social progress. Members are drawn from more than 30 countries and 20 major industrial sectors. www.wbcsd.org

Society and Business UK
The UK government's gateway to Corporate Social Responsibility. www.societyandbusiness.gov.uk/

SustainAbility
Based in the UK, SustainAbility focuses on how the sustainable development (SD) agenda fits within business strategy in

environmental, social and economic terms-the 'triple bottom line'. www.sustainability.com

Models of Success & Sustainability
Models of Success & Sustainability (MOSS) is Australia's peak body for Corporate Sustainability. It supports business through education, training, networking and advice to drive sustainability and competitive business success. www.moss.org.au

Voluntary Carbon Standard
The Voluntary Carbon Standard provides a robust, new global standard for voluntary offset projects. It ensures that carbon offsets that businesses and consumers buy can be trusted and have real environmental benefits. www.v-c-standard.org

PART 5

People

Spas and the future leadership climate

Anna Bjurstam and Marc Cohen

Spas and the future leadership climate

Megatrends 2010

Vision-quest; meditation; forgiveness training; heart-math; they sound touchy-feely, but conscious business pioneers are exploring results that will have significant impact on managers of the future. In her book 'Megatrends 2010 – the rise of conscious capitalism', Patricia Aburdene tracks the rise of 'conscious business' and describes a spiritual revolution that is currently transforming business from a model focused on capitalism and economic rationalism, to a new and more profitable model founded on ethics, values, and spiritual awareness. (Aburdene, 2007)

We appear to be entering into a new era; soft values such as quality of life, happiness, and love are entering not only our private life but our work life and spas are becoming more popular as people seek to achieve these qualities through the spa experience. Spas have evolved with this trend and there is an increasing emphasis on making them spiritual places where guests can find peace within. In order for the spa staff to transmit this 'peace within', it is necessary for spa managers to have found this within themselves and to install this within their organization.

In a highly personal service industry, there is a great need for both spa managers and therapists to actively work on their own personal and emotional development. It is difficult for a therapist to give advice, provide empathy, or truly 'be' with a client and explore their emotional life unless they have undertaken a similar exploration within themselves. Similarly it is difficult for managers to provide a safe environment where therapists can get in touch with their feelings unless they are also in touch with themselves. This means that the days of 'management by fear' are over and the above core concepts will be the guiding rules on how to deal with staff in the future.

Spa spas and the experience economy

We are now moving from a service economy to a more personal experience economy As Pines and Gilmore state: 'When a person buys a service, he purchases a set of intangible activities carried out on his behalf. But when he buys an experience, he pays to spend time enjoying a series of memorable events that a company stages – as in a theatrical play – to engage him in a personal way' (Pines and Gilmore, 1999, p2).

The growing trend for spas to sell 'experiences' or 'journeys' rather than simply treatments or services places spas at the forefront of the experience economy. A spa's profitability is directly linked to its ability to consistently delight guests by providing enjoyable and transformative experiences. Such experiences build the spa's reputation and drive return business and word-of-mouth advertising. These experiences are created through every aspect of the spa's operation including the ambience, customer service, value added benefits, the quality of the treatments and attention to detail before and after the treatment.

The very personal nature of spa services means that the emotional and spiritual commitment of staff may be higher than in other businesses. Equally, the guest visiting the spa is also investing more of themselves in what they are buying, compared with products such as groceries or consumer goods. This can result in excellent outcomes with staff being extremely fulfilled and satisfied by their career choice and guests being delighted by the service and experience received. Conversely, the heightened personal investment from both guest and staff may result in conflicts and insecurity, where the spa employees take critique, challenges, and complaints personally and where guests may be left feeling vulnerable and violated by unsatisfactory experiences.

It is the people that inhabit and serve at the spa that creates the magic of the spa experience and the temperament and demeanour of the staff go a long way towards creating this. The more passionate, empathetic and knowledgeable the staff, the greater their ability to serve and anticipate guests' needs and thus the more satisfied and uplifted the guests will be. The leadership challenge for the future is therefore to lead an experience economy in spas, where the product is based on the employee.

Specific leadership challenges in the spa industry

Why leadership in spas differs from other corporate business

The emphasis on experience makes spas different from many other businesses. In most businesses there is a lead-time between the point of creation of the product such as a garment, food item, or a piece of furniture and when the actual product is consumed. Sitting on the chair, you don't feel the hands of the carpenter nor what he smells like. When you put on your new shirt, you do not see the designer in action or feel the seamstress while she sows your shirt together. In a spa however, there is no lead-time. The product is essentially a direct one-on-one experience with a therapist where the guest

365

is paying for the therapist's ability to translate their tactile skill into a personalized service.

The intensely personal and experiential nature of the spa business provides a great challenge to managers. In a restaurant, the executive chef manages people, but the end product experienced by the guest is the food. If the chef has a bad day, you most likely won't know it when enjoying the dish. In contrast, if a guest is massaged by a therapist that is in conflict with their boss and/or dislikes their job situation, then this **will** come through in the treatment. Therapists that are happy, caring, balanced and experienced are best able to create a valued experience for the client. When therapists are unhappy, stressed, or uncaring, the guest experience suffers. The guest then does not get value for money and doesn't return and the business also suffers.

While the skill and experience of the therapist ultimately comes down to staff recruitment and training, maintaining happy, caring and grounded therapists, and thus maintaining a spa's profitability, requires good management and leadership. Badly managed therapists will enter into a phase of frustration with their manager, job situation or conditions. When they enter this phase, conflict, resignation or termination of contract will occur resulting in reduced revenue for the spa. Alternately, a good day, great working climate and happy, motivated staff will result in a very profitable spa. Happy employees are also much better equipped to handle workplace relationships, stress, and change. Companies that understand this, and help employees improve their personal well-being, can also boost their productivity. (Gallup Management Journal, 2006)

The right spa manager

Most spas are small stand alone businesses with only a few large chains and industry leaders. If the rapid industry growth continues, however, it is assured that in future, spas will become big business. Currently, one of the main factors holding the industry back is a lack of leadership and management skills. With the rapid expansion in the spa industry, there is difficulty finding qualified staff in general and an enormous shortage of qualified and experienced spa managers in particular.

Spa managers must not only understand the fundamentals behind the spa experience, and the requirements for operating a highly personal service-oriented business, they must also understand the fundamentals of leadership and business management and possess the skills necessary to perform financial, marketing and human resource functions.

Thus, the ideal spa manager must be conversant with the principles behind the new experience economy such as emotional intelligence (Cherniss and Goleman, 2001) and spiritual intelligence (Buzan, 2001), as well as understanding human resource management and organizational dynamics including the stages of group development, the principles of motivation theory, conflict resolution, and Strengths, Weaknesses, Opportunities and Threat (SWOT) and Political, Economic, Social and Technological (PEST) analysis (Armstrong, 2006). In addition spa mangers are required to run a business and achieve a bottom line result. They therefore need to understand and apply the principles of market analysis, budgeting, Key Performance Indicators (KPIs), yield management and be able to communicate with owners, investors and directors in standard business language.

The perfect spa manager therefore has a combination of both management and therapist experience. Table 21.1 outlines the differences in these managerial backgrounds. Currently, the most effective spa managers come from either a therapist background and obtain a spa-related business education, or they come from a business background and obtain therapist experience through attending a massage course. However, spa managers with experience in both therapy and management are hard to find, and the ones that do have this experience are in high demand enabling them to enjoy escalating pay scales and accelerated career opportunities.

Despite the demand for spa managers with both therapist and business experience and the opportunities available to such people, there are serious challenges in training and developing qualified managers. When it comes to hotel and destination spas, the average length of contract for a spa manager is 2 years. However, it is not uncommon for the spa manager to leave early

Table 21.1 Managerial backgrounds and resulting differences

Therapist-based	Business-based
Understands the therapists	Understands money
Can speak with the staff in their language	Can speak with the GM and owners using their language
Can drive business from a quality perspective	Can drive business from KPI's and statistics

due to attractive job offers elsewhere. As a result, employers are reluctant to risk making investments in a spa manager's ongoing education, as they may not be the ones to reap a return.

When an employer is faced with the choice of hiring a therapy- or business-based manager, most prefer the person with therapist experience as people skills and an in-depth understanding about the services that spas offer are considered more important than business skills which can be picked up on the job. Hence, most spa managers currently come from a therapist background and progress from therapist to head therapist and then spa manager without ever having spa-related business education. However, while therapy-based managers can manage spas effectively, they often lack the business acumen necessary to achieve maximum financial performance. Consequently, the spa industry is growing in terms of number of spas, but is being held back by a lack of experienced leadership.

The increasing demand for qualified spa managers has led some education providers to offer specific spa management degrees, yet most of these are business degrees focusing on the health and wellness industry and lack practical experience in massage or therapy (Cornell University, Sandhills Community College, University Campus Varberg). Spas increasingly recognize, however, that massage brings in more than 50% of their revenue and that the person in charge should be fully educated and preferably experienced in this field. Despite this, most business graduates are hesitant to go back and acquire a massage diploma when they do not plan to work as a therapist.

To address this issue some spa chains are now starting to announce trainee programs for graduates with a spa management degree (for example Mandarin Oriental see Spa Business 01/08 www.spabusiness.com in order to provide the practical experience needed to be able to lead a spa to success. As at this writing, RMIT University in Australia has also announced a series of post-graduate programs including a Master of Wellness program offered through distance education that allows students to combine therapist training with management subjects which also provide credit towards a Masters in Business Administration (www.rmit.edu.au/health-sciences/wellness).

Spa specific leadership principles

Spirituality in the work place

'The cornerstone of effective leadership is self-mastery and that the surest route to self-mastery is spiritual practice. Time spent in peaceful reflection or mindful meditation clarifies thoughts, sharpens intuition, and curbs unhealthy instincts' (Aburdene, 2007, p.11).

Spirituality in the workplace goes hand-in-hand with inspirational leadership which includes having a clearly defined vision and mission, strong core values and ethics, and a sense of Corporate Social Responsibility (CSR). While these may appear to be lofty goals, there is a growing awareness amongst business leaders that fostering a sense of spirituality in the workplace has many benefits including greater productivity improved staff attraction, retention and motivation, increased job satisfaction, greater customer loyalty and greater profitability (Tipping, 2004).

While modern spas are physically designed so as to embrace and enhance spiritual qualities (See Chapter 16), spirituality in a spa or any other work place does not just happen. There needs to be specific strategies in place to support staff to find their own power within and these strategies need to be supported by appropriate systems and paperwork. These strategies may include:

1. instilling a *sense of purpose* and meaning in staff through clearly articulated core values and ethics that are embraced by all levels of management;
2. fostering a *sense of peace*, well-being and community throughout the business through daily mediations, regular movement classes, weekly treatment exchanges and other group activities;
3. *supporting staff welfare* through provision of appropriate infrastructure including back-of-house areas and spa equipment as well as supporting social networking and local community activities;
4. providing ongoing *education and development opportunities* to ensure staff continually upgrade their skill levels and experience as well as maintaining staff motivation and retention, through clearly defined job descriptions, career paths and incentive programs.

Sense of purpose

Every spa should have clearly identified core values and ethics that help to define its goals and strategies. (see Chapter 11) Subscribing to values that are aligned with a higher good can also serve to inspire and motivate staff and foster a sense of purpose amongst the spa team thereby assisting with recruitment and retention. In contrast, values that not adhered to consistently will erode staff morale and create an unstable work environment.

Core values should ideally be placed prominently on the wall in the staff room, prep room and in weekly newsletters, etc. These core values are not merely words on a piece of paper however; they help to define the business and allow the business to be differentiated from the competition. Values need to be reflected in policies and procedures and be seen to be implemented in the spa on a daily basis. Thus a spiritually astute manager will use these values in daily language and will refer to them when solving conflicts.

Corporate social responsibility

It is likely that core values can be seen to align with specific CSR activities such as supporting local charities, community activities, medical research, environmental causes or aid programs. Such CSR activities can help to communicate core values to both staff and customer and actively engage them in ways that are meaningful to themselves and others. This helps to generate positive word-of-mouth and enhances both staff and customer loyalty. In spas, CSR activities can include opportunities to volunteer and provide spa services to marginalized or disadvantaged groups. It has been suggested that providing opportunities for volunteering workplace skills may provide recruiting advantages, particularly for staff in their 20s (Generation Y), with a recent Deloitte survey finding that nearly two-thirds of Gen Y employees preferred companies that let them volunteer their skills. (Deloitte, 2007)

Sense of peace

Spas are marketed as places where guests can experience a sense of peace. Spas therefore need to instill this through every aspect of their operation including their ambience, service and the demeanour of their employees. As such, achieving a sense of peace needs to be an integral element of working in a spa and there are several leadership practices and principles that can assist.

Daily meditation
Daily meditations help to set the energies and vision for the day, consolidate the team, focus the staff and enhance an atmosphere of co-operation and acceptance. A simple 10–15 minute

gathering conducted twice a day; one for the morning shift and one for the afternoon shift, can create a space where the people can leave their worries behind and collectively focus on creating a safe and healing sanctuary. Alternatively, the focus of a meditation could be on a challenge that the spa team is experiencing followed by a short discussion afterwards on what the team can do to address the issues.

This simple practice can be very motivating and powerful yet it is the leader that needs to ensure that a spiritual, yet safe space, is created and that the practice is adhered to on a daily basis.

Weekly movement

With receptionists standing up 8 hours a day and therapists using their muscles to treat others and giving as many as 6 massages on a daily basis, they need some 'me' time, only for them to give back to their bodies, mind and spirits. It is recommended that yoga, Qigong, Tai Chi or similar be offered to staff on a weekly basis. These holistic mind-body exercises are not just about physical movement, they are about breathing, connecting within and also embodying knowledge and may have the added advantage of fostering a sense of community amongst the team.

Weekly treatment exchange

It is not uncommon for spa receptionists to have never tried the treatments offered by the spa. This may reduce revenue as if they have not tried a treatment it is more difficult to provide detailed information about it or sell the treatment with passion. This situation can be remedied by the manager installing a system whereby staff exchange treatments on a regular basis. A system that can work well is to have a program where the therapist receives a treatment every third week and gives two treatments the following 2 weeks. This can be written into their job descriptions and may result in happier, more informed and more passionate staff along with a more profitable business with greater guest satisfaction and increased sales.

Supporting staff welfare

Back-of-house areas

In order for the staff to provide mindful and focused spa experiences, the manager needs to provide them with a supportive and nurturing working environment. This includes providing an attractive back-of-house area with lockers, natural or full-spectrum lightning and comfortable seating for the spa staff to rest, recuperate and build up their strength after having close and exhaustive encounters with the guests.

Conscious decisions on spa equipment
In addition to being provided with nurturing spaces in the back-of-house, the front-of-house should also support staff welfare through conscious decisions on spa equipment. Spa equipment should be chosen for its functionality and not only price and beauty. Although a rolling cart might not be the most beautiful piece of equipment, it saves the attendants backs. A hydraulic massage table is not only beneficial for the guest; it also saves the therapists bodies. Ergonomically designed chairs for receptionists, specialist shoes for all staff and organic uniforms is just a few examples of how the leader can take charge of the staff welfare.

Education and development opportunities

Pay is not the most important factor for most people when selecting an employer; rather most people view job satisfaction and the ability to grow and develop both personally and professionally as the key driver when making decision about entering or leaving employment. Recruitment and retention is becoming an important issue in the spa industry which is experiencing a severe shortage of staff. Thus, if spas want to attract and keep their staff, they must not only offer them a good salary and working environment, they must also offer the ability to continuously develop themselves.

Career path planning
Many companies do not fully appreciate that often staff reluctantly leave and go and work with another company because they do not see development opportunities that may exist with their existing employer (Trunk, 2007) This is certainly relevant to the spa industry where attendants may want to be receptionists, receptionists may want to be therapists, or therapists may want to develop management skills or learn a new therapy, believe they must change jobs in order to climb the career ladder. To avoid unnecessary staff attrition, it is prudent for the manager and human resources officer (in small spas, this is the same person) to sit down and identify potential career paths and the ongoing education and development they can offer their staff. This can then be communicated to staff with

individual development plans and regular appraisals being conducted for each staff member.

Ongoing education and training

Career opportunities in the spa industry are expanding all the time as are education opportunities which now include the possibility of university graduate and post-graduate education. Some universities also offer courses online so that staff can do them whilst remaining in the workplace and there are many private-based education providers such as spatrain (www.spatrain.com) spa lead (http://www.urbanhealing.net/) and Raison d'Etre (www.raisondetrespas.com) offering business and management training along with practitioner and customer service training.

The spa industry is alive with new science, therapies and technology emerging on a daily basis. It is important to keep both the business and its staff up-to-date through both formal and informal personal and professional development activities. In general, it is recommended to allow 2% of revenue to be allocated to these activities which can include formal training programs along with attendance at conferences, seminars and workshops. In addition, within the spa there may be specialists with unique knowledge within their fields that can be shared. For example, if a nutritionist is on staff, they can hold monthly sessions on healthy eating, or create individual programs for employees. Quarterly workshops using either internal or external expertise can also be productive and motivating.

Incentive programs

Incentive programs are a valuable tool to motivate staff and boost sales. These programs can be linked to professional and personal development activities as well as being directly linked to remuneration. Any variable remuneration program must take strategies, structure, values, processes and people into account and must be flexible and sufficiently mobile to adjust to the dynamic circumstances of the environment. Indicators that are valid for one spa might not prove valid for another and thus spas must take their own particular strategies and characteristics into consideration before adopting plans that have been used successfully elsewhere.

As sales in a spa are generally a team effort, they should be rewarded as such and it is recommended to include a team-based incentive system along with individual incentives. The structure of these programs can vary according to individual requirements, however, a common structure is a salary system based on a goal that is set each month (for example budget + 10%, where the

10% covers the extra cost of the system) and a team-based salary connected to this goal. Once this goal is reached the staff member also receives an individual commission on sales performed.

Systems and paperwork

A spa is a place of creation, and in order to focus on the creative tasks, there are basic structures that need to be in place. The following provides a list of systems and paperwork required to support the effective management of a high quality spa operation.

- Vision statement
- Core Values
- Corporate goals (qualitative and quantitative)
- Business plan
- Strategies
- Organization chart
- Employment contracts
- Job descriptions
- Induction plans for each position
- Appraisal system
- Pigeon holes for each staff member
- Incentive systems
- Career paths
- Weekly newsletters
- Educational events calendar

Conclusion

Where people are the product, effective leadership is required. Furthermore, all staff including leaders need continuous training, coaching and inspiration. No matter what background a spa manager comes from, in the new experience economy it is essential that they are able to embrace the 'touchy-feely' world of the therapist as well as the 'hard-nosed', bottom line driven world of the accountant.

Spa managers who lead by example and find their own inner peace, are best able to empower their staff to find their own inner peace. This can create a work environment where staff can feel rewarded and fulfilled and the guests can be consistently delighted by high quality personal service. The spa can then become more than just a work place aimed at satisfying the guest and become a place that nurtures the physical, emotional and spiritual needs of guests and staff alike. Such an environment will be characterized by happy clients, happy staff and happy mangers with staff high staff morale, low staff turnover and high profitability.

Acknowledgments

Thanks to Lena Frilund, who co-wrote the Raison d'Etre leadership manuals which were used as resources for this chapter.

Further reading

From Good to Great
Jim Collins, Collins, (October 6, 2001)

The 7 Habits of highly effective people
Stephen R Covey, Free Press, (November 9, 2004)

The 8th Habit: From effectiveness to greatness
Stephen R Covey, Running Press Book Publishers (May 31, 2006)

Outlines & Highlights for Group Dynamics
Donelson R. Forsyth, AIPI, (June 2, 2006)

Confronting Conflict. A first aid kit for handling conflict
F. Glasl, Hawthorne Press (1999)

Group Dynamics for teams
Daniel Levi, Sage Publications, Inc., (February 15, 2007)

The Dynamics of Conflict Resolution: A Practitioners Guide
Bernard Mayer, Jossey-Bass, (May 15, 2000)

The Eight Essential Steps to Conflict Resolution
Dudley Weeks, Tarcher (January 4, 1994)

References

Aburdene, P. (2007) *Megatrends 2010: The Rise of Conscious Capitalism*, Hampton Road Publishing Company Charlottesville.

Armstrong, M. (2006) *A Handbook of Human Resource Management Practice (10th edition)*, Kogan Page, London.

Buzan, T. (2001) *The Power of Spiritual Intelligence*, HarperCollins.

Cherniss, C., Goleman, D. (2001), *The Emotionally Intelligent Workplace: How to Select for, Measure, and Improve Emotional*

Intelligence in Individuals, Groups, and Organizations, (Eds.) Jossey-Bass, San Francisco.

Deloitte (2007) *Companies That Help Gen Y Employees Volunteer Their Workplace Skills to Non-Profits Can Gain Recruiting Advantages, Study Finds*, Press release 4/16/07; available at http://www.deloitte.com/dtt/press_release/0,1014,cid%253D152753,00.html

Gallup Management Journal (2006) *Gallup Study: Feeling Good Matters in the Workplace*, available at: http://gmj.gallup.com/content/20770/Gallup-Study-Feeling-Good-Matters-in-the.aspx

Pines, J., Gilmore, J. (1999) *The Experience Economy*, Harvard Business School Press, Boston.

Tipping, C. (2004) *Spiritual Intelligence at Work: A Radical Approach to Increasing Productivity, Raising Morale and Preventing Conflict in the Workplace*, Global 13 Productions, Inc.

Trunk (2007) *What Gen Y Really Wants, Time magazine*, Time Inc., available at: http://www.time.com/time/magazine/article/0,9171,1640395,00.html)

Human resource management in spas: staff recruitment, retention and remuneration

Marc Cohen and Daniella Russell

Introduction

The spa industry is a high-touch industry where people are the product. Managing people and recruiting and retaining appropriate staff is therefore critical for a spa business to be successful. This is becoming increasingly difficult as the rapid expansion of the spa industry into a global phenomenon has meant that spas must now compete for staff in a global market. Furthermore, as a high service industry, spas requires a distinct range of professional skills and qualifications along with practical experience and knowledge and the level and range of skills is expanding as new roles are defined.

The global spa industry is expanding rapidly in size and scope, as is employment in the industry. In 2002, the International SPA Association (ISPA) commissioned PriceWaterhouseCoopers to produce a report on the US spa industry which reported that between 2000 and 2002 the US spa industry saw an increase in employment of 87% with both the number of spas and the average number of employees per spa increasing (ISPA 2002). This report concluded that: 'Given the rapid growth in employment, it is not surprising that there is significant competition amongst spas for qualified staff in terms of both spa staff and management ... recruitment and training need to be priorities for the industry. Without deliberate cultivation of talent through training, the lack of qualified staff will become an increasingly significant constraint on further industry growth.' The report went on to conclude that: 'The spa industry needs to recruit qualified resources. The rapid growth of the industry has created significant competition for scarce qualified resources at all levels.' (PriceWaterhouseCoopers, 2002)

The rapid growth of the spa industry has been associated with an increasing expectation of spa goers. Years ago people would attend a spa and expect a beauty treatment or superficial make-over. The emphasis has now changed with more focus on relaxation and holistic treatments. This has led to a need for greater numbers of specialised staff with appropriate qualifications as well as changing business practices. Spas are therefore becoming larger and more complex to operate, requiring a greater emphasis on business operations, strategic planning, marketing and feasibility.

While there are many similarities between the human resource issues within the spa industry and the general hospitality industry in which it is embedded, they also have distinct differences. The spa industry has a similar requirement for high levels of customer service skills, presentation and communication skills, literacy with reservation software and international experience. Both industries are also constrained by a limited supply of staff and a general skills shortage with high staff turnover and both industries have an international scope with the potential for high mobility of employees.

However, unlike the hotel industry, where staff can often find suitable jobs with only theoretical knowledge, the spa industry requires staff with practical knowledge and experience of the treatments and procedures. Furthermore, the spa industry is less well established and recruitment drives for hospitality projects are generally on a much larger scale compared to those in the spa industry, despite a number of hotel brands now expanding their spa operations globally.

The range of careers

The spa industry is multifaceted and offers a wide range of careers and career paths with new roles and opportunities being constantly created. The spa industry is also now a global phenomenon creating opportunities for qualified staff to travel and obtain employment in both urban and remote locations across the world. Generally employees in the spa industry can be classified as either therapists, or management and customer service staff as outlined in Table 22.1, although there is often transfer between the two.

Career status

In many parts of the world the status of spa employees has changed dramatically. In the past, working in a spa would have been considered by many as a low status job. A career as a beauty therapist may have been seen being similar to that of a hairdresser of cabin crew; suitable for school leavers with little or no qualifications. A massage therapist in many parts of the world would also have may have been considered low status and may even have had connotations of akin to working in the sex industry; indeed in many regions 'massage parlours' were places of ill repute.

While in the past it may have been rare for people to aspire to work in the spa industry, with the increasing prominence of spas and the with more formal educational qualifications appearing in both the vocational training and university sectors, even entry level jobs in the spa industry may be seen as a stepping stone to higher paying and higher status positions.

Table 22.1 Examples of staffing positions in the spa industry

Management & customers service positions	Therapists positions
Spa Directors	Qualified & Senior Beauty Therapists
Spa Managers	Qualified & Senior Spa Therapists
Assistant Managers	Advanced Skincare Therapists
Group Operations/Directors & Executives	MediSpa Therapists
Operations Managers	Qualified and Advanced Massage Therapists
Marketing/Sales and Account Managers	Holistic Therapists: all types
Hospitality/Leisure-Senior Management	Fitness attendants
Retail Managers	Pilates instructors
Spa Co-ordinators	Yoga instructors
Educators and Trainers	Tai Chi instructors
Spa Concierge	Complementary therapists
Receptionists	Traditional Chinese Medicine practitioners
Front desk and reservation agents	Ayurvedic practitioners
Attendants	Lifestyle coaches
Café attendant	Naturopaths
Retail salespeople	Nutritionists
Spa butlers	Energy therapists
Group event organisers	Medical and allied health practitioners
Spa Hostess	Wellness directors
Revenue Managers	Spa coach

The role of therapist has also been re-evaluated as the world becomes more stressful. In the new millennium, treatments are being seen as a valuable part of health maintenance and promotion and there is an increasing ability for therapists to specialise in specific subject areas, especially within the holistic therapies area. Thus, therapists increasingly take pride in their profession and their ability to provide a quality service to their clients as well as realise the potential for further education and self-development.

The increasing range of career options, along with increasing status of the industry and a greater demand for work-life balance, has led to a wider demographic of employees. As therapy is quite a flexible role there is also an increasing mix of male and female therapists from many age groups, including

Table 22.2 Change in spa employees demographics over past 10 years

	Therapist	Mid management	High management
Age (in years)			
Current	18–22	24–30	28–40
Past	25-28	30-35	35 above
Experience (in years)			
Current	1 or less	3 &above	4+
Past	Min 2	Min 5	
Qualification			
Current	International qualification	International qualification and/or experience	International qualification and/or experience
Past	Any relevant qualification/ training. Sometimes Experience also counts	Any relevant qualification/training. Sometimes Experience also counts	Any relevant qualification/ training. Sometimes Experience also counts
Average duration in the job role (in years)			
	1–2	2–3	3–5
	3–5	8–10	10 & above

mothers who are wishing to enter the workforce on a part time basis. Table 22.2 outlines the changing demographics of spa industry employees over the past decade.

Management

Spa Managers and Spa Directors must be business driven with an understanding of the concept behind the unique spa service offered. While there are an increasing number of training and education providers that have begun offering spa management courses, graduates with management training are often lack specific spa and therapy experience. Thus, while management candidates are often considered for middle management positions, emphasis is also given to developing therapists internally to fulfil the growing need for experienced spa managers (See Chapter 21).

With the increasing size and complexity of the industry, the role of Spa Manager has become less operational as previously, the Assistant Manager may have had a dual role of either Receptionist/Assistant or Therapist/Assistant. Now managers are likely to be fully occupied with operational duties and the Spa Director has been introduced as a much needed role, driving the business forward, focussing on strategic planning, marketing and feasibility. Within the luxury hotel segment there has also been the creation of senior executive roles with Group Spa Directors being responsible for global spa operations for various 5-star hotel chains (see Chapter 10).

Therapists

The spa industry has created new career opportunities for beauty and massage therapists, and provided expanded career pathways. While the qualifications required for therapist varies widely across the globe (see Chapter 23) there is an increasing requirement for therapists with higher level and multiple skills.

As spas embrace wellness they are becoming centres for advice on health, complementary therapies and lifestyle enhancement and a resource for referrals to conventional and complementary health practitioners, thus there are also opportunities for complementary therapists, holistic exercise instructors and medical practitioners to enter the spa industry.

Spa recruitment

In the past 10 years the spa industry has grown to the size where it can support companies that specialise in spa-related recruitment, training, development and human resource management, yet these companies face the challenge of operating in a young and diverse market where there are few standards and qualifications, legal requirements and job descriptions vary across different regions.

The aim of effective recruitment is to adequately fill job vacancies and reduce the time and effort involved in training new staff as well as enhancing the effectiveness of staff in their respective roles. This requires a thorough understanding of each role in terms of it's specifications for technical ability, personal skills and emotional intelligence and the type of person best suited to perform it along with a detailed understanding of the skills, aspirations and needs of each job candidate.

Personality testing and behavioural profiling can assist in understanding people and how they behave and therefore help in choosing roles that are better suited to a particular individual. Behavioural profiling commonly uses the DISC instrument which measures behaviour in terms of a person's approach to problems, people, work pace and procedures, across the 4 dimensions of: Dominance, Influencing, Steadiness and Cautious. Personality testing on the other hand uses instruments such as the Myers-Briggs Type Indicator MBTI®, which assesses 'personality types' based on the extent of Introversion and Extraversion; Sensing and Intuition; Thinking and Feeling; and Judging–Perceiving (Inscape Publishing, 1996). There is a vast literature on the use of personality testing and behavioural profiling and many companies offers services in this area including companies that specialise in the spa industry such as SpaCareers (www.spacareers.com.au).

In addition to personality testing and behavioural profiling there is evidence to suggest that selection interviews for potential candidates should be structured so as to reduce bias, improve consistency and to better predict future job performance. Structured interviews also provide greater fairness and legal defensibility (Campion, 1991). A loyal staff member is essentially more valuable than a loyal customer because it is the staff member that ultimately creates the loyal customer. Recruiting, retaining and developing qualified staff is therefore a major determinant of a spa's success.

The global staff shortage

The spa industry is a highly personalised industry where 'people are the product'. Recruiting retaining and developing qualified staff is therefore a major determinant of a spa's success. A loyal staff member is essentially more valuable than a loyal customer because it is the staff member that ultimately creates the loyal customer. The sequence is: employee satisfaction drives employee retention and productivity which drives service value which drives customer satisfaction which drives customer loyalty which drives profitability and growth. There is a saying that if the owners look after the managers; the managers look after the staff; and the staff look after the guest; then the bottom line will look after itself.

While staff may be a spa's most valuable asset, the rapid industry expansion has seen growth outpace the supply of qualified personnel and as a result there is a global staff shortage and increasing competition between spas to recruit and retain the best staff. With the globalisation of the spa industry there is also an increasing mobility of spa professionals leading to competition between regions. For example in the Middle East the majority of the spa professionals come from Asian countries, such as Thailand, Indonesia, the Philippines and other parts of Asia and Central Asia where there are many trained therapists who are enticed away from their homelands by higher financial rewards. This situation is likely to continue as in the Middle East alone there are more than 300 5-star hotels in planning or construction each with a spa that will have a requirement for around 30 therapists. This will create a massive demand for new therapists that cannot be met locally.

The global staff shortage has also led to many job places remaining unfilled and forced some spas to compromise on their requirements or pay higher sums to secure staff with management experience, even if it is from a different field. It has also led to vacancies for pre-opening projects being filled with candidates without relevant experience or qualification, therefore intensifying the need for appropriate on the job training and access to qualified trainers.

In addition to staff shortages, the rapid industry growth has led to many new opportunities available to existing employees leading to a high staff turnover as employees change employers or locations in search of greater rewards. Furthermore, there is a trend for many spa professionals with 5 years of more of experience to want to open their own businesses as well as a trend in countries such as South Africa, Tunisia and India for therapists to go 'freelance' and convert a room in their house to do treatments or make home visits to clients. This has resulted in the mushrooming of several small-scale operations which further exacerbates the employee shortage.

Staff turnover

It is reported that for the period 2001–2006, the annual staff turnover rate for all industry sectors in the US averaged 39.6% (US Department of Labor 2007a), while the rate for the leisure and hospitality sector is reported to have averaged 74.6% (US Department of Labor 2007b) which is likely to reflect the large number of unskilled workers in part time employment. While there is currently no accurate data on employee turnover rates for the spa industry, it is suggested that for spas a healthy turnover rate should not the exceed 40% (ResortSuite, 2004).

Within the spa industry, high staff turnover rates are a major drain on the personnel and financial resources of operations and consequently have a negative impact on a spa's profitability. Advertising for, interviewing and training new recruits is timely and costly, as is having gaps in producing expected revenue during transitional periods. High staff turnover also creates difficulties in creating team loyalty, resulting in de-motivated and demoralised staff and a lack of quality and consistency for guests and reduced guest return rates.

For spa employees 'job hopping' may also create problems as there may be gaps without income during transitional periods, reduced income during probationary periods, difficulties in recreating a loyal clientele and time wasted retraining in new product lines and spa concepts. Job hopping also creates an unsettling lifestyle and demonstrates inconsistency to future employers.

Maximising recruitment and retention

There are a number of features that contribute to attracting and retaining the best staff and the companies that are able to achieve this can boast 'preferred employer' status and enjoy reduced staff turnover and enhanced productivity and financial performance. The features that contribute to recruitment and retention include: career development opportunities, remuneration, incentive programs, work environment and corporate culture.

Career development opportunities and training

There is a big difference in having a job and a having career. This difference lies in the ability of a career to provide a pathway for personal growth and development as well as increasing remuneration. In order for employees to take ownership of their career paths it is necessary to create an individualised career plan that outlines realistic growth and promotional opportunities and the appropriate time frames involved. Without a structured career path, many staff will leave the industry, become self-employed, or will simply move to another spa which may offer them a better chance for self-professional development.

Career planning for staff requires spas to engage in 'talent management' whereby they are able to assess the needs and skills of individuals and match these to specific jobs and career paths as well as training and development opportunities.

Talent management requires ongoing performance appraisals that can be used to clarify the strengths and weaknesses of individual team members and assessing what they enjoy and in which areas they excel, as well as where they see themselves progressing. This information can be maintained using career pathway forms that can be reviewed and updated during regular appraisal meetings.

It is important to involve line managers in the talent development process as 'talent spotting' can be done through continuous assessment of day-to-day activities and within training groups. It is also important to identify the qualities that are classed as 'talent' in a particular spa job role or business. Each role will have certain key skills that will enable individuals to excel. These skills may be a simple as being polite and friendly or use of software systems and continue through to high level strategic planning and financial skills. While talent spotting is important, talent management is more than just recognising team members who excel in certain fields; it involves the development of a strategic plan to ensure that staff are supported in using their talents to the best of their ability. Such a strategic plan includes a 'training needs analysis' in order to determine an individual's training requirements.

Training can be powerful motivator which enhances a business and at the same time empowers the team members. There is a wide range of training opportunities available including training provided by product companies, professional associations, and providers of both vocational and higher education as well as specialist training providers and training provided in-house (see Chapter 23). Ideally training should be continuous, professional and relevant to the business with training outcomes monitored and recorded. It is also advisable to vary training methods with a mix of internal and external training to maintain interest.

Remuneration

Remuneration packages and strategies vary tremendously in different locations and working environments such as cruise ships, island based resort spas, city centre salons, country homes, department stores, etc. Salaries and conditions also vary dramatically from country to country. For example a therapist working in the Middle East can expect to receive furnished accommodation, medical insurance, annual flights home as well as food allowance and possibly transportation allowance in addition to the basic salary. In Europe, however, it is not the norm to receive similar fringe benefits. Table 22.3 presents an indication of the monthly salaries offered in different regions.

As well as varying with location and working environment, renumeration can vary according to the particular strategy used. There are a wide range of remuneration strategies that are utilised within the spa industry including: salary, hourly, booth rental, straight commission and commission ladder, fixed fee-per-service, combination, team-based and non-traditional (ResortSuite, 2004).

Salary

A straight salary is one of the simplest remuneration strategies and can include fringe benefits such as holiday pay, superannuation, accommodation, etc. Salaries are often used to compensate fulltime Managers and Directors and may be increased based on experience or qualifications with attached bonuses based on the spas financial result. While salaries provide job security, they do little to motivate staff to achieve particular performance criteria.

Hourly rates

Similar to a salary, hourly compensation offers staff a stable pay structure yet fails to motivate staff to excel and this strategy is usually reserved for support staff such as receptionists and attendants or combined with other strategies.

Table 22.3   Indicative monthly (base) salaries in different regions (in $US) Most will also include accommodation, medical insurance, flights, etc. on top

Region	Therapist	Assistant Manager	Manager/Director
Far East	600 plus furnished accommodation and annual or six monthly vacation	800	1300+
Middle East	1000 plus housing, travel, flights	1800–2000	1500–2250
Europe and UK	2000–2500	2500–3000	3500–8000+
South Africa	500–600	650–1000	1300+
Australia	3000	3500–5000	4500–6000+
United States	4000	5000	5000–6500+

Booth rental

This is commonly used in conventional salons where an operator simply charges staff a rental fee to utilise a designated space. This effectively creates separate businesses for each staff member and does little to further the profitability or reputation of the spa and leaves it vulnerable to staff leaving and taking their clients with them.

Commission

Straight commission or a commission ladder involves staff receiving a percentage of services performed and products sold with the possibility of rates being varied based on different tasks or skill levels. A commission structure serves to motivate staff to perform more services and to up sell products and allows operators to define their margins and performance targets. Commission structures may also be used in combination with other strategies such as hourly pay but this can create complexities and requires appropriate software to manage effectively.

Fixed fee-per-service

Fixed fee-per-service involves defining a dollar value to each service performed or product sold and allows higher fees to be attached to services with higher margins or requiring specialised skills. This can provide motivation for staff to improve their skills as well as their retail performance and guest retention rate. Like commission ladders fixed fee-per-service may be used in combination with other strategies yet requires the appropriate software for effective management.

Combination strategies

Commonly utilised in the hospitality industry, larger hotels and resorts, combination strategies typically include a base hourly rate plus a straight commission, commission ladder or fixed fee on retail sales and/or services performed, with rates based on job category, performance goal levels and/or staff seniority and skill level. While complex to manage without appropriate software, combination strategies serves to motivate staff to perform ancillary duties and to improve their bookings and retail sales as well as improve their skill levels.

Team-based compensation

Team-based compensation programs rewards staff for their individual performance, their team's accomplishments and the spa's overall results by combining salaries with team-based incentives. This strategy needs to be adapted to each individual business according to it's objectives, values, staff competencies, culture and vision and therefore requires a considerable investment in time, planning, leadership, communication and risk management. It is particularly important that performance criteria and goals are communicated to staff in a clear and concise manner and that rewards are timely to reinforce the connection between performance and rewards. Where appropriate it is also important for teams to include back-of-house staff who do not have guest contact, as these staff are just as important in creating the guest experience.

There are many advantages of team-based strategies including: enhanced productivity, staff satisfaction, product sales and service quality, along with reduced staff turnover, and staff absences and costs. According to a ResortSuite white paper: 'Team based compensation quickly reveals poor performers and creates positive peer pressure from other staff working diligently to achieve performance goals. A team-based environment inspires staff to demonstrate positive behaviours, to eliminate selfish attitudes and to cultivate teamwork practices, ultimately increasing a spa's retention rates, service standards and profitability' (ResortSuite, 2004).

Incentive programs

In addition to financial rewards there are a number of incentives that can be used to promote and reward good performance, technical ability, enhanced experience and tenure. Incentives also can effectively enhance staff morale and contribute to the overall atmosphere and culture of the spa. Incentive programs include extending vacation days, providing health and wellness initiatives such as yoga classes or gym memberships as well as treatment exchanges whereby staff get to exchange and experience regular treatments either within their own spa or via exchanges with other spas.

Incentives programs can also include training opportunities with invited spa professionals or specialist speakers or through time release to attend a course or workshop. Product companies often use incentive programs effectively with some product companies offering free product to staff who exceed retails targets. Companies such as Thalgo and Comfort Zone have also rewarded high performers with international travel to attend week-long training workshops at their corporate headquarters. This serves not only motivates employees to excel, it also serves to increase their product knowledge and strengthens the relationship between the product company and their best salespeople.

Work environment

Time spent in the workplace is generally greater than time spent at home and therefore the working environment plays a vital role when choosing a place of work. While spas are designed to occupy spaces that instil a sense of relaxation and peace (see Chapter 16), they may not always provide the best work environments. Many hotel spas are built in basements with little natural lighting or access to fresh air and many spas have back-of-house areas that are not conducive to staff relaxing and recuperating after providing services that can be physically and emotional demanding. Furthermore, the selection of products and equipment may be chosen more for aesthetics rather than functionality, yet staff are required to use them day in and day out.

The work environment is more than just the physical environment it also includes the attitude of employees to their work tasks and their communication with each other and their supervisors. Establishing a positive work environment can boost employee morale and productivity, provide structure for employee's lives and create a sense of satisfaction, achievement, self-esteem and personal identity. (Moos and Billings, 1991) Factors that contribute to such a positive environment include flexible work arrangements that give staff some autonomy over their lives and providing work-life balance as well as creating an environment where staff are recognised and valued for their unique contribution.

The spa industry is not only a close-service industry it is also a global industry where both staff and clients are highly mobile. Thus an important aspect in creating a harmonious work environment in a spa is an appreciation for cultural differences. Cultural awareness affects all levels of staff and shows that an organisation is sensitive to the needs of both staff and guests as different cultures have very different sensibilities regarding touching, disrobing and gender issues. For example not all cultures permit female therapists to work on male clients and vice versa. Similarly, in the West a handshake is acceptable, man to man, woman to woman, man to woman, but in the Middle East a woman can only shake hands with another woman if the hand is offered.

Corporate culture and values

The work environment is greatly influenced by leadership at all levels which goes toward creating the corporate culture. A corporate culture is created by a combination of tangible and intangible factors including the company's values and mission, corporate social responsibility initiatives, volunteer programs, environmental policies, written policies and procedures and how they are implemented, along with opportunities for all levels of the organisation to contribute ideas and evidence that the company 'walks the talk'.

Perhaps the best retention and recruitment strategy is for a company to create a corporate culture that earns it a reputation within the industry as an outstanding employer that truly takes care of its employees. This will become evident from the comments of existing and previous employees who may rave about their positive experiences.

For example the Four Seasons Hotels and Resorts have created a reputation for having a strong corporate culture where all staff have a sense of dignity, pride and satisfaction in what they do and their staff are supported to treat all interactions with guests, customers, business associates and colleagues with the same high level of respect and service. As a result Four Seasons has a low staff turnover rate and many industry head-hunters will not attempt to poach their staff as they know that there is little chance of success of enticing staff away from such a positive work place, even when remuneration may be higher elsewhere (Greger, 2007).

Across many sectors, a company's values and ethics and attitude towards sustainability and corporate social responsibility have been shown to be major factors in attracting, retaining and motivating staff. In a recent report prepared by PWC for the World Economic Forum, titled 'Working Towards Wellness: Accelerating the prevention of chronic disease' (PriceWater-HouseCoopers, 2007) it is suggested that the workplace is an important location for successful prevention strategies and that wellness strategies provide the potential to; increase productivity; assist in recruitment and retention of staff; mitigate the risks of an ageing workforce; and have a positive impact on brand.

This report goes on to suggest that business leaders need to take a number of steps to promote long-term behavioural changes which will benefit employers, employees and communities. These steps include; assessing the health risk of employees and monitor their progress; embedding a culture of health so that wellness is inseparable from business objectives and long-term mission; managing change by committing resources and helping employees to change and sustain improvements in their lifestyles; collaborating with and supporting health programs in the wider community; and leading by example.

The adoption of wellness initiatives in the corporate sector suggests that such initiatives are even more crucial to the spa industry. The spa industry purports to be a caring industry that promotes wellness, it is imperative therefore that the corporate culture reflects this, anything less would be incongruous. 'Wellness workplace values' may be demonstrated through a range of initiatives such as providing staff with wellness products and services including nutritious organic food, yoga and exercise classes, and lifestyle intervention programs. Initiatives can also include activities where junior and senior staff can interact and observe each other's authentic dedication to health and well-being rather than simply bottom line results.

Conclusion

The spa industry is a highly service-oriented industry where people are the most important asset. The rapid global expansion of the industry has created a severe shortage of qualified management and therapy staff along with intense competition amongst employers both within and across different regions. This situation challenges operators to create supportive corporate cultures, positive work environments and flexible remuneration packages in order to attract and retain the best staff. There is also a great need for training programs and career development pathways to develop staff, yet despite these efforts, the rate of industry expansion across the globe in both size and scope, suggest that training and recruitment are likely to be constraints on the industry for many years to come.

References

Campion, M.A., Purcell, E.D., Brown, B.K. (1991) Structured interviewing techniques for personnel selection. In: Jones, J.W.,

Steffy, B.D., Bray, D.W. (Eds), *Applying Psychology in Business: The Handbook for Managers and Human Resource Professionals*, Lexington Books, pp. 251–259.

Greger, K. (2007) *Addressing the Global Labor Shortage Panel*, Global Spa Summit, New York.

Inscape Publishing (1996) *A Comparison of DiSC® Classic and the Myers-Briggs Type Indicator® Research Report. Item Number: O-231.* Available from www.starresources.biz/ebrochures.html

ISPA (2002) *The International Spa Association's 2002 Spa Industry Study*, PriceWaterhouseCoopers.

Moos, R.H., Billings, A.G. (1991) Understanding and improving work climates. In: Jones, J.W., Steffy, B.D., Bray, D.W. (Eds), *Applying Psychology in Business: The Handbook for Managers and Human Resource Professionals*, Lexington Books, pp. 552–562.

PriceWaterHouseCoopers (2007) *Working Towards Wellness: Accelerating the Prevention of Chronic Disease*, World Economic Forum, available at: http://pwchealth.com/cgi-local/hregister. cgi?link_reg/wellness.pdf

ResortSuite, (2004) *Spa Compensation Strategies, ResortSuite SPA Management Software: Optimal Tools for Peak Performance*, An Enablez White Paper available at: http://www.enablez.com/ html/enablez-whitepaper_main.html

US Department of Labor, (2007a) *Bureau of Labor Statistics, Job Openings and Labor Turnover Survey, Total non-farming separations (not seasonally adjusted)*, Series ID JTU00000000TSR; available at: http://data.bls.gov/cgi-bin/surveymost?jt

US Department of Labor, (2007b) *Bureau of Labor Statistics, Job Openings and Labor Turnover Survey, Leisure and Hospitality (not seasonally adjusted)*, Series ID JTU70000000TSR; available at: http://data.bls.gov/cgi-bin/surveymost?jt

CHAPTER 23

Spa-related education and training

Dieter Buchner, Alison Snelling and
Marc Cohen

Introduction

The spa industry offers a diverse range of services and at the time of writing, enjoys unprecedented growth rates of 16% annually (Global Spa Meeting, New York, 2007). Whilst this growth is exciting and provides new opportunities, it has also provoked a considerable shortage of experienced spa therapists and spa managers, and many spas are finding themselves with inexperienced or under-qualified teams of people. The recruitment and retention of qualified employees have become one of the industry's greatest challenges. The diverse nature of the industry, along with a lack of recognised standards and a growing need for employees, has also created both opportunities and challenges for education and training providers.

This chapter aims to give an overview of employment in the spa industry, the range of spa education providers and the factors that drive spa education, accreditation issues and the regulatory environment for spa education along with future trends in spa-related education.

Employment in the spa industry

Spa-related education essentially involves teaching students the knowledge and skills needed to gain employment in the spa industry. This requires education within the three key domains of the industry which are customer service, management and therapy. Each key section can be separated into categories as shown in Figure 23.1.

Spa therapy

The therapy area can be divided into beauty, massage and complementary therapies with complementary therapies including traditional Chinese medicine, Ayurveda, naturopathy and other forms of traditional medicine as well as instruction in yoga, tai chi, Pilates and holistic practices. Employees working in this area are by far the largest group of spa employees.

Many countries have specific licensing requirements for therapists which forces new employees to seek courses that provide accredited spa, beauty, massage or other health practitioner education. Graduates from these courses can then find employment as a junior or assistant spa therapist. Such courses can range from 60 hours in Thailand, to 700 hours in the state of Hawaii (AMTA 2008), to 2240 hours in British Columbia. In

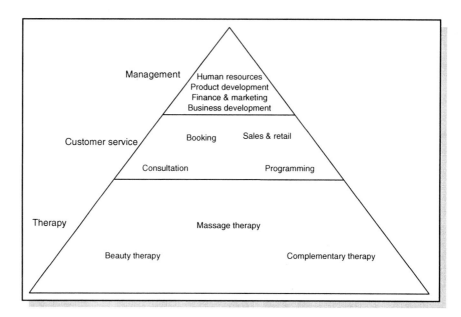

Figure 23.1
Spa employee structure

countries without any licensing requirement, therapists would often start to work in a spa after undergoing a 1–3 months in-company training program.

Most spas require newly recruited therapists to attend menu specific product and treatment training, which ranges in duration from 1 to 12 weeks depending on the size of the menu offered. Over time, as the junior therapists get more confident in delivering treatments to the standards and style of the spa, they may attend further treatment and product training and take a more senior role and advance to senior therapist and later therapy supervisor positions. The most senior position for therapists in the spa industry is currently the role of treatment manager, which often serves as a spring board into spa management positions. A typical career path for a therapist is shown in Figure 23.2.

Spa customer service

Customer service employees are recruited for their ability to communicate confidently with spa clients and to sell treatments and products. Spas are a highly service-oriented industry and customer service appears to be one of the major factors that drive guest satisfaction with research suggesting that guests rank great customer service as the most important factor in making their spa experience enjoyable (Intelligent Spas

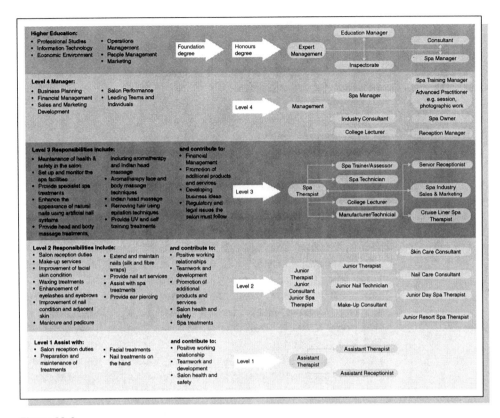

Figure 23.2
Career paths in the spa industry (Habia career ladder)

Singapore, 2005). Employees working in the customer service area may be engaged in reception duties, consultation and programming, the sale of treatments and products, along with facility and equipment preparation. Product houses may also send their own employees into spas to assist with the sales of their products and related treatments. Relevant subjects to be trained in this area include:

- treatment and product knowledge,
- spa cuisine and nutritional basics,
- anatomy and physiology,
- contraindications,
- selling skills,
- consultation skills,
- communication skills,
- taking reservations,
- use of software in the booking process,
- capacity optimisation,

- revenue Management,
- programming,
- scheduling and rostering,
- increasing capture rates and average spent,
- visual Merchandising,
- complaints handling,
- health and Safety,
- hygiene and Grooming,
- care of operating equipment and facility maintenance.

Typically, customer service employees start as Junior or Assistant Receptionists and progress to become Receptionist and Senior Receptionist. Recently established job titles include Spa Consultant, Spa Concierge and Spa Guest Service Representative. The highest customer service position is generally the front of house or Reception Manager, which also provides an entry into spa manager positions.

In most countries there are no legal licensing requirements to work in customer service and subsequently there is little or no formal training available in this area despite a need for the industry to have highly trained customer service employees. As a result, spas must rely on their own in-house training or training provided by product companies and consistently high standards for customer services can vary widely across the industry.

Spa management

The majority of spas are small stand-alone businesses, while large hotel spas have grown to become major profit centres within the hotel industry. There is evidence, however, that many spas are underperforming because of the lack of good management practices and commercial focus. A spa industry survey for Great Britain and Ireland reported that 20% of spas do not employ a full-time manager, leading the Spa Business Association to suggest that 'Lack of commercial management skills is a threat to industry development'. The report goes on to say that: 'Some operators view spas as a support service and a trophy facility rather than a proper business entity' (Topaz Consulting Group, 2006a).

Effective managers are required not only to run the financial and business side of the spa but also to lead and manage the spa team. Spa managers often come from a therapist background, reflecting the need to be in touch with the human side of the business where 'people are the product' (see Chapter 21). There is a growing trend to engage managers with specific customer service and business education in order to focus on making the spa a profitable business.

Managers and leaders generally handle product development, human resource management, marketing and business development and the financial aspects of the business. Management roles can be generic or specialist and spa management career paths generally start with Assistant Spa Manager leading to Spa Manager and Spa Director. Further job titles, depending on the scope and responsibilities, include Spa Operations Manager, Spa Business Development Manager, Director of Wellness or Group Spa Director. With the rapid expansion of the spa industry, there is also a trend for spa employees to see outside opportunities, leave their place of employment and use their management skills to open their own massage therapy studio or spa.

Salaries for spa managers appear to have increased significantly over the last 5 years, reflecting on the scarcity of supply and the contribution a good spa manager can make to the business results. To address this, an increased focus is being placed on the selection, training and development of spa managers. Spa-related education providers have also responded with a proliferation of specific spa management courses and programs, however; given the rapid expansion of the industry, it seems likely that a shortage of spa managers will continue to constrain the growth of the industry for years to come.

Spa-related education providers

Spa education is available through formal and informal channels and is wide ranging dependent on global location. Spa education is provided by both government and private education providers that offer either vocational or higher education as well as being provided 'in-house' by spas and product companies. Examples of spa-related education providers within key regions are outline in Table 23.1.

Vocational education

Vocational education prepares learners for careers that are related to a specific trade and based on practical skills. Rather than teaching broad concepts and principles, this type of education focuses on teaching specific competencies that can be practically assessed. The achieving of a specific set of competencies is then recognised by the awarding of a specific certificate or diploma that may be graded within disciplines according to the level of expertise acquired.

Table 23.1 Examples of spa-related education providers

Provider	Qualifications	Overview
Australian spa-related education providers		
RMIT University (www.rmit.edu.au)	Higher Education Awards including Graduate Certificate, Graduate Diploma and Master of Wellness as well as Vocational awards including Advanced diploma in Myotherapy, Diploma in Remedial massage and Certificate IV in massage	Offers postgraduate pathways via distance education Masters degree provides therapy and management education with the possibility of obtaining credit towards an MBA
Australasian College of Natural Therapies (ACNT) (www.acnt.edu.au)	Spa Degree Pathway	Leads to a degree in spa management by Sydney's Macquarie University – 3 years
Southern School of Natural Therapies (www.ssnt.vic.edu.au)	Degree courses in Naturopathy, Myotherapy and TCM and Massage Diplomas in TCM and Remedial Massage	Focus is on training practitioners Holistic approach Varying lengths of programmes
Nature Care College (http://www.naturecare.com.auwww.naturecare.com.au)	Bachelor Degrees in naturopathy, homeopathy and herbal medicines	Programme includes study in natural and complementary medicine and massage
UK and European spa-related education providers		
University of Derby, Buxton, UK (www.derby.ac.uk/udb)	BSc (Hons) International Spa Management	3 to 4 years with optional 1 year international placement
Coventry University, UK (www.coventry.ac.uk)	BA (Hons) Spa Management with Hospitality	3 years
University College Birmingham, UK (www.bcftcs.ac.uk)	Foundation Degree in Spa Management with Hospitality	2 years
City & Islington College, London, UK (www.candi.ac.uk)	Vocational qualification Beauty Therapy NVQ Level 1-3	Provide a range of courses from foundation to Level 3 which prepares students for a career in the spa industry

Table 23.1 (*Continued*)

Provider	Qualifications	Overview
JING Massage, Brighton, UK (www.jingmassage. com)	Vocational qualification Myofascial release courses Holistic Medical Massage Series	6 days 16 days in total for the full series
Middle East spa-related education providers		
Cleopatra & Steiner Beauty Training Centre (CSBTC) (http://www. cleopatra-steiner.com)	CIBTAC and CIDESCO Diplomas CSBTC Certificates	Middle East's first internationally endorsed beauty and holistic training facility Long- and short-term courses Full- and part-time courses
North America spa-related education providers		
Elmcrest College of Applied Sciences and Spa Management Toronto (www.elmcrestcollege.com)	Spa Manager/Director Diploma Programme	10 months programme
University of California, Irvine, USA (www.uci.edu)	Certificate Programme in Spa and Hospitality Management	Fully online Certificate Programme
Cornell University, USA (www.cornell.edu/)	Spa and Spa Hotel and Resort Development and Management	14 weeks 3 semesters
Cortiva Institute www. cortiva.com	Vocational qualification Therapeutic Massage Programme	33 weeks 300 classroom hours of biosciences including exercise science and kinesiology
Asia Pacific spa-related education providers		
Frederique Academy, Hong Kong (www. frederiqueacademy.com. hk)	ITEC/CIBTAC Diploma in Holistic Massage Frederique Certificate in Swedish Body Massage Frederique Aromatherapy Massage Certificate Course	Offer over 100 courses in English and Cantonese
Chiva-Som Academy, Bangkok (www. chivasomacademy.com)	Offer qualification focused on Spa, Holistic and Aesthetic Therapies	Department of the Chiva-Som International Health Resorts Co., Ltd

Of relevance to the spa industry are vocational qualifications for beauty and massage therapy. Management and vocational education providers include state run colleges and commercial academies. Within the spa industry, there have been a number of spa operators that have established their own academies such as the Shangri-La Chi Spa Academy in Manila (www.shangri-la.com/en/corporate/press/press-release/14858), the MSpa Centre in Bangkok (www.mspa-international.com/academy/training.htm), the Chiva-Som Academy in Bangkok (www.chivasomacademy.com), the Center Parcs Aqua Sana in the UK (www.aquasana.co.uk) and the Raffles Academy in Singapore (www.spaacademy.com.sg).

Higher education

Higher education generally refers to degree-level education that aims to develop a broad understanding of a field along with critical thinking and lifelong learning skills. Higher education leads to the awarding of both undergraduate degrees as well as postgraduate qualifications that include Graduate Certificates, Graduate Diplomas, Masters Degrees as well as PhDs and professional doctorates.

Providers of higher education are generally universities or private colleges that are accredited to award degree status. There are many degrees relevant to the spa industry including those relating to health practitioners and business graduates with the recent introduction of Masters level qualifications in wellness that allows these areas to be combined (www.rmit.health-sciences/wellness).

'In-house' and workplace education

In-house education refers to education provided by a company to its employees that focuses on the specific tasks, practical skills and services standards required by the company. This type of education may or may not lead to formal qualifications but forms a large bulk of the post-entry level education.

Many spa and products companies have developed their own in-house training programs to meet the specific needs of their operations and treatments. Companies may also provide ongoing lectures, seminars and employee exchanges to further their employee's education. For the spa employee, in-house education provides them with the skills to carry out their current role, but may not provide them with a recognised qualification, which would enhance their career development.

Workplace training

Workplace training includes placing students in the workplace to obtain practical business and/or therapy experience and develop and demonstrate specific competencies. Work placements, which can be paid or unpaid, are normally arranged between the employer and education provider as part of a vocational training or higher education award.

In the spa industry workplace training is seen as an essential part of developing the necessary practical skills to operate effectively. Workplace training may require a considerable effort on behalf of spa operators where existing employees are required to assist and mentor the student. If this does not happen, or if the student on work placement is viewed as a threat or a nuisance, or simply just another pair of hands, then the opportunity for effective learning and skills transfer can be lost.

Self-directed learning and distance education

Self-directed learning refers to study in which individuals guide their own learning through planning, implementing and even evaluating their efforts. Self-directed learning includes totally independent learning whereby individuals learn through their own experiences and through searching the internet, reading, visiting spas, experiencing treatments and talking to colleagues. Self-directed learning is included as part of formal higher degree qualifications where students are considered to be more independent learners and is particularly relevant for programs that are offered via distance education whereby education is delivered online or via correspondence.

As information technologies become more accessible and as pedagogical techniques develop, distance education is becoming a more accepted mode of delivery and this can be particularly attractive in the spa industry which is dispersed around the world and where individuals may wish to gain a qualification through part-time study while they are working and are unable to attend set lectures.

Factors that drive spa education

There are a number of factors that students must consider when choosing which qualification they want to study for. This includes location, legislation, employer demands, industry trends, price, availability of scholarships or industry sponsorship, the reputation and prestige associated with the particular teacher or school, the degree earned, the length of time required and the ability to articulate into other programs, recognise prior learning, study part time, full time or via distance education and participate in work-integrated learning.

When designing and/or implementing spa-related education, education providers are also influenced by a variety of factors including the needs of industry, student demands, the potential career paths within the industry as well as local, national and international legislation and accreditation requirements which are particularly relevant when providing massage, beauty and other health practitioner or therapist education.

The regulatory environment for spa therapists

Therapeutic activities in spas range widely and include beauty therapy treatments such as facials, body scrubs and wraps, manicure, pedicure, waxing and make up, massage treatments such as Swedish massage, shiatsu, reflexology, aromatherapy, hot stone massage as well as a wide range of complementary therapies and health practices. Spa therapists may therefore be classified under different titles such as beautician, aesthetician, cosmetologist, massage therapist, aromatherapist, acupuncturist, nutritionist, yoga instructor, etc. As such the legislation governing spa therapists may be considered under beauty practitioner, massage therapist or health practitioner regulation.

The regulatory environment for spa therapists varies widely and ranges from minimal or no legislative requirements in some countries to various models of industry self-regulation and government regulation which may act to protect specific job titles or scope of practice. For example, in some countries such as Germany some job titles are unprotected and anyone can claim to be 'Cosmetician' or 'Wellness Masseur'. However, once a therapy has a government recognised health benefit it must be practiced by a certified Masseur. Similarly, in countries such as Japan and Canada the practice of modalities with recognised health benefits such as shiatsu or acupuncture requires the practitioner to be specifically licensed.

As well as regulating the scope of practice, many jurisdictions also have regulations concerning therapists' educational requirements. Education for massage and beauty therapists is mostly offered as vocational training provided by licensed educational institutes that conform to legal standards set by the relevant authorities of the countries in which they operate. Legislation regarding licensing of spa therapists differs greatly around the world and ranges from no license required in some jurisdictions such as the State of Idaho in the US, to up to 3000 hours of massage training in British Columbia in Canada (www.cmtbc.bc.ca/index.shtml).

While the educational requirements for therapists may be covered by regulations, earning a therapist qualification does not necessarily guarantee the right to practice. There may be additional requirements that therapists must adhere to, such registration with a national board or association, signing up to professional codes of conduct, having adequate professional indemnity insurance and/or undertaking continuing professional education. Local governments may also have additional regulations regarding specific zoning or hygiene requirements that must be adhered to.

Where there is little or no regulation governing spa therapists such as in much of the Asia Pacific region, it is up to the spa industry to self-regulate in order to protect its reputation and maintain standards and credibility. To address this, specific companies have attempted to differentiate themselves by setting their own standards. For example Saint Carlos Medical Spa in Bangkok, hires exclusivey physiotherapist to deliver their spa treatments. Many national spa associations along with industry forums such as the Asia Pacific Spa and Wellness Council (APSWC 2008) are also taking initiatives to set regional standards to harmonise and raise the level of authenticity and quality of practice (www.spawellnesscouncil.com).

Spa education accreditation

Across the globe there are many different spa associations and accrediting bodies with diverse standards of education, assessment and licensing, leading to wide variations in the standards of therapists, service employees and managers. Whilst there are a number of highly regarded educational institutions around the world offering a range of spa therapist qualifications, there is a need to standardise these qualifications.

In a Spa Industry Survey Report for Great Britain and Ireland, the Spa Business Association reported 'The need for a standard approach to qualifications at all levels will become more important as the spa industry grows. The current mix of national and international qualifications, the increasing presence of many overseas workers now employed as therapists, together with the expanding number of product houses and demand for unique treatments, means that employing the right employees and then training them according to the needs of the business will be an even bigger challenge in the future' (Topaz Consulting Group, 2006b). While the range of qualifications available to therapists is vast and beyond the scope of this chapter to discuss, examples of qualifications are described in Table 23.2 while the following outlines the main accrediting bodies in key regions.

Table 23.2 Examples of Therapist Vocational Qualifications

Qualification	Length	Overview
ITEC Level 3 Diploma in Anatomy and Physiology	50 hours	This award is the 'foundation' upon which all other ITEC complementary, beauty and sports therapy awards are based.
ITEC Diploma in Holistic Massage	50 hours	This is the foundation course for complementary therapy and includes holistic massage incorporating the classical movements treating the whole body.
ITEC Level 3 Diploma in Aromatherapy	80 hours	Advanced aromatherapy techniques are included in the course including lymphatic drainage and acupressure points as well as the holistic approach.
National Certification Examination for Therapeutic Massage (NCETM)	500 hours	This is the award required to receive certification from the US National Certification Board for Therapeutic Massage & Bodywork (NCBTMB).
Therapeutic Massage Therapy Diploma (South Africa)	2 years	In South Africa therapists are legally required to be registered with the Allied Health Professions Council of South Africa (AHPCSA) (www.ahpcsa.co.za).
Diploma of Remedial Massage and Spa Therapy – ACNT, (Australia)	1 year	This course is the integration of remedial massage therapy techniques with spa therapy. It combines the Diploma of Remedial Massage course with a Postgraduate Advanced Certificate in Spa and Stone Therapy.
Advanced Diploma of Myotherapy – RMIT University, Australia	3 years	This course builds on the Certificate IV in Massage and the Diploma in Remedial Massage (www.rmit.edu.au/programs/c6064).

UK and Europe

The UK is perhaps leading the way in Europe with several new initiatives being introduced which will have an impact on both European and global education.

The international therapy examination council (ITEC)
This is the largest international examination board offering a variety of beauty, business, complementary therapy and

sports-related qualifications worldwide. ITEC sets its own examinations and sends out its own examiners to colleges around the world where its curriculum is taught. ITEC provides 31 qualifications which are highly regarded and supported by industry and are easily transportable nationally and internationally (www.itecworld.co.uk).

Confederation of international beauty therapy and cosmetology (CIBTAC)

This is an international examination board responsible for the education and training of beauty and holistic therapists worldwide (CIBTAC Awards). CIBTAC works by accrediting schools which must meet the minimum requirements in terms of accommodation, facilities, equipment and products and levels of teaching. Currently there are over 150 schools in 18 countries accredited to offer CIBTAC Awards which are recognised internationally (www.CIBTAC.com).

Comité international esthetique et de cosmétologie (CIDESCO)

This is the world's major international beauty therapy association founded in 1946 with its head office in Zurich, Switzerland. CIDESCO is represented in over 33 countries with over 200 approved schools around the world being independently audited for adherence to CIDESCO's curriculum, the quality of its facilities, training employees, teaching and assessment standards.

Approved schools have to provide a training period of at least 1200 hours and successful candidates are required to gain at least 600 hours of salon experience before being awarded their CIDESCO Diploma and CIDESCO Badge. Estheticians who have not been trained at an approved school but have at least three years salon experience can gain the CIDESCO Diploma by independently taking the CIDESCO Examination (www.cidesco.com).

Hairdressing and beauty industry association (HABIA)

This association is the UK government's approved standard setting body for hair, beauty, nails and spa therapy. HABIA creates the standards that form the basis of all qualifications including UK National Vocational Qualifications (NVQs), Scottish Vocational Qualifications (SVQs), Apprenticeships, Diplomas and Foundation degrees, as well as industry codes of practice (www.habia.org.uk).

City and Guilds

City and Guilds is the leading vocational awarding body in the UK, awarding over 50% of all NVQs and operating in up to

100 different countries. Awards are generally short and allow for recognition of prior learning (RPL) so that individuals can gain recognised qualifications for skills they already have (www.city-and-guilds.co.uk).

Vocational Training Charitable Trust (VTCT)
This is a government approved Awarding Body offering NVQs, SVQs and other vocationally related qualifications (VRQs). VTCT qualifications are provided in the areas of beauty therapy, hairdressing, holistic and complementary therapies and sports and fitness, and delivered at over 500 colleges of further education, private training providers and schools throughout the UK as well as expanding to include countries such as Turkey, Romania, Malta and Kenya (http://www.vtct.org.uk).

USA

The National Certification Board for Therapeutic Massage & Bodywork (NCBTMB)
This was founded in 1992 to establish a certification program and uphold a national standard of excellence in therapeutic massage and bodywork in the USA. Certification with the NCBTMBs requires completion of a minimum of 500 hours of instruction, demonstration of core skills, abilities and knowledge, the passing of a standardised NCBTMB exam and a pledge to uphold the NCBTMB's Standards of Practice and Code of Ethics (www.ncbtmb.com).

The Commission On Massage Therapy Accreditation (COMTA)
This is a US-based non-profit independent body, aiming to improve the quality of education in the fields of massage therapy and bodywork. COMTA accredits schools and programs that provide post-secondary certificates, diplomas or degrees in the practice of massage therapy and bodywork. Accreditation is a voluntary process that requires schools to compare their performance against established standards and to undergo an on-site inspection to evaluate the quality of the program and the institution. To be accredited, institutions are required to offer at least one massage therapy program with a minimum of 600 hours of instruction and to have operated for more than 2 years and graduated at least 20 students from a non-degree program (www.comta.org).

Federation of Massage Therapy Boards (FMBT)
This is a non-profit organisation established in 2005. It launched a new Massage & Bodywork Licensing Examination, MBLEx, on October 1, 2007 which is currently available in 14 US states. Its mission is to support Massage Therapy Boards across the US in their work to ensure that the practice of massage

therapy is provided to the public in a safe and effective manner (www.fsmtb.org).

Figure 23.3 shows a graphic representation of all US states regulating massage therapy.

Australia

The Australian Qualifications Framework (AQF) is a nationally recognised accreditation framework that links together all qualifications issued by secondary schools, vocational education and training (VET) providers and higher education institutions with the aim of promoting lifelong learning and a seamless and diverse education and training system (see Figure 23.4 for an outline of nested spa-related qualifications).

Vocational training in Australia is governed by Industry Skills Councils that are responsible for the development of training packages which outline the vocational qualifications and competencies used for setting nationally recognised educational curricula and qualifications (www.aqf.edu.au). In addition to the standardised qualifications in defined industry sectors, the AQF also allows individual educational institutions

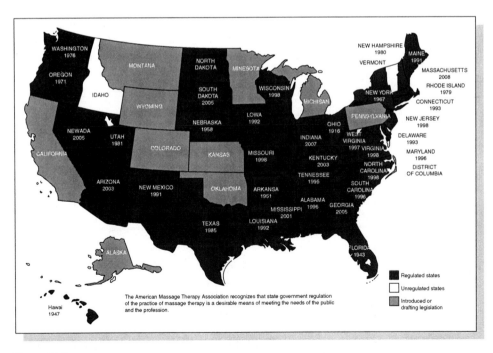

Figure 23.3

US states regulating massage therapy AMTA, 2006. www.amtamassage.org/about/lawstate.html

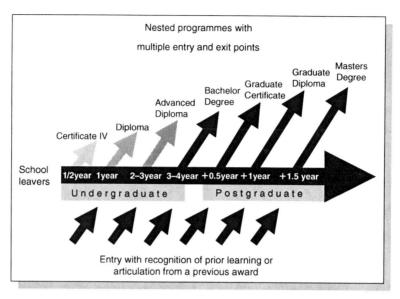

Figure 23.4
Spa education pathways in Australia which include vocational and higher education awards

to develop their own qualifications and recently a number of specific spa-related qualifications have been developed including an Advanced Diploma of Natural Beauty, Spa and Nail Therapy (www.acnt.edu.au), a Diploma of Resort Management (Spa) (www.angliss.vic.edu.au) and an Advanced Diploma of Spa (www.headmasters.com.au).

Service Skills Australia and Community Services and Health Industry Skills Council (CSHISC)

Services Skills Australia is the national Industry Skills Council for a range of service industries including tourism, hospitality, hairdressing and beauty, fitness and recreation (www.service-skills.com.au), while the CSHISC specifies the training packages for the Australian community services and health workforce.

The Health Training Package includes 86 qualifications and more than 1000 units of competency that cover a range of spa-related qualifications including certificates (generally 6 month full time) and diplomas (generally 1 year full time) in massage, aromatherapy and kinesiology, separate diplomas in reflexology, Shiatsu and Oriental Therapies, Traditional Chinese Medicine Remedial Massage (An Mo Tui Na) and advanced diplomas (generally 3 years full time) in naturopathy, nutritional medicine, western herbal medicine, aromatic medicine, Ayurveda and homoeopathy (www.cshisc.com.au).

In addition to spa education in the Australian vocational training sector, there is also the possibility of accredited spa education in the higher education sector including both undergraduate and postgraduate qualifications. There are a number of Australian universities that offer Bachelor degrees in naturopathy which generally include massage, nutrition and herbal medicine and recently RMIT University in Melbourne has announced the first postgraduate programs in wellness including Graduate Certificate, Graduate Diplomas and Masters qualifications that can be undertaken via distance education and includes both therapy- and business-related subjects (www.rmit.edu.au/health-sciences/wellness).

South Africa

The Allied Health Professions Council of South Africa (AHPCSA)
This is a statutory health body established to control all allied health professions, which includes Ayurveda, Chinese Medicine and Acupuncture, Chiropractic, Homoeopathy, Naturopathy, Osteopathy Phytotherapy, Therapeutic Aromatherapy, Therapeutic Massage Therapy, Therapeutic Reflexology and Unani-Tibb (www.ahpcsa.co.za).

The Massage Therapy Association – South Africa (MTA)
This was founded in 1989 to work towards the professional recognition of Therapeutic Massage Therapy in South Africa. MTA is managed by an annually elected Committee and is a non-profit making organisation with its own Constitution, Code of Ethics and Conditions of Membership to govern the conduct of its members. It is to date, the only professional association representing the interests of Therapeutic Massage Therapists in South Africa (www.mtasa.co.za).

The future of spa education

With the growth of the spa industry expected to continue, it is likely that we will see a number of important changes and trends, which will impact on spa education. Such trends include increasingly astute clients, higher educational standards and continuing education, a greater focus on customer service training, insurance reimbursements for spa services and more interaction with the mainstream healthcare system.

Expectations of spa users are continually rising as their ability to compare advertising and marketing claims with the realities of treatment is increasing. Clients are also looking for treatments with long-term impact that extend beyond their stay at the spa. Such treatments require more interactive and customised experiences and educational sessions that can help clients embrace healthier lifestyles and, therefore, demand higher levels of education from therapists.

The demand for higher levels of education has created a need for more qualifications to be offered at advanced levels including postgraduate qualifications. Higher qualifications will provide avenues for continuing professional development, thus helping to develop career paths and keep existing employees in the industry. Higher educational status will also enable advanced therapists to set themselves apart from their junior and less educated colleagues, enabling them to improve their status and income. 'Star therapists' with advanced education and skill levels and a high reputation are also likely to develop their own client base or 'following' which will travel with them if they change employer. Spas may therefore be on the look out for 'star therapists' to differentiate themselves from their competitors.

As differentiation is the key to success in an increasingly saturated market, there is a trend for higher levels of customer care and service, more professional, authentic and customised treatments combined with innovative marketing approaches. This will lead education providers to focus more on spa management and customer service education with an emphasis on business generation and personal and team leadership training. This may eventually result in the development of specific standards and qualifications in these areas as well as harmonisation of standards across diverse geographical regions. It is also likely that there will be an increasing number of new spa-related education providers including existing providers who extend their educational offerings as well as new education providers funded either by industry or governments who want to capitalise on wellness tourism.

With massage therapy gaining increasing recognition from the healthcare sector and the health insurance industry, spas may become accessible to a much larger market, and some of the more therapeutic treatments may become eligible for reimbursement by health insurance companies. This may result in spas needing to conform with the insurers requirements, which may have an impact on the content of spa education in this area.

The global spa industry is still in its infancy and similarly we are just witnessing the birth of formal spa education. The appearance of new qualifications and standards as well as new standard setting bodies is a vital part of this industry's growth and timely relevant and accessible spa education will be required to ensure that standards within the industry are not just met, but exceeded.

References

AMTA (American Massage Therapist Association), 2008, www. amtamassage.org

Asia Pacific Spa and Wellness Council, www.spawellness-council.com (Site accessed 30 January 2008)

Global Spa Meeting, New York, 2007, http://www.blog. spafinder.com/archive/2007_05_01_spafindertest2_archive. htmlhttp://blog.spafinder.com/archive/2007_05_01_spafind-ertest2_archive.html

Intelligent Spas Singapore, Female vs Male Spa Consumer, 2005 http://www.intelligentspas.com/cart/cart_main.asp?detail=28

Topaz Consulting Group, 2006a, British Spa Business Association, Spa Industry Survey Report for Great Britain & Ireland, Summary Document, and Topaz Consulting Group, p4

Topaz Consulting Group, 2006b, British Spa Business Association, Spa Industry Survey Report for Great Britain & Ireland, Summary Document, and Topaz Consulting Group, p5.

CHAPTER 24

Traditional knowledge and spas

Gerard Bodeker and Gemma Burford

Introduction

In the evolving spa world, indigenous themes have emerged as a significant trend, especially in destination spas and in rural and regional settings where traditions are strong and local health knowledge is lively. In December 2006, SpaFinder. com noted in its 'Ten Spa Trends to Watch for in 2007': 'Spa guests are rewarding a spa's efforts to incorporate authentic indigenous treatments, hire local staff, and contribute to the community. They are also welcoming education about local cultures and healing traditions.'

Approximately half of the population of most industrialized countries is now using complementary medicine as a part of their general healthcare and also for wellness and preventive purposes (Bodeker et al., 2005). A growing body of research published in the scientific literature (e.g. www.ecam.oxford-journals.org, www.jacm.acm.org) attests to the clinical benefits of acupuncture, Ayurvedic and Chinese herbal treatments, various forms of massage, meditation, yoga, qi gong and many of the other traditional or indigenous therapies that are increasingly utilized in the spa industry.

At the same time, traditional medicine continues to exist in the developing world as a major source of healthcare for the majority of the population, often serving as the primary or only source of healthcare for the world's poor (Bodeker, 2007a). The contrast between this reality and the incorporation of indigenous themes into luxury spas is a real one. Accordingly, it would seem timely to bring these realities together into a single focus with a view to better benefitting both the discretional users of natural healthcare and those who practice and use traditional forms of healthcare for their everyday livelihood and family health.

In Asia, the Americas, Africa, Australia and the Pacific as well as in Europe there are groups that identify themselves as 'indigenous'. Indeed, the term 'indigenous peoples' is used to characterize a reported 300–350 million people worldwide – from the Arctic to the South Pacific, from the Kalahari Desert in southern Africa to Tierra Del Fuego at the southernmost tip of the Americas. With ancient roots in their local areas, these peoples are also among the world's most marginalized populations – politically, economically, and territorially (Bodeker, 2008). Ironically, in the face of growing interest in indigenous therapies in the natural medicine and spa worlds, indigenous peoples also suffer the highest burden of health challenges (WHO 2007). This is a point to which we will return later in the chapter and also in the chapter on Ethics and values (Chapter 25)

415

when we consider issues of social responsibility and the use of indigenous therapies in the spa industry.

This chapter will review some of these trends in different regions of the world. Inevitably, due to space limitations, coverage of the many and rich new initiatives in indigenous-themed spas will be brief and it is possible that some important innovations may be overlooked.

Key issues include the scientific evidence base for traditional therapies, the conservation of indigenous traditions, the role of innovation within tradition, and the sharing of benefits between those commercializing traditional knowledge and the custodians of these traditions. Also, the effects of globalization and the trend for blending of traditional practices and philosophies with those from other regions – known as 'syncretism' – need to be analysed and articulated within the spa community.

If the spa industry is profiting from indigenous traditions, it is reasonable to ask what the industry is returning to these cultures. It is also valid to ask whether the rapid and often superficial spread of these therapies contributes to strengthening or weakening the tradition itself, through propagation of a piece of the tradition rather than of the whole philosophy and the formal process of training historically required of practitioners. Clearly, this is a field that is largely unaddressed by the industry and there is a need for an industry response. In Asia, this has begun, as will be noted in considering the work of the Asia Pacific Spa and Wellness Council's task force on indigenous therapies.

Traditional medicine in healthcare

Asia has seen the most progress in incorporating traditional health systems into national health policy. In China, this began in 1951 with the establishment of a traditional Chinese medicine division within the Ministry of Public Health, upgraded to a department in 1954. In 1988, the State Council established the State Administration of Traditional Chinese Medicine as an independent administrative body in its own right, with eight major departments. The government's commitment to 'develop modern medicine and traditional Chinese medicine' has been written into the National Constitution and the two are regarded as of equal importance (Baoyan, 2005).

In India, formal recognition for Indian systems of medicine came with the Indian Medicine Central Council Act of 1970. In 2002, India developed a specific national policy to facilitate the integration of these healthcare systems into national health programmes. The policy emphasizes affordability, safety, efficacy and the sustainable use of raw materials (Lavekar and Sharma, 2005).

The African Union declared a decade for the development of traditional medicine in 2001. It is estimated that 80% of the population of Africa regularly use traditional medicine for their everyday healthcare (Kassilo et al., 2005).

Asia

Ayurveda

While Ayurveda is known to have existed in India and neighbouring countries for some thousands of years, the concept of 'spa' has only recently been applied to the age old Ayurvedic rejuvenation system known as *panchakarma*. 'Pancha' means five in Sanskrit and 'karma' means action. Panchakarma then refers to the five principle therapeutic strategies or actions employed in Ayurvedic rejuvenation. Widely promoted by Maharishi Mahesh Yogi in the 1980s and 1990s, panchakarma has become well known in the West as an indigenous therapy system from India.

The five treatment approaches of Ayurveda, conducted over three phases of treatment, are designed to both eradicate the basic cause of disease and to also treat or reduce existing diseases and their symptoms. The term 'rejuvenation therapy' is used to illustrate that Ayurvedic panchakarma does more than promote detoxification – or removal of harmful elements from the body – but also revitalizes the body's tissues.

Current spa programmes offer Ayurvedic packages in well designed luxury settings, a far cry from the original clinic in which they would have been performed in rural villages of India. Perhaps India's most internationally renowned Ayurvedic spa is the multiple award-winning Ananda Spa in Rishikesh in the Himalayan foothills (www.anandaspa.com). Based in a restored royal palace, Ananda offers individualized treatments, diet and daily routine according to classical Ayurvedic principles. The many Western guests who visit Ananda have often learned about Ayurveda in their own countries and read widely on the subject before taking their Ayurvedic sojourn in India.

With Ayurvedic centres in Germany, Austria, Britain, North America as well as in many parts of Asia, Ayurveda is very much a globalized indigenous system. In the USA, for example, The Raj, in Iowa, has for 14 years offered comprehensive Ayurvedic rejuvenation based on Maharishi Vedic Health programmes. The recipient of numerous awards, including Spa-Finder's readers award for 'Best Healing Treatments' and a

417

New York Times listing as one of the four recommended silent/meditative retreats, The Raj takes an evidence-based approach to explaining its programmes.

Guests at The Raj are advised that 'lipophilic toxicants (fat-soluble toxins), such as PCBs, DDEs, DDT, and other chemicals and pesticides tend to accumulate in our fat tissues. They have been associated with hormone disruption, immune system suppression, reproductive disorders, cancer, and other diseases' (www.theraj.com). Drawing on published research, clients at The Raj are informed that The Raj's Ayurvedic programmes 'are capable of dislodging lipophilic and other toxins from the tissues and reducing their concentration in the body'. This convergence of traditional treatment and scientific insight into the workings of the traditional system is the result of the fusion of Eastern and Western influences that has accompanied the globalization of some traditional health systems, such as Ayurveda. It responds to the demands of a discerning global clientele that demands quality care and informed insight into the nature of their care.

With respect to Chinese traditions, the seminal text of traditional Chinese medicine, the Yellow Emperor's Classic of Internal Medicine (Nei Ching Su Wen) dating c. 300 BCE, details a cosmology in which the universe is described as composed of ethers of heaven and earth, which are *yang* – which have the attributes of bright, light, and male – and *yin*, with the attributes of dark, heavy, and female (Veith, 2002). Chinese medical theory identifies the Five Agents (*wu-hsing*) or elements that are created by the interaction of yin and yang. These are: water, fire, metal, earth, and wood, which mutually create and destroy each other. In this system, the concept of *qi* refers to subtle energy or life force. Here, energy is seen as more fundamental than matter (i.e. the body) and is thus the starting point of medical intervention. *Qi gong*, acupuncture, *tui na* massage, Tai Chi Chuan, and the Chinese marital arts all draw on this perspective. Other Asian countries whose systems are built in part on Chinese medical theory and tradition – for example Japan, Korea, Vietnam – take a similar orientation to medical theory and treatment.

Acupuncture, as noted in the first global mapping exercise on the growth of traditional and complementary medicine worldwide (Bodeker et al., 2005), has become a globalized form of traditional healthcare. Many countries now provide licensure for acupuncturists and there are societies for medical acupuncture which offer training only to medical doctors, who in turn are reimbursed for their services by private and public health insurers.

In the spa world, Chinese-themed treatments and products are very much globalized. The Mandarian Oriental Group's The Spa, as noted in Chapter 10, and the Shangri La Group's Chi spas all incorporate elements of these traditions.

In wellness programmes, traditional Chinese medicine clinics and, increasingly, in spas, Tai Chi is used to assist people, particularly the elderly, with circulatory problems, hypertension, joint conditions such as rheumatism and arthritis, and a range of other chronic conditions (Kin et al., 2007; Voukelatos et al., 2007). Summa Spa in Beijing has incorporated Tai Chi into its massage practice (www.summaspa.com). Integrating Tai Chi principles into massage therapy, Summa Spa therapists maintain mental focus and move their body during massage by using Tai Chi breathing techniques and postures. In this new evolution of the Tai Chi art form, therapists are described as being like dancers, and clients reportedly experience deep satisfaction with the rhythmic movement and pressure, drawing on the yin-yang concept of complete balance.

Elsewhere in Asia, the Japanese Onsen tradition is centred around hot springs in this volcanically active country. Traditionally used for public bathing, Onsen have become major features of Japan's tourism industry and include indoor and outdoor pools, all characterized by what the Japanese describe as 'the virtues of naked communion'. Purity of water, mineral richness, and heat are key features of the Onsen experience. Reflecting the globalization of Asian health cultures, Onsen are found in spa settings in many different parts of the world.

Perhaps the earliest form of Onsen spas were the *ryokans*, which are traditional Japanese inns originating from the Edo period (1603–1868). Ryokans located near hot springs invariably had an Onsen. The tradition and standards of the ryokans and their Onsen, as authentic Japanese residential spas are perpetuated by the Japanese Ryokan Association (www.ryokan.or.jp), which maintain standards for the inns and for the Onsen and their traditional retinue of attendants and products. Here, tradition, tourism, and preservation of standards across changing times and consumer groups converge in a regulated and cooperatively managed model of cultural preservation.

Elsewhere, principles of modernity and fusion are at work. In Australia, the Onsen Retreat and Spa in Victoria offers Onsen bathing along with a menu that includes caviar scrubs, hot stone therapy, western massage, and pre-natal therapies (www.onsen.com.au). Reflecting the eclectic tastes of Western spa and casino guests, the Montbleu Resort Casino in Tahoe, California (www.montbleuresort.com), provides cardiovascular machines and weight training devices as well as an Onsen Spa offering Aveda products and whirlpool baths.

Thai Massage

South East Asia has perhaps seen the greatest proliferation of indigenous or traditionally themed spas, with Thailand leading the field with a large array of centres, services, products, and aesthetics. Deriving from basic principles of the Wat Pho tradition of Thai massage and the Lana traditions of Northern Thailand, Thai spas draw on local as well as generic national concepts and products to integrate into their treatment regimens. Wat Pho, the Temple of the Reclining Buddha, in Bangkok, adjoins the Grand Palace and is known as the birthplace of traditional Thai massage. In the era before the temple was established, the site was a centre for training in traditional Thai medicine, which in turn has it roots in Ayurveda. Preservation of the tradition, purity of teaching, and links to a temple-based origin of the tradition are central to the core values of Thai massage. Conservation efforts in Thailand have resulted in such initiatives as Thai Massage Restoration Project which has revised the texts of Thai traditional massage and the Foundation for Restoring Thai Traditional Medicine and the College of Ayurvedic Medicine which have developed educational curricula according to traditional standards (Disayavanish and Disayavanish, 1998).

Palace and Village (kampung) Traditions of the Malay Kingdoms

The indigenous health traditions of Malaysia and Indonesia have also been the source of a unique set of spa programmes and ambiances that have taken village or kampung traditions, as well as those from royal courts, and placed them within a spa and wellness setting.

Malay health and beauty traditions are undergoing a resurgence of interest in Malaysia and have been showcased in the YTL Group's spa resort, Tanjong Jara (www.spavillage.com/tanjongjara), in collaboration with the Malay traditional products company Nonaroguy.

Drawing on both royal and village (kampung) traditions, Tanjong Jara's spa menu is based in traditions that have ancient roots in Malay culture. These include a range of herbal baths: the royal flower bath or *mandi bunga*, a foot bath, a lime bath and a sitz bath for female reproductive care. Traditional *urut* (long-stroke and pressure point Malay massage) is the centrepiece of the services available and a women's health programme is also offered, including traditional post-natal care. Underpinning these is a causative theory which builds on organizing principles of hot and cold, damp and dry and of the elements earth, fire, water, and air, drawn from ancient links with Ayurveda.

In Indonesia, Jamu herbal traditions have remained the mainstay of the population in managing healthcare as well as in promoting beauty and wellness. Based on fresh herbal ingredients and combined with traditional massage and spiritual approaches to wellness, these methods are now being incorporated as features of Indonesian and Balinese spas. Dr. Martha Tilaar, over a period of decades, has recorded and applied royal Javanese and other Indonesian traditions for beauty and health, and incorporated these into a range of franchised indigenous Indonesian spa programmes (www. marthatilaar.com).

Traditional Philippine medicine has its roots in the many ethnic groups of the Philippine islands. The traditional massage system of the Philippines, known as *hilot*, is equally diverse in practice and tradition, but is becoming standardized as part of a modern incorporation of hilot into contemporary spa programmes in the Philippines (Maraña and Tan, 2006). These are featured by the large hotel groups, such as The Spa at the Mandarin Oriental and Chi at Shangri La, as well as at the numerous smaller urban day spas and rural destination spas, often along with some traditional herbal body treatments and herbalized drinks.

Vietnam's burgeoning economy is often represented in south east Asian investment circles as 'the new Thailand', with its surge of new golf and health resorts and beach developments. Historically, two medical traditions have co-existed in Vietnam. The first *thuoc nam* – meaning the medicine (*thuoc*) of the South (*nam*) – is the indigenous Vietnamese tradition, based largely on folk herbal knowledge. The introduction of Chinese medicine with Chinese rule in Vietnam, coming as it did from the North (*bac*), led to traditional Chinese medicine being referred to as *thuoc bac* – Northern medicine. The development of *thuoc nam* into a national system was effected by a scholar and Buddhist monk, Tue Tinh, who gathered local medicinal knowledge from all over Vietnam and set up health clinics in monasteries and also established herbal gardens to provide the *materia medica* and to educate the public on herbal home medicine (Dung and Bodeker, 2001). A number of new spas in Vietnam are drawing on these two traditions to offer Vietnamese-themed treatments in both urban and rural settings.

Africa

It is recognized that in Africa, the traditional medical sector serves the everyday healthcare needs of 80% of the population (Kassilo et al., 2005). Traditional medical practitioners are widely consulted and regarded as offering personalized care that is readily available, accessible, and affordable, taking into account the feelings of patients, their ability/inability to pay for the health services and their socio-cultural and economic realities (UNAIDS 2002; Mbindyo, 2007). Traditional medicine, drawing on local plants and generational knowledge about their application for healthcare, is often the first and last resort to healthcare for the poor.

At the other end of Africa's economic spectrum, indigenous themes are becoming increasingly popular in the growing spa industry, especially in South Africa. These themes are reflected in the décor and ambience of spas as well as in the treatments themselves. Music, dance and traditional clothing are often used to set the scene, with African mythology sometimes incorporated. The Spa Afrique Day Hydro in Northcliff, Johannesburg, has created fibre-optic caves in which the legend of the river god Nyaminyami, protector of the Tonga tribe, is told (www.spaafrique.co.za). Many of the spa's treatments and rituals refer back to this theme. At the Osero African Living Spa based at Gibb's Farm in Karatu, Tanzania, guest literature draws on Maasai proverbs and values, such as *Inkishu oo Inkera* ('cattle and children'), which refers to the custom of children massaging their parents when they return to the homestead after a hard day's work. Treatments may be offered in an authentic Maasai hut constructed by local people or under an *oreteti* tree (*Ficus* sp.), which is regarded by the Maasai as sacred (Bradford Zak, Founder, Osero African Living Spa, personal communication; see also www.gibbsfarm.net).

In some African spas, treatments inspired by indigenous plants and their uses are transformed into marketable products and acquire new layers of meaning in the process. At Fourdoun Spa in KwaZulu-Natal, for example, a resident traditional healer has developed two distinct product ranges based respectively on *Leonotis leonorus* and *Artemisia*, which include soaps, shower gels, body lotions and sprays, and bath salts. The Fourdoun website not only discusses the ethnobotanical uses of these two plants in indigenous Zulu culture, but also uses the language of 'New Age' spirituality and the self-help industry, as illustrated by this example: '*Make bath time a special time when you can wash away negativity and let go of the things that do not serve your purpose in life. Breathe in the aroma of your body soap and be mindful of breathing in life'* (www.fourdoun.com). The ethnobotanical information does not refer to bathing, but rather to decoctions, infusions, and use of incense. The concept of immersing the body in warm water perfumed with these plants would certainly be a novel one to the Zulu people. Other spa treatments that reference indigenous therapies (unfamiliar though they may be to the communities concerned) include rubbing the body down with ground coconut shells and diamond dust at the Benguerra Island Eco-Lodge in Mozambique, and hot stone massage with volcanic basalt at the Track and Trail River Camp in Zambia's South Luangwa National Park.

The language of science is increasingly being employed by indigenous-themed spas in Africa to increase acceptance of their products and therapies in the global market, and both Fourdoun and Osero drawn on this strategy. The Fourdoun website provides information on the medicinal properties of *Hypoxis* (African potato), marula oil, aloe vera, and rooibos tea, as well as eight 'essential minerals' reportedly contained in the spa treatments. Osero African Living Spa provides a detailed guide to the medicinal properties of plants used in its treatments, based on an extensive search of scientific literature relating not only to the plants themselves, but also to their active ingredients, and is developing a partnership with the Department of Phytochemistry at the National Museums of Kenya to conduct its own research (field work by Gemma Burford).

The Americas

Throughout the Americas, a 'sense of place' is becoming increasingly important in the spa industry. Spa developers and consultants such as Sylvia Sepielli, recipient of the 2006 International Spa Association Visionary Award, are building an international reputation by creating distinctive destination spas characterized by indigenous-themed architecture, signature treatments, and often locations traditionally held as sacred. Sepielli's Mii Amo Spa in Sedona, Arizona, for example, is located in a canyon revered by the Havasupai Indians as a place of healing, where spa clients are invited to join a 'Walk with the Ancestors' led by a former Havasupai tribal chief. Sepielli has described the emerging focus on indigenous therapies and authentic regional atmosphere as 'an extension of [the client's] desire for a unique travel experience' (Albanese, 2007).

Also emerging is a trend for blending influences from different indigenous groups and historical periods. The Spa of Colonial Williamsburg in Williamsburg, Virginia, also created by Sepielli, combines traditions and ingredients used by Native Americans, English settlers, African-Americans, and immigrants. Healing practices from each of the last five centuries inspire its five signature treatments, reflecting the spa's motto, 'A Continuum of Wellness' (www.colonialwilliamsburg.com). Another example can be found at The Spa at Shingle Creek, in the Florida Everglades, where spa developers first researched the intertwined histories of the Spanish and Native Americans in central Florida (www.rosenshinglecreek.com).

In the field of indigenous North American spa products, Native Naturals offers a professional range based on Native American ethnobotanical knowledge, featuring scents such as sweetgrass, sage, and cedar. The company, owned and operated entirely by Native Americans, also provides consultants who can train and certify spa therapists. Its website includes detailed information on 'Essence Folk Lore' and 'Native Bath Customs', relating to a number of different Native American tribes in different parts of the continent (www.nativenaturals.com).

In Central and South America, as in Africa, the concept of indigenous themes in spas is sometimes extended to include genuine local practitioners performing traditional rituals. At the Inca Utama Spa in Huatajata, Bolivia, for example, the Kalawaya spiritual healer Tata Lorenzo practices divination by 'casting sacred coca leaves' (www.ladatco.com/titi-uta.htm). The Maya Spa Patagonia in Mapuche, Chile, features indigenous treatments performed by local shamans and herbalists (www.maya-spa.cl). These include Mayan astrology, based on the elaboration of the five powers (*kins*), that together comprise the oracle of destiny, as well as the ancient practice of ear candling. At La Mirage Garden Hotel and Spa in Imbabura, Ecuador, a female shaman offers a purification ritual involving crystals, candles, and smoke (www.larc1.com/ecuador/lamirage/lm_spa_treatments.html).

Australia

The Daintree Eco-Lodge in northern Queensland, Australia, draws on the traditional knowledge of the Kuku Yalanji people, who are indigenous to the Daintree Forest region and are believed to have inhabited the rainforest for more than 9000 years. The Daintree Forest itself, at 135 million years old is reportedly 65 million years older than the Amazon. The Daintree Eco-Lodge acknowledges the ancient history of the Kuku Yalanji group in their spa and resort literature and a history notes the five seasons which guided hunting, gathering and mobility patterns, and also shaped the sources and type of products used as medicines (www.daintree-ecolodge.com.au). In recognition of its work, Daintree was recognized as the World's Leading Eco-Lodge in the World Green Category at the 14th World Travel Awards (WTA), in January 2008.

Offering a range of organic spa products, the Daintree Eco-Lodge spa programme 'incorporates the principles of aromatherapy, colour therapy, phytotherapy and thalassotherapy in combination with local Kuku Yalanji Aboriginal principles aimed at balancing the five elements of earth, water, fire, air, and ether'. This reference to the five elements is identical to the Ayurvedic framework of the five elements or *panchamahabhutas*. Also available is Japanese shiatsu massage. Members of the Kuku Yalanji community are employed in the lodge and spa, and their traditions are honored as part of the guests education to the entire ecological and social environment.

Skin Therapeia day spa, in New South Wales, Australia, launched in June 2006 what the company describes as 'holistic Australian indigenous therapies', which include 'cleansing indigenous teas and edible bush tucker (food)' (www.skintherapeia.com.au).

Drawing on the local Aboriginal term 'Li'Tya', meaning 'of the earth', Skin Therapeia's Li'Tya treatments draw on knowledge from the Ya'idt-midtung tribe, originating in a rugged high country area in the south eastern region of Australia. Li'Tya spa therapists are extensively trained by indigenous trainers on the source on traditional use of native ingredients, and traditional application methods.

Similar to the Daintree group, Skin Therapeia provides indigenous treatments from Australia along with those from other regions, offering chakra therapy derived from India's Vedic tradition and hot stone therapy from native American southwest traditions.

Europe

Although Europe is generally considered the home of more cosmopolitan traditions such as the baths of Germany, France, and Britain, originating from ancient Roman bath traditions, there are also very local traditions, some belonging to groups classified as indigenous, that are being incorporated into contemporary spa services.

In southern Sweden, the coastal spa resort, Varberg, has a tradition dating back to the 19th century. The wooden cold bath house, dating from 1902, offers both classic spa treatments – based on salt water, mud, and seaweed – and various new therapies from around the world, including an Asian spa and a special Sami spa treatment. The Sami, the indigenous people of the arctic region of Scandinavia, have previously been known as the Lapps or Lapplanders. Their traditional medicine is reported to have connections with Siberian shamanistic traditions and includes laying on of hands, stoppage of bleeding, and traditional herbal medicine. This is an original use of indigenous European health traditions by a European spa.

Throughout Europe, Asian spa traditions are offered – Ayurvedic oil massage, Thai massage, Chinese herbal treatments and acupuncture, Japanese shiatsu massage, etc. – speaking to the globalization of tradition through the spa world. American, African, Indian and Sri Lankan spas are marketed in Europe based on reference to tradition since the concepts of tradition and antiquity are highly marketable to a values-oriented and educated clientele. This is contributing to the eclectic mix of indigenous or traditional therapies on offer in Europe and globally.

Syncretism – the fusion of traditions

There is clearly a global trend of the traditions of one region being offered along with those from other regions in today's spas. While some spas simply offer a diversified menu of treatments from around the globe, sometimes with an emphasis on those services and products which have a local origin, others offer overarching frameworks, such as the Asian theories of elements, as a way of harmonizing these diverse treatments into a single philosophy of the spa. While the former represents more of a smorgasbord approach, the latter fits with what, in sociology, is referred to as 'syncretism'. Syncretism is essentially the fusing of diverse or disparate philosophies and practices into an overarching framework that focuses on commonalities by referencing a unifying philosophy.

As with other globalizing Asian traditions, Thai massage and herbal spa products have also undergone their own metamorphosis during the globalization process. While schools such as the Old Northern Medicine Hospital in Chiang Mai offer short courses according to formal Thai massage procedures, the fact that a reported 10 000 foreign students have taken these courses, suggest that there is great opportunity for unsupervised modification of tradition once the learning is applied in non-Thai settings. Indeed, Thai massage is widely available along with Swedish and Ayurvedic massage as a standard option in many European and North American spas.

The varied indigenous programmes on offer fit into one or other of these two categories: the smorgasbord approach and the syncretic. The key difference is the presence or absence of an underlying philosophy to unify the programme.

Indigenous issues, spa industry policy and international law

By way of reference to international law, the United Nations in 2007 passed the UN Declaration of the Rights of Indigenous Peoples, which refers to rights and responsibilities pertaining to the traditional health knowledge of indigenous peoples (Bodeker, 2008).

According to the International Work Group for Indigenous Affairs (IGWIA), Asia is home to the vast majority (70%) of the world's indigenous peoples. In India alone, there are 68 million Adivasis, or indigenous peoples. The Orang Asli, the Mon-Khmer-speaking peoples of the Malaysian peninsula, by contrast, have a population of 150 000 and claim continuous presence in the world's most ancient rainforests. In East Asia, Taiwanese aboriginal groups are held to be the source of the Austronesian language family, which is now found throughout Oceania. And indigenous peoples in West Asia include the Bakhtiari, Laks, Lurs, and Qashqai of Iran, and Assyrian peoples of Iran, Iraq, and Turkey. In North and South America, every nation has indigenous peoples. In the USA, census data indicate that there are approximately 2 million native Americans. And in Canada, where Aboriginal people, including the Inuit of the Arctic region, have been designated as members of First Nations, the population is approximately 1 million. In South America, indigenous populations now range from Bolivia with up to 70% of the nation to approximately half of the nation in Peru and Guatemala to a reported 8% in Uruguay (The World Factbook, 2007).

In Africa, the term 'indigenous' has come to refer to nomadic peoples, such as the Tuareg of the Sahara and Sahel, hunter gatherers such as the San people of the Kalahari and pastoralists, including the Masai of East Africa. Their claim to indigenous status has been endorsed by the African Union's *African Commission on Human and Peoples Rights*, which has noted their status of under representation in government and the need for affirmative action to ensure their survival.

Despite this large population that identifies itself as indigenous, the term 'indigenous' has been contested for the simple reason that almost all Asians and Africans consider themselves indigenous.

In a global context, then, the term 'indigenous' has political meaning, as encapsulated in the United Nations Declaration on the Rights of Indigenous Peoples, which was adopted by the UN on September 13, 2007 (www.iwgia.org/sw248.asp). More broadly, the rights of indigenous peoples are of ongoing significance to the Untied Nations and its members states (www.un.org/issues/m-indig.html).

Yet in the sphere of natural therapies, wellness and spas, 'indigenous' has come to mean 'local', 'traditional', 'from the local culture'. The political view and that of the wellness therapies have a degree of overlap that is important for both indigenous communities and spa owners and operators to recognize. This overlap lies in the principle that knowledge is a commodity which can be owned and that owners of knowledge have entitlements relating to the use of their knowledge. Related to this is the position that knowledge from a tradition must be guided by the tradition if development is to take place. Training also should be in accord with the standards of the tradition if the term 'traditional' is to continue to be applied to practices that have crossed cultural and international borders.

Human rights issues are of relevance to the spa industry as well (See Chapter 25). As the industry profits from the use of indigenous knowledge, there is an accompanying ethical and, under international law, a legal imperative to share these benefits with indigenous groups and with the individual owners of the knowledge that is commercialized. There are many frameworks available for doing this, for example that of the International Society for Ethnobiology (www.ise.arts.ubc.ca/global_coalition). These issues are addressed further in the following chapter on Ethics and Values.

Conclusion

The trend towards including indigenous themes in spas around the world can assist indigenous and traditional communities to create economic opportunities as well as to gain respect for their traditions and culture. This is the opportunity offered by the spa industry. The responsibility of the industry is to ensure that international standards of ethics are applied when drawing on the knowledge of traditional or indigenous cultures.

It is also noteworthy that differences exist in national and cultural approaches to these issues. China is clear in wishing to promote its healthcare traditions and to globalize these freely, given adherence to certain standards of quality control. India, however, has made it clear that while it is promoting a sharing of its traditional medical knowledge with the world community, it is not offering ownership and will protect its cultural property in the face of foreign attempts to claim a proprietary position on original or modified forms of Indian traditional knowledge. More discrete indigenous groups in various parts of the world are fierce in the protection of their traditional knowledge and there is a history of litigation related to the protection of these from what has been referred to by critics as 'biopiracy'.

Of central importance is the involvement of traditional custodians of cultural knowledge as the gatekeepers of standards. Training curricula, indigenous spa therapies, herbal and related products designed from traditional knowledge should all be developed with reference to indigenous standards of best practice. The trend towards syncretism found in the global spa industry may attract customers with its sense of exotic variety. But in so doing it may homogenize culturally discrete packages of beneficial knowledge and dissociate them from their guiding theory in a way that loses much of their richness and ability to contribute to the wellness and wellbeing of spa clients. Early signs are that standards of 'best practice' with respect to indigenous therapies are emerging in Asia, which may in turn serve as a template for similar developments elsewhere.

Acknowledgement

We would like to acknowledge the catalytic input of Kelda and Kathy Maloney of Daintree Eco-Lodge in Queensland, Australia, whose original insights helped in focusing the research and development for this chapter.

References

Albanese, E. (2007) Sense of place: Indigenous connections and unique environs are key ingredients to the bodywork done here, *The Boston Globe*, January 14.

Baoyan, L. (2005) People's Republic of China. In: Bodeker, G., Ong, C-K., Grundy, C., Burford, G., Maehira, Y. (Eds), *World Health Organization Global Atlas of Traditional, Complementary and Alternative Medicine*, World Health Organization, Geneva.

Bodeker, G. (2007a) Traditional medicine. In: Cook, G., Zumla, A. (Eds), *Manson's Tropical Diseases.*, WB Saunders Elsevier Health Sciences, London.

Bodeker, G. (2007b) Intellectual property rights. In: Bodeker, G., Burford, G. (Eds), *Public Health & Policy Perspectives on Traditional, Complementary & Alternative Medicine*, Imperial College Press, London.

Bodeker, G., Burford, G. (Eds) (2007) *Public Health & Policy Perspectives on Traditional, Complementary & Alternative Medicine*, Imperial College Press, London.

Bodeker, G. et al (Ed.) (2008) Indigenous Medicine. In: Heggenhougen, K., *Encyclopedia of Public Health*, vol. 7, Elsevier Press, New York.

Bodeker, G., Ong, C-K., Burford, G., Grundy, C., Shein, K. (Eds) (2005) *World Health Organization Global Atlas on Traditional & Complementary Medicine: 2 volume set*, World Health Organization, Geneva.

Disayavanish, C., Disayavanish, P. (1998) Introduction of the treatment method of Thai traditional medicine: its validity and future perspectives, *Psychiatry Clin Neurosci Suppl*, 52:S334–S337.

Dung, T.N., Bodeker, G. (2001) Tue Tinh: founder of Vietnamese traditional medicine, *Journal of Alternative and Complementary Medicine*, 7(5):401–404.

Kasilo, O., Soumbey-Alley, E., Wambebe, C., Chatora, R. (2005) Regional Overview, African Region. In: Bodeker, G., Ong, C-K., Burford, G., Grundy, C., Shein, K. (Eds), *World Health Organization Global Atlas on Traditional & Complementary Medicine*, World Health Organization, Geneva.

Kin, S., Toba, K., Orimo, H. (2007) Health-related quality of life (HRQOL) in older people practicing Tai Chi – comparison of the HRQOL with the national standards for age-matched controls, *Nippon Ronen Igakkai Zasshi*, 44(3):339–344.

Maraña, M.R., Tan, J.Z. (2006) *Hilot: The Filipino Traditional Massage*, Creative Concoctions Inc, Pasig City, Philippines.

Mbindyo, P. (2007) Public private partnerships for the development of traditional medicine in Kenya. In: Bodeker, G., Burford, G. (Eds), *Public Health & Policy Perspectives on Traditional, Complementary & Alternative Medicine*, Imperial College Press, London.

UN Declaration on the Rights of Indigenous Peoples: http://www.un.org/esa/socdev/unpfii/en/declaration.html Accessed, Jan 26, 2008

Veith, I. (2002) *The Yellow Emperor's Classic of Internal Medicine*, University of California Press, Berkeley and Los Angeles.

Voukelatos, A., Cumming, R.G., Lord, S.R., Rissel, C. (2007) A randomized, controlled trial of tai chi for the prevention of falls: the Central Sydney tai chi trial, *Journal of American Geriatric Society*, 55(8):1185–1191.

World Health Orgnisation. (2007) *Health of indigenous people.* http://www.who.int/mediacentre/factsheets/fs326/en/ (accessed 26 Jan 2008).

CHAPTER 25

Ethics and values

Gerard Bodeker

Introduction

History is full with accounts of the wealthy giving away money to charity. John of Balliol, a notorious robber baron in 13th century England, redeemed his name, and, in his hope, his soul, by leaving his fortune to Oxford University to support a theological college now named after him, Oxford's renowned Balliol College. JD Rockefeller, at the time when he was being widely criticized for ruthless business practice in the move to monopolize the American oil industry, was giving 10 percent of his annual income to his church and establishing what was to become one of the world's largest philanthropic foundations, the Rockefeller Foundation. The well-known case of Microsoft and its oft-legally-challenged monopolistic practices has generated a fortune that Microsoft founder Bill Gates has channeled into the Bill & Melinda Gates Foundation to support research to eradicate malaria, HIV, and TB from the world's most afflicted and poorest nations. Most recently, Pepsi Cola, which has been challenged by health campaigners, along with other multinational beverage manufactures, for exposing children to sugar addiction and to a series of health risks associated with obesity, made an $8 million donation at the 2008 Davos Summit to Columbia University's Earth Institute and $2.5 million to Matt Damon's H2O Foundation to support water in Africa. The funds will be used to improve sanitation, access to drinking water and crop yields through irrigation. Pepsi offered not only money, but corporate resources for planning, infrastructure development, and evaluation to ensure the success of these African water projects (www.bitc.org.uk/news_media/world_economic_forum.html).

Is philanthropic giving by industry's captains or by corporations donations equivalent to Corporate Social Responsibility (CSR)? Or, as suggested by Models of Success & Sustainability (MOSS) (www.moss.org.au) Australia's industry body for Corporate Social Responsibility (CSR) and Corporate Sustainability, modern CSR more about how a company makes its money rather than how it spends its money? This and a range of related perspectives will become clearer as the chapter considers the broader context of corporate social responsibility and then its application to the world of spas.

What is CSR?

The responsibility of industry to recognize through outreach its role in the community, the environment and indeed to its own employees, consumers and suppliers, has come to be termed 'Corporate Social Responsibility' or CSR as it is abbreviated.

Definitions of CSR have been offered by business writers and analysts for at least the past 50 years. The 1950s are considered the beginning of 'the modern era' of CSR, where a shift from generic philanthropy to relevant responsibility came into place. Definitions expanded from this time across the 1960s and 1970s, when a shift to empirical evaluation of CSR practice took over from definitions and values frameworks in the business literature. Key themes to emerge included corporate social performance (CSP), stakeholder theory, and business ethics theory (Carroll, 1999). More recently, CSR has evolved to a point where leading exponents of the strategy are now calling for a new term and set of concepts to characterize what has evolved from earlier approaches to CSR.

At Cranfield University, one of Britain's leading business schools, CSR is conceptualized as follows: 'Corporate responsibility is about ensuring that we take into account the social, community and environmental consequences of our activities.' (www.cranfield.ac.uk/about/csr/index.jsp).

At Harvard University, the CSR Initiative at the Kennedy School of Government was established in 2004 as a multi-disciplinary and multi-stakeholder program that seeks to study and enhance the public contributions of private enterprise. The Harvard CSR Initiative takes a strategic approach to conceptualizing CSR:

'Corporate social responsibility encompasses not only what companies do with their profits, but also how they make them. It goes beyond philanthropy and compliance and addresses how companies manage their economic, social, and environmental impacts, as well as their relationships in all key spheres of influence: the workplace, the marketplace, the supply chain, the community, and the public policy realm' (www.ksg. harvard.edu/m-rcbg/CSRI/index.html, accessed 30 Jan 2008).

The Harvard CSR Initiative explores the intersection of corporate responsibility, corporate governance, public policy, and international development and, in so doing, bridges theory and practice. The project was founded in 2004 with support from Walter H. Shorenstein, Chevron Corporation, The Coca-Cola Company, and General Motors.

The impetus behind the Initiative is that companies face increasing demands to participate in public–private partnerships 'and are under growing pressure to be accountable not only to shareholders, but also to stakeholders such as employees, consumers, suppliers, local communities, policymakers, and society-at-large'.

Recognizing that Government bears the ultimate responsibility for ensuring public welfare the Harvard CSR Initiative is equally cognizant of the reality that globally, there is no formal legal or regulatory system governing many of the activities of multinational corporations. Self-governance is a reality and commitment to societal well-being is an ethical track that CSR is designed to orient companies towards.

The public sector context of CSR

While most international focus has been on the private sector and its social responsibilities, a World Bank report on CSR (Fox et al., 2002) has considered the role of public sector (i.e. government) agencies in providing the necessary 'enabling environment' for CSR to evolve.

Focusing on the developing world, in accord with its mandate, the World Bank calls for a definition of CSR that goes 'beyond compliance' to one in which business is genuinely committed to sustainable development. Given the growth of the spa industry in Asia and its emerging presence in Africa – especially South Africa (see Chapter 24) – a developing country perspective is worthy of consideration here.

Within a framework of four public sector functions – Mandating, Facilitating, Partnering, and Endorsing – the World Bank report identifies 10 public sector themes for CSR:

1. Setting and ensuring compliance with minimum standards
2. Public policy role of business
3. Corporate governance
4. Responsible investment
5. Philanthropy and community development
6. Stakeholder engagement and representation
7. Pro-CSR production and consumption
8. Pro-CSR certification, 'beyond compliance' standards, and management systems
9. Pro-CSR reporting and transparency
10. Multilateral processes, guidelines, and conventions.

Five key themes emerge from the World Bank's analysis as necessary for a future CSR role for developing country government agencies:

1. Work to build awareness of the contemporary CSR agenda within developing country agencies.
2. Initiatives that enable public sector bodies in developing countries to become effective players in setting the terms of the CSR debate and its associated standards.

3. Work to build a stable and transparent environment for pro-CSR investment.
4. Engage the private sector more directly in public policy processes, such as national sustainable development or poverty reduction strategies.
5. Develop frameworks for assessing local or national priorities in relation to CSR.

There are very real constraints for this to come about, including poor government infrastructure, corruption, conflicting political agendas such as military expansion, etc. While acknowledging this, the World Bank considers that the opportunities are significant and that there is a wealth of experience to draw on.

The Harvard framework for CSR: relevance to the global spa industry

The Harvard CSR Initiative has developed a framework for governance and accountability in CSR which has five broad themes:

1. The role of business and human rights
2. Business and human rights: accountability mechanisms for resolving complaints and disputes
3. The role of private governance institutions
4. Corporate responsibility reporting and public accountability
5. New directions in environmental accountability.

This is a useful framework for considering the early initiatives of the global spa industry in the field of ethics and social responsibility. Accordingly, the following section will consider some of the initiatives within the Harvard framework and draw out implications from this for the industry as a whole. However, it should be noted that the ideal situation will be for the spa industry itself to build from such frameworks as the Harvard model and to tailor a CSR framework that fits the industry comprehensively and comfortably.

The role of business and human rights

If, as the World Health Organization considers it to be, health is a basic human right, the work of doctors at The Farm at San Benito in the Philippines is human rights work by a spa for the higher good of rural healthcare. The resident physicians in this medical spa, which offers holistic treatments and a dietary based approach to detoxification and wellness, volunteer part of their time to provide healthcare to poor rural communities in their vicinity (www.thefarm.com.ph).

The Shangri-La Group of hotels and resorts has formally articulated a human rights policy as a cornerstone of its CSR agenda
(www.shangri-la.com/en/corporate/aboutus/socialresponsi-
bility). The group publicly commits to 'not knowingly engage or
be complicit in any activity that results in human rights abuse'.
In addition to equal opportunity and non-discriminatory HR
policies, the Shangri-La group, whose Chi spas are planned to
operate in 27 locations, 'will contribute to local communities by
initiating and supporting philanthropic, biodiversity, cultural,
and civic projects'.

Business and human rights: accountability mechanisms for resolving complaints and disputes

As noted in Chapter 24, the issue of globalization of traditional
or indigenous health practices raises questions of quality control, depth of training, adherence to traditionally acquired
experience, and ownership of the traditional knowledge.

An illustration of this set of issues is highlighted by the Indian
Government which has challenged the right of other countries
to modify and claim as inventions any variations of traditional
yoga postures. News services reported in May 2007 that 'Indian
officials announced that; 'they' would lodge official complaints
with US authorities over hundreds of yoga-related patents,
copyrights and trademarks that have been issued in recent
years. The dispute has exposed the differing attitudes towards
yoga – and intellectual property rights over 'traditional
knowledge' – in India and the US. As yoga has moved from
marginal to mainstream, US authorities have issued 150 yoga-
related copyrights, 134 patents on yoga accessories and 2315
yoga-related trademarks. Yoga is one of thousands of traditional Indian products – including basmati rice and turmeric –
that the Indian Government has been fighting to protect from
Western patents in recent years (Page, 2007).

Elsewhere, herbal treatments from indigenous communities
have been studied both as the source of novel pharmaceutical
drugs and as sources for new herbal or phytomedicines. This has
generated legal debate and lawsuits and is played out against
an unclear backdrop of international intellectual property law.
Here, two major international agreements – the International
Convention on Biological Diversity (1992) (www.cbd.int),
also known as the CBD, and the World Trade Organization's
Agreement on Trade Related Aspects of Intellectual Property
Systems (1994) – known as TRIPS (http://www.wto.org/english/
tratop_e/trips_e/t_agm1_e.htm)–present diametrically opposing

positions on the ownership and protection of indigenous knowledge (Bodeker, 2007). While the CBD takes the position that long-term traditional use of knowledge, or a product or a process, use constitutes a form of legal ownership. TRIPS, however, takes the position that unless a product or process is patented, it is not owned. Until this broader international legal framework is resolved, the legal issues will remain contentious.

The spa industry, however, is in a position to develop an ethical framework that sets a moral high ground, consistent with the values of spa consumers and consistent also with the trend for ethical practice in the areas of environmental and social responsibility.

In February 2008, the Asia Pacific Spa and Wellness Council's (APSWC) task committee on Indigenous Therapies and Intellectual Property Rights, held its inaugural meeting and established a founding vision which includes:

- recognizing a traditional therapy for the country,
- recognizing the Master therapists of this modality,
- linking with country tourism boards to help promote the cultural history and significance of this modality, the living practitioners of this modality, and its therapeutic benefits (www.spawellnesscouncil.com).

The goal of the APSWC's task committee on Indigenous Therapies and Intellectual Property Rights is to recognize indigenous traditions as a regional natural resource, helping them to gain respect while creating economic opportunities for the communities that have harbored and cultivated them. This is a foundational development which though only having the power to recommend and develop voluntary standards, will serve as a process that will recognize rights and responsibilities in the wider area of traditional knowledge and indigenous themed spas.

The role of private governance

The Harvard group is studying the trend whereby companies, acting on their own or in groups, have established codes of conduct, management systems standards, certification schemes, and reporting requirements. In the spa industry, Six Senses in Asia has taken a lead (see Chapter 20). In addition, Six Senses has developed codes of conducts and management systems, accompanied by affiliation with certification bodies such as Green Globe with the associated reporting responsibilities. This is an example of a spa company taking a lead in not only performing according to principles of CSR, but reporting on this and being held accountable for its adherence to its own standards. Further examples are cited in the following Section on 'Reporting and Public Accountability'.

Corporate responsibility reporting and public accountability

The Harvard CSR Initiative notes that a growing number of large firms now publish corporate responsibility reports to share their strategies and performance with stakeholders. These are studied by the Harvard group to explore the role of corporate responsibility reporting in governance and accountability.

In the hospitality and spa world, Six Senses stands out again as an early leader. Six Senses, through linking with rating bodies such as Green Globe, provides an external audit of its performance and then allows this to be published (see Chapter 18).

In Thailand, the Six Senses Spa, Evason, Hua Hin, has a commitment to investing back into local village communities that provide the herbs, local produce, and workforce for the spa (www.sixsenses.com/evason-huahin). Contributing to children's education, local micro-enterprise activities, and village development is part of the wider philosophy of 'putting back'. 'Fair Trade', 'recognizing the intellectual property entitlements of traditional knowledge holders who share their secrets for new spa products and treatments', and 'economic well-being of people at the local level', are all concepts that appeal to the values of their guests. In this instance then, CSR reporting and public accountability converge with marketing. Being accountable and being seen to do the right thing work hand in hand to appeal to values-sensitive consumers.

Six Senses also provides support to HIV positive children in Thailand through guest donations and partners with Care for Children (www.careforchildren.com.cn) in projects which engage their guests in supporting the company's social and environmental initiatives. Care for Children exists to relieve abandoned and orphaned children by the introduction of strategic initiatives and has projects in China and Thailand supported in part by Six Senses and their guests. This is reported publicly by Care for Children as well as by Six Senses.

Many of these highly ethical CSR programs of Six Senses, may be considered to relate to how a company spends its money rather than how it makes it money.

On the side of how they make their money, Six Senses report that they offer job opportunities to the local communities in which their spas operate and give preference to local suppliers and locally sourced products. The company also reports that, in accord with their equal employment opportunity statement, there are currently seven hearing and speech impaired personnel working in the Hua Hin, Thailand spa's laundry and food and beverage departments. Key here, is the principle of not only having a policy and implementing it, but also reporting publicly on it for the sake of social accountability.

New directions in environmental accountability

As noted in the chapter on traditional knowledge (Chapter 24), Daintree Eco Lodge, with its Australian indigenous spa concepts, personnel and products has a commitment to protect, preserve and promote the natural environment, biodiversity and ecosystem as well as the indigenous Australian cultural heritage of their region. Its success has been acclaimed through being recognized as the World's Leading Eco-Lodge in the World Green Category at the 14th World Travel Awards (WTA) in January 2008, an award program referred to by the Wall Street Journal as 'the travel industry's Oscars'. Daintree's programs of sustainable environmental use and conservation and cultural engagement and respect reflect its unique position in having one of the world's most ancient cultures, the world's oldest living rainforest and the Great Barrier Reef at its doorstep.

The Shangri-La Hotels & Resorts Group, whose Chi spas are open in Bangkok, Cebu, Shanghai, Penang and Muscat, has 22 spas scheduled to open in premier city and resort locations over the next 5 years. Chi Spas share the Shangri-La group's wider commitment to biodiversity conservation. Shangri-La's stated goal is 'to mitigate impacts on the environment by working with all stakeholders to promote and implement responsible environmental practices and continuous improvement' (www.shangri-la.com/en/corporate/aboutus/socialresponsibility).

Some examples of the group's projects include a nature reserve at the Shangri-La Rasa Ria Resort & Spa in Sabah, Malaysia. This is a unique private sector initiative, in Sabah, which includes a rehabilitation centre for baby orang utans. In Oman, Shangri-La's Barr Al Jissah Resort and Spa employs a turtle ranger to raise awareness of the country's endangered sea turtles through guest education. A coral garden replanting project plays a central role in marine conservation at Shangri-La's Fijian Resort and Spa, Yanuca Island. Shangri-La's policy requires all employees to be responsible and accountable for operating in an environmentally responsible manner. By January 2008, nineteen Shangri-La hotels had received ISO 14001 certification, the International Environmental Management System standard. The group was the first to receive such certification for hotels in P.R. China, Taiwan, Thailand, and the Philippines.

In Australia, MOSS www.moss.org.au has been established to help business owners, CSR and sustainability practitioners understand the various aspects of CSR and how to imbed it into business strategy to enhance one's bottom line. It focuses on sustainability in the marketplace, workplace, community and environment in line with the Global Reporting Initiative, and other globally recognized reporting programs.

Dominant motivators towards CSR include: better economic performance, employee retention and motivation, brand reputation, and risk management especially in relation to climate change.

MOSS also endorses the Green Globe accreditation program for spas and runs workshops on how to achieve sustainability and best practice around the world.

Perceived failure of CSR – public backlash

The Body Shop is recognized as an industry pioneer in the field of corporate social; responsibility (www.bodyshop.com). In the arena of natural products for external use on the body, its core values concentrated around opposition to animal testing, developing community trade, building self-esteem, campaigning for human rights, and protection of the planet. Over a period of two decades, the Body Shop cultivated a loyal customer base who shared the same values and Body Shop founder, Anita Roddick became a global spokesperson for ethical business and for having CSR as part of the fabric of global companies. When the Body Shop was sold to L'Oreal in March 2006 for $US1.14 billion, the support base turned against the Body Shop in a very public manner. Over the years, the supporters of the Body Shop included activists who had strongly criticized L'Oréal, for testing its cosmetics on animals, exploiting the sexuality of women, and selling its products by making women feel insecure.

An advocacy group, McSpotlight (www.mcspotlight.org) has made a series of claims in contradiction of the Body Shop's claim that its ethical position continues under L'Oreal ownership. These include:

- an allegation that the Body Shop's products are not actually natural but are almost wholly synthetic,
- the opinion that while Body Shop claims to oppose animal testing, its products contain ingredients that other companies have tested on animals,
- the Body Shop is accused of paying exploitative wages and of being opposed to trade unions,

- McSpotlight also charges that the Body Shop's Community Trade program is simply a cynical marketing strategy since less than 1% of sales are generated by Community Trade producers,
- echoing opinions of some ethnobiologists and community development workers, McSpotlight also charges that the Community Trade program creates tensions and division within indigenous communities and undermines self-sufficiency, encouraging an unhealthy situation of dependency.

Another British example of a deeply ethically oriented corporation is Cafédirect. Cafédirect is the UK's largest Fairtrade hot drinks company and one of the largest in the world. The company's shares are traded on the Triodos Bank's 'matched bargain market' Ethex152, together with shares in the Ethical Property Company, Green Lane Housing Ltd and Triodos Renewables. This is a trading system by social enterprises that attracts shareholders who do not prioritize profit over ethics. A total of 45% of Cafédirect is owned by its founders (Oxfam, Traidcraft, Equal Exchange, and Twin Trading) and its producers (www.cafedirect.co.uk).

This is widely viewed as a model of fair trade. It is too early to know whether recent findings (2008) of serious medical risks associated with caffeine consumption may come to challenge the standing of the company and its products, even if its trade practices remain fair and equitable.

Clearly, CSR is not a once-only position. The Body Shop example demonstrates that the perception that a company has fallen away from its ethical commitment can hurt its image and alienate its loyal customer base. Advocacy and watchdog organizations are certainly vigilant for evidence of failure of commitment by corporations and of attempts to use a CSR position to market a company that is not, in reality, as committed to a core CSR orientation as its PR might suggest.

Is CSR a limiting framework?

Leading theorists are united in pointing to the need for new conceptualizations of CSR and new approaches. However, their views vary on what those approaches should be.

Professor Jeffrey Sachs, Director of The Earth Institute at Columbia University in New York and Special Advisor to United Nations Secretary-General, is widely considered to be the leading international economic advisor of his generation. Commenting on PepsiCo's commitment to both finance and inject management expertise into the two Africa water projects, Sachs commented that the initiative reflected a new approach to CSR, moving beyond the charitable donations of the past, to one where corporations are now actively engaging in social change and development (www.bitc.org.uk/news_media/world_economic_forum.html).

Cranfield University professor and British corporate ethicist and campaigner, David Grayson, has taken this view a step further and has called for a shift from an 'obligation' orientation to one of 'opportunity' (Gettler, 2007). Grayson considers that the term CSR may have outlived its usefulness. Noting that CSR implies some sort of charge on businesses, he has argued that companies should instead be seeing CSR as a vehicle for innovation and for opening new markets. Drawing on what, in the past, has been characterized as a position of enlightened self-interest, Grayson has pointed to GE's 'Eco-imagination' – an initiative in which GE invested in technologies aimed at reducing greenhouse gas emissions. In one year, revenues from GE's environmental products had risen from $US6.2 billion in 2004 to & US10.1 billion in 2005. The company's advance orders had risen to $US17 billion.

Professor Michael Porter of the Institute for Strategy and Competitiveness at the Harvard Business School places profitability and corporate leadership at the forefront in determining a company's values and priorities. Porter, a co-author of The Global Competitiveness Report 2007–2008, has argued that business has the means to make a substantially greater positive impact on social issues than most other institutions. By contrast with generic CSR approaches, Porter favors addressing social issues through shared value strategies in which a company identifies the particular set of societal problems that it is best equipped to help resolve and from which it can gain the greatest competitive benefit (www.isc.hbs.edu) (Porter, 2008).

Frank Dixon (2007), a Harvard MBA graduate and consultant on innovative CSR for leading US corporations, has argued that 'voluntary CSR provides benefits only to a limited extent. Beyond a certain point, voluntary impact mitigation increases costs relative to firms that are not fully mitigating. Without intending to do so, modern economic and political systems essentially make it impossible to fully mitigate impacts and remain in business. In effect, firms are compelled to negatively impact society. As a result, growing pushback from society is inevitable'(www.globalsystemchange.com/GSC/Articles_files/SSI%201-8.pdf). Dixon argues that achieving high level sustainability change (HSLC) is possible through an approach he calls 'Sustainable Systems Implementation (SSI)'. SSI is described as a collaborative approach that engages key stakeholders, such as

443

system change experts and leaders from business, government and civil society, in dialogue and action to identify key system change leverage points. It focuses on raising awareness of the most promising system change strategies already developed but not widely implemented. Dixon asserts that 'SSI is unique in that it takes a true whole system focus and renders complex ideas and strategies down to simple terms and concepts, with the goal of greatly expanding public awareness and action'.

While engaging public officials in dialogue to develop CSR programs may seem beyond the scope of most spa companies, the wider context that spas inhabit in the hospitality and wellness industries does offer a forum for industry-wide initiatives, possibly initiated through industry associations and professional bodies.

Spas and the ethical future

Models for ethical responsibility – within or outside what may be perceived by the theorists as a core CSR framework – have begun to emerge in the global spa industry.

As discussed, these range from a company-wide commitment to CSR by groups such as the Shangri-La Hotels and Resorts group, to very local projects with indigenous groups and biodiversity conservation by a single resort and spa such as Daintree Eco-Lodge. Clearly, the spa story in the world of ethics and responsibility is in its infancy and these are the early trailblazers.

What would seem to be called for is for spa associations throughout the world to address the CSR issue: to develop a framework for action and to establish a system for reporting and recognizing innovation as well as highlighting abuses – such as exploitative labor practices towards developing country spa therapists, patenting of indigenous products without prior benefit sharing agreements with traditional owners, etc.

By taking the high road and setting a vision, backed with standards, reporting systems and possibly even sanctions for abuses (such as suspension from Association membership), the industry will elevate itself in the eyes of its highly values-sensitive clientele and draw in more guests of the same values orientation. In the absence of such initiatives, there are risks that pockets of the industry will be branded as exploitative, thus dragging down the image of the wider industry as a result. Clearly, the spa industry is facing a cross roads with respect to values and ethics. How this is addressed will have a significant impact on the credibility, and hence the viability, of the industry in the future.

Acknowledgment

Anne-Maree Huxley, CEO, Models of Success & Sustainability (MOSS) (www.moss.org.au) provided valuable assistance for this chapter by way of reference material and CSR perspectives. Her generous contribution is greatly appreciated.

References

Bodeker G. (2007). Intellectual Property Rights. In: Bodeker G. & Burford G. (Eds.) 2007. Public Health & Policy Perspective on Traditional, Complementary & Alternative Medicine. Imperial College Press, London.

Caroll A.B. (1999). Corporate Social Responsibility: Evolution of a Definitional Construct. Business & Society, Vol. 38, No. 3, 268–295

Dixon, F. (2007) Sustainable Systems Implementation: Building a Sustainable Economy and Society. *CSRwire.com and GlobalSystemChange.com*: http://www.globalsystemchange.com/GSC/Articles_files/SSI%201-8.pdf (site accessed 7 February 2008)

Fox, T., Halina Ward, H., Howard, B. (2002) Public Sector Roles in Strengthening Corporate Social Responsibility: A Baseline Study. World Bank Group, Washington DC.

Gettler, L. (2007, March 15) The Age, Victoria, Australia: www.theage.com.au/news/business/dogooders-accrue-benefits-not-losses/2007/03/14/1173722558436.html

Kaiser Permanente Division of Research (2008, January 22). Caffeine Is Linked To Miscarriage Risk, New Study Shows. *ScienceDaily.* www.sciencedaily.com/releases/2008/01/080121 080402.htm (site accessed 1 February 2008)

Lane, J.D., Feinglos, M.N., Surwit, R.S. (2008) Caffeine increases ambulatory glucose and postprandial responses in coffee drinkers with type 2 diabetes, *Diabetes Care*, 31:221–222.

Page, J. (2007) American attempt to patent yoga puts Indians in a twist. The Times Online, 31 May. http://www.timesonline.co.uk/tol/news/world/asia/article1862524.ece (site accessed 26 January 2008).

Porter, M., Sala-I-Martin, X., Schwab, K. (2008) *The Global Competitiveness Report 2007–2008*, Palgrave Macmillan, Basingstoke, UK.

Conclusion

Gerard Bodeker and Marc Cohen

The spa industry has evolved from a series of small businesses and cottage industries existing in parallel in many different locations around the world based on local bathing, beauty, wellness and healing practices. Around the turn of the millennium, spas were adopted by the international hotel and resort industry which has applied its international expertise in hotel management, architecture and design, along with significant financial resources to make the spa industry a fully global phenomenon. The industry is still evolving and, while hotels spas and day spas are becoming more established, there are new models developing including specialty spas, residential spa communities and medi-spas that are beginning to integrate western medical expertise, as well as a growing market for home spa products and services.

Spas are now riding the wave of the baby boomers and the Lifestyles of Health and Sustainability (LOHAS) and conscious consumer movement. A spa business model has been built based on personal service, human connection and a growing wellness ethic combined with the aspirations of luxury, spirituality and personal transformation.

As addressed in the opening chapters, much of the momentum of the current global spa boom is best understood from the perspective of the wider wellness movement. The quest for well being, for taking charge of one's own health, recognition of the importance of relaxation and inner focus, an understanding of balance in the body and life, a sense of responsibility for the quality of one's healthcare, an awareness of looming world crises and the need for environmentally and socially sustainable products and processes. These are the wider societal forces driven by the group described by sociologists as 'cultural creatives'. And as is the case with cultural creatives, what they do today becomes the norm for society tomorrow.

In adapting and responding to these trends, the spa industry faces many challenges. As a highly service-based industry that requires qualified practitioners and managers, the rapid global expansion has produced challenges in staffing, recruitment and training. There are also significant challenges in developing standards for qualifications, management benchmarks, as well as financial, social and environmental practices and reporting systems. There is a need for harmonization of standards across regions and between different business models. There is also a risk that the spa industry is being seen as frivolous pampering or wasteful luxury, as well as being relatively invisible to the eye of institutional investors.

While there are now moves to develop new training programs, including university-based postgraduate courses, along with social and environmental reporting guidelines and financial reporting frameworks, there is a long way to go. The spa industry currently lacks robust methodologies for monitoring its international growth. Therefore, there is a dearth of hard data on the industry itself. The industry is also yet to engage seriously with the wealth of medical technology, including diagnostic testing and emerging virtual systems for health and wellness monitoring and maintenance. Accordingly, hard data is scarce on the health outcomes that the spa experience generates.

At the core of the excitement within the global spa industry is a sense that the new spa trends will have impacts far wider than the industry itself – that spas are part of a new direction of living life in a way that nurtures and supports individuals as much as it does their communities and their environment. This new life orientation brings together deep personal values, a sense of beauty and balance in one's physical environment, and a relationship of harmony, rather than of discontinuity, between commercial, social and environmental values. The promise – and the challenge – of spas is, therefore, to demonstrate that living well and living sustainably are fully compatible; that it is possible to live in luxury yet tread lightly on the earth.

Some of the key themes to emerge from this first analytic book on the global spa industry are as follows:

- The need for more robust reporting systems for financial, social and environmental performance.
- The need for self-regulatory moves by the industry to harmonize standards across regions and to ensure best practice is identified and encoded into industry standards and benchmarks.

- The importance of valuing the human dimension first and last in the spa development process – both the client and spa personnel.
- The emergence of cultural themes in spas, borrowing from indigenous traditions and from the major established healing traditions of Asia. This raises issues of preservation of traditional knowledge, particularly the appropriate use and development of local knowledge so that traditions are preserved and benefits are returned to local communities, traditional knowledge holders, and to the cultures themselves.
- Responsibility to the environment and sustainable practices– not just in use of eco-friendly products but in the whole environmental footprint of the operation.
- The importance of an innovative principle at all stages of spa development – the need to be creative, open to new ideas and the translation of this into skilled marketing strategies.
- The opportunities created by technological innovations and integration with the wider healthcare system, including conventional, complementary and traditional medicine.
- The importance to spa guests of concepts such as balance, communication through touch, and a healing environment – and the related imperative that spas take a leadership role and embody these principles in all aspects of their own value systems and personnel policies.
- The aspirational aspect of spas, being able to showcase what is possible in terms of health as well as sustainability.

This first book is a start on the journey to fill the knowledge gap in the growing world of spas. Doubtless, other authors and editors will generate other, related works. While this book has addressed design, commercial, management, operational, technological, environmental, human and ethical dimensions, a sequel is planned that will take up the themes of wellness and spa services. This next book will examine the key spa wellness programs, the evidence base for health claims, issues of best practice, quality control and safety and horizons for future development. Furthermore, to enable the contributors in this current book to share their knowledge and experience more comprehensively, as well as to bring in other experts in the spa industry, some topics in the present book will be developed into full books as part of an ongoing series.

While Utopian visions have a way of coming and going in history, deep changes in the way societies shape their lives are often precipitated by them. The spa world does seem to fit that bill and merits continued understanding and recalibrating according to its core values, wider vision and carefully measured performance.

Index

Page numbers followed by "f" denote figures; those followed by "t" denote tables

451

Lightning Source UK Ltd.
Milton Keynes UK

177477UK00006B/1/P